The Common People
of
Great Britain

The Common People
of
Great Britain

A History
from the Norman
Conquest to the
Present

J.F.C. Harrison

Indiana University Press

Bloomington

The Common People of Great Britain
A History from the Norman Conquest to the Present
First Midland Book Edition 1985

Library of Congress Cataloging in Publication Data
Harrison, J. F. C. (John Fletcher Clews)
The common people of Great Britain.
Bibliography: p.
Includes index.
1. Labor and laboring classes—Great Britain—History.
2. Peasantry—Great Britain—History.   3. Great Britain—
Social conditions.   I. Title.
HD8388.H36 1985   305.5′62′0942   84-48820
ISBN 0-253-20357-0

1   2   3   4   5   89   88   87   86   85

For Margaret

Contents

Maps and Tables

Preface

During the writing of this book I have incurred many obligations. To the University of Sussex I am indebted for two terms' leave of absence, and to the Rockefeller Foundation for a month as scholar in residence at the Bellagio Study and Conference Centre in 1982. The British Academy made a grant towards the cost of typing and preparation of the manuscript.

Many friends, colleagues and acquaintances have helped me with information, comments and expert opinion, and I would like particularly to thank Ian Roy, Rodney Hilton, Willie Lamont and Michael Hawkins. I owe much to the encouragement of my colleagues at Sussex, whose friendly enquiries as to how 'the book' was going spurred me on. Willie Lamont read the first two Parts and I have benefited greatly from his advice.

I have written elsewhere about some of the topics mentioned in this book. In Chapter 5 and in Part III I have drawn upon some material which I used previously in my books, *The Second Coming: Popular Millenarianism, 1780–1850* (1979) and *Early Victorian Britain, 1832–51* (1981).

J.F.C.H.

Introduction: the Contours of Popular History

This book is about the people who are usually left out of history. For the last thousand years or more at least 70 per cent and sometimes as many as 90 per cent of the population have been ordinary (common) people who had to work to make a living and who were ruled by a small minority who lived off the labour of the majority. Most history is concerned with this minority, who owned most of the wealth, exercised supreme power, and made all important decisions in the country. When the common people appear in history at all they are not central but only in the background, almost like characters off-stage. To write a book which reverses this usual practice of historians therefore requires some explanation and perhaps justification. There are several questions which can fairly be put.

Why write a history of the common people? The short answer is that most of us read history because we see it as related in some way to the world in which we live. Through history we can widen our experience of men and society beyond our own generation and culture. All historical knowledge, in this sense, is knowledge about ourselves; and we identify more easily or comfortably with ordinary people than with kings and prime ministers. We may believe secretly that we are really neither common nor ordinary; but at the same time there is the lingering romantic belief in the common people as the repository of real-life experience: 'My heart was all given to the people, and my love was theirs.'[1] In our day, when the emphasis is on grass-roots democracy and cultural pluralism, and elites are regarded with suspicion, there is a natural desire to know more about the people at the bottom of the social heap. They after all were the ones who were largely ignored because it was thought they did not matter; but for that very reason they were the ones who experienced the true values of a society, not its pretensions.

13

If one does write a history of the common people, will it be different from other histories? In some ways it will; in others, not. We cannot, for instance, ignore the historian's basic requirement of chronology, for history is essentially the study of change over time. But it will not necessarily be the same chronology as is appropriate for other types of history. Probably the traditional chronology and periodization of English history, being based on the political and economic decisions of the ruling classes, distorts or confuses the history of the common people, whose lives were largely determined by other considerations. We need an alternative periodization based on changes in popular experience and perceptions. Unfortunately the danger of forcing popular history into a procrustean bed of traditional historiography cannot be entirely avoided. Until we have much more evidence to work on, we have to take some of the accepted historians' categories and periods, even though they may not be truly relevant. Moreover, although the history of the common people should not be submerged in general history, the two are obviously interrelated. The common people were always faced with the problem of living in a world they did not create.

A history of the common people will also be different in its selection of themes. All history is a pattern made by interweaving chronological and thematic evidence from the records of the past; and for the common people the themes will be those which seem to show most closely how they lived and what they made of their lives. This will mean (at least ideally) that the history of the common people will not be simply traditional history with highlights on the contributions of ordinary men and women, but a completely different pattern, starting from different assumptions and ideas of what is important and what not. Historians will never be able to recreate, no matter how sympathetic or imaginative they are, anything more than a tiny fragment of the experiences and sentiments of that infinite host of men and women 'which have no memorial, who are perished as though they had never been born'.[2] But if we start by asking the right questions and looking for answers in new directions we may at least stand a chance of uncovering more than has been discovered about the common people in the past. The starting point must be those things which were central in the life of labouring people.

14

Following these precepts will result in a history whose contours appear somewhat unfamiliar to readers accustomed to the standard histories of England. Well-known landmarks will be missing; obscure happenings will appear as important signposts. There will be strange silences in places where the din of conflicting voices was anticipated; and equally unexpected and apparently eclectic emphases and details which seem to invite distortion. Thus there will be nothing on Magna Carta, Tudor despotism, Shakespeare, the rise of the gentry in the seventeenth century, the nineteenth-century revolution in government, or foreign policy. But there will be plenty of space for manorial life in the Middle Ages, the Peasants' Revolt, enclosures, chapbooks, Chartism, and domestic service. John Ball will receive more attention than King Richard the Lionheart, John Bunyan than Oliver Cromwell. We should expect to find nothing on Public Schools, but a fair amount on trade unions; no account of cabinet discussions, but perhaps a reference to the Tichborne claimant. The basis of selection will be the degree to which events and experiences illuminate the lives of ordinary men and women and their perceptions of themselves and their world. We cannot be sure what the priorities in their lives were; but it would appear reasonable to deal in each historical period primarily with work, family, popular mentalities, and indigenous forms of organization. The test always must be: what at the time did common people feel was important to them, and what, with the privilege of hindsight, seems to have been significant for the common people beyond their own generation and environment?

A third question which arises is, what are the peculiar problems and difficulties in writing this kind of history, and can they be overcome? The first and greatest problem is the scarcity of sources. We are dealing with that part of the community which was largely inarticulate. They did not for most of their history leave written records in which they described their thoughts and feelings and the events in which they were involved. The literary sources upon which historians rely so heavily do not at present exist in the same form and quantity for the common people as for their social superiors. This, more than any other, has been the argument advanced by professional historians against the possibility of writing a history of the common people. The historian is bound by his evidence, and if it is not there he can make no headway. This of course is correct; but it is not the whole story. First, the amount and variety of material, especially for the last two hundred years, is much greater than was once supposed: for example, many hitherto unknown autobiographies of working men and women have come to light in the past fifteen years when scholars have deliberately gone out to look for them. No truth is greater for the historian than that he who seeketh, findeth. Second, new information about the common people can sometimes be gained from reworking known sources. A prime example is recent work in the 'archives of repression', from which accounts of crowd movements, details of medieval peasant life, and the belief system of a sixteenth-century miller have been extracted. Third, the tyranny of literary sources can be escaped by turning to other types of evidence: oral testimony, folklore, the work of men's hands, the comparative researches of archaeologists and anthropologists. This material is not easy to use and has its pitfalls for the historian. But it is there and awaiting ingenious exploitation. A fourth way of dealing with the problem is to argue that we do not have enough material to write about the common people as individuals but we can deal with them in the aggregate. With the aid of statistical techniques and computers economic historians and demographers have been able to establish trends and structures at all levels of society. Work in reconstructing the family life of villagers in the sixteenth and seventeenth centuries is now possible in a way unthinkable a few years ago. This puts the common people back into history but sometimes only as masses, not as individuals.

If the history of the common people has not been written it is not primarily because it cannot be done but because historians have chosen not to do it. Historians in general, remarked an eminent member of the profession recently, are great toadies of power.[3] They prefer to write about the great and successful, the people who decided the fate of others. The common people are, almost by definition, those who do not exercise power. Why bother about people who do not matter? So, the common people were excluded from history: they were for the most part illiterate and therefore assumed to be inarticulate. But this 'inarticulateness' may be the result of more than a shortage of documentary records. It may stem from the historian's unfamiliarity with the culture of working people, and even more from a refusal to take their ideas and actions seriously. Many of the historian's stereotypes of the common people come from third parties, and are not the perceptions of the people themselves. In other words, the evidence may be there but the historian cannot see it. There is also a special kind of intellectual snobbery among traditional historians which works in the same direction. They assume a hierarchy of types of evidence, with the written word very much at the top; ideas are superior to artefacts; and it's crafts for the people and fine art for the intelligentsia. This sort of approach precludes any extensive popular history. The historian shuts himself off from ever finding the common people as they saw themselves, and then proclaims that the common people have no history, or history worth taking seriously.

But this said, very real problems remain for even the most sympathetic would-be historian of the common people. Is it enough simply to let the common people have their say and leave it at that? At the present stage of scholarship about the common people it is probably wise to lay the main stress on the experiential, or lived quality of history. Our task is to try to recreate the past as it felt to peasants working in the fields and artisans in their workshops. The materiality and trivia of daily life have for too long been neglected in favour of the elite culture of the educated classes, and it is time to restore the balance. But can we really be satisfied with what is no more than a kind of proletarian version of the old 'men and manners' type of social history? Surely not. Habit, gossip, artefacts all have their place; but in themselves they broaden rather than deepen our understanding of the people's history. At some point the historian is required to transcend the perceptions of contemporaries, suggest a pattern of the interconnectedness of events, and offer a tentative explanation. This pattern may be an elaborate and sophisticated theory of history, such as some version of Marxism. Or it may be little more than an implicit belief that in the long run things get better all the time: in the words of the immortal Mr Dooley, 'The past always looks better than it was. It's only pleasant because it isn't here.'[4]

A belief in progress, in some form or other, seems inescapable today, despite the almost universal repudiation of a Whiggish or optimistic, nineteenth-century view of history. Most readers will find it acceptable to think about the history of the common people in terms of development and evolution. Indeed, so strong is the hold of the concept of organism, which implies growth and development, that it seems impossible to think about social classes and institutions in any other way. But growth is by stages, from birth, through infancy, to maturity; and this implies a destination and a logical purpose towards an end. We may define that end as we choose; but once we have accepted the historian's discipline of chronology there is no escape from its logic. Since many of us are utilitarians at heart, we shall not have too much difficulty in arriving at the pleasing conclusion that the happiness of the greatest number (the common people) has increased, albeit very slowly and with many set-backs, during the past nine hundred years; that, in short, it is better to be alive today than in 1066.

An alternative to some form of evolutionary theory is the idea of the people as an eternal presence. They undergo metamorphoses, but do not basically change: their history is analogous to a dream sequence. In a sense they stand outside the past or the future, but exist always in the present. For them time is irrelevant. This is Thomas Hardy's vision of the eternal labourer:

> Only a man harrowing clods
> In a slow silent walk
> With an old horse that stumbles and nods
> Half asleep as they stalk.
>
> Only thin smoke without flame
> From the heaps of couch grass;
> Yet this will go onward the same
> Though Dynasties pass.[5]

It was also Hardy who once suggested that the measurement of life should be proportioned rather to the intensity of the experience than to its actual length: 'A moment chronologically [may be] a season in history.'[6] Pursuing this line of argument we should have to present the common people through a series of images rather than in a narrative. Strange, romantic, and even mystical as such hypotheses may sound, they remind us that to put the common people into a central place in history we require more than an emphasis on work and daily life.

In the pages that follow there will be no attempt to use any particular theory of history or model of social change; but the assumptions and prejudices of the author will soon become apparent. It would be convenient if the historian could pretend that, in trying to make articulate the experiences of people from the past, he is only a midwife to their history. The experiences and perceptions of the common people, however, are the material for their history, not the history itself. It is the historian who selects, suggests and implies; who through his imagination and reading constructs the pattern. The history, alas, will be only as good as the historian.

The book is divided chronologically into four parts, and within each part are themes central to the experience of the common people. The parts are unequal in their time spans for the reason that much more is known about the later periods than the earlier, and the story becomes altogether denser as we approach the twentieth century. As Mr Dooley observed, 'The further you get away from any period the better you can write about it. You aren't subject to interruptions by people who were there.'[7] But the parts are not rigid boundaries, and there is considerable overlap: peasants are found in the seventeenth and eighteenth centuries, not only in the Middle Ages; and handworkers continued long after the Industrial Revolution. The titles of the parts are no more than labels for the dominant section of the common people during the period. They are to be thought of as developments which continued before and after the defining dates. The themes in each part are concerned generally with social structure and demography, the making of livings, family relationships, ideas and beliefs, indigenous institutions, and popular movements. Here again the emphasis is on continuing process rather than categorization. The continuity of labouring life needs to be remembered as well as the changes: ploughing, shepherding, handweaving, cobbling, wheelwrighting and other crafts changed very little over long periods of time. New social institutions and forms existed side by side with older ones, which were not suddenly displaced.

There is of course a price to be paid for compressing nine hundred years of history into a book of this length. Whole areas have been left out: the common people of Ireland, Scotland and Wales require special treatment which I have neither the space nor competence to give them. In many places only a sentence has been possible where there could have been a paragraph, or a paragraph where there could well have been a chapter. Topics are introduced but not followed up; decades, even whole generations, are glossed over without a mention. The decision to give priority to those things which concerned the common people most immediately and directly, wherever possible in their own words, or failing that from what it seems likely was their point of view, is itself a limitation. History, to use an old metaphor, is a seamless garment, and any attempt to treat it otherwise must be imperfect.

In a work such as this, which is primarily interpretative, I have had to rely heavily on the work of other scholars. My debt to them is not always acknowledged in the footnotes, which have been kept to a minimum. But in the suggestions for further reading my main authorities will be obvious.

PART I

The English Peasantry (1066–1500)

1. Villeins and Serfs

Ten sixty-six is the best known – perhaps the only widely known – date in English history. On 28 September of that year William the Conqueror and his army landed at Pevensey Bay in Sussex. The story of how Harold, the English king, fresh from his victory at Stamford Bridge in Yorkshire over an invading Viking force, hurried south, how the English and Norman armies fought a bloody battle near Hastings on 14 October, and how Harold was killed by an arrow through his eye, is made familiar in innumerable school history books. The Battle of Hastings is *the* battle of English history; and to this day the little town which grew up on the site is named simply Battle. Medieval chroniclers and later historians alike have emphasized the watershed nature of 1066: before and after the Norman Conquest is the accepted mode of explaining many facets of life in the early Middle Ages. Nine hundred years later we can try to impose on events that pattern which we call history. With the convenient advantage of hindsight and the merciful simplification resulting from vast areas of oblivion a history of the eleventh century can be reconstructed.

But if we inquire whether, and if so how, the Battle of Hastings affected the lives of the great majority of the English people, no very straightforward answer is forthcoming. Only a small number of them actually fought in the battle: estimates of the size of the opposing armies are no more than five to seven thousand. Many more of the population soon encountered William's army of occupation, as in the following five years the king suppressed revolts, devastated large areas of the north, and terrorized the inhabitants. The fact of conquest was impressed most nakedly by the building of great castles throughout the land: within the next twenty years there were seventy to eighty castles constructed in England, dominating the county towns, the harbours, the borders and much of the countryside. The immediate effects of 1066 were

23

felt mainly by the upper echelons of English society, for William dispossessed the English nobility of their land and distributed it among his followers. We do not know what the common people thought about 1066, nor to what extent they were aware of any resulting changes in their daily lives. No ploughman or housewife has left us an account of that fatal 14 October. We might guess that they heard rumours from afar and carried on with the routine tasks of getting a living in the same way as they had always done. In one sense 1066 is not a real date in the history of the common people. Yet in a long-term perspective it is significant in that it made important changes in the ruling class, whose decisions, directly and indirectly, affected the mass of the people. To this extent the conventional wisdom that 1066 was a major turning point in English history may be accepted.

The Norman aristocracy which replaced their English predecessors was small in numbers, but completely dominant. The English were now a subject nation, separated from their rulers by birth and language. Even today we are reminded by synonyms that the Anglo-Saxon peasantry tended the cows, calves, swine and sheep, but that it was the Normans who ate them as beef, veal, pork and mutton. The alienation of the rulers from the majority of the population was emphasized in the theory of the Norman yoke, which interpreted the Norman Conquest as a loss of Anglo-Saxon freedom and the imposition of a foreign tyranny. Whether such ideas were part of medieval folk memory is uncertain; but the Norman yoke appeared in the seventeenth century as part of the democratic theory of the Levellers, and was taken up again in the eighteenth and early nineteenth centuries by Thomas Paine and the advocates of popular radicalism.

The kingdom that William rapidly conquered looked very different from the England of today. Although the basic geography was the same (with all that rich diversity which makes Britain a true miniature, complete in itself, and not merely a part of a larger whole) the landscape would have seemed unfamiliar. In general the country was wilder and less tamed. A very much larger part than today was forest and woodlands: Epping Forest, for instance, is all that now remains of a royal forest that once covered most of Essex. Vast areas of oak and ash covered much of the clay areas, and on the chalk uplands beech woods stretched for miles. But there were no sycamores, which were not introduced until the late sixteenth century. Marshes and fens, heather and scrublands were also much more numerous than today. Along the Sussex and Kentish coast, in the Fens of East Anglia, and everywhere in low-lying areas were thousands of acres of uninhabited marshland. In the north and west the high moorlands remained in their natural state. Eagles nested in Devon, Shropshire and the West Riding of Yorkshire. From an aerial view much of England would have seemed to be a wilderness, from which villages and areas of cultivation had been won. Indeed, this is the way in which we should think of England in 1066: a country in a state of colonization, with forests being cleared, marshes drained, and the frontiers of occupation steadily extending. This process had been going on for the previous six hundred years and was to continue for many more generations.

Amidst the forests, heaths and fens the villages were small and relatively isolated, linked to each other by tracks or roads which were little more than bridlepaths. The neat patchwork field pattern of the modern countryside in the south and midlands, beloved by foreign visitors as typically English, was largely absent. Instead, the arable land lay open, without hedges or walls, round each settlement. Beyond these few hundred acres was the frontier of woodland, moor and bog. By comparison with today the country was grossly underpopulated. Recent estimates have suggested a total population of between 1·2 and 1·6 million; today the figure is 50 million. Nine-tenths of the population in the eleventh century lived in villages and hamlets, mostly in the eastern and southern counties. East Anglia was the most densely populated part of the country, with perhaps an average of forty or fifty people to the square mile. By contrast northern England probably had no more on average than four persons per square mile. Even the most populous county, Norfolk, had only 95,000 people – less than one medium-sized town has today. The towns in 1066 were few and far between, and reflected an order of priorities quite different from twentieth-century needs. Some were little different from villages. Perhaps twenty towns had populations of more than a thousand. After London (which was unique in every respect) came York (about nine thousand), Lincoln, Norwich (between six and seven thousand each), Winchester (perhaps between six thousand and

Where People Lived in the Middle Ages

LINCOLN — Town
Sturbridge — Fair
Walsingham — Pilgrimage centre

0   50   100
Miles

YORK

CHESTER   •LINCOLN

Nottingham•   Boston•   Walsingham

•SHREWSBURY Stamford   Lynn   NORWICH
LEICESTER•   •WISBECH
                      •Peterborough
COVENTRY•   •Ely
WARWICK•   St Ives•
WORCESTER• Northampton Sturbridge•   •BURY ST
                                      EDMUNDS
•Hailes   COLCHESTER•
GLOUCESTER•
              •Oxford
          Abingdon•
•BRISTOL   LONDON•

                    St Bartholomew
                    Smithfield   CANTERBURY
                    Southwark
SALISBURY•
          •Winchester
EXETER

•PLYMOUTH

In the fourteenth century 78 per cent of the population lived south and east of a line drawn from York to Exeter.

From J.F.D. Shrewsbury, *A History of Bubonic Plague in the British Isles* (Cambridge University Press, 1970), p. 33. Reproduced by permission.

eight thousand), Oxford (over five thousand), Thetford (nearly five thousand), Ipswich and Gloucester (about three thousand).

Other familiar features of the English scene were also absent in 1066. The glorious heritage of several thousand medieval parish churches is mostly post-Conquest. Saxon churches were generally built of wood and roofed with thatch (as at Greenstead, Essex, to this day), and only occasionally (as in some Northamptonshire and Sussex churches) was stone used. There were no graceful church spires rising above the huddled village houses and visible for miles around, for they were not built until the early thirteenth century. As some compensation, however, we might have found the climate somewhat warmer than today. In 1086 vineyards are recorded in about forty-five places, mostly in the south; and in the early twelfth century vines were grown as far north as Derbyshire. Yet despite these differences many parts of England would have been perfectly recognizable to us. The majority of the villages we know today were there when William the Conqueror landed. In some places, where we know sheep have been grazed for a thousand years, the landscape has probably changed little. As Professor Hoskins has reminded us, the Cotswold uplands and the Wiltshire downlands were in the eleventh century much as they are now.[1]

The majority of people in William's kingdom – and indeed for many generations thereafter – were peasants. We do not normally think of our ancestors in this way. Peasants in France, Mexico, China – yes; but not in England. We talk rather of farmers, labourers and cottagers. It is useful however to use the term peasant, because it enables us to conceptualize the process of production and social relationships, and also suggests the possibility of comparative study. If we have difficulty in grasping some of the realities of life in the eleventh century it may be helpful to look at peasant conditions in other places and at different times. The basic facts of a peasant economy are the starting point for our understanding of medieval society. Peasants are small-scale agricultural producers, living on individual holdings, which they work mainly or entirely with the labour of their families. The primary object of growing crops and rearing animals is to provide subsistence for the family; but as society does not consist exclusively of peasants but includes non-agricultural producers of various kinds, the peasantry have also to produce a surplus which can be transferred to other groups or classes. These processes are effected through institutions which differ between types of agrarian society. The way in which land is held, the size of holdings, the role of the family, the nature of the village, hamlet or isolated farmstead, the agricultural system practised are such institutionalizations of peasant production. This is the rationale of many of the complexities and obscurities of medieval society which follow. Nine-tenths of the medieval population lived in the countryside, and it is with them that we are concerned first, leaving until later some consideration of the one-tenth who lived in towns.

It is by no means easy to discover all the details of this peasant economy in the eleventh century. King William, faced with the same problem, ordered a complete survey of his kingdom to be made. In 1086 his commissioners collected information in immense detail, county by county, and from it was compiled Domesday Book – popularly so-called because it seemed as thorough and inescapable as the book of judgement in Revelation 20:12. From this unique document we have an unparalleled picture of early medieval society in England, including much about the peasantry. Domesday Book does not by any means tell us all that we would like to know; and some of what it tells us seems ambiguous and hard to interpret. Like most historical records it was written not to inform historians but for quite other purposes. Moreover, it is a view of England from the top down, and that through the eyes of foreigners (Normans). Nevertheless, we can learn from it a good deal about the realities of peasant life.

Let us look at the entry for just one of the 13,000 villages and settlements mentioned in Domesday. It is for Halesowen in Worcestershire and may be taken as typical of hundreds of similar descriptions.

> Earl Roger holds of the King one manor, Halesowen. There are 10 hides there. On the demesne there are 4 ploughs and 36 villeins and 18 bordars, 4 radmans and a church with 2 priests. Among them all they have 41½ ploughs. There are there 8 serfs and 2 bondwomen. Of this land Roger Venator holds of the Earl one hide and a half, and there he has one plough and 6 villeins,

and 5 bordars with 5 ploughs. It is worth 25s. In the time of King Edward this manor was worth 24l. Now 15l. Olwin held and had in Droitwich a saltpan worth 4s. and in Worcester a house worth 12d.

The same Earl holds Salwarpe, and Urso of him. Elwin Cilt held it. There are 5 hides there. On the demesne there is one plough and 6 villeins, and 5 bordars with 7 ploughs. There are there 3 serfs and 3 bondwomen and a mill worth 10s. and 5 saltpans worth 60s. Half a league of wood and a park there. In the time of King Edward it was worth 100s. Now 6l. There can be two ploughs more there.[2]

The form of this entry follows the questions which the commissioners put to the local inhabitants:

what is the name of the manor?; who held it in the time of King Edward?; who holds it now?; how many hides are there?; how many teams, in demesne and among the men?; how many villeins?; how many cottars?; how many serfs?; how many free men?; how many sokemen?; how much wood?; how much meadow?; how much pasture?; how many mills?; how many fisheries?; how much has been added or taken away?; how much was the whole worth?; how much is it worth now?; how much had or has each freeman or sokeman?; all this is to be given in triplicate, that is in the time of King Edward, when King William gave it, and at the present time; and whether more can be had than is had?[3]

Some of the words and ideas in the passage are unfamiliar, and not all are relevant to our purpose. For instance, the word hide, which is a unit of tax assessment, reminds us that the main object of Domesday was to facilitate the collection of the king's taxes, or geld. With this we are not directly concerned. But other words, such as manor, demesne, villein, bordar, serf can only be explained in terms of the manorial system and feudalism, and lead us to the heart of peasant life.

'Earl Roger holds of the King one manor . . . Of this land Roger Venator holds of the Earl one hide and a half . . . The same Earl holds Salwarpe, and Urso of him . . .' This is the language of feudalism, and it introduces those two keys to early medieval society, land and lordship. King William asserted the principle that he was the absolute owner of all the land in the kingdom. He made grants of large amounts of land to his chief followers (barons) on the condition that they provided a certain number of knights (horse soldiers) for his army. Some of the largest grants of land were to the church, and William treated his bishops and abbots as barons. The tenants-in-chief then granted estates to knights in return for military service. The knights, or sub-tenants, in turn made land available to smaller men, who held it on condition of performing various services. All holders of land were thus linked in a chain stretching from the king to the lowliest peasant. There was also a personal bond in this arrangement of land tenure between a superior (the lord) and an inferior (the vassal). Every holder of land, except the king, held it of some lord whom he was obliged to serve and obey. The lord, on his part, was required to protect and maintain the means of livelihood of 'his' man. Vassals 'did homage' to their lords. This vast system of dependent relationships – for everyone (except the king) who held land held it of someone else, and owed allegiance to a lord – was known later as feudalism, the word being derived from the Latin *feudum* meaning fief or landed estate held by a vassal in return for service.

Earl Roger, holding his manor of Halesowen direct from the king, was at one end of the feudal chain. The cultivators of the soil – the villeins, bordars and serfs – were at the other. They, together with three other categories of people who do not happen to be mentioned in the Halesowen entry, but who figure prominently in some other parts of Domesday – the freemen, sokemen and cottars – constituted the English peasantry. For many generations before William's arrival there had been considerable differentiation among the peasantry. There were also important regional differences and changes in time. The Norman clerks who compiled Domesday did not have a very easy task in understanding some of the distinctions they found; and the situation was soon further obscured by the efforts of contemporary lawyers to impose clear-cut categories where they originally did not exist. Nevertheless, the main outlines of the social structure of the peasantry are reasonably clear.

Most numerous were the villeins. They amounted to over one-third of the total rural population recorded in Domesday. In many counties they were over half, and in Yorkshire, Derbyshire, Huntingdonshire and Sussex over 60 per cent. A villein may be thought of as a farmer who had a holding of thirty acres (called a virgate or yardland), but some might have as much as sixty acres and others only ten to fifteen acres. The word villein is used in Domesday to cover a wide variety of people, and sometimes seems to mean simply villager. Below the villeins were the cottars and bordars. They were cottagers, who had only their house and a small parcel of land, anything from one to five acres. They accounted for about a third of the total population in Domesday. Superior in status to villeins and cottagers were the freemen and sokemen, who were most numerous in the eastern and northern counties which had been settled by Scandinavians (the Danelaw) in the ninth and tenth centuries. Their holdings were not necessarily larger than those of villeins; but they enjoyed the benefits of a tenure free from most of the burdensome restrictions under which, as we shall see, the villeins laboured. Lastly, at the bottom of the economic and social scale, were the serfs, who numbered a little over 10 per cent of the Domesday population. They were slaves and did not normally hold land, but worked on the lord's demesne. In all, these various categories formed a Domesday peasantry of 262,500. Of these, 36,900 were freemen and sokemen; 109,000 villeins; 88,500 cottagers; and 28,100 serfs. Assuming that the persons enumerated were heads of households (though this may be doubtful in the case of serfs), we have to multiply these figures by four or five to arrive at the total peasant population of England.

The manor of Halesowen: this description of Earl Roger's holding brings us to the basis of the organization of the peasant economy. Victorian historians, relying heavily on Domesday, presented a clear and relatively simple picture of rural society in terms of the manor. This picture is today no longer entirely acceptable, for recent research has shown the need for important modifications. Nevertheless the conventional view is still the most useful starting point, even though we may not unreservedly endorse G.G. Coulton's claim of fifty years ago that the manor was 'the web within which the medieval peasant lives and moves and has his being'.[4] According to the classic model, the peasants lived in small houses, grouped together in a nucleated village. Behind each house was a garden or small plot of land, sometimes called a close; but the main arable farm land lay some distance away in great common fields surrounding the village. These fields, two or three in number (depending on whether one field was left fallow every second or third year), were divided into strips, which were a furrow long and contained an acre or half-acre. The strips were separated from each other only by hazel twigs or balks of unploughed land. At right angles to the strips ran the turf head-lands which gave access to the fields and provided space for turning the teams of plough oxen. By the stream were the meadows, the Lammas lands as they were often called. They were enclosed from soon after Christmas until the hay was harvested about Lammas (1 August), and then thrown open for grazing. Beyond the open fields was the common or waste. This was uncultivated land and woodland, which provided rough grazing for cattle, sheep and pigs, and also fuel and timber for building.

In this manorialized village part of the arable land was reserved for the lord of the manor, and was called the demesne or (later) the home farm. The remainder was held by the peasantry, each man having a number of strips allocated in various parts of the common fields, so that his holding was not a compact block but scattered over a fairly wide area. Such was the nature of the typical villein's virgate of thirty acres. Coupled with this went rights of grazing on the common and a share in the meadows proportionate to the size of the holding. A majority of the peasants were, as we have noted, villeins, and they held their land in return for labour services. Each week they were required to provide so many days' work for the lord on his demesne, and at sowing and harvest times extra or boon work. The villein was not allowed to leave the manor, and was legally bound to the soil. He was an unfree or servile tenant. The cottagers and smaller tenants were similarly bound, though as their parcels of land were only small they owed fewer labour services to the lord. Their holdings were too small to support their families, and they had therefore to work for richer peasants or for the lord, providing a pool of reserve labour. Where there were freemen they paid a rent for their land and helped the lord at busy seasons, but did not do weekly labour service. The manor was administered for the lord by his officials: steward, bailiff, reeve, hayward and beadle; and manorial affairs were settled in the manor court (or hall moot), which all were required to attend regularly.

Among the small tenants or cottagers holding five acres or less was an important section of the peasantry: the craftsmen. Every village needed its blacksmith, carpenter and, if possible, miller (over six thousand watermills are recorded in Domesday). Thus at Amberley in Sussex we read later of Benet Smith who holds 'four acres belonging to the smithy', for which 'he shall mend with the lord's iron all the iron-gear belonging to two ploughs, but do nothing new. He shall shoe two horses, and the sergeant's horses with the lord's iron, and receive nothing. . . . He shall grind all the scythes used in the lord's meadows, and all the shears while they shear the lord's sheep.'[5] Most peasants, as part of their husbandry, are able to carry out small repairs to their tools and equipment, and to undertake rough building jobs. Spinning and (to a lesser extent) weaving are traditional peasant home crafts. But specialized craft skills are required for certain types of work, and the tendency is therefore to increasing differentiation of jobs in a rural community. In the Middle Ages such specialist workers were often migratory. Masons, thatchers, tilers – and indeed all building workers – as well as potters moved around from job to job. On the edge of the village or in the forests, but still part of the rural economy, were miners, charcoal burners, iron workers, and salt-makers.

The model of the manorialized village has the great advantage of simplicity, and accurately describes the main features of English agrarian organization. It does not however give a complete picture of medieval rural life. First, the manor and the open-field system flourished mainly in central and southern England, in the grain-growing areas of the fertile plains. Elsewhere geographical realities and peculiarities of ancient settlement dictated other patterns. In areas of mountain, forest and marsh there were no open fields – none in the northern counties of Cheshire, Lancashire, Cumberland and Westmorland, nor in the Weald of Kent and Sussex, and Cornwall. Hamlets and scattered farmsteads, not nucleated villages, were common in Devon and Cornwall. Wherever sheep-grazing and not arable farming was dominant the open fields were absent. Even within the main area of the open-field system and manorial organization there were local exceptions and variations. Thus the villagers in Sherwood Forest, which lay in the middle of the open-field county of Nottinghamshire, practised an ancient system of agriculture usually known as infield and outfield. To meet their need for arable land they periodically enclosed bits of grazing land, called 'breaks' or 'brecks', which they ploughed for a few years and then returned to pasture.

Secondly, manor and village did not always coincide, which somewhat upsets the manorial pattern of our model. In many cases there was more than one manor in a village, and conversely some large manors covered more than one settlement. Historians have argued at length over the precise meaning of the term manor in Domesday and subsequent documents. In general we may think of it as an estate, organized as an economic unit, with the peasantry bound to the lord and contributing labour services or rent. To the medieval lawyer (and later to the economic historian) the manor was the dominant element in rural organization; but to the peasant it is probable that the village was a more immediate reality. From the top we have a view of medieval England as a land of great estates; from the bottom as a land of peasant farms. Thirdly, the free peasantry do not fit easily into the manorial stereotype. In East Anglia, Lincolnshire, Nottinghamshire and Leicestershire, the existence of free tenants (freemen and sokemen) meant that peasant society in many villages did not conform to the classic model of the manor. For example, at Wigston, near Leicester, in 1086 about 40 per cent of the land was held by free tenants and they constituted some 45 per cent of the population of the village. Since the lords of the manor were not resident, but ruled their tenants through bailiffs, the villagers were 'never subservient to one man or family but . . . were free and roughly equal, socially if not economically'.[6] The Norman clerks and lawyers, in their desire to categorize and codify, to some extent superimposed a concept of manorialism upon the economic and social reality that they observed. Their classification of the peasantry may well not have been the same as the perception that the peasants had of themselves. In any case, there is a confusion of criteria in Domesday which does not help us. On the one hand the peasants are classified by legal status (free or unfree); and on the other by economic position (amount of land held or occupation);

and this by no means uniformly between different counties. Legal distinctions about degrees of freedom naturally took priority with feudal lawyers and have occupied constitutional historians ever since. How the peasants themselves viewed these issues we do not know. To the peasant the size of his holding and its productive capacity may have been equally if not more important, though as we shall see, the Norman development of servile distinctions worked to the detriment of many villeins in the twelfth and thirteenth centuries.

Domesday catches for us a view of the peasantry at one particular time. It is a still from a continuously running film. Although it shows change between 1066 ('in the time of King Edward') and 1086, it cannot of course help us beyond that date. For the next three hundred years, until about 1350, we have to rely on other, mainly manorial records. These documents – account rolls, surveys and court rolls – were not written by peasants nor from a peasant angle; but despite this limitation they can provide valuable information about many aspects of peasant life. The following description of the village of Pytchley, Northamptonshire, in 1125 is from a survey of the lands of Peterborough abbey. It records the work and payments that the peasants had to render to the lord of the manor:

There are there 9 full villeins and 9 half villeins and 5 cottagers. The full villeins work 3 days a week up to the feast of St. Peter in August and thence up to Michaelmas every day by custom, and the half villeins in accordance with their tenures; and the cottagers one day a week and two in August. All together they have 8 plough teams. Each full villein ought to plough and harrow one acre at the winter ploughing and one at the spring, and winnow the seed in his lord's grange and sow it. The half villeins do as much as belongs to them. Beyond this they should lend their plough teams 3 times at the winter ploughing and 3 times at the spring ploughing and once for harrowing. And what they plough they reap and cart. And they render 5 shillings at Christmas and 5 shillings at Easter and 32 pence at St. Peter's feast. And Agemund the miller renders 26 shillings for his mill and for one yardland. And all the villeins render 32 hens at Christmas. The full villeins render 20 eggs and the half villeins

10 eggs and the cottagers 5 eggs at Easter. Viel renders 3 shillings for one yardland and Aze 5; the priest, for the church and 2 yardlands, 5 shillings. Walter the free man pays 2 shillings for a half yardland. Leofric the smith pays 12 pence for one toft. Ægelric of Kettering pays 6 pence for the land he rents and Ægelric of Broughton 12 pence and Lambert 12 pence. And Ralf the sokeman lends his plough 3 times a year. Martin gives a penny and Azo a penny and Ulf and Lambert a penny. On the home farm there are 4 plough teams with 30 oxen and 8 oxherds who each hold a half yardland of the home farm. There are 2 draught horses, 220 sheep, 20 pigs, and 10 old sheep in their second year.[7]

This extract, with its talk of villeins, custom, plough teams and oxen, takes us to the heart of peasant life. It reminds us that the overwhelming majority of the common people were farmers. They were concerned, almost wholly, with making a living off the land. Their skills were those of the ploughman, herdsman and shepherd – skills with which most of us today have no direct experience. There are things about animals and the soil known only to those who work closely with them, day in day out, for a whole lifetime. But these things are not written down; they are known intuitively and almost subconsciously. The true record of the husbandman's skills is to be found, if at all, not in documents but in remains of the medieval landscape: ditches, dry-stone walls, ancient ponds, field systems, the pattern of arable strips ('ridge and furrow') beneath the grass. It is inescapable that our understanding of medieval farming will be at best partial, and that whole areas of peasant experience may well elude us. We can nevertheless establish the external structure of labouring life.

The villeins of Pytchley were required 'to plough and harrow one acre at the winter ploughing and one at the spring' for the lord of the manor. Ploughing was the basic, most widely required skill of the peasant, and the ploughman was regarded throughout the Middle Ages as the archetypal worker. When the villein appeared in literary form it was as Piers Ploughman. 'God speed the plough' was a prayer to be echoed by all. It was hard and (in the wet English climate) often unpleasant work, as the following dialogue between a master and his pupil makes clear:

M. What do you say, ploughman, how do you do your work?

P. Oh, sir, I work very hard. I go out at dawn, driving the oxen to the field, and I yoke them to the plough; however hard the winter I dare not stay at home for fear of my master; but, having yoked the oxen and made the plough-share and coulter fast to the plough, every day I have to plough a whole acre or more.

M. Have you any companion?

P. I have a boy who drives the oxen with the goad, and he is even now hoarse with cold and shouting.

M. What more do you do in the day?

P. A good deal more, to be sure. I have to fill the oxen's cribs with hay, and give them water, and carry the dung outside.

M. Oh, oh, it is hard work.

P. Yes, it is hard work, because I am not a free man.[8]

The medieval plough was a heavy, clumsy tool of wood and iron, drawn by a team of oxen or horses. On light soils a pair of horses or a yoke of oxen was sufficient; but on heavy clays a team of as many as eight oxen in four yokes might be necessary. The control of such a team must have been no easy task. Up and down the long narrow strips the ploughman and his boy plodded, while the plough threw the earth towards the centre of the strip, thus producing the characteristic 'ridge and furrow' of open-field farming. 'Holding plough' was for many generations of Englishmen synonymous with doing a man-sized, adult job. Starting at first light, the work went on until noon or early afternoon, by which time the amount of land expected by custom had been ploughed. Not all villeins had a full plough team of their own, and some had therefore to pool their oxen with those of their neighbours to make up a team. With the ploughing went other tasks, such as sowing and harrowing. And always the work had to be done on both the lord's demesne and the peasant's own holding.

Ploughing and harrowing, however, were but part of a villein's work. Like peasants everywhere he was bound by the rhythm of the seasons, the nature of the soil and the demands of his animals. These were the imperatives that dictated the husbandman's year, and virtually all aspects of medieval life were directly or indirectly geared to the needs of agriculture. The working year began after

Michaelmas (29 September) with the winter ploughing and sowing of corn (wheat and rye). Animals had to be brought in from the pastures, and some of them slaughtered and salted down. Throughout the winter there was corn to be threshed in the barns, dung to be carted and spread on the fields, ditches cleaned out and fences repaired. Christmas and the twelve days that followed marked the chief break or holiday in the year: the weather was too bad for much work in the fields, and the crops were in the dormant period of their growing cycle. With the early spring, ploughing began again, this time for the spring crops of oats, barley, peas and beans, and also the first ploughing of the fallow field. In June and July haymaking kept all hands busy; and from August to Michaelmas the farming year reached its climax in the harvest. An immense amount of hard labour was required to get in both the lord's and the peasants' corn crops, and every available man, woman and child was pressed into service. After this prodigious effort Harvest Home was not surprisingly an occasion for feasting, fun and community celebration. But then the cycle of the year began again, season relentlessly following season. For the peasant there was no respite from the daily and yearly routine: as far as he knew it had always been so and the future would be no different. Labour on the land was a condition of life itself. For him the curse of Adam had a literal quality which to us is denied: 'Cursed is the ground for thy sake; in toil shalt thou eat of it all the days of thy life; thorns also and thistles shall it bring forth to thee; and thou shalt eat of the herbs of the field; in the sweat of thy face shalt thou eat bread, till thou return unto the ground.'

The tyranny of the seasons and the inevitability of toil are characteristics of all peasant societies. What distinguished the medieval peasantry was that they were part of a manorial and feudal system. This meant that the English peasant did not own his farm, nor was he a member of a collective farm or commune. Instead, he 'held' his land in return for rents and services. Broadly speaking, there were three main social groups in the peasantry – the freemen, the villeins and the cottars (or cottagers) – and all are mentioned in the Pytchley survey. Most numerous was the middle group: 'There are 9 full villeins . . . [who] work 3 days a week.' This labour service was performed on the lord's demesne throughout most of the year, and was known as week-work. At the busy time of harvest (from 'the feast of St. Peter in August . . . to Michaelmas') extra work was required. The amount of work due corresponded to the size of holding: the 'half-villeins' and cottagers, for example, owing less than the 'full villeins' at Pytchley. A day's work was defined by the custom of each manor in terms of cutting so much corn, threshing so much wheat, or some similar job. In most cases this did not amount to working for the whole of a day. It would also seem that a villein was not always bound to do the work himself, but could depute one of his sons or some other member of his household, provided that his obligation to the manor was fulfilled. The system allowed time for the cultivation of the villein's own holding on the assumption that the peasant family worked as a unit. Nevertheless at harvest time the lord demanded extra or 'boon' work, on top of the already increased week-work during August and September. Boons could be demanded to suit the lord's convenience, and entailed the services of the maximum number of workers. As some recompense the lord usually provided food and drink for boon work. The peasant was required, at the very height of the farming year, to put the lord's needs first, to get the lord's crops in at all cost – and in theory he did this out of love for his lord (hence the boons were sometimes called love-boons). At such times the condition of the villeins and cottagers contrasted strongly with the more enviable position of the freemen (such as those men named in the Pytchley survey) who paid a money rent for their holdings and were free from the obligations of week-work.

The villein was constantly reminded of his servile status by the burden of payments (fines) in kind or money, in addition to the provision of labour services. The Pytchley men owed their lord hens at Christmas and eggs at Easter. Before he could take over his holding the villein had to pay an entry fine. When his daughter married there was another payment to be made, known as merchet. If he sent his son to school a fine was due. Manorial records are full of the endless details of these exactions, some of which were petty, others considerable. Here is a typical extract, this time from the account roll of the manors of the bishopric of Winchester in 1292, detailing the payments (court fines) made at Staplegrove in Taunton, Somerset:

Entry and Marriage Fines Likewise, they render account for 4s. from Robert le Muchele for marrying his daughter Alice. And for 60s. from Adam Cole to have Emelota the widow of Folkemer with half a virgate of land. And for 12d. from William son of Adam Cole to have one acre of land, by his father's concession. And for 60s. from Thomas son of Walter Folkemer to have half a virgate of land, by the concession of Adam Cole. And for 40s. from Simon Glide to have one half of a half-virgate of land, which was Stephen Glide's, for he has paid a fine for the other half some time ago (*temporibus retroactis*). And for 20s. from William Kynth' of Coddesheye to have 5 acres of land, by the concession of John of Chilewardeswode. And for 12d. from Robert Wynter to have one half of one messuage and one curtilage, by the concession of Walter Colling. And for 4s. from Thomas Kyng the baker to have one house and curtilage, by the concession of Walter Carter. And for 6d. from Alice Colling for getting herself married. And for 12d. from John son of John Warman to have a part of a house, by the concession of Margery of Ak'. And for 6d. from the same John to have one house with a curtilage, by his father's concession. And for 13s. 4d. from Agnes the widow of William *longus* to retain 1 fardel of land which was her husband's. And for 10s. from Adam Kempe and Richard Sprut to have 3 acres of land in Wodelond, by the concession of Richard le Palmer. And for 30s. from the communal fine at Hockeday (*de Hockedayeswyte*).

Total: £12. 5s. 4d.[9]

The marriage fine was regarded as a sure sign of unfree status: the villein had to 'buy his own blood', as the legal phrase put it. Similarly a fine called leyrwite was imposed for female sexual incontinency. In legal theory the villein belonged to his lord, and any action such as marriage or unchastity which might affect the villein's value had to be met by a payment. Other common servile burdens were the monopolies of the lord's mill and bread-oven.

The villein was obligated to have his corn ground only at the manorial mill, for which he paid a certain proportion of the grain, known as multure. This was felt to be a particularly onerous and irritating imposition. It was levied on the most basic item of food, was inefficient (often involving the transport of the corn over long distances and then having to wait at the mill), and was subject to the fraudulent practices for which millers were notorious. Popular opposition to 'owing suit to the lord's mill' is attested by the large number of cases before the manorial courts in which the accused was alleged to have ground corn on a quern or handmill at home. We hear less about failure to use the lord's oven or bakehouse, perhaps because the cottagers and poorer villeins did not have ovens but only open fires in their homes. Nevertheless men were fined for not baking in the communal oven, and it may have been as much of a burden as a convenience.

More oppressive were the feudal dues of tallage and heriot. The former was a rent or tax which varied annually in amount and frequency, assessed according to size of holding and number of animals. Theoretically the lord's right to 'tallage at will' was unlimited. The uncertainty which it entailed was resented by the peasantry, whose main endeavour over the years was to get the tallage regularized 'according to the custom of the manor'. Once this had been established tallage became in effect an extra rent charge. Yet even after it had become fixed by custom, a special tallage could be levied arbitrarily, as for instance for a sort of 'housewarming' when a new lord of the manor took over his estates.

Heriot was paid when a peasant died. His lord claimed the best beast or chattel of the deceased; and (to make matters even worse for the bereaved widow or heir) the church took the second best as a 'mortuary'. On his death as much as a third or a half of a poor villein's animals and household goods could be lost in payment to the lord of the manor and the rector. The heriot had to be paid at the same time as the entry fine or 'relief' for taking over the holding; and in course of time the two payments of heriot and relief came to be regarded as the price for transfer of the holding from one villein to the next.

The manorial documents which constitute the main evidence of medieval peasant life suggest that a conflict of interest between lord and peasant was endemic in the manorial system. A never-ending struggle over rents, services and payments is recorded. Always the steward or bailiff sought to increase his lord's (and his own) power over the lives of the peasantry; and they tried to resist or nullify all such attempts with a cunning and obstinacy born of long experience in the methods of evasion. To contain this struggle and maintain the stability of society some institutional device or ideological framework was required. This took the form of the 'custom of the manor', which provided the social cement of manorial society. Custom, in the general sense of following traditional and proven ways of doing things, is strong in most agricultural societies. But in twelfth- and thirteenth-century England it was elaborated into a body of law governing virtually all social and economic relationships. In the first instance custom gave some degree of protection to the villein, in that it limited the arbitrariness of the lord's decisions. What had been uncertain rents and services were declared to be fixed and 'customary'. And the customs were determined by the peasants themselves, meeting in the manorial court and presided over by the lord or his official. When points in dispute were put to sworn juries of peasants the collective verdict was given (or 'found') by the people most likely to be directly affected by it. But once custom had been put into writing – as it was increasingly in the thirteenth century – it tended to strengthen the lord in exacting his rights to the full. The custumals, in which the services and dues were set down, often went into great detail, for once a service had been minutely described it was the more difficult to avoid its complete fulfilment. Custom was essentially local, and variations between manors were immense. But everywhere the reign of custom prevailed. It regulated every aspect of peasant life to such an extent that a villein was sometimes described in documents as a customer (*consuetudinarius*).

None of these documents, of course, was written by a peasant. The things that concerned him most were never presented by him but by others. It was the lord who took the initiative in compiling the custumals and rentals; and we see custom only as it appeared to his skilled lawyers. Nowhere is this truer than in the matter of peasant freedom. One of the results of that appetite for definition which obsessed the new race of Anglo-Norman lawyers between 1100 and 1300 was the classification of the rural population into two categories: free (*liber homo*) and unfree (*villanus*). The complicated economic and legal differences among the peasantry at the time of Domesday were ignored in the interests of simplicity and exactness, and in the process the status of the villein was downgraded. All who were not wholly free were declared to be villeins, and at the same time some of the personal disabilities of the serfs (*servi*) were extended to the villeinage. Serf and villein became synonymous. For three hundred years after the Norman Conquest more than half the population were serfs, men who in the famous definition of the thirteenth-century lawyer, Henry de Bracton, 'ought not to know in the evening what work might be demanded of [them] tomorrow'. Or, as the abbot of Burton brutally told his villeins in 1280, they had no belongings but their bellies (*nihil praeter ventrem*).

Despite, or perhaps because of, the best efforts of medieval lawyers, the dividing line between free and unfree remained hazy, and this presumably complicated social relations in the village. The daughter of a freeman might marry a villein; or a freeman might take a villein holding. Complications arose because unfreedom of two different types was involved. A person might be unfree because he was born a serf; his servile condition was thus personal. But unfreedom could also arise when a man held land for which labour services were due; unfreedom in this case was tenurial. Put another way, villeinage was distinct from villein tenure – although in practice the two most frequently went together. Historians have speculated that the tenurial aspect of freedom was probably of greater concern to peasants than the personal or legal disabilities, since labour services were what loomed largest in the daily lives of most villeins. Manorial records place heavy emphasis on rents and services. This may well be taken as an accurate reflection of what the compilers of the records regarded as most important; though whether this was also what mattered most to the peasants we cannot be sure. Certainly villeins were eager to commute their labour services for money payments whenever the lord was agreeable; and as we shall see later, commutation was the way to peasant freedom. But when the struggle for emancipation reached a climax in the fourteenth century the demand was more fundamental. It was for freedom from the degrading personal aspects of serfdom and the right to recognition as a full human being, not a chattel: 'We are men formed in Christ's likeness and we are kept like beasts.'[10]

The assumption that the peasant was little better than a beast occurs in medieval jokes and stories. There was a stigma attached to serfdom, and in time people resented being called serfs, natives or villeins. What could be more telling than the change of meaning of these medieval words? Villein, which became transmuted into villain, was originally a Norman-French importation signifying a tenant holding by labour services. It was then used to mean a rural, boorish, lowly person; and by Shakespeare's time had acquired its modern meaning of a scoundrel. Servile, which was simply an adjective denoting unfree status, came to mean cringing or mean-spirited. Naif (*nativus*) was a word sometimes used synonymously with serf or villein; but today it denotes, rather condescendingly, something which is amusingly simple. The word boor in Old English meant simply a peasant. But now a boor is a clumsy or ill-bred fellow. The direction of change in all these cases is unmistakable: it is towards a downgrading or denigrating of the peasant's condition and qualities. Such a change of meaning – largely impersonal and over many generations – represents a consensus of informed (or at least recorded) opinion. The verdict of superior and educated persons was that the villein, in comparison with other classes in the community, was at best to be pitied and at worst to be guarded against.

Perhaps this view was a reaction to the inevitable hardness and coarseness of a life on the land without any mechanization to mitigate the ceaseless and backbreaking toil. Or it may have stemmed from an awareness of the stultifying effects of peasant poverty. For medieval England was, by modern standards, a poor country – poor, that is, in the same sense that many countries of the third world today are poor. The total amount of wealth produced was relatively small, and the possibilities of increasing it were severely limited. There was (if we may use the language of the economists) a ceiling on the level of attainable output per head. To see why this was so we need to look a little more closely at some of the determinants of peasant farming.

Calculations made from manorial records in different parts of the country indicate that the yield of mixed grain per acre was about eight to ten bushels. This compares with a figure of fifty-eight to sixty bushels in England today. A bushel of wheat sown in medieval times could be expected to produce about three bushels, whereas a modern farmer has a return of twenty. The medieval peasant had only three ways of maintaining or increasing the fertility of his land: marling, dunging and fallowing. Marl (a mixture of clay and carbonate of lime) is found in many, though not all, parts of England and when available was spread on the fields. But the labour involved in digging out, carting and spreading marl was very great, and manure was therefore the principal fertilizer. The supply of dung, however, was very limited. The peasant was not able to keep many animals because of the difficulty of feeding them in the winter; and even such as he had were folded on the lord's land (*jus faldae*) for the benefit of their dung. Peasants who wished to keep their sheep, and sometimes cattle, on their own holdings were either prevented from doing so or granted the privilege only in exchange for a money payment. There remained the system of fallowing, by which a half or a third of the land was left fallow every second or third year to regain its fertility. The use of roots and grasses to maintain a crop rotation which would not exhaust the soil was unknown until the eighteenth century. Nor was grass sown as a crop to increase the supply of hay, which was limited to natural areas of water meadow. Thus at any given time a large percentage of the arable land was producing nothing; the land under cultivation was producing only a meagre amount; and there was no margin to allow more fodder for more animals whose manure could have increased crop yields. Medieval agriculture was trapped in a vicious circle of low productivity.

Peasant poverty then is to be accounted for in the first instance by the limitations of medieval husbandry. To these have to be added the burdens of manorialism and the church: rents, tallage, entry fines, merchet, tithes. How much these compulsory outgoings amounted to is hard to determine, and they obviously differed from place to place and individual to individual. But that lord and church took a considerable proportion of the peasant's produce in rent and services is clear, and some historians have put the amount as high as 50 per cent of his gross output. In assessing peasant poverty we also need to know the minimum amount of food required for subsistence per person, and the acreage requisite to produce such an amount. Since the peasant holding had to support a household, which could vary in size from one person to many, the average number of persons per household needs to be taken into account. Using figures compiled from manorial accounts of the thirteenth century the situation looks something like this.[11] On a two-field system three acres per person, and on a three-field system two and a half acres were required to produce the minimum cereal diet necessary for subsistence, taking into account compulsory outgoings of 33 per cent of the gross output. Assuming 4·5 persons per household, the total acreage required for subsistence by a peasant household was between ten and thirteen and a half acres, or somewhere between a quarter- and a half-virgate. The villein who held a full virgate of thirty acres was well above subsistence level. But many holdings were much smaller than this. Researches have shown that on 104 manors which were part of eight estates in different parts of the country in the thirteenth century, 45 per cent of the tenants held only a quarter-virgate or less.[12] Many of these were the cottagers mentioned above. Their holdings would as a rule have been insufficient to maintain a family even at the minimum (subsistence) level; and the additional income required would have been obtained – if it was obtained – by working for the lord or a more substantial peasant. The significant thing about this group of the poorest peasantry is that it was so numerous. Nearly a half, and on some individual manors many more, of the peasants must have lived close to subsistence level at the best. Even the middle group of peasants – those holding a half-virgate, who formed 33 per cent of the tenants on the 104 manors surveyed – would have had only just enough to provide for their families, with nothing left over to meet unforeseen contingencies or exceptionally poor seasons. Only the top layer of peasants, holding a full virgate or more, and amounting to 22 per cent of the sample, had much margin beyond the needs of daily living.

A minimum subsistence level expressed in terms of cereal diet only would be unacceptable today, though it would not have seemed unreasonable to medieval writers. For many centuries the standard of living of working people has been measured by the number of loaves of bread available to them, since bread was the main item of their diet. 'Give us this day our daily bread,' was the most familiar of all prayers. The medieval peasant's diet contained a very high proportion of carbohydrates, mainly barley and oats, from which both foodstuffs and drink were made. Although he grew wheat, when the land was suitable, the peasant did not normally consume it but used it for payment of his rent and taxes. Like most peasant communities burdened with payments, medieval villagers grew both a cash crop for special purposes and inferior grains for food and fodder. Fine wheaten bread was therefore not seen on the peasant's table, but coarse, dark loaves, tough as shoe-leather. The bread or oat cake was eaten with the inevitable soup (pease pottage), washed down with ale brewed from barley or oat malt and without the use of hops. Peas and beans, onions and garlic were staples; but meat of any kind was scarce, as animals were too few and valuable to be eaten regularly. Chickens and salt pork were more available; but probably the main source of protein was eggs. The poor widow in Chaucer's *Nun's Priest's Tale* had only 'milk and brown bread, broiled bacon and sometimes an egg or two'. It was a diet that was monotonous and also deficient by modern standards. The poorer peasantry and labourers were almost certainly undernourished, which may help to account for the high mortality rates of the thirteenth century.

The peasant's housing was as basic as his diet. Very few medieval peasant homes survive today, mainly because they were replaced or altered in the great rural rebuilding boom between c.1570 and 1640. From what archaeological and documentary evidence we have, it would seem that few villeins' houses had more than two rooms, one for living and one for sleeping, and with the byre immediately adjacent or built as an extension of the dwelling house. A barn and other outbuildings, together with a yard, completed the messuage, as this plot of land round the house was called. The construction of houses varied according to regions. Where timber was available an oak frame was built, using either the cruck method (by which large curved timbers, meeting at the centre, supported both roof and walls) or a truss design (posts, rafters and tie beam). The cruck or truss formed a gable end, and a ridgepole, running the length of the house, joined the crucks or trusses together. Timber studs or uprights strengthened the frame, and the spaces between them were filled with wattle and daub or a mixture of clay and straw to make the walls. The roof was of thatch. But in some upland areas, such as the Cotswolds, houses were built of stone, and to a different pattern. Here the richer peasants lived in 'long' houses, a type of building in which the family and animals were all under one roof, with the living and sleeping quarters next to and interconnected with the byre. The walls were low, four or five feet in height, and similar to the dry-stone walling of the fields but packed with clay to make them wind and water proof; and the roof was steep and thatched. The poorer peasantry had one-roomed stone houses, comparable to the single-bay, timber-framed houses elsewhere. Some of the poorest people in medieval villages lived in round huts, made of mud; but none of these has survived, and we know little about them.

Peasant houses did not have glass windows or chimneys. The fire burned on an open hearth in the middle of the 'hall' or living room, and the smoke found its way out through an opening in the roof. How true must have been Chaucer's comment on his poor old widow's cottage: 'Full sooty was her hall and eek her bower.' The floor was of beaten earth, sometimes covered with sand or rushes. Furnishings were scanty, though precise information from probate inventories or other sources is not available before the sixteenth century. A table, chest and stools were probably the main items, and kitchen utensils, such as brass pots and pans, were considered valuable enough to be mentioned in documents. Comfort there was none: only simple wooden benches to sit on, and bags of straw or flock to sleep on. Animals and poultry (with their accompanying vermin) were free to wander in and out; the stench of dung, animal sweat and smoke was pervasive.

It needs little imagination to picture the realities of daily life in such surroundings. Larger houses might have a separate kitchen in a lean-to; but in the majority of peasant homes cooking and eating – and indeed most other activities – took place in the one living room. With water from an outside well or spring, and no form of sanitation, the level of personal hygiene was unlikely to be very high. There could be virtually no privacy when a family of five or more persons lived in one or two rooms. The traumas of childbirth, illness and death were acted out amidst domestic squalor. Physical deterioration came much earlier in the Middle Ages than it does to most of us today. After the age of forty a peasant man or woman looked old, and was often in poor health.

Life expectancy was shorter than today, and relatively few people reached what we should now consider a ripe old age. The image of the typical medieval peasant, emerging from his hut, is a wizened, wrinkled creature, with skin browned by exposure to the sun and wind as he ploughs his strips and by the smoke when he is indoors. In an age when for the educated classes the standard of physical beauty emphasized whiteness and fairness, the poor peasant was an object of pity. Few passages are more moving than the description in the fourteenth-century poem, *Pierce the Ploughman's Crede*:

> As I went by the way, weeping for sorrow, I saw a poor man hanging on to the plough. His coat was of a coarse stuff which was called cary; his hood was full of holes and his hair stuck out of it. As he trod the soil his toes stuck out of his worn shoes with their thick soles; his hose hung about his hocks on all sides and he was all bedaubed with mud as he followed the plough. He had two mittens, scantily made of rough stuff, with worn-out fingers and thick with muck. This man bemired himself in mud almost to the ankle, and drove four heifers before him that had become feeble, so that men might count their every rib as sorry-looking they were.
>
> His wife walked beside him with a long goad in a shortened cote-hardy looped up full high and wrapped in a winnowing-sheet to protect her from the weather. She went barefoot on the ice so that the blood flowed. And at the end of the row there lay a little crumb-bowl, and therein a little child covered with rags, and two two-year-olds were on the other side, and they all sang one song that was pitiful to hear: they all cried the same cry – a miserable note. The poor man sighed sorely, and said, 'Children be still!'[13]

About the medieval peasant family, and related problems of marriage, love and sex, we know very little. Surviving records, being mainly legal, fiscal or judicial, are concerned with landholding, inheritance and crime. From them we can infer some of the external aspects of the family but little about its inner, emotional life. Until we have the equivalent of Professor Le Roy Ladurie's study of the French peasantry in *Montaillou* we have to wander largely in the dark.[14] Such accounts as have been written have relied mainly on inferences drawn from later material, usually no earlier than the sixteenth century. It is quite probable that some of the patterns and customs of marriage, family hierarchy and childrearing which have been studied for the early modern period were also prevalent three hundred years earlier. But we do not have hard evidence of this, and it is always dangerous for the historian to extrapolate examples from one period to substantiate claims about another. Generalizations about peasant mores in 'traditional' (meaning all pre-industrial) societies are also unreliable when applied to the Middle Ages. The most that can be done at present is to indicate the nature of the problem and the areas of partial knowledge.

Until fairly recently it was generally assumed that medieval families were large and of the extended stem type, consisting of two or three generations of kin living under the same roof. This was in contrast to the small modern nuclear or conjugal family, made up of parents and unmarried children only. The household, especially in the case of the richer peasantry, could be larger than the family because it included domestic servants, unmarried labourers who lived in, and lodgers. From what we know of medieval society it is plausible to imagine various types of family and household among the peasantry, depending upon the amount of land held, the chronology of the family, and local customs of inheritance. Villeins who held a full virgate or more might be expected to support an extended family or large household. Poor cottagers who had insufficient land for minimum subsistence were more likely to live as nuclear families. The middling peasantry could move from extended to nuclear family status and back again, according to how long the grandparents lived and the number and spacing of children. In view of the high mortality rate and shortened life expectancy, the family cycle passed through its various stages more rapidly than in modern society.

The type and size of peasant families is closely related to their economic role, and in particular to the nature and condition of their landholdings. Here the matter of inheritance is crucial. A villein was not free to leave his holding to whom he pleased, but only according to the custom of the manor. Throughout the manorial heartland of central and southern England (called champaign or champion in the Middle Ages) the commonest system was of impartible inheritance, by which the holding was handed on, undivided, to one of the peasant's sons. Usually this heir was the eldest son (primogeniture); and if there were no sons the land descended to the eldest daughter or was divided among all the daughters equally. In the event of there being no children to inherit, the holding went to the deceased's eldest brother, and after that to the male heirs in succession. By the custom known as Borough English the holding was inherited not by the eldest but by the youngest son (ultimogeniture); or in the absence of sons by the youngest daughter or all the daughters. On some manors there is evidence of a third custom, by which the holder was allowed to choose which of his sons should inherit, and could moreover pass on the land to that son during the holder's lifetime. An alternative to these three types was the custom of partible inheritance or gavelkind, as in Kent. Under this system the land was divided equally among all the sons, or in default among the daughters, of the last holder. The heirs then either farmed jointly and lived together or else divided up the land physically, each taking a share. The latter custom could result in a profusion of very small holdings, as among the Irish peasantry in the nineteenth century; whereas joint occupation preserved the original holding intact. Partible inheritance is found mainly in Kent and East Anglia, and also in Wales. But in all these types of inheritance the holding was associated only with blood relations, the kin.

Family organization accorded with the needs and consequences of the particular system of inheritance. Taking the most widely observed custom of primogeniture, we can see how this worked in three areas of importance: old age, the lot of younger sons and daughters, and marriage. If the heir was able to take over the holding before the death of his parents, the first problem for the family was where and how the old couple were to live. One solution was for them to be allocated a separate part of the house – the traditional 'west room' on Irish farms – and to continue to be supported out of the family economy. In the Middle Ages this would presumably have been acceptable, provided the house was large enough, which seems doubtful in the case of poorer peasants. The problem however would be mitigated insofar as fewer people survived to old age. Even in the seventeenth century a majority of children had been bereaved of at least one parent before they were

51

fully adult. The likelihood was that only one grandparent would survive into retirement, who would be the grandmother, since men tended to marry later and to have a shorter life expectancy than women. The second problem was psychological: how could or did the old peasant and his wife adjust to their new, demoted status and accept the son's and his wife's primacy? We do not know. Surviving documents give us no clues as to how this was handled; nor indeed do we really know if it was conceived as a problem at all. A somewhat different situation arose when, as was sometimes allowed by custom, a widow inherited her late husband's holding. Usually this took the form of a life interest only, and might be limited to a third or a half of the property. This was sometimes called 'free bench', a term which conjures up a picture of the widow sitting by the family hearth in her special place. Under this arrangement the son and heir assumed his father's role, and his mother was assured of a place in the family home.

Less enviable was the position of younger sons and all daughters. After the heir had taken the pick of his father's goods and chattels (the heirlooms, since in Old English loom meant any tool) and the heriot and mortuary had been paid, the remainder was available for division between the other sons if they had not already received their share or portion during their father's lifetime. The legendary younger son, when he came of age, received his portion, left his father's home and went off into the world to seek his fortune. 'Father, give me the portion of goods that falleth to me,' requested the prodigal (and younger) son in the parable. No doubt some younger sons migrated to the nearest town, especially if it was London, and a few might enter the church through the encouragement of a kindly priest. But those who remained in husbandry had either somehow to acquire a holding (hopefully perhaps by marrying a widow or heiress) or to remain simply as farm labourers. In this last condition a man could work for his elder brother, or some other peasant who held land, or for the lord. But it was difficult for him to marry until he had at least a bit of land and a cottage. Daughters were treated similarly to younger sons. When they came to marry and leave home they received a portion of their father's goods and chattels, the dower. In all peasant societies the dower was a vital part of the marriage compact.

Marriage in England today is for most people romantic, an affair of the heart. In peasant England it was also, and in some cases no doubt primarily, a business deal involving property. The order of priorities is made clear in a passage from the fourteenth-century poem by William Langland, *Piers the Ploughman*: 'Thus marriage was made – first by the consent of the father and the advice of friends, and then by the mutual agreement of the two partners. So marriage was established, and God himself made it.'[15] In peasant societies the availability of land acts as a regulator of marriage. Until a man has a holding of some sort he is not able to support a wife and found a family, and custom therefore dictates that he should not marry without such land. A villein was not free to marry without the lord's consent, which was obtained by application to the manorial court and payment of a fee. From court rolls of the thirteenth and early fourteenth centuries it is clear that it was the practice for the heir to marry, or to contemplate marriage, when he inherited the holding. This could take place either on the death of his father (in which case marriage might be considerably delayed) or more usually when the father decided that the time had come to hand over to his son and make provision for old age. The selection of a suitable wife (or husband), bargaining over the dower, and considerations of inter-family politics were (and are) of central concern in peasant life – at any rate for those peasants with property, or whose holding was large enough to function as an economic unit. But what of that possibly quite large number of villagers for whom such considerations were largely irrelevant: the poor cottagers with two or three acres, the labourers who worked on the lord's demesne, the craftsmen? For them, too, marriage was presumably as much an economic as an affective matter, involving a partnership and division of labour in the fields, home and workshop. But we have little knowledge of how, when and why partners were chosen.

Marriage in the early Middle Ages as far as the laity were concerned seems to have been regarded as a private and civil matter. It was essentially a contract between two families or persons. After agreement about property had been reached (the marriage covenant) a ceremony of betrothal or handfasting took place, in which the man and woman joined hands and plighted their troth. The couple might then go to bed, and the ceremony in church followed, if at all, some time later. From the thirteenth century the church increasingly asserted its control over marriage, but the ancient custom of espousal was recognized as legally binding in ecclesiastical law. Marriage and the family, from the community's point of view, were also powerful means of controlling sexuality. Fornication, adultery and incest – condemned as sins by the church, and disapproved of officially by the village – could undermine social stability. In a unit as small as the medieval English village (averaging perhaps three hundred people in some sixty families) the number of possible marriage partners was severely limited. Marriage to a person outside the manor was discouraged by the lord but was allowable on payment of a fine. To a high degree villages and manors were endogamous, and peasant families were closely interrelated. The church, which cherished a somewhat exaggerated fear of in-breeding, prohibited marriage within four degrees of consanguinity, that is between third cousins who had a common great-great-grandparent. But it seems doubtful whether this could have been enforced. In a normal village at least half the villein population were related to this degree. How far sexual norms were observed (or indeed what, at the peasant level, those sexual norms actually were) is hard to determine. Manorial documents contain entries for payment of leyrwite or lecherwite, and disputes over inheritance sometimes involve the status of bastards. But we have nothing as definite as statistics of illegitimacy, and Chaucer's references to love, marriage and lechery in his *Canterbury Tales* tell us little about sexual behaviour at the peasant level.

The limitations in the choice of a marriage partner were but part of a more general limitation of the peasant's world, both mental and physical. There is no reason to suppose that most villagers ever had need to travel more than ten or fifteen miles from home, except possibly when carrying produce between the different manors of a far-flung ecclesiastical estate, or when compelled to serve in the king's army. Their range of human contacts and experiences was much restricted. They were effectively cut off from the outside world of learning by ignorance of Latin, in which all theological and historical works, the liturgy of the church, and all legal and business documents were written. We almost never hear of peasants possessing books nor any suggestion that they could read. Only through the priest, sometimes himself the son of a peasant, did they have access to this wider world of human knowledge. Whether there were oral traditions and mental cultures separate from and unknown to the educated classes (on whose records historians rely), we can only speculate. In some other peasant societies and at different times this was the case.

But when the historian reaches the stage of speculation, and argues what must have been instead of what was, it is time for him to move on. We have gone as far as sources will at present allow us to go in searching for the realities of peasant life in the twelfth and thirteenth centuries; and those realities are only such as can be inferred from the structure and organization of village and manorial life. Below the level of feudal and manorial structures were decisions about family matters, the ramifications of consanguinity, quarrels with neighbours, friendships and sexual liaisons. That the people were poor, illiterate, tied to the land, and living in small and primitive houses leads to certain obvious conclusions about the sort of life that was possible for them. On the inner rituals and subtle relationships of daily life and the mental world of the peasantry our sources are silent.

2. Craftsmen and Journeymen

The common people in medieval England were mainly peasants. But an important minority (between 5 and 10 per cent of the total population) were townsmen. They are to be seen not as an anomaly but rather as an essential characteristic of a peasant economy. The townsmen created a market demand which was met by the peasantry who, although they produced primarily for their own subsistence, also provided some agricultural produce for sale to the towns. This was the source of the townsmen's food (grain, meat, eggs, cheese, vegetables) and raw materials (wool, hides, timber). Economically the bond between town and country was close. With the exception of London, the towns had a rural atmosphere. Although even small towns had their walls, the houses were surrounded by gardens, orchards and sometimes farmyards. Outside the walls were open arable fields and pastures, shared by the burgesses like the peasants in their villages. The townsman lived close to the land, both physically and spiritually. As late as the sixteenth century the weavers of Norwich were forbidden to practise their craft during harvest time because they were required to work in the fields.

Nevertheless, the pattern of urban life was different from that of the countryside. The requirements of trade and industry fitted uneasily into the structure of feudalism, and medieval towns developed, wherever they could, into independent and non-feudal centres. The twelfth and thirteenth centuries saw a marked growth of towns and therewith demands for privileges and exemptions from normal feudal practices. These privileges were defined in charters, granted by the king or great baron to the town (or borough, as it was technically called) in return for a payment. Details varied between towns, but three main liberties or franchises were everywhere sought. First was burgage tenure, which meant that householders (burgesses) were deemed to be personally free and able to buy and sell urban land. Second was the concession of the *firma burgi*, the right to discharge all financial obligations due to the king or other lord by payment of a fixed annual sum levied collectively by the townsmen themselves. In this right of self-taxation lay the germ of municipal self-government. Third, towns acquired control of rights of toll and jurisdiction, including the right to hold their own courts under their own officials and according to borough custom. Commercial privileges meant in effect local monopoly, most commonly expressed in the institution of the gild merchant (market gild), consisting of the burgesses and controlling all commercial activities in the town. Chartered towns thus operated in an atmosphere very different from the feudal society around them. The merchant's and craftsman's need for personal mobility, freedom to buy and sell, and to enter into contracts could not be met by the rural world of lord and peasant. The medieval town developed characteristics of its own, variously interpreted as aspects of freedom. It was, for instance, held by Ranulph Glanville, the great lawyer-minister of Henry II, writing near the end of the twelfth century, that if a serf dwelt unclaimed for a year and a day in any chartered town, and was received into the community or gild of that town as a citizen, he was thereby made free. Medieval towns have been described as oases of freedom in a desert of feudalism. What that freedom meant for the common people remains to be examined.

The network of medieval towns can be ranked in a hierarchy according to their wealth and size of population. Exact figures do not exist, and rough estimates have therefore to be calculated from such sources as the poll-tax returns. London was far and away the largest and wealthiest urban centre, with a population in 1377 of perhaps thirty-five to forty thousand, and more comparable to one of the great continental towns than to any other town in England. Next after London came the provincial capitals, York and Bristol, the former with rather more and the latter with somewhat less than ten thousand inhabitants. Coventry had about seven thousand two hundred, Norwich about six thousand; followed in descending order by Lincoln, Salisbury, Lynn, Colchester, Boston, Beverley, Newcastle, Canterbury, Bury St Edmunds, Oxford, Gloucester, Leicester and Shrewsbury, ranging from about five thousand two hundred down to three thousand. Smaller county towns, like Hereford, Cambridge, Worcester and Nottingham, numbered between two and three thousand; and after these came a large number of market towns, some of them very rustic, but functioning as centres of exchange for the agricultural products of the district and the craftsmen's goods which were not available in the villages.

How many of the inhabitants of a particular town can be classified as belonging to the common people is difficult to determine precisely. But we do know something of the kind of work which was done in towns and the sort of people who did it. Most medieval towns had a range of workers in metals, textiles, leather and wood, as well as in building and in the supply and preparation of food and drink. Colchester in the early fourteenth century, for instance, had sixteen shoemakers, thirteen tanners, ten smiths, eight weavers, eight butchers, seven bakers, six fullers, six girdlers, five mariners, four millers, four tailors, three dyers, three fishermen, three carpenters and three spicers or grocers. Other trades were also enumerated in the same list: cooper, white-leather seller, potter, parchment-maker, furrier, cook, tiler, bowyer, barber, mustarder, woolcomber, lorimer, wood turner, linen draper, wheelwright, glover, fuel dealer, old-clothes dealer, sea-coal dealer, glazier, brewer, ironmonger and vintner.[1] The commonest of English surnames, from the early thirteenth century when such names became generally used, has always been Smith – a reminder of the ubiquity of workers in metal. The Taylors, Walkers, Fullers, Skinners, Tanners, Coopers, Bakers, Carpenters, Wrights, Masons and dozens of similar surnames bear witness to the occupations of our medieval ancestors. Every town was likely to have some of these; but where there was specialization in say woollen textiles or the iron trades or leather working, the number and variety of specialist craftsmen was correspondingly greater. In all trades too the artisans were supported by unskilled helpers and a large number of more or less casual labourers.

The work of many, but not all, craftsmen was organized through a characteristically medieval institution, the gild. In a chartered town the trading privileges which had been won were exercised through the gild merchant, which was in effect the leading burgesses functioning as a monopolistic body. Some towns, including London and Norwich, did not have a gild merchant, but their top citizens nevertheless exercised commercial no less than political control of the city's affairs. From the early twelfth century gilds exercising similar functions, but restricted to one craft, began to appear. Such craft gilds, beginning with the weavers in London and the larger provincial towns, and then spreading to other trades and places, were associations of specialized handworkers. They arose when the level of demand (and therefore the number of workers in the trade) was sufficient to justify a measure of specialization and industrial organization. In a town which specialized in textiles there might be separate gilds for each of the crafts connected with cloth-making; or in the case of iron manufactures the various metal crafts would each have their own gild. Between about 1350 and 1450, when the gild system was in its prime, London had over a hundred craft or 'mystery' organizations. York, Bristol and Coventry all had many craft gilds. Norwich had relatively few.

The aims and practices of the craft gilds were set down in their ordinances, which thus provide evidence of some aspects of the conditions of labour. The following extract is from the ordinances of the white tawyers (leather workers) of London, in 1346:

In the first place, they have ordained that they will find a wax candle, to burn before Our Lady in the Church of All Hallows near London Wall. Also, that each person of the said trade shall put in the box such sum as he shall think fit, in aid of maintaining the said candle.

Also, if by chance any one of the said trade shall fall into poverty, whether through old age, or because he cannot labour or work, and have nothing with which to help himself; he shall have every week from the said box 7d. for his support if he be a man of good repute. And after his decease, if he have a wife, a woman of good repute, she shall have weekly for her support 7d. from the said box, so long as she shall behave herself well and keep single.

And that no stranger shall work in the said trade, or keep house [for the same] in the city, if he be not an apprentice, or a man admitted to the franchise of the said city.

And that no one shall take the serving man of another to

work with him, during his term, unless it be with the permission of his master.

And if any one of the said trade shall have work in his house that he cannot complete, or if for want of assistance such work shall be in danger of being lost, those of the said trade shall aid him, that so the said work be not lost.

And if any one of the said trade shall depart this life, and have not wherewithal to be buried, he shall be buried at the expense of their common box; and when any one of the said trade shall die, all those of the said trade shall go to the Vigil, and make offering on the morrow.

And if any serving-man shall conduct himself in any other manner than properly towards his master, and act rebelliously towards him, no one of the said trade shall set him to work, until he shall have made amends before the Mayor and Aldermen; and before them such misprision shall be redressed.

And that no one of the said trade shall behave himself the more thoughtlessly, in the way of speaking or acting amiss, by reason of the points aforesaid; and if any one shall do to the contrary thereof, he shall not follow the said trade until he shall have reasonable made amends.

And if any one of the said trade shall do to the contrary of any point of the Ordinances aforesaid, and be convicted thereof by good men of the said trade, he shall pay to the Chamber of the Guildhall of London, the first time 2s., the second time 40d., and the third time half a mark, and the fourth time 10s., and shall forswear the trade.

Also, that the good folks of the same trade shall once in the year be assembled in a certain place, convenient thereto, there to choose two men of the most loyal and befitting of the said trade, to be overseers of work and all other things touching the trade, for that year, which persons shall be presented to the Mayor and Aldermen for the time being, and sworn before them diligently to enquire and make search, and loyally to present to the said Mayor and Aldermen such defaults as they shall find touching the said trade without sparing any one for friendship or for hatred, or in any other manner. And if any one of the said trade shall be found rebellious against the said overseers, so as not to let them properly make their search and assay, as they ought to do; or if he shall absent himself from the meeting aforesaid, without reasonable cause, after due warning by the said overseers, he shall pay to the Chamber, upon the first default, 40d.; and on the second like default, half a mark; and on the third, one mark; and on the fourth, 20s. and shall forswear the trade for ever.

Also, that if the overseers shall be found lax and negligent about their duty, or partial to any person, for gift or for friendship, maintaining him, or voluntarily permitting him [to continue] in his default, and shall not present him to the Mayor and Aldermen, as before stated, they are to incur the penalty aforesaid.

Also, that each year, at such assemblies of the good folks of the said trade, there shall be chosen overseers, as before stated. And if it shall be found that through laxity or negligence of the said governors such assemblies are not held, each of the said overseers is to incur the said penalty.

Also, that all skins falsely and deceitfully wrought in their trade, which the said overseers shall find on sale in the hands of any person, citizen or foreigner, within the franchise, shall be forfeited to the said Chamber, and the worker thereof amerced in manner aforesaid.

Also, that no one who has not been an apprentice, and has not finished his term of apprenticeship in the said trade shall be made free of the same trade; unless it be attested by the overseers for the time being or by four persons of the said trade, that such person is able, and sufficiently skilled to be made free of the same.

Also, that no one of the said trade shall induce the servant of another to work with him in the same trade, until he has made a proper fine with his first master, at the discretion of the said overseers, or of four reputable men of the said trade. And if any one shall do to the contrary thereof, or receive the serving workman of another to work with him during his term, without leave of the trade, he is to incur the said penalty.

Also, that no one shall take for working in the said trade more than they were wont heretofore, on the pain aforesaid, that is to say, for the *dyker* [a package of ten] *of Scottes stagges*, half a mark; the *dyker of Yrysshe*, half a mark; the *dyker of Spanysshe stagges* 10s.;

for the hundred of *gotesfelles*, 20s.; the hundred of *rolether*, 16s.; for the hundred skins of *hyndescalves*, 8s.; and for the hundred of *kiddefelles*, 8s.[2]

Here, in the idiom of the fourteenth century, are the main elements of gildsmanship. The first paragraphs remind us of the religious and social origins of the medieval gild, and of the need for mutual aid in times of poverty, sickness, old age and death. Early on in the document monopoly rights in the trade are asserted, notably against all 'strangers'. Apprenticeship is laid down as the normal method of entry into the trade. This had the double function of restricting recruitment and controlling the standard of craftsmanship. In some gilds apprenticeship was for a full seven years, culminating in an examination and the production of a 'masterpiece'. Rates of payment are also fixed; and in later years the craft gilds elaborated further codes governing hours and conditions of work and numbers to be employed. The prime function of the gild was to protect and enforce the monopoly and rights of the members; but the fixing of fair prices and the control of quality was also of benefit to the community as a whole. This has made it possible in modern times to idealize the craft gild as an institution protecting the interests of producers and consumers alike in a society free from the acquisitive values of capitalism. In fact the qualitites of the craft gild sprang not only from medieval notions of justice and fairness, but also from the limitations of a restricted market which made it imperative that production should be tightly regulated.

Nor were the gilds quite the repositories of democracy and corporate harmony that used to be imagined by romantic historians. It is noticeable that the white tawyers' ordinances are concerned with the relations of 'serving men' towards their masters. Ideally, after a boy had served his apprenticeship to a master craftsman he became for a time a journeyman, paid by the day (*journée*), and in due course a master himself. Where this ideal approximated to the reality, as it perhaps did in some smaller towns, the craft gild represented the interests of artisans opposed to a commercial oligarchy which ruled through the gild merchant. But in London and the larger seaports some of the craft gilds developed into fraternities of rich speculating merchants; and the twelve great London livery companies such as the Goldsmiths, Mercers, Grocers, Drapers, and so on, which emerged in the late Middle Ages, were far removed from humble craftsmen. From the mid-thirteenth century some journeymen were no longer potential masters but wage workers employed by richer gild members. Such journeymen attempted to form their own combinations – and were fiercely resisted by the masters. In a well-known case of 1396 the London Master Saddlers complained to the mayor and aldermen of the City that

> the serving men, called *yomen* . . . without leave of their masters, were wont to array themselves all in a new and like suit once in the year, and often times held divers meetings, at Stratford and elsewhere without the liberty of the said city, as well as in divers places within the city; whereby many inconveniences and perils ensued to the trade aforesaid; and also, very many losses might happen thereto in future times, unless some quick and speedy remedy should by the rulers of the said city be found for the same.[3]

The journeymen protested that they were simply a pious fraternity which had existed from 'time out of mind', and that they 'arrayed themselves all in like suit' (that is, wore their livery) to walk in procession annually on the feast of the Assumption of the Blessed Virgin Mary from Stratford, east of London, to the church of St Vedast to hear mass. To which the masters replied that the journeymen 'under a certain feigned colour of sanctity' had formed 'covins' to raise wages, 'to such an extent . . . that whereas a master in the said trade could before have had a serving-man or journeyman for 40 shillings or 5 marks yearly, and his board, now such a man would not agree with his master for less than 10 or 12 marks or even 10 pounds, yearly'. The mayor and aldermen promptly forbade such a journeymen's combination, declaring that 'in future they should have no fraternity, meetings or covins or other unlawful things'.

Widespread and various as was the medieval habit of forming gilds, not all craftsmen were members of such fraternities. Even in London, which had the most developed gild system, there were many more trades than gilds, and probably no more than a quarter of the townsmen were freemen who exercised political rights through gild membership or other qualifying franchises. In small towns the number of workers in some crafts would be too small to warrant the formation of a separate craft gild. Other trades, such as shipbuilding, iron-smelting, mining and salt-making, which were carried on outside the towns, seem not to have been organized in gilds. The highly skilled stonemasons, who moved about the country from one job to another, had their own special system of lodges. Overall, only a minority of artisans – and an even smaller minority of the total working population – belonged to gilds. The classical gild system (like the classical manor) has to be regarded not as a description of how medieval artisan life was actually organized in a particular town but as a model or ideal-type to which reality approximated in a greater or lesser degree. We do not know whether the working life of a craftsman in York, which had many gilds, was substantially different from that of his counterpart in Norwich which had few. It would seem likely that common technical processes imposed a dominant pattern of activity throughout the trade, gild or no gild.

That dominant pattern of industry was basically domestic. For several hundred years, until the great changes brought by the Industrial Revolution, manufacture was centred in the home. This was the overriding feature which determined the nature of the working life of craftsmen and tradesmen, and which made it so different from life for the majority of workers in modern times. Home and workplace were one and the same. The breadwinner did not 'go out to work' each day, leaving his wife and family behind in the home. Instead, the weaver or shoemaker or baker carried on his business in a part of the house set aside as a workshop, or sometimes in the main room of the dwelling. The family could be an extended one: man and wife, their children, apprentices, journeymen and maidservants. It was an economic as well as a social and affective unit. There was work for all members of the family, including the children. While the weaver worked at the loom, his wife and children carded and spun the wool. Spinning was so characteristic an occupation for girls that un-married women became known as spinsters. In other trades the work of the master craftsman was similarly supported by prepar-atory, ancillary or finishing tasks performed by members of the family. At its head, in his multi-role of husband, father, employer and entrepreneur, was the master. His wife was in varying degrees his partner, though clearly subordinate to him. To the apprentices he stood *in loco parentis*. In this indenture, made in 1459, between John Gibbs, a fisherman of Penzance, and John Goffe,

the aforesaid John Goffe has put himself to the aforesaid John Gibbs to learn the craft of fishing, and to stay with him as apprentice and to serve from the feast of Philip and James [May 1] next to come after the date of these presents until the end of eight years then next ensuing and fully complete; throughout which term the aforesaid John Goffe shall well and faithfully serve the aforesaid John Gibbs and Agnes his wife as his masters and lords, shall keep their secrets, shall everywhere willingly do their lawful and honourable commands, shall do his masters no injury nor see injury done to them by others, but prevent the same as far as he can, shall not waste his master's goods nor lend them to any man without his special command. And the aforesaid John Gibbs and Agnes his wife shall teach, train and inform or cause the aforesaid John Goffe, their apprentice, to be informed in the craft of fishing in the best way they know, chastising him duly and finding for the same John, their apprentice, food, clothing linen and woollen, and shoes, sufficiently, as befits such an apprentice to be found, during the term aforesaid. And at the end of the term aforesaid the aforesaid John Goffe shall have of the aforesaid John Gibbs and Agnes his wife 20s. sterling without any fraud.[4]

The patriarchal family was central to the medieval world of work. Not all workers in towns of course were craftsmen; but the general assumption was that in productive industry the manufacturing unit would approximate to the family group. It was a hand-made world. The scale and speed of work, the range and type of product were determined by what men and women could make with hand tools and (with the exception of watermills for grinding corn and fulling cloth) without power-driven machinery. The worker stood in a very close relationship to his work and its product; and the alienation of the worker from the product of his labour, which has been diagnosed as a major ill in modern capitalist societies, was not present for the medieval craftsman. Moreover, the work was undertaken in an environment built upon the close and subtle relationships of a family. How this affected the nature and quality of working life we can only guess. Perhaps the nearest we can get to it is through the dimly remembered folk consciousness preserved in ancient legends. The world of masters and servingmaids and apprentices is enshrined in the story of Cinderella. In the tale of Dick Whittington (who in real life died in 1423) we have the archetype of the poor boy who made good. Nursery rhymes are full of tailors, bakers, pretty maids, old women, cats, London Bridge and Charing Cross. The industrious apprentice who marries his master's daughter, or the widow of a master craftsman who bravely continues the business with the aid of faithful journeymen, flit in and out of the picture. But the image is generalized and blurred, and much of it is possibly no older than the sixteenth century. The finer details of the lives of working people and their own perceptions remain hidden.

One industry made a greater impact than any other on the national life in the Middle Ages, and that was wool. From time immemorial spinning and weaving had been part of the peasant economy, carried on in the villages and to meet local needs. The production of wool, however, was far in excess of these requirements, and a thriving export trade to Flanders and Florence developed. At the same time the production of woollen cloth also expanded and this too was exported. By the late twelfth and early thirteenth centuries weavers were busy in many English towns and their gilds in some cases grew rich and powerful. In the fourteenth century there was a marked shift from the export of raw materials (wool) to the export of manufactured goods (cloths); and for the next three hundred years the industry was a pre-eminent part of the economy. Symbolically the Lord Chancellor himself sat upon a wool sack; and the wealthy wool merchant spoke for many when he engraved on the windows of his new house,

> I praise God and ever shall
> It is the sheep hath paid for all.

This growth of the cloth industry necessitated certain technical and organizational changes which directly affected the lives of the craftsmen and their families.

As long as the craftsman was producing for a local and limited market he was able to sell his goods directly to the customer. But when the market became national and international he could no longer do this but had to sell to merchants, who thus came to dominate the trade. Within the gilds of the larger towns the richer masters ceased to be craftsmen and became entrepreneurs. They bought the cloths from the working weavers, supervised the all-important finishing processes, and marketed the finished product. When in addition to this the clothier, as the entrepreneur was called, also supplied the raw material, his control of the industry was complete. The weaver, even though he remained a master craftsman owning his own loom and working in his own home, became dependent on a middleman. In some cases by the later Middle Ages he was virtually no more than a piece worker dependent on a wage.

Technological innovation also reinforced the position of the capitalist clothier. After the cloth was taken off the loom it had to be 'fulled', a process of washing, cleaning and felting which was traditionally performed by 'walkers' who trod on the cloth in large vats full of water and fuller's earth. From the late twelfth century fulling mills were introduced, and in these the stamping of the cloth by the bare feet of the walkers was replaced by heavy hammers driven by water power. The early fulling mills were located mainly in the northwest and west of the kingdom, where there was a natural supply of water power in fast-flowing streams. These of course were rural areas, and in the thirteenth and fourteenth centuries there was a movement to transfer cloth production from the towns to country districts, where also wages were lower and gild control absent. By the fifteenth century we can distinguish two quite distinct types of clothier. First was the master weaver who bought or grew his fleeces, had them carded and spun by his family and neighbours, and employed journeymen in his home to help with the weaving. Such was the pattern in Yorkshire, where the clothier sold his cloths in Wakefield and Halifax, mainly for the home market. The second type was the capitalist clothier, who gave out the raw material, collected the cloth from jobbing weavers, had it fulled and finished, and then marketed it. These men were found in East Anglia and in the West Country, the main export areas.

Cloth, as England's major export, employed an important minority of the working population. An estimate of the numbers employed in the production of cloth for export in the early fifteenth century puts the figure at between fifteen and twenty-five thousand, calculated on a full-time basis. Since many textile workers were in fact part-time, and production for the home market has also to be taken into account, the actual number of persons involved in the cloth industry may have been twice this figure. From the worker's point of view the cloth trade was not a single industry, but a number of separate trades or crafts. We are reminded of this when we look at the number of mysteries in a medieval town: the woollen weavers, coverlet (worsted) weavers, fullers, dyers, wool chapmen, wool packers, shearmen, woadmen and cardmakers all had their own gilds.

In the long run the cloth trade is significant because of its organization. The domestic or putting-out system, in which production was carried on in the homes of the workers but controlled by middlemen or putters-out, was a prototype of the industrial organization which developed in other trades too. In the sixteenth and seventeenth centuries it expanded greatly, and flourished in varying forms until the Industrial Revolution and later. This was the system through which the daily work of men and women in productive industry was organized. It gave them a certain measure of freedom to regulate their own pace and rhythm of work, to make their own decisions about details, and to select their own partners or workmates. But they were ultimately dependent on middlemen who effectively decided what should be produced and who should produce it. They had lost the independence of the master craftsman who dealt directly with his customers. In its final, declining years in the nineteenth century the domestic system was to become a terrible instrument of oppression. In medieval times it provided a minority of the common people with a perhaps enviable alternative to peasant life.

Comparison with the peasantry might provide a way of assessing the standing of town craftsmen and labourers. The medieval town only existed as a town in relation to its surrounding hinterland, against which it appeared as in many respects privileged and superior, and it would not be surprising to find that town workers were more favourably situated than peasants. In practice it is rather difficult to make such a comparison because of the insufficiency of data which is strictly comparable. Thus although we have daily wage rates for various categories of craftsmen, the income of the peasantry was only partially expressed in cash terms. Other non-quantifiable constituents of a standard of living, such as housing, conditions of labour, variety of diet, health, are similarly difficult to compare. Nevertheless some scraps of information are available and worth setting down.

At the end of the thirteenth century a skilled worker such as a carpenter or mason was paid 3d. or 4d. a day. An unskilled labourer, whether man or woman, might have 1d. or 1½d. Artisans' wages in London were anything between 25 per cent and 60 per cent higher, and reached 4d. or 5d. Special work was paid at a differential rate. At the building of Newgate gaol in 1281, one set of carpenters had 5½d. per day, another 5d., and a third 4d.; the sawyers were paid 9½d. the pair, and the masons 5d. a day each. In the countryside the daily rate for reaping an acre of wheat was 5d. This included binding and reaping, and could be done in a long harvest day by a good man with his wife helping to bind. The rate for a thatcher and his helper (who might be a woman) was a little over 3d. a day. To give meaning to these wage rates we have to see what they would buy. For the (scriptural) penny a day the labourer could buy thirty or forty eggs, or three or four pigeons and about 2 lb of cheese. A hen cost 1¼d. and a fat pig about 3s. (By comparison, the daily wage of a farm labourer in 1900, which was 2s., would also buy forty eggs.) Wage rates of course are not the same as earnings, which depend upon the number of days actually worked. In all outside occupations the weather reduced the number of working days in the year. For artisans in such trades the winter's wages were about 25 per cent less than in other seasons. Sunday was supposed to be observed as a day of rest. Religious festivals were also days off from work. Walter of Henley, the author of a thirteenth-century treatise on husbandry, assumed a working year of 308 days, which after allowing for Sundays gives only five holidays. But during the building of the Cistercian Abbey of Vale Royal at Delamere in Cheshire the masons observed twenty-seven feastdays and holidays in 1279 and twenty-two in 1280. At the repair of Beaumaris castle, Anglesey, in 1319–20 the number was twenty.

Although economic statistics give but a weak indication of the daily realities of labouring life, figures of wages and prices are more useful in showing trends. From wage records in various occupations it is clear that there was a general increase in wage rates in the later Middle Ages, reaching a peak between about 1430 and 1460, the explanation and social effects of which we shall have cause to examine later. Between the mid-fourteenth and mid-fifteenth centuries the piece rates paid for agricultural labour such as threshing and winnowing increased 50 to 75 per cent; and the daily rates of building workers rose by 75 to 100 per cent for craftsmen and 100 to 125 per cent for labourers. Taking price movements into account, we find that the real wage rates of building craftsmen in Oxford rose by nearly 50 per cent between the 1340s and the last quarter of the fourteenth century, and by almost 100 per cent by the later fifteenth century – a figure not equalled again until the later nineteenth century.

Building workers are among the best documented of medieval craftsmen, thanks to the large number of fabric rolls of royal and ecclesiastical buildings which have survived. The masons are, of all medieval workers, the ones who have left the greatest and most enduring legacy of their work.[5] They built the nine hundred to a thousand monasteries, cathedrals, colleges and hospitals of England and Wales, to say nothing of the thousands of parish churches, most of which after the Norman Conquest were built or rebuilt in stone. They constructed huge castles for the king and his barons, town walls as at York and Chester, gild halls, quays and bridges. After the original construction followed centuries of extension, rebuilding and repair work. Some of these projects were on a very large scale. The building of Eton College required over a million bricks in one year, 1443–4. At a time of peak (and exceptional) activity Beaumaris castle provided employment for 400 masons, 30 smiths and carpenters, 1000 unskilled workers and 200 carters. Undertakings of this nature, needing large sums of capital, were mostly reserved for the king or the church. But even on smaller buildings the industry operated in an atmosphere different from the world of small master craftsmen and gildsmen of the towns. Stone was seldom used for domestic architecture, and the medieval town consisted of timber-framed houses with wattle-and-daub walls and straw or reed thatch. A majority of masons therefore tended to be employed on large buildings such as churches, castles and bridges, though there was some work on a smaller scale such as building chimneys and laying stone floors or paving. The capitalist organization of the industry, its large-scale operations, and the particular conditions of work removed the medieval mason from the familiar pattern of peasant life. Like the townsman, he fitted uneasily into the feudal mould.

Masons were peripatetic, moving on from one job to the next. It seems unlikely that most of them enjoyed permanent employment. For casual and seasonal work they were paid by the day or week, but on a big job they might be hired for several years or even for life. The building of Vale Royal abbey took fifty years, Caernarvon castle thirty-eight years, London bridge fourteen years. Works such as these provided regular and continuous, if not permanent, employment. Indeed, so great was the demand for masons that at times the king resorted to impressment. For the building of Windsor castle in 1360–2 instructions were sent to the sheriffs in all the surrounding counties and as far away as Lancashire and Yorkshire commanding them to send a quota of masons to Windsor, totalling in all 1360 men. What the masons felt about this method of recruitment, reminiscent of the press gang for the army and navy in the eighteenth and nineteenth centuries, we can only guess. Cases of desertion are recorded, and also of opposition from local craftsmen who feared the impressed men would lower rates. Impressment, like tramping and living away from home, was presumably one of the hazards or conditions of the mason's life.

Within the trade itself there were several categories of mason. Most exalted of all was the master mason, who superintended the work and functioned in effect as the architect. Under him were the operative masons, divided into freemasons and roughmasons. The latter were concerned with laying stones, and sometimes also bricks. The freemasons are thought to have been so called because they originally worked on freestone, a finely grained stone suitable for carving and moulding. They were highly skilled craftsmen and artists, and were perhaps free in more senses than the original one. Their work is to be seen in the splendid legacy of medieval carving and Gothic tracery and vaulting in churches, gild halls and palaces. All skilled men were supported by their servants or labourers, who did the fetching, carrying, mixing, digging, and all kinds of rough work.

At the centre of the mason's working life was the lodge. Physically this was a wooden shed, erected on the site, which served as a workshop. Organizationally it controlled the conditions of work, and elaborate rules were laid down for the governance of the masons' affairs. Outwardly this looks similar to a craft gild, but in one vital respect it was different. The gild was an association of independent master craftsmen; the lodge was composed of journeymen, most of whom would never become master masons. For this reason apprenticeship was not common among masons, since it could not be a stepping stone to mastership as in other crafts. Although there seem to have been some masons who were in the position of independent master craftsmen, undertaking small or limited pieces of work, the majority remained in the status of wage workers. Only a small number of very outstanding masons could hope to rise to the few positions of master mason or master of works.

Many writers have noted the grotesque humour or sly satire in some medieval carvings and have concluded that the stonemason or wood carver must have got fun out of his work. Surely the gargoyles on the exteriors of churches which are often fantastic creatures spewing out the rain water, or the interior decorations on capitals and screens such as a fox in abbot's clothing or a pig playing bagpipes, could only have been executed by men who enjoyed their work, it is argued. Perhaps it was so; but we do not know what they were thinking as they worked, nor why they did what they did. All we can do is substitute our feelings for those of the anonymous craftsmen; or in other words exercise our historical imagination.

Not all craftsmen, then, were townsmen; some were employed in industries which were not located in towns, and there were also some craftsmen in the villages. Nevertheless the characteristic medieval gild organization of craftsmen, journeymen and apprentices is associated primarily with the towns. The English people were already divided between town and country, each developing in time a different social structure, a different political system (borough and county) and different cultural patterns. It is a dichotomy which has persisted into recent times and which we shall meet recurrently throughout this history.

It was suggested at the end of the first chapter that the inner world of medieval peasant belief is to us a closed book. The same is true for the craftsmen and townsmen. We can study the institutions of society within which the common people lived; but their thought systems are much more elusive. Christian belief and practice provided the framework within which men were expected to live. The physical presence of the church was everywhere apparent. In practically every village in the land the largest and most substantial building was the parish church, used for meetings of the community as well as for worship. In the small space of the medieval city of York were forty parish churches, as well as the minster and St Mary's abbey. Town gilds were embedded in religious observances. Abbeys and monasteries exercised their power as wealthy landowners throughout the countryside. We do not have statistics of medieval church attendance, only the constant complaints of preachers that not everyone who could have been was at mass on Sundays and feastdays.

It has been suggested that religion in the Middle Ages was for most people primarily a practical matter; the mass was a semi-magical ceremony from which the hearers could hope to derive some (perhaps undefined) benefit. Even more valuable (because more personal) were the rituals associated with the rites of passage: baptism, confirmation, marriage, churching (that is, purification after childbirth) of women, extreme unction and burial of the dead. In all societies important changes in personal condition are marked with ceremonies, which function as a recognition and stabilization of the change. A practical expression is given to the sentiments connected with the new status. In a Christian world the church gave meaning to and guidance on the problems of sexuality, family relationships, the upbringing of children and death. This practical aspect of religion continued into recent times. Even among non-churchgoers the parish church has remained the place for christenings, marriage and funerals. All this of course was public religion, not family prayers round the fireside, about which little is heard before the Reformation. It tells us about outward observances and what people were supposed to believe; but not what was actually in their hearts and minds.

Until 1549 the central act of worship of the church – the mass – was in Latin, and the bible was officially available in English only from 1539. Medieval Christianity was for most people oral and visual religion. Popular knowledge of the scriptures and basic doctrines came from preachers and the images and wall paintings in the church. Regular attendance at the mass, year in year out, was supposed to familiarize people with the great central truths of the faith; and the more devout might be expected to memorize the *Pater, Ave* and the creed. But what this meant to labouring people is impossible to say.

3. The Growth of Freedom

A dominant characteristic of all agricultural societies is their stability and continuity. Over long periods of time there is relatively little change in either the countryside or rural life. Peasant conditions may be comparative over several generations or even centuries – so much so that some writers have felt justified in using material from one age to illuminate conditions in another. If we are short of evidence on peasant life in the fourteenth century, may we not extrapolate from Thomas Hardy's novels of Wessex in the nineteenth, finding there the selfsame villagers of five hundred years earlier? Be that as it may, in such societies at all times men are accustomed for the most part to the assumption that their lives will be the same as their fathers'. Some social change, however, even though slow in pace, did take place in medieval peasant societies, and occasionally external events obtruded themselves into daily life. These were unsettling and difficult to deal with. Ideology explained and justified stability and equilibrium in society, not change. Most men's thinking was not attuned to a concern for social change. Proponents of change usually presented it as a restoration of former conditions, not as something new. These problems came to the fore in the fourteenth century.

In the past historians have presented the changes of the later Middle Ages as a growth of freedom. At the risk of sounding somewhat old-fashioned, we could do far worse than adopt this interpretation, though always with the proviso that freedom is to be defined in context. A combination of economic, demographic and political upheavals in the fourteenth century impinged on peasant life in many important ways, but the single most significant change was in status. Whereas in 1300 the majority of peasants were villeins, by 1500 very few were still servile. However this change came about, and whatever qualifications we need to add, for the peasant this was a gain in freedom. The bondman had become free. A vital link in the chain of feudal relationships was broken, and the English peasantry was set on a path of development leading to the ending of feudalism earlier than in some other parts of Western Europe. The steps by which this momentous change was effected must now be considered, and in particular how far the decline of serfdom was due to the peasants' own conscious actions and how far to impersonal factors of demography and economics.

From the time of Domesday the manor as an economic (though not as a legal) entity had shown tendencies to dissolution. On some estates the lord of the manor decided for various reasons not to farm the demesne by means of the customary labour services of his villein tenants. Instead he commuted the labour dues into a money rent and worked the demesne with wage labour. Or, if he wished no longer to cultivate the demesne himself, he could let it to a tenant, who thus became the occupant of what in many villages was later called the home or manor farm. These developments were not systematic or complete in any particular place, nor was there any uniformity between regions. In the later twelfth and thirteenth centuries the process was interrupted: a combination of expanding trade, rising prices and increase in population encouraged some landlords to work their demesnes themselves with labour services. But the conditions favourable to this direct exploitation of their estates did not last; and in the fourteenth century the contraction of demesne farming and its labour services continued. This did not in itself destroy villeinage, but it seriously undermined its economic basis. When labour services were commuted into a money rent, villein tenure sooner or later became copyhold, that is tenure by copy of the court roll according to the custom of the manor. Gradually and unevenly the conditions of customary villein tenure grew more like free tenure, and therewith villeinage began to wither away.[1] Moreover these long-term changes in manorialism were greatly accelerated in the fourteenth century by two events which affected directly the lives of great numbers of the common people: the Black Death and the Peasants' Revolt.

The visitation of bubonic plague in 1348–9, known popularly as the Great Pestilence or Black Death, was arguably the greatest catastrophe suffered by the common people in the Middle Ages, or perhaps in the whole of their history. If this seems an exaggerated claim for a happening which is treated in many histories as simply an influence or factor in economic or demographic change, rather than as an event in itself, we need only ponder the statistics of mortality to realize the unprecedented nature of the calamity. Within a few months after August 1348 between 30 and 45 per cent of the total population died – killed suddenly by a pestilence they could not understand or counter. Men, women and children were seized with violent pains in their chests; they developed hard swellings or boils, usually in the groin or armpits; others vomited blood, became feverish and delirious. A man who felt perfectly well in the morning could be dead by nightfall. Others took three or four days to die. They were victims of bubonic plague, which is now known to be carried by rats and transmitted to humans by fleas. In its pneumonic form plague is highly contagious, and can only be treated with extreme precaution. Nothing of this was known in the fourteenth century, with the result that the disease exacted a terrible toll. No part of the kingdom escaped and all classes suffered; but inevitably those most at risk were the poor, the malnourished and the most crowded. And here we come yet again upon the paradox familiar in the history of the common people, that the greater the event the less we seem to know about it from the point of view of the people themselves. Although over a third of the population perished we have little idea how or to what extent this terrible experience entered into the consciousness of the ordinary people. Somewhere in folk memory or local tradition one would expect to find at least vestigial remains of the upheaval; but if there are such clues they are at present undiscovered. For guidance we have to turn elsewhere, to the testimony of chroniclers and the manorial and ecclesiastical records.

The plague is generally supposed to have originated in China and spread to Europe along the trade routes. It ravaged Constantinople and Sicily in 1347 and reached France and Germany the following year. About 1 August 1348 the disease appeared in the seaport towns of Dorsetshire, brought probably by a ship from France, and travelled westwards and northwards through Devon and Somerset. 'It passed most rapidly from place to place,' recorded Robert of Avesbury, Keeper of the Registry of the Court of Canterbury, 'swiftly killing ere mid-day many who in the morning had been well, and without respect of persons (some few rich people excepted), not permitting those destined to die to live more than three, or at most four, days. On the same day twenty, forty, sixty and very often more corpses were committed to the same grave.'[2] Bristol was very badly hit; according to a later chronicler the plague left scarcely enough survivors to bury the dead, and the grass grew several inches high in High Street and Broad Street. The men of Gloucester, fearful of contagion, tried to cut themselves off from all contact with Bristol, but in vain. By 1 November London was affected, and in the following January the first outbreaks occurred in Norwich. Throughout 1349 the plague spread northwards. Every town soon had its common pit for the burial of plague victims; and the chroniclers record harrowing stories of parents burying their children, the stench of death in the churchyards, and the terrified attempts to escape by fleeing from place to place.

The most vivid contemporary account of the plague was written not by an English chronicler but by the Italian, Giovanni Boccaccio, in the preface to his *Decameron*. The conditions he describes are those of Florence in 1348, but they might equally well have been in England.

[The] maladies seemed to set entirely at naught both the art of the physician and the virtues of physic; . . . those that recovered [were] few, but almost all within three days from the appearance of the said symptoms, sooner or later, died, and in most cases without any fever or other attendant malady.

Moreover, the virulence of the pest was the greater by reason that intercourse was apt to convey it from the sick to the whole, just as fire devours things dry or greasy when they are brought close to it. Nay, the evil went yet further, for not merely by speech or association with the sick was the malady communicated to the healthy with consequent peril of common death; but any that touched the clothes of the sick or aught else that had been touched or used by them, seemed thereby to contract the disease. . . . The condition of the lower, and, perhaps, in great measure of the middle ranks, of the people shewed even worse and more deplorable; for, deluded by hope or constrained by poverty, they stayed in their quarters, in their houses, where they sickened by thousands a day, and, being without service or help of any kind, were, so to speak, irredeemably devoted to the death which overtook them. Many died daily or nightly in the public streets; of many others, who died at home, the departure was hardly observed by their neighbours, until the stench of their putrefying bodies carried the tidings; and what with their corpses and the corpses of others who died on every hand the whole place was a sepulchre.[3]

While the catastrophic proportions of the Black Death are adequately recorded by contemporaries (who could find no parallel short of God's chastisement of his people in Old Testament times) their figures of mortality cannot usually be accepted at face value. More accurate calculations have to be made from other sources, such as diocesan registers which record the institutions of priests to benefices. Historians using this method have produced death rates of beneficed clergy for the year of the plague of about 40 per cent; and other figures for monastic clergy are as high as 45 per cent. Another method is to use manorial records to calculate rural death rates from the numbers of holdings which fell vacant during 1348–9. The payment of death duties (heriots) yields figures which can be set against the total number of holdings on the manor liable to heriot. On this basis it has been calculated that two-thirds of the customary tenants on four manors in Hampshire, Wiltshire and Oxfordshire died; and between 50 and 60 per cent on seven manors in Cambridgeshire, Essex and east Cornwall. Using calculations derived from the fall in the numbers of payments of customary dues, the death rate on twenty-two Glastonbury Abbey manors was 55 per cent, and on three Essex manors 43 per cent.[4] We can also see the devastation of the peasantry through individual case studies. Thus on the manor of Cornard Parva in Suffolk, where there were never more than fifty holdings, sixty people died and twenty-one families were entirely obliterated. At Hunstanton in Norfolk one hundred and seventy-two tenants of the manor died in eight months: seventy-four of them left no male heirs, and nineteen others had no heirs at all.[5] On the manor of Halesowen, Worcestershire, where the number of tenants had risen from seventy-one in 1086 to two hundred and three on the eve of the plague, eighty-one of them died: 40 per cent of the male tenantry was thus destroyed and whole families were wiped out. On the manor of Alvechurch, some eight miles southwest of Halesowen, 44 per cent of the tenants died in the Black Death.[6] In some cases even the records themselves tell a story, for at the height of the plague they are often imperfect, and the handwriting changes during the course of the year.

In the towns the horror and devastation equalled (or perhaps exceeded) the plight of the manors. Henry Knighton, a canon of St Mary's Abbey, Leicester, described conditions in that town:

> Then this cruel death spread on all sides, following the course of the sun. And there died at Leicester, in the small parish of St. Leonard's, more than 380 persons, in the parish of Holy Cross, 400, in the parish of St. Margaret's, Leicester, 700; and so in every parish, in a great multitude. Then the bishop of Lincoln sent notice throughout his whole diocese giving general power to all priests, both regulars and seculars, to hear confessions and give absolution with full episcopal authority to all persons, except only in case of debt. . . . There was no recollection of so great and terrible a mortality since the time of Vortigern, king of the Britons, in whose day, as Bede testifies, in his book concerning the deeds of the English, the living did not suffice to bury the dead.[7]

The last sentence catches the note which is repeated in all accounts of the Black Death: that it was an overwhelming horror, in which all the known decencies and normal expectations of society disappeared. Daily life in its accustomed form broke down, and men's minds were gripped by a deadly fear. After the plague had subsided and the survivors began to repair the damage to society and the economy, they came to see the Black Death as a watershed, and in popular memory events were dated as before or since 'the pestilence time'.

The overall effect of the Black Death was to strengthen the condition of peasants and artisans as against lords and masters. Labour was now in short supply and therefore in a stronger bargaining position than formerly. This sudden reversal of fortunes was the more welcome to the common people in that the early fourteenth century was a period of overpopulation. Evidence from the cultivation of marginal land, the small size of holdings, and labour plentiful to the point of underemployment, all points towards a crisis of Malthusian proportions. Estimates of medieval population are extremely tentative and subject to wide degrees of variation. A generally accepted estimate would put the figure at the time of Domesday at 1·5 to 1·8 million. By the early fourteenth century this had increased to about 3·75 million; but by the 1390s it had declined to 2·25 million, and only began to rise slowly from the 1430s and more rapidly in the later fifteenth century. More recent calculations put the figures somewhat higher: 1·75 to 2·25 million in 1086; 4·5 to 6 million in 1348; a decline to 2·5 to 3 million by 1377 when returns for a poll-tax were made; and a low point in the mid-fifteenth century of 2 to 2·5 million, scarcely more than in Domesday.[8] Whatever the exact size of the population, the trend downwards after the Black Death is clearly established, aggravated by further outbreaks of plague and other epidemic diseases on a national or regional scale, and also (if we accept the testimony of the chroniclers) by the especially high mortality among the young and the males.

The first sign of the more favourable position of the labouring poor (at least for those who survived) was a demand by both artisans and agricultural workers for higher wages. This was immediately seen by the government as a serious threat to the status quo and a Royal Ordinance of Labourers was issued in June 1349 even before the plague had died away. In the first parliament after the Black Death the Royal Ordinance was made permanent in the Statute of Labourers, 1351, thus initiating a long line of labour legislation designed to regulate in considerable detail the conditions of working life in towns and countryside. The Statute was passed by a parliament representative of the lords of the manors and rich town merchants who were concerned to promote their own interests, not those of the common people. Nevertheless it provides important information about labouring life in the second half of the fourteenth century, for as the great French social historian, Marc Bloch, noted, documents are witnesses, sometimes hostile, which have to be forced by cross-examination to speak, even against their will.

Against the malice of servants who were idle and unwilling to serve after the pestilence without taking outrageous wages [begins the Statute of Labourers], it was recently ordained by our lord the king, with the assent of the prelates, nobles and others of his council, that such servants, both men and women, should be obliged to serve in return for the salaries and wages which were customary (in those places where they ought to serve) during the twentieth year of the present king's reign [1346–7] or five or six years previously. It was also ordained that such servants who refused to serve in this way should be punished by imprisonment, as is more fully stated in the said ordinance. Accordingly commissions were made out to various people in every county to investigate and punish all those who offended against the ordinance. But now our lord king has been informed in this present parliament, by the petition of the commons, that such servants completely disregard the said ordinance in the interests of their own ease and greed and that they withhold their service to great men and others unless they have liveries and wages twice or three times as great as those they used to take in the said twentieth year of Edward III and earlier, to the serious damage of the great men and impoverishment of all members of the said commons. Therefore the commons ask for a remedy.[9]

The remedy was to regulate wages and conditions of work on a national scale. Specific groups of workers are mentioned:

First, that carters, ploughmen, leaders of the plough, shepherds, swineherds, domestic and all other servants shall receive the liveries and wages accustomed in the said twentieth year and four years previously; so that in areas where wheat used to be given, they shall take 10d. for the bushel, or wheat at the will of the giver, until it is ordained otherwise. These servants shall be hired to serve by the entire year, or by the other usual terms, and not by the day. No one is to receive more than 1d. a day at the time of weeding or hay-making. Mowers of meadows are not to be paid more than 5d. an acre or 5d. a day; and reapers of corn are to be limited to 2d. in the first week of August, 3d. in the second week and so on to the end of August. Less is to be given in those areas where less used to be given and neither food nor any other favour is to be demanded, given or taken. All such workers are to bring their tools openly in their hands to the market towns; and there they are to be hired in a public and not in a secret place.

Also, that no one is to receive more than 2½d. for threshing a quarter of wheat or rye, and more than 1½d. for threshing a quarter of barley, beans, peas or oats, if so much used to be given. In those areas where reaping was paid by means of certain sheaves and threshing by certain bushels, the servants shall take no more and in no other way than was usual in the said twentieth year and previously.

Artisans' rates are similarly prescribed:

Carpenters, masons, tilers and other roofers of houses shall not take more for their day's work than the accustomed amount; that is to say, a master carpenter 3d. and other [carpenters] 2d.; a master mason of free-stone 4d. and other masons 3d.; and their servants 1½d. Tilers are to receive 3d. and their boys 1½d.; thatchers of roofs in fern and straw 3d. and their boys 1½d. Plasterers and other workers on mud walls, as well as their boys, are to receive payment in the same manner, without food or drink. These rates are to apply from Easter to Michaelmas: outside that period less should be paid according to the assessment and discretion of the justices assigned for the purpose. Those who perform carriage by land or water shall receive no more for such carriage than they used to do in the said twentieth year and four years before.

Other groups specifically named are cordwainers, shoemakers, goldsmiths, saddlers, horsesmiths, spurriers, tanners, curriers, pelterers, tailors 'and all other workmen, artificers and labourers, as well as all other servants not specified here'. The Statute was to be enforced by justices in each locality, on the evidence of stewards, bailiffs and sheriffs. Both those who demanded and those who offered wages above the level of 1346 were to be punished by fine, imprisonment, or the stocks. ('For this purpose stocks are to be constructed in every vill between now and Whitsunday.') Labourers were to be hired for the year, not by the day, thus restricting labour mobility; and 'if any of the said labourers, servants or artificers flee from one county to another

Wage Rates, 1301–1540

	Piece rates for threshing and winnowing 3 rased quarters of grains (wheat, barley, oats)			Daily wage rates of craftsmen and labourers — Average of rates on 8 Winchester manors				Rates paid for building work in Westminster			
	Westminster manors d.	Winchester manors d.	Thorold Rogers d.	Carpenter d.	Thatcher and helper d.	Labourer d.	Tiler and helper d.	Carpenter d.	Labourer d.	Mason d.	Tiler and helper d.
1301–10	6·51	3·85		2·82	3·19	1·49	6·19				
1311–20	8·01	4·05		3·41	3·55	1·87	6·44				
1321–30	6·68	4·62		3·39	3·78	1·84	5·91				
1331–40	7·35	4·92		3·18	3·82	1·78	5·73				
1341–50	7·41	5·03		2·96	3·73	1·86	4·70	3·89	2·12	6·13	
1351–60	13·02	5·18		3·92	5·00	2·85	6·25	6·06	3·08	6·52	
1361–70	12·76	6·10	7·20	4·29	5·95	3·25	7·01	7·94	4·27	7·35	9·00
1371–80	12·23	7·00	8·70	4·32	5·98	3·19	6·89	6·00	3·39	7·21	11·92
1381–90	10·82	7·22	9·03	4·40	6·01	3·35	7·54	6·42	3·33	6·48	10·50
1391–1400	10·44	7·23	7·66	4·13	5·85	3·30	7·36	5·68	3·46	6·67	10·00
1401–10	11·00	7·31	8·37	4·64	6·31	3·53	8·17	—	3·33	6·67	11·51
1411–20	12·40	7·35	8·50	4·51	6·40	3·69	8·50	6·22	4·00	6·67	12·50
1421–30	10·00	7·34	8·13	4·52	6·19	3·83	8·56	6·77	3·84	6·67	11·88
1431–40	13·00	7·30	9·75	4·75	6·89	3·87	8·81	7·00	4·87	6·67	12·99
1441–50	13·00	7·33	9·13	5·18	8·19	4·11	9·24	8·17	4·91	6·67	13·20
1451–60		7·25	8·75	5·23	8·24	4·03	9·60	7·57	4·64	6·67	13·17
1461–70			8·50					8·00	4·42	6·67	12·74
1471–80			8·00					7·45	4·06	6·67	13·00
1481–90			7·00					6·63	4·03	6·67	13·00
1491–1500			9·25					6·27	4·00	6·67	12·31
1501–10			11·63					6·66	4·07	6·67	11·50
1511–20			10·00					6·64	4·02	6·67	12·75
1521–30			11·25					7·61	4·04	6·67	12·24
1531–40			12·25					8·00	4·00	6·67	—

From John Hatcher, *Plague, Population and the English Economy, 1348–1530* (London and Basingstoke: Macmillan, 1977), p. 49. Reprinted by permission.

because of this ordinance . . . such fugitives [shall be] apprehended' and gaoled.

The Statute was met with hostility and evasion by the working population; and almost all contemporary commentators agreed that it did not succeed in its main purposes, despite constant re-enactment with ever-increasing penalties. It manifestly failed to check the rise in wages. What the Statute called the 'malice of servants' could not be gainsaid. An indictment from a Suffolk village shows that a demand for higher wages could be backed up by collective action on the part of the peasantry; for Walter Halderby 'took of divers persons at reaping-time sixpence or eightpence a day, and very often at the same time made various congregations of labourers in different places and counselled them not to take less than sixpence or eightpence'.[10] This was three times the rate decreed by Statute. The dramatic increase in wages in the decade following the Black Death is most clearly presented by statistics covering different types of work. The table on page 84 shows daily wage rates for craftsmen as well as agricultural workers. Prices generally during the later Middle Ages tended to remain stationary or to fall, though with fluctuations in specific decades. There were therefore real gains in the wages of peasants and artisans.

The second objective of the legislation – to provide an adequate labour supply for lords of manors – was equally unattainable. Faced with a sudden and unexpected shortage of labourers and demands for higher wages the lords reacted by trying to compel villeins to work for them as before. Every able-bodied man and woman under sixty 'not living by trade nor exercising a certain craft, nor having of his own whereof he shall be able to live, or land of his own' was bound by the 1349 Ordinance of Labourers to serve his lord if required. But as the preamble to the 1351 Statute noted, 'such servants completely disregard the said ordinance'; and provisions were made to deal with villeins who attempted to move ('flee') to another part of the country. When labour was dearer than before it was in the lords' interest to exact the traditional labour services, but the process of commutation was generally too far advanced to make this practicable. Historians once thought that it was the attempt by lords to reimpose servile labour services which had been commuted that led to the rising of 1381; but more recent research in manorial records has largely discounted this view. Where the demesne was already being worked with hired labour, the lord of the manor could decide that in view of the rise in wages he would no longer cultivate it himself, but lease it to tenants. This was the case in Halesowen, where the abbot, who was lord of the manor, leased his demesne piecemeal to peasant farmers in the 1350s.[11]

Landowners were under pressure to exploit all possible ways of countering the new strength of labour; and when their seigneurial rights were no longer adequate they turned to legislation to deal with their labour problems. The peasants resisted stubbornly. If the free labourer could not get the wages he demanded or the villein tenant the commutation of his services for money rent, he defied both the Statute and immemorial custom and simply 'fled' to another village or town. 'As soon as their masters accuse them of bad service, or wish to pay them for their labour according to the form of the statutes,' complained the Commons in the parliament of 1376, 'they take flight and suddenly leave their employment and district, going from county to county, hundred to hundred and vill to vill, in places strange and unknown to their masters.'[12]

Such action was not new. But the increasing mobility of the peasantry was a challenge to the lords' power. It was also regarded as a threat to law and order and therefore to be punished by outlawry. Geographical mobility was closely associated with social mobility, which had to be suppressed or tightly controlled lest it undermine the foundations of the social structure. That the behaviour, attitudes and expectations of labouring people changed in the decades following the Black Death is attested by many contemporary commentators, though none of them was a peasant or artisan. William Langland, the most sympathetic, put the matter baldly: 'Nowadays the labourer is angry unless he gets high wages, and he curses the day that he was ever born a workman . . . he blames God, and murmurs against Reason, and curses the king and his Council for making Statutes on purpose to plague the workmen.' With gentle irony Langland observed that 'the day-labourers, who have no land to live on but their shovels, would not deign to eat yesterday's vegetables. And draught-ale was not good enough for them, nor a hunk of bacon, but they must

86

have fresh meat or fish, fried or baked and *chaud* or *plus chaud* at that, lest they catch a chill on their stomachs.'[13]

The verdict of the affluent classes was that the lower orders were getting above themselves. Moralists inveighed against the 'outrageous and excessive' expenditure of the age, and chroniclers complained that the master could not be distinguished from his servant since the 'inferior people' had taken to dressing and behaving like their superiors. Parliament responded in 1363 with a sumptuary statute, designed to regulate expenditure and personal possessions according to status and wealth: agricultural workers with less than 40s. worth of property were to wear no cloth but blanket and russet wool at 1s. the cloth. But, like the Statutes of Labourers, its constant reiteration failed to increase its effectiveness. 'The world goeth fast from bad to worse, when shepherd and cowherd for their part demand more for their labour than the master-bailiff was wont to take in days gone by,' complained the poet John Gower, about 1375. 'Labourers of old were not wont to eat of wheaten bread; their meat was of beans or coarser corn, and their drink of water alone. Cheese and milk were a feast to them, and rarely ate they of other dainties; their dress was of hodden grey; then was the world ordered aright for folk of this sort. . . .'[14]

From the perspective of the shepherd, cowherd and labourer, however, this state of things had a different significance. The outstanding fact to which all the documents quoted bear witness is the new independence and self-assertion of the labouring population. Demographic changes beyond the control of individuals provided the opportunity for this, but the specific behaviour of peasants and artisans was the result of conscious decisions. The labourers who combined to demand higher wages or fled through the woods to make a new life elsewhere were no longer the passive recipients of decisions made for them by others. What was rebelliousness in the eyes of lords and justices was for the peasantry an assertion of a greater degree of control over their own lives. It was a bid for a certain amount of freedom, perhaps the beginning of a new consciousness.

The most dramatic expressions of this demand for freedom were the events of what is usually, though somewhat misleadingly, called the Peasants' Revolt of 1381 – sparked off by military defeat and heavy taxation. For almost fifty years the English kings had been at war with France in pursuit of dynastic and feudal claims. English armies, recruited or pressed from villages all over the kingdom, campaigned and raided in France and as far away as Castile. War, however, is extremely expensive, its burdens and rewards are unevenly spread, and only spectacular success can ensure its popularity. During the early phase of the Hundred Years War, Edward III and his son, the Black Prince, won resounding victories at Crécy (1346) and Poitiers (1356); and the operations were financed largely, though not entirely, out of taxes on exported wool. But from 1369 the war went increasingly badly for the English, producing little to show for its enormous expense. Indeed, the enemy was now able to raid and loot towns on the south coast, and there was fear of a French invasion. The government, hard-pressed to know where to turn for money to continue the war, levied three poll-taxes in 1377, 1379 and 1381. When the returns for the 1381 poll-tax were in, it was apparent that there had been widespread tax-evasion, and commissioners were therefore appointed to enforce payment of the full tax. In the last week of May 1381 one of the new commissioners went to Brentwood in Essex and summoned the inhabitants of the three marshland villages of Fobbing, Corringham and Stanford for examination. The peasants and fishermen of these places said they would not pay any more taxes, and when the commissioner ordered arrests he and his party were beaten and chased out of town. The Chief Justice of the Common Pleas was then sent to punish the contumacious villagers, but he too met with resistance and was driven back to London. Moreover three of his clerks were beheaded, as also were three local jurors who had been called to present the accused. Their heads were set on poles and paraded round the neighbouring villages. The men of south Essex were now thoroughly roused, and resistance quickly spread from village to village during the first week of June.

Across the river in Kent the revolt began a few days later. A small band led by Abel Ker from Erith attacked the abbey of Lesnes, and the next day, 3 June, crossed the Thames and recruited men in Essex. Thus reinforced they returned and incited the townsmen of Dartford to join them. Elsewhere in Kent the rebellion rapidly gathered momentum. The king's commissioners were prevented from reaching Canterbury and, as in Essex, were driven back to London. At Gravesend a dispute arose out of the arrest and imprisonment in Rochester castle of a runaway serf, claimed by Sir Simon Burley, a knight of the king's household. On 6 June the Kentishmen entered Rochester, forced the capitulation of the royal castle, and released the imprisoned serf. The next day the rebels appeared in Maidstone under the leadership of Wat Tyler; and on 10 June they marched on Canterbury and took control of the city. The archbishop's palace and the castle were sacked, the gaol broken open and the prisoners released, and quantities of legal documents and records of all kinds destroyed. The mayor and bailiffs were forced to join the rebels and take an oath of loyalty to 'King Richard and the true Commons', which from now on became the password of the rising. At this point the wider aims and implications of the rising began to appear: the king had to be rescued from his treacherous advisers. They – and the king – were in London, and it was therefore logical to go there and seek them out.

> Let us go to the king, he is young, and shew him what servage [servitude] we be in, and shew him how we will have it otherwise, or else we will provide us of some remedy; and if we go together, all manner of people that be now in any bondage will follow us to the intent to be made free; and when the king seeth us, we shall have some remedy, either by fairness or otherwise.[15]

Thus did John Ball advise his hearers, according to the chronicler Jean Froissart. On Tuesday, 11 June, Tyler and the rebels left Canterbury, and late on the following evening were encamped on Blackheath. Advance contingents pushed on to Southwark and Lambeth, where they were joined by sympathizers from the suburbs and the city itself. The two prisons in Southwark, the Marshalsea and King's Bench, were broken open and their inmates set free, and the archbishop's palace in Lambeth and the house of the warden of the Marshalsea were burnt.

In Essex the rising followed a course parallel to that in Kent during the week preceding 12 June. The homes of unpopular officials and ministers, as well as religious houses were attacked. Colchester was taken without resistance and several Flemings in the town were put to death. Everywhere court rolls, charters and manorial documents were sought out and destroyed. On 11 June the Essex men moved towards London, and the next day, while the main body encamped at Mile End, their leaders made contact with the Kentishmen at Blackheath. Exactly how many insurgents were mustered on both shores of the Thames is impossible to determine. The chroniclers' estimates vary widely, and are almost certainly as exaggerated and unreliable as their numbers who died in the Black Death. The *Anonimalle* [anonymous] *Chronicle* which is generally regarded as the most reliable account of the revolt, puts the numbers at Blackheath at 50,000 and of the Essex men at 60,000; while Thomas Walsingham writes wildly of 200,000 listening to Ball at Blackheath. A more realistic guess might put the total who entered London at under 10,000.

It was on the morning of 13 June that John Ball, the 'mad priest of Kent', is said to have preached his famous sermon to the rebels on Blackheath, using as his text the couplet:

> When Adam delved and Eve span
> Who was then a gentleman?

He had but recently been released by the rebels from Maidstone gaol, where he was imprisoned in April 1381 for his invectives against pope and prelates. Little is known about his early career, but he was probably a secular priest in York and then in Colchester. In the 1360s he was formally prohibited from preaching; but for twenty years he was well known in the southern counties as a radical, itinerant preacher. His message to the rebels, as reported by the chroniclers, was an expression of egalitarianism and a call to action:

> In the beginning all men were created equal: servitude of man to man was introduced by the unjust dealings of the wicked, and contrary to God's will. For if God had intended some to be serfs and others lords, He would have made a distinction between them at the beginning. Englishmen had now an opportunity given them, if they chose to take it, of casting off the yoke they had borne so long, and winning the freedom that they had always desired. Wherefore they should take good courage, and

behave like the wise husbandman of scripture, who gathered the wheat into his barn, but uprooted and burned the tares that had half-choked the good grain. The tares of England were her oppressive rulers, and harvest-time had come, in which it was their duty to pluck up and make away with them all – evil lords, unjust judges, lawyers, every man who was dangerous to the common good. Then they would have peace for the present and security for the future; for when the great ones had been cut off, all men would enjoy equal freedom, all would have the same nobility, rank, and power.[16]

On the same morning that Ball delivered his address the young King Richard came by boat from the Tower, where he had taken up residence, to meet the Kentish rebels. The king was accompanied in the royal barge by the chancellor and the treasurer, and four other boats contained members of his household. A parley was attempted at Rotherhithe between the rebels and the king who remained in his barge offshore, being advised not to trust himself to the vast crowd assembled beneath their banners and pennons. The rebels declared their loyalty to Richard but demanded the heads of John of Gaunt (the king's uncle), and other 'traitors', some of whom were at that moment in the royal party. Concluding that further discussion under these conditions was not likely to be profitable, the king and his advisers put back to the Tower, followed by curses and shouts of 'treason'.

The breakdown of negotiations was followed by the occupation of the city. The Kentishmen crossed London bridge, unopposed, and the Essex rebels entered through Aldgate. They were welcomed by the London poor – artisans, labourers, apprentices – and immediately set about destroying the property of those associated with unpopular policies, injustice, and the poll-tax. John of Gaunt's great palace, the Savoy, was completely destroyed. The Temple and its hated legal records were sacked. Clerkenwell priory (headquarters of the Order of St John of Jerusalem of which Sir Robert Hales, the king's treasurer, was prior) was set on fire. At Newgate the prisoners were released and offered their chains in thanksgiving at the church of the Greyfriars nearby. A certain selectivity in the attacks suggests that the rebels had definite objectives; though, as with all crowd action, once the violence and arson had started it was possible for acts of private vengeance or local grievance or simple plunder to be caught up in the general state of riot. Anti-alien feeling, for example, was expressed in hunting out and killing Flemings, perhaps because in London (and in East Anglian towns) the rivalry of native weavers could be disguised in xenophobia.

Once the rebels had occupied London the king and his council found themselves trapped in the Tower. Attempts from there to negotiate with the rebel leaders broke down, and the king then offered to meet them outside the city at Mile End. Early on the morning of 14 June Richard and his entourage rode out from the Tower. The rebels assembled at Mile End demanded the abolition of serfdom and the commutation of all servile dues for a rent of 4d. an acre per year. They also asked for a general pardon for any action committed during the rising. Richard agreed to these demands, and promised to give a royal banner to the representatives of each county as a sign of his protection. Thirty clerks were engaged to draw up forthwith the charters granting freedom from serfdom and pardon for all treasons and felonies committed. But to the rebels' demand that the ministers they regarded as traitors should be punished, the king replied evasively. This did not suit the rebels; and either during or after the meeting a party of them broke into the Tower, seized the archbishop-chancellor (Simon Sudbury) and the treasurer (Sir Robert Hales), dragged them outside and beheaded them. Two others suffered a like fate. The heads of the victims were set on poles and carried round the city before being fixed over the gate of London bridge. Other killings of government servants and aliens followed.

It had been the object of the king's temporizing to get the rebels to disperse, but many of them were reluctant to go home. The king therefore proposed another conference the next day, 15 June, this time at Smithfield. In this open space outside the walls of the city the insurgents, led by Wat Tyler, were drawn up on the west side facing the king and his party on the east. Richard ordered the mayor of London, William Walworth, to announce that he wished to hear their leaders' demands. Tyler thereupon rode out to him on a little horse, dismounted, bowed, and then shook the king's hand, telling him 'to be of good cheer, for within a fortnight he would have thanks from the commons even more than he had at the present hour'. When the king asked why the rebels had not gone home after the concessions granted at the Mile End meeting Tyler replied with a more radical set of demands. He asked, according to the *Anonimalle* chronicler,

that there should be no law except for the law of Winchester and that henceforward there should be no outlawry in any process of law, and that no lord should have lordship in future, but it should be divided among all men, except for the king's own lordship. He also asked that the goods of Holy Church should not remain in the hands of the religious, nor of parsons and vicars, and other churchmen; but that clergy already in possession should have a sufficient sustenance and the rest of their goods should be divided among the people of the parish. And he demanded that there should be only one bishop in England and only one prelate, and all the lands and tenements of the possessioners should be taken from them and divided among the commons, only reserving for them a reasonable sustenance. And he demanded that there should be no more villeins in England, and no serfdom nor villeinage but that all men should be free and of one condition. To this the king gave an easy answer, and said that Wat should have all that he could fairly grant, reserving only for himself the regality of his crown. And then he ordered him to go back to his own home, without causing further delay.[17]

This reply apparently did not satisfy Tyler, who reacted provocatively. He called for a drink, rinsed his mouth out, and remounted his horse. According to one source he also kept his head covered with his hood while before the king. From the chroniclers' accounts it almost seems as if Tyler was then deliberately provoked into violence. One of the king's retainers remarked that he recognized Tyler as 'the greatest thief and robber in all Kent'. Tyler angrily demanded that the man who said that should stand forward, and drew out a dagger to avenge himself. Walworth, the mayor, tried to arrest Tyler for drawing a weapon in the king's presence, whereupon Tyler stabbed at his stomach. But the mayor was unharmed as he was wearing a coat of mail under his gown and replied by wounding Tyler in the shoulder. During this scuffle one of the king's squires drew his sword and ran Tyler two or three times through the body, mortally wounding him. Tyler managed to turn his horse and ride halfway across the square, before falling to the ground. When the rebels saw their leader fall, they bent their bows and prepared to shoot; whereupon the king spurred his horse forward into the open, raised his right hand to the rebels, and cried, 'Sirs, will you shoot your King? I will be your chief and captain, you shall have from me that which you seek. Only follow me into the fields without.' And he led them northwards into Clerkenwell fields.

What passed between King Richard and his true commons while he was alone with them is not known. But during that time the mayor rode back into the city and raised a band of loyalists to rescue the king. He also hunted down Tyler, whom he dragged from St Bartholomew's hospital into Smithfield and beheaded him. Tyler's head was displayed to the king and the rebels at Clerkenwell and then taken to London bridge to replace that of the archbishop. The rebels were now faced by well-armed troops, and accepted the king's command that they should go back to their homes. The rising in London was thus over – to be followed by the arrest, imprisonment and execution of such leaders and rioters as were still in the city. Jack Straw, who was Tyler's principal lieutenant, was summarily beheaded, as also were John Kirkby and Alan Threder, both leaders of the Kentishmen. The same end was meted out to John Sterling, a religious fanatic from Essex who went about boasting that he had executed the archbishop. Royal commissions were issued to punish rebels and rioters; and Walworth the mayor (knighted at Clerkenwell for his loyal services) was given dictatorial powers over the city.

As soon as the king could collect an army together he moved into Essex to crush the insurgents there. He denied any promises that the rebels thought he had given and warned against believing rebel claims that he approved of their doings. At Waltham a deputation who asked for the ratification of the Mile End promises were brutally told, 'Serfs you are and serfs you will remain.' At Billericay on 28 June the rebel forces were routed; and at Chelmsford on 2 July the king issued a proclamation which revoked all charters of manumission and amnesty which he had granted at Mile End. John Ball, who left London after Tyler's death, was caught in

Coventry and sent to St Albans for trial before the Chief Justice. On 15 July Ball was hung, drawn and quartered.

The early stages of the rising of 1381 centred on Essex, Kent and London; the later stages on East Anglia. Elsewhere the insurrection was more sporadic and uncoordinated, concerned often with separate but parallel grievances. Throughout the home counties the villagers burnt manorial records and attacked unpopular lords and their property. In Hertfordshire the main centre of trouble was St Albans, where the activity in 1381 was part of a traditional struggle between the abbot, as lord of the manor, and the townsmen. With support from the peasantry of the abbey estates the townsmen on 14 June renewed their attempts to win liberty from the monks. Led by William Grindcobbe, a man of some education and property in the town, they contacted Tyler in London, obtained one of the prized charters authorized by the king, and attacked the abbot's property. During the next few days the abbot was forced to give in to the demands of the townsmen and villeins. But three weeks later the revolt was repressed and the townsmen surrendered the charters granted to them by the abbot. On 12 July the king arrived in person, having just subdued the Essex rebels. Grindcobbe was executed. Before his death, but foreseeing his fate, he addressed his followers in words which shine through even the hostile chronicler's account:

Fellow citizens, for whom a little liberty has now relieved the long years of oppression, stand firm while you can and do not be afraid because of my persecution. For if it should happen that I die in the cause of seeking to acquire liberty, I will count myself happy to end my life as such a martyr. Act therefore now as you would have acted if I had been beheaded at Hertford yesterday.[18]

The rising in East Anglia took place about ten days to a fortnight after the first action in Essex and Kent. In Suffolk the lead was taken by John Wrawe, a parish priest of Ringsfield near Beccles, who on 12 June directed the sacking of the manor of Richard Lyons, a financier, at Liston. The next day the rebels, after attacking a manor belonging to Sir John Cavendish, the Chief Justice, marched to Bury St Edmunds. The town was a centre of cloth-making, and had a history of struggle against the local prior similar to St Albans. Wrawe's forces were welcomed by the poorer townsmen and the opportunity was taken to try to extract a charter from the monks. Cavendish was tracked down and beheaded on 14 June and the prior was executed on the day following. For eight days Bury was occupied by the rebels. In Norfolk armed bands appeared in several villages in the west of the county on 14 June; and in the east the rebels mustered in force on Mousehold Heath, outside the city of Norwich, on 17 June. Their leader was Geoffrey Litster, a dyer from Felmingham, supported by Sir Roger Bacon, a discontented landowner from Baconsthorpe. The mayor and aldermen of Norwich would have liked to close the city but feared the strength of the poorer citizens who sympathized with the rebels. Norwich therefore offered no resistance and Litster and Bacon entered in triumph. During the week following 17 June rebel bands moved into neighbouring towns and villages. Yarmouth was entered on 18 June and there was a rising in Lowestoft. At Cambridge the burgesses took the opportunity of support from rebels in the county to attack their old enemies, the university and the prior of Barnwell. Three days of violence from 15 to 17 June resulted in the sacking of Corpus Christi college and the burning of the university records. 'Away with the learning of clerks, away with it,' cried an old woman, Margery Starre, as she flung to the winds the ashes of the documents. On 17 June the rebels at Ely captured and beheaded Edmund Walsingham, a local justice; and at Peterborough there was a rising by the peasantry and townsfolk against the abbot.

For about a week there was virtually no resistance to the rising (or perhaps more accurately risings) in the eastern counties. But then the warlike bishop of Norwich, Henry Despenser, rallied the local gentry and put himself at the head of an avenging army. He marched rapidly from place to place in pursuit of the rebels, whom he summarily dispersed, imprisoned or executed. On 24 June he arrived at Norwich but found that Litster and his force had moved to North Walsham. Despenser caught up with them there, attacked their fortified camp and completely routed them. Litster was captured and promptly hung, drawn and quartered. A few days later Wrawe was captured in Suffolk, and after trial in London was put to death in the same way.

Repercussions of the rising were felt beyond these areas of its greatest intensity. Throughout June and July unrest and disorders were reported from the West, the Midlands and the North. In Somerset the hospital of St John at Bridgwater was attacked. There were revolts by the tenants of the prior of Worcester and a rising in the Wirral by the abbot of Chester's villeins. Urban riots occurred in Winchester, Northampton, Scarborough, York and Beverley. Although these were not strictly part of the Peasants' Revolt they were perhaps encouraged by news of the rebellion in London. Wherever peasants struggled to change the relationships with their lord, townsmen sought to wrest a charter of liberties for themselves, or the poor saw an opportunity to improve their lot at the expense of the rich and privileged, there was the possibility that local grievances could be fanned into a flame of revolt.

It has been necessary to recount the events of June 1381 in some detail for several reasons. First, the story is worth telling for its own sake. It has all the elements of high drama, as the chroniclers, especially Froissart, realized. Second, Wat Tyler and John Ball have become part of English folk mythology. Later reformers were able to refer back to them as legendary heroes. Third, and most importantly, this is the first time that the common people have appeared consciously as a national force in this history. The common people could be, and often were, involved in events on a national scale, such as plagues, famines or wars, but always for reasons beyond their control. They did not make the decisions which brought about those events; nor did they participate in the conscious making of political or economic policy. They were, to use a cliché favoured by social historians, the victims not the makers of history. For a few days in June 1381 this role was suddenly reversed. Instead of accepting the initiatives of their social superiors the common people made the decisions themselves. They aspired to become the agents of, not simply the material for social change. Yet for this important moment in their history we have to rely almost exclusively on evidence from the side of their enemies. The monastic chroniclers, whose writings provide the main chronology of the rising, were naturally hostile to rebels who challenged the rights of monastic lords of manors and attacked ecclesiastical life and property. Thomas Walsingham, whose chronicle is a basic source, was a monk of St Albans. The author of the secular *Anonimalle Chronicle* is thought to have been a government official. Jean Froissart, whose account is at once the most detailed and fanciful, was an admirer of courtly life and had little sympathy for the people. Other records such as cases before the commissions to inquire into and punish participants in the revolt, copies of pardons to individual rebels, and details of local troubles revealed in manorial estate documents, are also accounts from above rather than below. Nevertheless these hostile and frequently irrelevant witnesses can be cross-examined and made to produce evidence which puts the rising in a light different from that intended. We have also to remember that the medieval chronicler was not trying to write a history in the modern sense, however biased, but rather to record, largely from hearsay and rumour, a series of events from which he could deduce moral truths relevant to his own generation.

The traditional interpretation of the 1381 rising, derived mainly from the chroniclers, is deficient in several respects, including the matter of context. Neither geographically nor chronologically was the Peasants' Revolt the unique event sometimes inferred. All across Europe there were popular risings in the fourteenth century: the *Jacquerie* (peasantry) in the region round Paris in 1358, the *ciompi* (poor) in Florence in 1378, the revolts in Flanders in 1323–7 and 1378, to name but the best-known examples. There is no evidence that any of these movements directly affected the 1381 rising. But the existence of a European dimension indicates the possibility (to put it no higher) of comparative study, and the need to bear in mind that the English revolt was not an isolated phenomenon. This is even more obvious when the comparison is chronological rather than geographical. Long before and after 1381 there is ample evidence of peasant protest and urban discontent, and it is not difficult to present the rising as a larger but logical version of earlier movements. The demands of the rebels and some of the obscure or puzzling aspects of the revolt become more intelligible in the light of earlier and sometimes continuing struggles. For instance, the villeins of the abbot of Vale Royal on his manors in Darnall and Over rose in 1336 and in the course of their struggle against serfdom vainly tried to appeal to the king. At Bury St Edmunds there had been risings against the monastic lords on four or five separate occasions during the sixty years before 1381. The St Albans townsmen had risen against the abbot of the day in 1274, 1314 and 1327.

An incident at St Albans during the 1381 rising provides a rare insight into popular perceptions of the affair. Walsingham records:

> some ribald people, breaking their way into the Abbey cloisters, took up from the floor of the parlour doorway the millstones which had been put there in the time of Abbot Richard as a remembrance and memorial of the ancient dispute between the Abbey and the townsmen. They took the stones outside and handed them over to the commons, breaking them into little pieces and giving a piece to each person, just as the consecrated bread used to be broken and distributed on Sundays in the parish churches, so that the people, seeing these pieces, would know themselves avenged against the Abbey in that cause.[19]

This is not how one usually imagines insurrections being conducted. It becomes intelligible in the light of over a hundred years of conflict between the abbots of St Albans and their villein tenants over the use of handmills. Peasants and townsmen 'owed suit' to their lord's mills, that is they were required to have their corn ground and their cloth fulled in the abbot's mills. But they preferred to grind their corn at home in their small handmills and full their own cloth, because it was cheaper and more convenient. In 1274 the men of the town 'rising up against us like wild people', wrote Walsingham, 'fulled their cloths and ground their own corn to please their own wishes and also . . . ventured to erect handmills in their own houses.' From then on the struggle was continuous. In 1327 the monastery was besieged by the townsmen, who forced the abbot to grant them a charter. But the next abbot, Richard of Wallingford, repudiated his predecessor's concessions. The people 'surrendered their millstones in the church as a sign of the absolute renunciation of their right to mill'. To rub in the lesson the abbot had the millstones cemented into the floor of his parlour. The action of the rebels in 1381 in breaking up the floor thus acquires a ritualistic quality. It was a symbolic expression of deep-rooted grievances, stretching back for several generations. A similar significance may be seen in other actions of the crowd at St Albans. They destroyed enclosures and gates in the abbey woods; and, as a token of the 'giving of seisin of the warren and common of woods and fields', took branches from the trees, and put a live rabbit on a pole on the town pillory. Walsingham records how the villeins went out to the woods 'in great splendour', how they marched to the monastery gates 'in great pride', and how the townsmen and peasants 'joining their right hands' promised to be faithful to one another. These were local issues (rights to common land, woods and game) expressed in a ritualism of revolt. They may seem far removed from the wider freedom envisioned by William Grindcobbe or John Ball. The apparent paradox, however, probably arises more from the limitations of our knowledge of popular modes of perception than from a confusion of understanding by the rebels. We have yet to learn how to recognize the signs of popular communication embedded in the documents of an unsympathetic culture.

At present the only evidence from the rebels themselves is a little collection of six letters preserved in the chronicles of Thomas Walsingham and Henry Knighton. Written in the vernacular, with internal rhyme and allegorical references, they are very difficult to interpret. The chroniclers took them to be orders or appeals for action, and this has been the generally accepted view among historians. It seems likely that they were all written by one man, probably John Ball. In the tunic of one of the executed Essex rebels was found a note which read:

Iohon Schep, som tyme Seynte Marie prest of York, and now of Colchestre, greteth wel Iohan Nameles, and Iohan the Mullere, and Iohon Cartere, and biddeth hem that thei bee war of gyle in borugh, and stondeth togidre in Godes name, and biddeth Peres Ploughman go to his werk, and chastise wel Hobbe the Robbere, and taketh with yow Iohan Trewman, and alle hiis felawes, and no mo, and loke schappe you to on heued, and no mo.

Iohan the Mullere hath ygrounde smal, smal smal;
The Kynges sone of heuene schal paye for al.
Be war or ye be wo;
Knoweth your freend fro your foo;
Haueth ynow, and seith 'Hoo';
And do wel and bettre, and fleth synne,
And seketh pees, and hold you therinne;
And so biddeth Iohan Trewman and alle his felawes.[20]

John Schep may plausibly be interpreted as John Shepherd, a synonym for priest (i.e. John Ball); but the other Johns (Nameless, Miller, Carter, Trueman) sound more like pseudonyms or, even more probably, allegorical names, than actual rebels. Hobbe the Robber has sometimes been identified with the treasurer, Sir Robert Hales; and it has been suggested that 'beware of guile in borough' may be a warning either to avoid being tricked in London or against getting involved in town quarrels such as those in Canterbury. Literal interpretation of these 'dark sayings', however, is probably misguided: their real significance lies elsewhere.

A clue is to be found in the reference to Piers Ploughman, that great symbolical figure of the common people whom we have already encountered several times. Do Well and Do Better [do wel and bettre] are allegorical figures in Langland's poem, and it would seem therefore that the letter belongs to the same cultural tradition. Langland's *Piers the Ploughman* is believed to have been written in the 1370s, that is before the great revolt. The poet was a poor, unbeneficed priest – a class noticeably to the fore among the leadership of the rising – but the poem is not a revolutionary document. It is in the form of a moral allegory and as such has meaning at several different levels. Like a later epic of the common people, Bunyan's *The Pilgrim's Progress*, 'delivered under the similitude of a dream', *Piers the Ploughman* is concerned with the Christian's search for salvation: 'What shall I do to be saved?' In Piers's vision the world is to be saved by a ploughman, who becomes in fact a Christ-like figure. Although he was not a peasant it is obvious from the poem that Langland was well acquainted with peasant life – witness the rollicking description of an alehouse in Book V. His sympathies are with

the prisoners in dungeons and the poor in their hovels, over-burdened with children, and rack-rented by landlords. For whatever they save by spinning they spend on rent, or on milk and oatmeal to make gruel and fill the bellies of their children who clamour for food. And they themselves are often famished with hunger, and wretched with the miseries of winter – cold, sleepless nights, when they get up to rock the cradle cramped in a corner, and rise before dawn to card and comb the wool, to wash and scrub and mend, and wind yarn and peel rushes for their rushlights. – The miseries of these women who dwell in hovels are too pitiful to read, or describe in verse.[21]

What then is the status of *Piers the Ploughman* as a document of the common people? It seems unlikely that many of Ball's followers could have actually read the poem, so his references must be to a body of knowledge with which they were already familiar. The idea of the good ploughman as a model of Christian virtue was already used in current preaching. The opening vision of the 'fair field full of folk', the tower of truth and the pit of falsehood presents a setting not unlike the stage of a miracle play. Other aspects of the poem, such as its mildly conservative attitude towards authority, enthusiasm for reforms, biting class satire and continuous criticism of churchmen, are also to be found in the literature of late medieval preaching.[22] *Piers the Ploughman* is in this respect representative of social attitudes which were disseminated fairly widely among the lower classes, including presumably some of those who took part in the rising. It may be therefore that in the poem we have an expression of the same sort of beliefs as are contained in Ball's enigmatic letters and the rebels' demands. In the prologue Piers's dream includes the following:

> Then there came into the field a king, guided by the knights. The powers of the Commons gave him his throne, and Common Sense provided men of learning to counsel him and to protect the people.
>
> The king, with his nobles and counsellors, decided that the common people should provide them with resources; so the people devised different trades, and engaged ploughmen to labour and till the soil for the good of the whole community, as honest ploughmen should. Then the king and the people, helped by Common Sense, established law and order, so that every man might know his rights and duties.[23]

This surely was close to the ideal of the rebels, expressed in their password, 'with King Richard and the true Commons'. In place of the ancient division of society into the three ranks of those who pray, those who fight and those who labour, the rebels' demands at Mile End and Smithfield seem to envisage a society without lords and prelates, a kind of people's monarchy in which there would be no intermediate classes of lawyers, officials and gentry standing between the king and his people.[24] When Richard at Smithfield called on the rebels to follow him (instead of Tyler, who had just been struck down) they did so, for this was perhaps what they most wanted, to be led by their king himself.[25] Walsingham reports that the St Albans rebels believed that 'there would be no lords thereafter but only king and commons'.

There is a further element in *Piers the Ploughman* which is also present in the letters, namely the apocalyptic. A millenarian vision of the Day of Judgement, when the poor as the children of God would overcome their oppressors (identified as the hosts of Satan), seems implicit in Ball's sermon, with its eschatological references to the parable of the wheat and the tares. Such chiliastic hopes and visions were common in medieval protest movements all over Europe, and have indeed persisted into modern times.[26] Ball's cryptic letters appear to be in this tradition:

Jon Balle gretyth yow wele alle and doth yowe to understande, he hath rungen youre belle. Nowe ryght and myght, wylle and skylle. God spede every ydele. Nowe is tyme. Lady helpe to Ihesu thi sone, and thi sone to his fadur, to make a gode ende, in the name of the Trinite of that is begunne amen, amen, pur charite, amen.

And again:

Jakke Mylner asketh help to turne hys mylne aright. He hath grounden smal smal; the kings sone of heven he schal pay for alle. Loke thy mylne go aright, with the foure sayles, and the post stande in stedfastnesse. With ryght and with myght, with skyl and with wylle, lat myght helpe ryght, and skyle go before wille and ryght before myght, than goth oure mylne aryght. And if myght go before ryght, and wylle before skyle; than is oure mylne mys adyght.

The phrase 'now is time' occurs in four of the six letters; and 'John the Miller hath ground small, small, small/The king's son of heaven shall pay for all' in two of them. In Walsingham's version of the Blackheath sermon, Ball, with prophet-like assurance, told his hearers that God 'had now appointed the time' for them to claim their liberty.

Nevertheless, after all attempts at exegesis the letters remain obscure – probably deliberately so. Likewise the references in indictments and by the chroniclers to a Great Society (*magna societas*) – which earlier historians interpreted as a great union or organization of the lower classes – have so far successfully resisted attempts at elucidation. If the name is anything more than a misreading of the Latin (for *societas* can mean simply gang or band), the Great Society may have been some form of conspiratorial organization – perhaps even a forerunner of the 'opaque society' of the early nineteenth-century working class.[27] But in the absence of any new evidence we can at present go no further along this particular road.

Other paths, however, are still open. By using the same material as earlier historians but asking new questions of it, and by supplementing this with new research in manorial and other records, it should be possible to deepen our understanding of the 1381 rising. Slowly, as individual studies are published, a palimpsest will be built up and a new view of the Peasants' Revolt will emerge.[28] Already we can see that to call it a peasants' revolt is a misnomer. In London the lower classes made common cause with the men of Kent and Essex, and in other towns the rising resulted from an alliance between townsmen and peasants from the surrounding county. The rural rebels were not all agriculturalists but included village craftsmen and tradesmen. An artisan element is indicated clearly enough by the names of Wat the tiler, Geoffrey the litster (or dyer), Thomas the baker (of Fobbing, Essex, where the rising began) or Thomas the fletcher (meaning arrow-maker, from Bergholt, who was beheaded). More unexpected is the support from gentry such as Sir Roger Bacon, Sir Thomas Cornerd and James Bedingfield, or substantial yeomen landowners like John Hanchache and Thomas Sampson. Their participation is best explained by desire to settle personal scores and take advantage of the general collapse of order in East Anglia. The peasants for their part seem to have been by no means averse to gentry leadership, despite Ball's condemnation of the 'gentleman' in his well-known text.

The name of John Ball reminds us of another social group that was noticeably active in the rising: the lower clergy. John Wrawe, leader of the Suffolk rebels, and John Batisford, rector of Buckle-sham, are but two of nearly a score of clerics known to have been implicated. The role of 'poor priests' in stirring up and leading the people is a familiar theme in the chroniclers' accounts. Economic and social grievances, which turned them into an ecclesiastical proletariat, may have made some of these clerics sympathetic to the rebels. Walsingham was convinced that Ball taught 'the perverse doctrines of the perfidious John Wycliffe'; and other contemporaries sought to establish a connection between the religious radicalism of Wycliffe and the Lollards (as his followers were called) and the social radicalism of the rebel leaders. In fact Wycliffe repudiated the rising, though there is some controversy about the possible revolutionary effect of his writings. At the popular level a distinction between religious and social radicalism is hard to make, and, if Ball can be taken as representative, the poor priests contributed an element of ideological radicalism to the revolt.

In general the ideology of the rebels, insofar as it can be deduced from their demands and actions, contained strong elements of what is best described as radical-traditionalism[29] – a characteristic of popular protest movements which continued into the nineteenth century. Social and economic changes were claimed on the basis of ancient rights and liberties. The idea that rights had once existed but had been taken away from the people by lords and rulers appears to have been widespread. At St Albans the rebels were convinced that King Offa, who founded the monastery in the eighth century, had granted a 'charter of liberties' to the townsmen, and demanded that the abbot produce it. In his speech at Smithfield Tyler demanded 'that there should be no more villeins in England'; and in their attempts to establish free status many peasants in the fourteenth century appealed to Domesday. They believed (usually erroneously) that if they could prove 'ancient demesne' (which was land held by the crown at some time in the past, and which retained royal protection for the tenants) they would gain privileges and a greater degree of freedom. Tyler's mysterious demand for the 'law of Winchester' may refer to this, as Domesday was kept in that town and was sometimes called the

Book of Winchester. The belief that traditional institutions could work in favour of the common people is apparent in their appeal to the king as protector, and their eager acceptance of his charters granting freedom.

The attitude of the rebels towards documents is not easy to interpret. On the one hand they valued them as possible guarantees of rights and privileges. On the other there was widespread destruction of muniments: indeed in Essex the revolt was commonly called The Burning of the Rolls. The logic of the burning was that as the records (rolls) of manorial courts provided evidence of villein tenure and services due to lords, destruction of the evidence would be a blow against seigneurial rights and an increase in peasant freedom. Associated with these attitudes may have been the hostility to law and lawyers which the chroniclers comment on. Since very few, if any, peasants and artisans could read Latin documents, belief in their efficacy must have been on the level of folklore. The ancient function of documents was to serve as symbolic objects; and it may be that the rebels in 1381 valued written records primarily as symbols rather than for their contents in the modern literate way.[30] The strangeness today of such an attitude shows the gap between our totally and blindly literate outlook and the perceptions common in a medieval non-literate society. Literate people assume that illiteracy is restrictive and narrowing to the point of being a form of unfreedom. But this was not the way in which lack of freedom was perceived by the rebels. They asked not for schools and literacy, but charters. Freedom was something to be won, to be granted immediately; and charters were a symbol rather than the basis of it.

What then did freedom mean to the common people in the late Middle Ages? From the evidence of the 1381 rising there is no single answer to this question. Instead we find a variety of grievances, expectations and demands, the meeting of which was defined as freedom for the individuals concerned. Some of these demands were entirely local and predated 1381 by many years. Others were common to a much wider area. It was the widespread nature of the rising which made it different from other revolts and which so alarmed the ruling classes. When the men of Kent linked up with the men of Essex, and both were supported by the Londoners and then by the commons of East Anglia, the worst fears of a general rising seemed to have been realized. The chronicler, John of Worcester, tells a story about a nightmare of King Henry I, in which he was threatened by desperate peasants and woke up in an agony of terror;[31] and the poet John Gower had warned in the 1370s that 'three things, all of the same sort, are merciless when they get the upper hand; a water-flood, a wasting fire, and the common multitude of small folk. For these will never be checked by reason or discipline.'[32] The pattern of a bundle of local and special revolts loosely associated in a national movement with general aims was a brief forerunner of later movements of popular protest in England. Contrary to a fairly common assumption, movements of revolt do not usually occur at the times of greatest depression, but when expectations are rising. It is when men can see new possibilities of their own betterment, or when they fear that newly won gains will be taken from them, that they are prepared to rise in protest. Such was the position in England in the decades following the Black Death, when the power of labour was greatly strengthened and lords reacted to assert their control. The chronicler Froissart shrewdly hazarded the opinion that the 1381 rising took place 'because of the ease and riches that the common people were of', not because of poverty. New hopes and possibilities had been nurtured, culminating in the great request to the king at Mile End: 'We will that ye make us free for ever, ourselves, our heirs and our lands, and that we be called no more bond [serf] nor so reputed.' To Froissart, who thus records the incident, the demand was the ultimate proof of the 'foolishness' of the common people. Granting this degree of freedom would have completely undermined the social order. It was, in the context of the late fourteenth century, a revolutionary demand.

Nevertheless, there was no revolution; and the question remains, what, if anything, did the common people gain from the 1381 rising? The answer must be, in the short term very little. Their leaders were executed, and any concessions granted were speedily revoked. Historians are generally agreed that the rising had no immediate effect on economic and social conditions. The rebel demands for the ending of villeinage were not met, and it is difficult to prove that the extension of free status and tenure in the fifteenth century owed much to the peasants' actions in 1381. However, the enormity of the occasion, the horror of the very idea that peasants and artisans should challenge their rulers, comes through clearly in the chroniclers' accounts. The refusal by contemporaries to examine the rebels' demands seriously, the persistent attempt to discredit the leaders and finally to consign the whole affair to the realm of folk tales suggest that the rising had a very frightening effect on lords and rulers. Local revolts continued after 1381 and throughout the fifteenth century; and their message was clear:

> If thou art pore, than art thou fre.
> If thou be riche, than woo is the.[33]

Defeat of the rebels did not extinguish the aspirations of the common people. One thing, however defined, they wanted above all else: freedom. A fifteenth-century Malmesbury bondman, who had achieved a modest standard of material comfort, remained nonetheless dissatisfied. In his old age he said that 'if he might bring that [his freedom] aboute, it would be more joifull to him than any worlie good'.[34]

It is possible that some echo of this longing for freedom is retained in the legend of Robin Hood. The earliest reference to the most popular folk hero in English history is in Langland's *Piers the Ploughman*, some four years before the Peasants' Revolt. Direct connection between peasant protest and the early Robin Hood ballads is hard to establish, and attempts to trace an individual Robin Hood are confusing and inconclusive. The value as historical evidence of such largely oral legends, however, is not as literal statements of fact, but as expressions of folk memory and popular history. There may never have been a single historical figure of Robin Hood who performed all the exploits of the stories; rather, the memory of one or several outlaws from Barnsdale and Sherwood Forests provided a basis from which the legend grew. The freedom of life as an outlaw in the greenwood under the leadership of a brave man who robbed the rich and gave to the poor was a dream not limited to England in the later Middle Ages; but its appeal was likely to be strong in a society concerned with issues of personal freedom as well as economic and social grievances. Robin Hood embodied the notion of justice in an unjust world, and his arch-enemy, the sheriff of Nottingham, the idea of oppression and persecution. In a wider sense Robin Hood is the archetypal social bandit or noble robber who is able to right wrongs and who champions the poor and oppressed. For over five hundred years his legend has flourished. In ballads and songs, in the May Games of the Tudor period, in mummers' plays, in street literature, in chapbooks, in the writings of late eighteenth- and early nineteenth-century radicals, and finally through children's stories and modern films, Robin Hood survived down the ages – perhaps a tenuous link with some of the forgotten hopes and aspirations of medieval people.

PART II

Labouring People (1500–1780)

4. Living and Working

For a majority of the English people the central experience of life has always been the business of making a living. The lifelong waking hours of all but a small minority of the population have, until very recently, been dominated by work of some kind. This truism would hardly be suspected from the books of many historians who have given preference to other things like wars and high politics. Yet as a notable historian of Tudor England has remarked of the fifteenth century, 'The Wars of the Roses, like the politics which gave rise to them, were scarcely more than a sport which great men indulged in while the country as a whole stuck doggedly to the more important business of feeding, warming and clothing itself.'[1] Although we know more about how the common people fed and warmed and clothed themselves in the sixteenth and seventeenth centuries than in the Middle Ages it is still little enough, and even less if we are looking for the testimony of labouring people themselves. We can nevertheless try to establish certain basic categories of labouring life in the period 1500–1780.

After the decline of the late fourteenth and first half of the fifteenth centuries, population slowly increased, and by 1530 had perhaps reached 2·5 or 3 million in England and Wales. By 1600 the figure was over 4 million; in 1700, 5·5 to 6 million; and by 1750, 6 to 6.5 million. These of course are overall figures, useful for giving perspective and showing long-term trends, but not telling us very much about the common people as such. For that we have to turn elsewhere, particularly to the remarkable calculations of the herald and genealogist, Gregory King. His survey, made in the 1690s and based on data from the hearth-tax returns, shows the social structure in 1688. Some of his terminology and his method of dividing up the material may seem a little strange; but it does provide both a quantitative estimate and a record of how an informed contemporary thought about the problems of 'political arithmetic'. From the table on pages 114–15 several points emerge.

Gregory King's Scheme of the Income & Expense of the

Number of families	Ranks, degrees, titles and qualifications	Heads per family	Number of persons
160	Temporal lords	40	6,400
26	Spiritual lords	20	520
800	Baronets	16	12,800
600	Knights	13	7,800
3,000	Esquires	10	30,000
12,000	Gentlemen	8	96,000
5,000	Persons in greater offices and places	8	40,000
5,000	Persons in lesser offices and places	6	30,000
2,000	Eminent merchants and traders by sea	8	16,000
8,000	Lesser merchants and traders by sea	6	48,000
10,000	Persons in the law	7	70,000
2,000	Eminent clergymen	6	12,000
8,000	Lesser clergymen	5	40,000
40,000	Freeholders of the better sort	7	280,000
120,000	Freeholders of the lesser sort	$5\frac{1}{2}$	660,000
150,000	Farmers	5	750,000
15,000	Persons in liberal arts and sciences	5	75,000
50,000	Shopkeepers and tradesmen	$4\frac{1}{2}$	225,000
60,000	Artisans and handicrafts	4	240,000
5,000	Naval officers	4	20,000
4,000	Military officers	4	16,000
500,586		$5\frac{1}{3}$	2,675,520
50,000	Common seamen	3	150,000
364,000	Labouring people and out servants	$3\frac{1}{2}$	1,275,000
400,000	Cottagers and paupers	$3\frac{1}{4}$	1,300,000
35,000	Common soldiers	2	70,000
849,000		$3\frac{1}{4}$	2,795,000
	Vagrants; as gipsies, thieves, beggars, &c.		30,000
	So the general account is		
500,586	Increasing the wealth of the kingdom	$5\frac{1}{3}$	2,675,520
849,000	Decreasing the wealth of the kingdom	$3\frac{1}{4}$	2,825,000
1,349,586	Neat Totals	$4^{1}/_{13}$	5,500,520

From Peter Laslett, *The World We Have Lost* (London, 1965), pp. 32–3.

Several Families of England Calculated for the Year 1688

Yearly income per family	Yearly income in general	Yearly income per head			Yearly expense per head			Yearly increase per head			Yearly increase in general
£ s	£	£	s	d	£	s	d	£	s	d	£
3,200	512,000	80	0	0	70	0	0	10	0	0	64,000
1,300	33,800	65	0	0	45	0	0	20	0	0	10,400
880	704,000	55	0	0	49	0	0	6	0	0	76,800
650	390,000	50	0	0	45	0	0	5	0	0	39,000
450	1,200,000	45	0	0	41	0	0	4	0	0	120,000
280	2,880,000	35	0	0	32	0	0	3	0	0	288,000
240	1,200,000	30	0	0	26	0	0	4	0	0	160,000
120	600,000	20	0	0	17	0	0	3	0	0	90,000
400	800,000	50	0	0	37	0	0	13	0	0	208,000
198	1,600,000	33	0	0	27	0	0	6	0	0	288,000
154	1,540,000	22	0	0	18	0	0	4	0	0	280,000
72	144,000	12	0	0	10	0	0	2	0	0	24,000
50	400,000	10	0	0	9	4	0	0	16	0	32,000
91	3,640,000	13	0	0	11	15	0	1	5	0	350,000
55	6,600,000	10	0	0	9	10	0	0	10	0	330,000
42 10	6,375,000	8	10	0	8	5	0	0	5	0	187,500
60	900,000	12	0	0	11	0	0	1	0	0	75,000
45	2,250,000	10	0	0	9	0	0	1	0	0	225,000
38	2,280,000	9	10	0	9	0	0	0	10	0	120,000
80	400,000	20	0	0	18	0	0	2	0	0	40,000
60	240,000	15	0	0	14	0	0	1	0	0	16,000
68 18	34,488,800	12	18	0	11	15	4	1	2	8	3,023,700
								Decrease			*Decrease*
20	1,000,000	7	0	0	7	10	0	0	10	0	75,000
15	5,460,000	4	10	0	4	12	0	0	2	0	127,500
6 10	2,000,000	2	0	0	2	5	0	0	5	0	325,000
14	490,000	7	0	0	7	10	0	0	10	0	35,000
10 10	8,950,000	3	5	0	3	9	0	0	4	0	562,500
	60,000	2	0	0	4	0	0	2	0	0	60,000
68 18	34,488,800	12	18	0	11	15	4	1	2	8	3,023,700
10 10	9,010,000	3	3	0	3	7	6	0	4	6	622,500
32 5	43,491,800	7	18	0	7	9	3	0	8	9	2,401,200

First, the exact identity of the common people becomes a little clearer. So far in this history it has been assumed that by the common people was meant the great majority of the population, all those in fact who had to work in some way for a living, who were in no way distinguished, and without power beyond their immediate family and occupational circle. This definition excluded the aristocracy, gentry, richer merchants, and supporting professional classes; but leaves open the tricky question of certain borderline groups. King's figures and categories give substance to such a scheme. Nine-tenths or more of the persons he enumerates are below the status of gentry. They are the commonalty – freeholders (yeomen), farmers, shopkeepers, artisans, tradesmen, soldiers and sailors, labourers, servants, cottagers and paupers. They were the 'plain mean people' among whom the puritan divine, Richard Baxter, had been bred. Unlike the gentry, they worked with their hands, and they had virtually no leisure except on Sundays and holidays. Even the most prosperous among them, such as the yeomen farmers, to whom the Elizabethan chronicler William Harrison accorded 'a certain pre-eminence', were sharply distinguished from the gentry: 'They be not called "Master", as gentlemen are, or "Sir", as to knights appertaineth, but only "John" and "Thomas", etc.' Lower in the social scale according to Harrison were

day-labourers, poor husbandmen and some retailers (which have no free land), copyholders, and all artificers, as tailors, shoemakers, carpenters, brickmakers, masons, etc. [They] have neither voice nor authority in the commonwealth, but are to be ruled and not to rule other; yet they are not altogether neglected, for in cities and corporate towns, for default of yeomen, they are fain to make up their inquests of such manner of people. And in villages they are commonly made church wardens, sidesmen, ale conners, now and then constables, and many times enjoy the name of head boroughs.[2]

So great was the gulf between this majority of ordinary people (the plain John Harrisons and Elizabeth Browns) and the tiny minority who owned most of the wealth, made all the decisions, and exercised exclusive class power, that one eminent social historian has concluded that in England before the Industrial Revolution there was effectively only one class, and that in the sixteenth and seventeenth centuries the country was a one-class society.[3]

The second interesting point in King's table is that his unit of social accounting is not the individual but the family. He thinks of England as comprising 1,350,000 families rather than 5,500,000 separate persons. By family is meant the extended family or household, including servants, apprentices, and such labourers and journeymen as lived-in, in addition to the kin group. Hence, as reflected in column 3 (Heads per family), the higher the rank in the social hierarchy, the larger was the family. In the great house, on the farm and in industry, the household was the central unit of economic life, and King's presentation is based on this assumption. It means, however, that one large section of the labouring population – the servants who lived-in – does not appear separately, but is concealed among other categories. The reality behind King's family figures is well illustrated by the example of a London bakery in 1619. In this typical establishment there were thirteen or fourteen people: the baker, his wife, their three or four children, four journeymen, two apprentices and two maidservants. They all worked, ate, and (except for the journeymen) slept in the house.[4]

A third and very striking point is the number of people shown by King to be in a state of poverty. This would appear to be the only interpretation of his otherwise puzzling division between those who increase and those who decrease the wealth of the kingdom. Over half the total population, including the two largest categories of labouring people and cottagers, do not have sufficient income to live on. If King's calculations are correct (and the general view of historians is that they have on the whole worn remarkably well) 2·8 million people must have been either in want or reliant on poor relief and charity, since their yearly expenses exceeded their income. This suggests that there was not enough productive work for them to do, and that poverty, as in medieval times, was built into the economic system. Low productivity (by modern standards), underemployment and seasonal unemployment combined to produce a low output per head.

The dimensions of this structural poverty will become apparent when we consider one further point which emerges from the table: namely, the extent to which England was still a rural society.

Three-quarters of the whole population lived in villages and earned their living by agriculture or by occupations directly related to agriculture. Their lives were at the mercy of floods, harvest failures, famine and pestilences. In King's figures the rural and agricultural population is shown in the categories of freeholders, farmers and cottagers, and to these must be added many of the 'labouring people and out servants', for he does not distinguish between agricultural and non-agricultural labour. Much of handicraft industry was semi-rural and sometimes combined with agricultural pursuits, so that some of the 240,000 artisans and craftsmen may also have to be counted as part of the rural world. Clearly if we are to investigate how the majority of the common people lived and worked we have to begin with the countryside.

Here we immediately run into a difficulty: how to generalize about the common people when they were far from homogeneous. Geographically, and therefore agriculturally, England and Wales is not one uniform area but a number of separate regions. A line drawn approximately from York to Exeter divides the kingdom into two different zones (see map, page 26). To the north and west is an area of mountain and moor, with few valleys and plains, poor soil and a wet climate. The south and east is lowland with gentle hills, richer soil and a drier climate. The former produces mainly grass and is therefore animal country; the latter can grow corn as well as grass, and is therefore suitable for mixed husbandry. Farming practices, field systems, customs of inheritance, the social framework, and rural industries developed differently in the two zones; and (to complicate the picture even further) there were small parts of the lowland zone which resembled the highland pattern, and vice versa. We have already noted the limitations which this division imposes on generalizations about the medieval manorial and open-field system. It now suggests the need for caution when delineating peasant conditions in the sixteenth and seventeenth centuries. Ideally, to recapture the realities of labouring life, we need studies of scores of communities, county by county. Even that would be insufficient until we have learned how to appreciate the skills and culture of dozens of local crafts and rural jobs. The diversity of the ways in which the common people made their livings is seldom emphasized. Blanket ignorance of the complexities of farming and of the difficulties and subtleties of hand-craftsmanship, combined with easy generalizations about the masses, obscure important aspects of the nature of work in pre-industrial society. Agricultural labourers, for instance, did not think of themselves as an undifferentiated mass, but as shepherds, cowmen, horsemen, ploughmen or specialists in any of the other skilled jobs on the farm. Meanwhile we have to rely on such material as is to hand. Precious little of it is from the common people themselves; but occasionally voices from below can be heard if we listen hard for them.

Often these are voices of protest. Only when something has gone wrong to such an extent that people riot and rebel do their voices come through the deadening silence of official documents. Grievances and demands can no longer be ignored, and in them we are able to glimpse perceptions of social reality different from those of the ruling classes. For a brief moment the dominant social and political mould is broken. Alternative priorities and policies erupt and become visible to us, before being hastily suppressed. Riots and rebellions will for this reason tend to figure prominently in any history of the common people, quite apart from any theory of class struggle. There is a danger that this prominence may cause distortion if it creates the impression that the common people were unduly prone to revolt and that their history is mainly a matter of unsuccessful risings. The material is included not because the events themselves were necessarily of decisive importance in the development of the common people but because of what it reveals about the social and personal expectations and assumptions of those involved. Revolts are those rare moments when, if we are lucky, we may catch the mood of people whose very existence we might otherwise hardly notice. Much of what historians write is simply a record of what succeeded, with no suggestion that things could have been otherwise. In our attempts to understand the past (and through it the present) we have to remind ourselves continually of the unreality of that peculiar construct, history.

For six weeks in July and August 1549 several thousand Norfolkmen were encamped on Mousehold Heath outside the city of Norwich, where their forefathers had gathered in 1381.[5] Under the leadership of Robert Ket, a prosperous man of property from Wymondham, they drew up a list of grievances amounting to a programme of agrarian reform with some political and religious overtones. An examination of the programme will give a fair indication of where the peasantry thought the shoe was pinching, and what were for them the chief issues of the day. But first it will be convenient to recount briefly the course of the rising. Ket's rebellion began in the area round Attleborough and Wymondham in south Norfolk, between 20 June and 10 July 1549, as a movement against recent enclosures. The rioters destroyed fences in the neighbourhood, and then moved to Norwich, where they set up camp outside the city from 12 July to 26 August, and were joined by men from other parts of Norfolk. The city fathers of Norwich were at first hostile, but the rebels had supporters within the city, and the mayor and some leading citizens therefore thought it prudent to cooperate, even to the extent of signing the articles of complaint drawn up by Ket and his lieutenants. At Castle Rising in the western part of the county the peasantry also rose, and after moving south to the Suffolk border turned eastwards and joined Ket at Mousehold Heath. An attempt to take over Yarmouth failed, and the eastern rebels too came into the Great Camp at Mousehold. What had started as a series of local riots developed into an alternative form of government. A council composed of two representatives or 'governors' from each of twenty-four county hundreds, plus a representative of Suffolk, issued orders and saw that justice was dispensed. Under Ket's leadership the affairs of the rebels were conducted with decorum and in due form, even to the extent of claiming to act in the king's name.

The government at first responded in a conciliatory manner, offering a pardon to all who would disperse peacefully. This was rejected on 21 July and the rebels occupied Norwich after fighting their way in. A force of about 1400 men under the command of the marquess of Northampton was then sent to restore order but was defeated and had to abandon the city. The government therefore sent out instructions for the levying of troops in the neighbouring counties, and the earl of Warwick at the head of some 12,000 English troops and 1200 German mercenaries advanced into Norfolk. On 24 August he entered Norwich, which suffered from the street fighting and burning. Ket and his forces decided to strike camp and move to Dussindale. They were pursued by Warwick's cavalry and foot-mercenaries and ruthlessly cut down; and so on 27 August an ancient prophecy was fulfilled:

> The country gnooffes [i.e. knaves], Hob, Dick, and Hick,
> With clubs and clouted shoon
> Shall fill up Dussindale
> With slaughtered bodies soon.[6]

There were perhaps 3000 peasant casualties in the battle of Dussindale, and many were taken prisoner. Forty-nine were hanged at Norwich, and others were perhaps executed elsewhere. Robert Ket, who had twice refused a pardon on the grounds that he had done nothing that needed pardoning, was captured after the battle and subsequently convicted of treason. His body was hung in chains outside Norwich city gates, and his brother William was hanged from Wymondham steeple.

Until more work has been done on local sources it is not possible to go very far in identifying the rank-and-file participants in the rebellion. A list of forty-seven rebels includes seventeen husbandmen, two labourers, and an assortment of tradesmen and artisans. The general impression is that the rising was a protest by the Norfolk peasantry, supported by townsmen from Norwich and Yarmouth. It was conducted by the insurgents (until the final bloody suppression) without savagery, and even with sardonic humour, as witness the note left on the carcasses of the animals of an offending landlord:

> Mr Pratt, your sheep are very fat,
> And we thank *you* for that;
> We have left you the skins to pay your wife's pins,
> And you must thank *us* for that.[7]

The rebels' grievances were formulated in twenty-nine articles of complaint, signed by Robert Ket, Thomas Aldrich (a respected citizen of Norwich) and Thomas Cod (the mayor):

> We pray your grace that where it is enacted for enclosing that it be not hurtful to such as have enclosed saffron grounds, for they be greatly chargeable to them, and that from henceforth no man shall enclose any more.

We certify your grace that whereas the lords of the manors hath been charged with certe free rent, the same lords hath sought means to charge the freeholders to pay the same rent, contrary to right.

We pray your grace that no lord of no manor shall common upon the commons.

We pray that priests from henceforth shall purchase no lands neither free nor Bondy, and the lands that they have in possession may be letten to temporal men, as they were in the first year of the reign of King Henry the VII.

We pray that reed ground and meadow ground may be at such price as they were in the first year of King Henry the VII.

We pray that all marshes that are holden of the King's Majesty by free rent or of any other, may be again at the price that they were in the first year of King Henry VII.

We pray that all bushels within your realm be of one stice, that is to say, to be in measure viii gallons.

We pray that [priests] or vicars that be [not able] to preach and set forth the word of God to his parishoners may be thereby put from his benefice, and the parishoners there to choose another, or else the patron or lord of the town.

We pray that the payments of castleward rent, and blanch farm and office lands, which hath been accustomed to be gathered of the tenements, whereas we suppose the lords ought to pay the same to their bailiffs for their rents gathering, and not the tenants.

We pray that no man under the degree of a knight or esquire keep a dove house, except it hath been of an old ancient custom.

We pray that all freeholders and copyholders may take the profits of all commons, and there to common, and the lords not to common nor take profits of the same.

We pray that no feodary within your shires shall be a councillor to any man in his office making, whereby the King may be truly served, so that a man being of good conscience may be yearly chosen to the same office by the commons of the same shire.

We pray your grace to take all liberty of let into your own hands whereby all men may quietly enjoy their commons with all profits.

We pray that copyhold land that is unreasonably rented may go as it did in the first year of King Henry VII, and that at the death of a tenant or at a sale the same lands to be charged with an easy fine as a capon or a reasonable [sum] of money for a remembrance.

We pray that no priest [shall be chaplain] nor no other officer to any man of honour or worship, but only to be resident upon their benefices whereby their parishoners may be instructed with the laws of God.

We pray that all bond men may be made free, for God made all free with his precious blood-shedding.

We pray that rivers may be free and common to all men for fishing and passage.

We pray that no man shall be put by your escheator and feodary to find any office unless he holdeth of your Grace in chief or capite above x1.1 by year.

We pray that the poor mariners or fishermen may have the whole profits of their fishing as porpoises, grampuses, whales or any great fish, so it be not prejudicial to your Grace.

We pray that every proprietary parson or vicar having a benefice of xv.1 or more by year shall either by themselves or by some other person teach poor men's children of their parish the book called the catechism and the primer.

We pray that it be not lawful to the lords of any manor to purchase lands freely and to let them out again by copy of court roll to their great advancement and to the undoing of your poor subjects.

We pray that no proprietary parson or vicar, in consideration of avoiding trouble and suit between them and their poor parishoners which they daily do precede and attempt, shall from henceforth take for the full contentation [i.e. satisfaction] of all the tenths which now they do receive but viiid of the noble in the full discharge of all other tithes.

We pray that no man under the degree of [blank] shall keep any conies upon any of their own freehold or copyhold unless he pale them in so that it shall not be to the commons' nuisance.

We pray that no person, of what estate, degree or condition he be, shall from henceforth sell the wardship of any child, but that the same child if he live to his full age shall be at his own chosen concerning his marriage, the King's wards only except.

We pray that no manner of person having a manor of his own shall be no other lord's bailiff but only his own.

We pray that no lord knight nor gentleman shall have or take in farm any spiritual promotion.

We pray that your Grace to give license and authority by your gracious commission under your great seal to such commissioners as your poor commons hath chosen, or as many of them as your Majesty and your council shall appoint and think meet, for to redress and reform all such good laws, statutes, proclamations, and all other your proceedings, which hath been hidden by your justices of your peace, sheriffs, escheators, and other your officers from your poor commons, since the first year of the reign of your noble grandfather King Henry VII.

We pray that those your offices that hath offended your Grace and your commons, and so proved by the complaint of your poor commons, do give unto these poor men so assembled iiijd. every day so long as they have remained there.

We pray that no lord, knight, esquire nor gentleman do graze nor feed any bullocks or sheep if he may spend forty pounds a year by his lands, but only for the provision of his house.

By me, Robt. Kett.

   ,,   ,,   Thomas Aldryche.   Thomas Cod.[8]

The first impression on reading this document is that we have butted in upon some long-standing quarrel between tenants and landlords. There is dispute over the rents and fines to be paid, complaints that rights of common are being eroded or abused by lords, and that pigeons and rabbits are allowed to damage tenants' crops. The plea is that conditions be restored to what they used to be in the first year of King Henry VII (1485–6); and there is obviously some feeling that the clergy are not all they should be. These demands are all very specific; they call for a curbing of various actions by landlords which the peasants see as something new and undesirable. Individually such acts have happened before and perhaps in isolation have had to be tolerated. But together they pose a threat, for they seem to challenge the basis of much of peasant life as it has hitherto been known. Underlying the exasperation at particular abuses was a widespread feeling against the general nature of changes in the economy.

These changes in the sixteenth century went by the name of enclosures. Every age has its slogans or catch-phrases which serve to encapsulate some important principle or idea but which are sufficiently vague to allow the mobilization of wide support. Enclosure was simply the process of putting a hedge or fence round a parcel of land. But this could be – and was – done in different ways and for different reasons, with correspondingly different consequences. For instance, the actions of the rebels in 1549 indicate their resistance to enclosure by landlords for the keeping of sheep; but the first of their articles is a request that although 'from henceforth no man shall enclose any more', those tenants who have gone to the expense of enclosing land for the better cultivation of saffron should be exempt from enactments against enclosure. Here we have two quite different types of enclosure: the first by lords of manors and large farmers, and opposed by the peasantry; the second by the peasants themselves and considered acceptable.

Of all agrarian grievances the one we hear most about from contemporary observers is the enclosure of land for purposes of sheep pasture. In a famous passage in his *Utopia* (1516) Sir Thomas More condemned the changes in no uncertain terms:

Your sheep that were wont to be so meek and tame, and so small eaters, now, as I hear say, be become so great devourers and so wild, that they eat up, and swallow down the very men themselves. They consume, destroy, and devour whole fields, houses, cities. For look in what parts of the realm doth grow the finest and therefore dearest wool, there noblemen and gentlemen, yea and certain abbots, holy men no doubt, not contenting themselves with the yearly revenues and profits, that were wont to grow to their forefathers and predecessors of their lands, not being content that they live in rest and pleasure nothing profiting, yea much annoying the weal public, leave no ground for tillage, they inclose all into pastures; they throw down houses; they pluck down towns, and leave nothing standing, but only the church to be made a sheep-house. And as though you lost no small quantity of ground by forests, chases, lawns, and parks, those good holy men turn all dwelling-places and all glebeland into desolation and wilderness. Therefore that one covetous and insatiable cormorant and very plague of his native country may compass about and inclose many thousand acres of ground together within one pale or hedge, the husbandmen be thrust out of their own, or else either by cunning and fraud, or by violent oppression they be put besides it, or by wrongs and injuries they be so wearied, that they be compelled to sell all: by one means therefore or by other, either by hook or crook they must needs depart away, poor, silly, wretched souls, men, women, husbands, wives, fatherless children, widows, woeful mothers, with their young babes, and their whole household small in substance and much in number, as husbandry requireth many hands. Away they trudge, I say, out of their known and accustomed houses, finding no place to rest in. All their household stuff, which is very little worth, though it might well abide the sale: yet being suddenly thrust out, they be constrained to sell it for a thing of nought. And when they have wandered abroad till that be spent, what can they then else do but steal, and then justly pardy be hanged, or else go about a begging. And yet then also they be cast in prison as vagabonds, because they go about and work not: whom no man will set a work, though they never so willingly proffer themselves thereto. For one shepherd or herdsman is enough to eat up that ground with cattle, to the occupying whereof about husbandry many hands were requisite.[9]

Here is the classical indictment, repeated by pamphleteers and preachers, and legislated against by governments continuously from 1489 to 1656, of enclosure leading to depopulation. The growth of the cloth trade increased the demand for wool, to which landlords responded by enclosing arable land and turning it into pasture for sheep. Whereas tillage employed many hands, sheep farming needed relatively few. Men and their families were therefore turned off the land and driven from their villages in search of food and work. The first phase of what Marx called the expropriation of the peasantry from the soil was thus effected.

Economic historians have been at pains to mitigate the harshness of this picture by pointing out that enclosure at this time affected only a small percentage of the total land of the country and that the regional differences noted earlier precluded any uniform pattern of enclosure. Not all enclosure was for pasture; and there is evidence that the peasants themselves at times carried out enclosures before the sixteenth century. In some southern counties (Sussex, Surrey, Essex, Suffolk) the open fields had by 1500 largely been replaced by consolidated (enclosed) farms. But we are also reminded that much open field and common land (perhaps as much as half the total) remained to be enclosed in the late eighteenth and early nineteenth centuries. Should we therefore conclude that the dozens of contemporary writers who complained that enclosures 'bred a decay of people', the legislators who set up royal commissions to investigate agrarian distress or enacted laws for the repression of vagrancy, and the thousands of peasants who revolted, were all mistaken? By no means; but we are warned that under the umbrella label of enclosure there was taking place a variety of economic and social changes whose motivation was complex and confused, but whose immediate consequences were only too clearly perceived. The grievances of the rebels of 1549 were genuine enough, and their twenty-nine articles are a sure pointer to the problems facing the peasantry in the sixteenth century.

The document assumes the familiar social structure of lords of manors, freeholders, copyholders and bondmen, all of whom are mentioned by name. However, the relationships between these groups are not the same as when we last met them in medieval times. By the sixteenth century the substance of feudalism had virtually disappeared though outward forms remained; and the rural population had become more differentiated. At the apex of the rural commonalty was that much-lauded Elizabethan figure, the yeoman. In legal parlance he was the holder of free land to the annual value of forty shillings; but more generally the term was used to denote a well-to-do farmer below the rank of gentleman. Yeomen were usually, though not necessarily, freeholders – descendants of those free tenants of the manor who held their land in perpetuity and not for a stated number of years or at the will of the lord. The security of their tenure was the basis of their prized independence; and since the thirteenth century they were privileged politically in that the forty-shilling freeholders were entitled to vote for members of parliament. Freeholders, however, were a very heterogeneous class, ranging from a sort of peasant-aristocracy to cottagers with only three or four acres. Gregory King shows three times as many freeholders of the 'lesser' as of the 'better' sort. In the sixteenth century freeholders as a whole probably constituted about a fifth of the tenants in the country, and even in the eastern counties where they were most numerous they were perhaps little more than a third.

The bulk of the peasantry (three-fifths overall and more in some counties) were not freeholders but customary tenants. A majority of these were copyholders who held their land according to the custom of the manor, on the terms set out on a copy of the manorial court roll. They were the descendants of the villeins of the medieval manor and their tenure retained traces of its villein origins. Because the custom of the manor varied so much from place to place it is difficult to generalize about the degree of security enjoyed by copyholders, and it is evident that their prosperity and holdings could be very diverse. Unlike their ancestors they were now personally free – though traces of vil-leinage by blood lingered on. There may have been as many as 250 villein families in the reign of Elizabeth, which would account for the rebels' demand that 'all bond men may be made free'. For several centuries the peasantry had relied upon the custom of the manor, which functioned in effect as the law of village life, to protect their rights as well as to lay out their obligations. A firm claim, it was thought, could be established by a successful appeal to custom, 'whereof the memory of man runneth not to the contrary'. But in the sixteenth century it became clear that this was insufficient protection against such changes as the 1549 rebels complained of. Even more at risk from the activities of grasping landlords and enclosing 'cormorants' was the class below the copyholding husbandmen on the social scale, the farm labourers.

In medieval England landless wage labourers (farm servants) were a minority of the manorial population, and they continued so throughout the Tudor and Stuart period. The typical peasant farm was worked by the family, with hired labour brought in only occasionally at peak times. But where the demesne or home farm was worked as a single unit there was a steady demand for labourers. At the beginning of the sixteenth century the labouring population included tenants with holdings of less than five acres who had to supplement their income with wage work. Others had only a cottage and garden or close. Such labourers were not entirely landless and, even more important, they had rights of common. This permitted them to graze their sheep, cattle, pigs and geese – either stinted or without limit – on the common lands of the village. They also enjoyed the right to timber for building, fuel for their fires, rabbits and birds for food, bracken for bedding, and reeds for thatching. In some parishes they were allowed to quarry stone or dig gravel and coal from pits on the common. These rights were carefully regulated by custom. They were not 'extras', or a sort of village charity for the poor, but part of an integrated economy. To upset the balance of any single part of the regime was liable to have consequences far beyond the point of immediate impact. In the sixteenth century the labouring population amounted to between a quarter and a third of the total rural population; by the end of the seventeenth century this figure had increased, and Gregory King shows labouring people, out-servants, cottagers and paupers as 47 per cent of the entire population.

The 1549 articles of complaint refer to rights of common several times: no lord of the manor is to use the commons but only the freeholders and copyholders, the king himself is to ensure that all men may quietly enjoy their common rights, and so on. The Norfolk rebels do not actually mention enclosure of the commons, but in other areas where this occurred the effect upon the labourers and small husbandmen was catastrophic. Large landowners and wealthy tenants were able to carry through enclosure of the commons and the open fields without agreement from the peasantry. Compensation for loss of common rights was either inadequate or non-existent. Without access to the commons the previous way of life of the labourers was made impossible. They were reduced to living solely upon wages and lost that measure of independence they had once enjoyed. For those who could not find sufficient wage-work to support themselves and their families there was the prospect of joining that army of vagrants which so frightened Tudor governments and which Gregory King later assessed at no less than 30,000 persons.

The plight of these farmworkers was but a part of the 'agrarian problem' in the sixteenth century. Although outwardly much of the structure of manorialism and the medieval village remained, inwardly the system disintegrated under the combined impact of diverse developments: the leasing of the demesne and the amalgamation of two or more holdings (called engrossing) to create large farms, either arable or pasture; the buying and selling of land among the peasantry with a consequent widening of the differential between rich and poor peasant farmers; the consolidation of strips in the open fields and their enclosure by landlords or the tenants themselves; the enclosure of commons and wastes, both large scale (by landlords) and small scale (by the encroachment of poor peasants); the conversion from arable farming to sheep pasture and resultant 'depopulation'; a rise in total population which increased demand for food and put pressure on the available land. In retrospect these changes appear as a continuous process, the transition from a largely subsistence husbandry to capitalist agriculture. The process was uneven and incomplete but the dominant tendency was unmistakable. Before the transformation from peasant cultivator to capitalist farmer could be effected, however, various obstacles to change had to be removed. Many of the grievances of the peasantry may be seen as opposition to attempts to dismantle the defences of the poor. The struggle over common rights and the endless legal disputes over tenure are cases in point.

A complaint of the Norfolk rebels goes to the heart of the matter: 'We pray that copyhold land that is unreasonably rented may go as it did in the first year of King Henry VII, and that at the death of a tenant or at a sale the same lands to be charged with an easy fine. . .' The copyholders had discovered to their cost that their tenure was vulnerable, and they were trying to get safeguards for the future. It is not easy to disentangle the legal complexities and local variations which surround the question of tenant right. For many years social historians have taken the view that in some cases copyhold did not offer security of tenure.[10] It has been argued that the crucial factors were first, whether the copyholder held his land by inheritance or only for a number of years or lives; and second whether the rent and fines were fixed or alterable by the landlord. In the second case, where payments were variable, a copyholder could be forced to give up his land by a prohibitive increase in the rent. Even in the first case, where the copy passed from father to son, if the fine (payment on entry) was at the will of the lord it could be used to exclude the successor. It was in the landlord's interest to substitute leases in cases where copyholders had estates of inheritance, and to force eviction of small tenants. In this way rents could be raised, holdings amalgamated into large farms, the restrictions of custom evaded, and the way cleared for enclosure and engrossing.

Recently this view has been challenged.[11] It has been argued that copyholders did have legal security against wrongful eviction, and that the substitution of leases for copyholds could be to the advantage of the tenant. This conclusion is based on a careful examination of the precise legal meaning of copyhold, and on the apparent scarcity of cases of copyholders being ousted and left without redress. The problem we are faced with is that tenants were evicted, either legally or illegally, and that enclosures, conversion to pasture and depopulation did take place. Perhaps from a peasant perception of these events the legal rights and wrongs are something of a red herring. If his interests were set aside, if he were dispossessed of something he had previously enjoyed, or if what seemed like legitimate expectations were denied, it mattered little to him that legally he had suffered no wrong. In the following case it would appear that John Wilson of Buston in Northumberland had no legal case at all, but his muted protest voices a genuine sense of grievance nonetheless. He had been persuaded to give up his copy in return for a lease at double rent, and now regretted it:

To the Right Honourable the Earl of Northumberland, the humble petition of John Wilson, his wife and 8 poor children. Humbly complaining showeth . . . your petitioner . . . that whereas your said petitioner and his predecessors being ancient tenants to your honour, holding one tenement on ferme in Upper Bustone, by virtue of copyhold tenure out of the memory of man, which copies both of your said poor petitioners' great grandfather, his father's father, and his own father are yet extant to be seen: and now of late your said poor petitioner, being under age, helpless and none to do for him, and forced (God knows) by some of your honour's officers to take a lease and pay double and treble rent, in so much that your said poor petitioner, his wife, and 8 poor children is utterly now beggared and overthrown, unless your worthy good honour will be pleased to take a pitiful communication thereof, or otherwise your said poore petitioner, his wife and poore children knows no other way but of force to give over your honour's land, by reason of the deare renting thereof, and so be constrained to go a-begging up and down the countrie.[12]

How many John Wilsons there were we shall never know. The series of peasant risings in the sixteenth and seventeenth centuries point to continuing agrarian grievances. Ket's rebellion was not an isolated instance. In 1536 the northern counties and Lincolnshire were ablaze, with perhaps as many as 40,000 armed men involved at the height of the risings. This outburst, the Pilgrimage of Grace, was a massive protest against the dissolution of the monasteries, but the complaints of the rebels concerned agrarian as well as religious changes: enclosures, tenant rights, increases in rent. Similarly the 1549 rising in Devon and Cornwall which preceded Ket's rebellion was directed mainly against the new Prayer Book but also against enclosures and high prices. In 1550 there were disturbances in Kent, and in 1552 in Buckinghamshire. Sir Thomas Wyatt's rebellion in 1554 was an anti-Catholic revolt but his Kentish followers demanded the restoration of pasture lands which had been forcibly seized. The Midland revolt of 1607 was a peasant rising provoked entirely by enclosure. In the counties of Leicestershire, Northamptonshire, Bedfordshire and Warwickshire the high prices of wool, meat and leather prompted landlords and farmers to enclose their land and convert ploughland to pasture. It only needed a series of poor harvests, beginning in 1594, and a period of high food prices to cause distress among the labourers and small farmers. Enclosures were a symbol – perhaps also a scapegoat – for a combination of ills, which together could threaten hunger and starvation. The hazards of peasant tenure and the tragedies that could ensue from it continued into modern times. In Thomas Hardy's novel *The Woodlanders*, set in the nineteenth century, Giles Winterborne was dispossessed of his holding because the lease was inadvertently not renewed before the death of the last holder and so reverted to the lord of the manor:

'He [Winterborne] marvelled what could have induced his ancestors at Hintock, and other village people, to exchange their old copyholds for life-leases.'[13]

Perhaps the most unfortunate victims of the agrarian changes and rising population were the unemployed. All societies are faced with the problem of looking after those who cannot work: the aged and impotent, orphans and widows, and the chronically diseased – those who came to be known in the language of a later age as the deserving poor. Traditionally in England they were supported by their families, by the parish, and by Christian almsgiving. But the sixteenth century was concerned with a new problem: the able-bodied unemployed who could not find work in their own locality and who therefore went on tramp. The vagrant became the terror-figure of the Tudor period. In the old nursery rhyme there may be an echo of this:

> Hark, hark, the dogs do bark,
> The beggars are coming to town;
> Some in rags, and some in jags,
> And one in a velvet gown.

The spectre of gangs of 'sturdy idle rogues and vagabonds' haunted legislators, to whom the issue seemed to be more a matter of law and order than the treatment of poverty. The distinction between the man who was unemployed because he could not get work (and who should therefore be relieved) and he who was unemployed because he did not want to work (and who might therefore merit punishment) was only recognized in the later years of the sixteenth century. Vagabonds were to be severely, in fact brutally, punished: 'to be grievously whipped and burned through the gristle of the right ear with a hot iron of the compass of an inch about, as a manifestation of his wicked life,' says William Harrison.[14]

At the end of Elizabeth's reign, after half a century of earlier legislation, social policy was consolidated in the great Poor Law Act of 1601. For the common people few acts have been of greater significance. It lasted until 1835; and together with the complementary Act of Settlement of 1662 governed the very conditions of existence for thousands of humble people at crucial periods of their lives. Each parish was made responsible for the relief of its own poor, the administration being entrusted to the churchwardens, seving *ex officio*, and two or more overseers of the poor chosen annually by the vestry. The system was superintended by the local justices of the peace. Provision was made for supplying work to the able-bodied and for a stock of materials; for giving relief to 'the lame, impotent, old, blind and such other . . . being poor and not able to work'; and for binding children as apprentices. The whole system was financed by a rate levied on the occupiers of property. Entitlement to relief was restricted to persons who had settlement in a parish, and immigrants could be removed provided that they had been resident for less than forty days. Mobility of labour was in this way impeded. The Act was a recognition that poverty and vagrancy constituted a new problem which required new measures for its control. As R.H. Tawney put it, villeinage ends and the Poor Law begins.

The working of the Poor Law provides a faithful reflection of the differentiation that had been taking place in the rural population. The gulf between those who paid and those who received relief was institutionalized. On the one hand were the yeomen and farmers on whom the poor-rate was levied and from whom were recruited the churchwardens and overseers; on the other were the poor, made up of labourers and cottagers and their families. The desire of landowners and farmers to keep the poor-rates as low as possible clashed with the interests of the humbler members of the community, and introduced a divisive element into village life. This division between the richer and poorer villagers, between well-to-do farmers and labourers with little or no land, was evident in the outward signs of material prosperity or lack of it. Between about 1570 and 1640 the standard of housing and domestic comfort in rural England rose markedly, but the increase was not enjoyed equally among all classes.

The most noticeable improvement was in the amount of building and rebuilding of the farmhouses of yeomen and better-off husbandmen. Medieval peasant houses were usually of the one- or two-room variety, and they were now either replaced by new structures or remodelled to provide more rooms. Upper floors were inserted to make bedrooms, staircases then became necessary, and large medieval rooms were divided by partitions to form rooms for specific purposes, such as a kitchen, buttery, parlour and servants' sleeping chamber. Chimneys were built and windows glazed. By the mid-seventeenth century the typical farmhouse had three to six rooms, though some yeomen's houses had as many as ten. The evidence is still with us in the vernacular building traditions of the English regions: the stone farmhouses of the Yorkshire Dales with their date and initials carved in the lintel over the door; the fifteenth-century hall houses of Kent and Sussex modernized in Elizabethan times; the black and white timber-framed houses of the west Midlands. From wills and household inventories the evidence is the same: whereas in the early sixteenth century the list of furnishings in farmers' households is meagre, in the later years of the century the number and variety of items of furniture, bedding, utensils and implements is much greater and their value higher. A case study of the Leicestershire village of Wigston suggests that in the period 1529–60 the household goods of the ordinary farmer averaged 10 to 15 per cent of his total personal estate, but in the closing years of the sixteenth century this figure had risen to between 20 and 40 per cent of the total.[15]

Lower down the social scale the picture was not quite so rosy. Although there was plenty of new house building it was of a less substantial nature than the yeomen's farmhouses. At their poorest the cottages of landless labourers could be flimsy one-roomed hovels, built on heaths and woodlands. It was a belief common in many parts of the country that if such a cottage were erected on the waste overnight by a squatter and his friends he had a right to undisturbed possession. Local materials were used for all types of cottage building: stone and clay in some northern counties, flints and clunch in the southeast, cob (clay strengthened with straw and used very thick) in Devon and parts of the Midlands, and most frequently a wooden frame filled in with wattle and daub. A writer in 1602 described older cottages in Cornwall as having 'walls of earth, low thatched roofs, few partitions, no planchings [i.e. floorboards] or glass windows, and scarcely any chimneys other than a hole in the wall to let out the smoke . . .'[16] And in an often-quoted verse Bishop Hall referred to the poor man's cottage,

Of one bay's breadth, God Wot, a silly cote
Whose thatched spars are furred with sluttish soot

A whole inch thick, shining like blackmoor's brows
Through smoke that through the headless barrel blows.
At his bed's feet feeden his stalled team,
His swine beneath, his pullen o'er the beam.[17]

Between the landless labourer and the husbandman proper was the class of rural workers – variously known as cottagers, cottage farmers, or peasant labourers – who made a living partly from their smallholding and partly from wage work. Their cottages usually had at least two rooms, and also a buttery and sometimes a dairy or cheese room. But few had separate kitchens, and cooking was done in the main living room, called the hall or house. From probate inventories it would seem that the furniture and furnishings were similar to those of the husbandmen but on a smaller scale. The inventories however cover only the better-off members of the labouring population; the majority were too poor to need an inventory. We can only guess at the level of their domestic comfort (or, as it seems to us, discomfort) from stray hints of contemporary commentators. William Harrison, for instance, says that old men in his village of Radwinter in Essex remembered the days when if servants 'had any sheet above them, it was well, for seldom had they any under their bodies to keep them from the pricking straws that ran off through the canvas of the pallet and rased their hardened hides'.[18] There was no sanitation; people relieved themselves out-of-doors or in the cowshed. Water was obtained from wells, springs, or the local stream or pond. The staple food was bread, usually made from barley, though occasionally from wheat, oats, rye or maslin (a mixture of wheat and rye). But among the very poor – and in hard times among others too – the barley was mixed with peas, beans, acorns or buckwheat. Milk, cheese and lard, together with vegetables and herbs from the garden figured largely in the labourer's diet. Meat was a rarity, and then mostly pig's meat or the result of poaching rabbits, deer, fish or wildfowl. As with all poor peasants they could not afford to consume the best of their produce. Richard Baxter, in his *Poor Husbandman's Advocate* (1691), explains:

If their sow pig or their hens breed chickens, they cannot afford to eat them, but must sell them to make their rent. They cannot afford to eat the eggs that their hens lay, nor the apples nor the pears that grow on their trees (save some that are not vendible) but must make money of all. All the best of their butter and cheese they must sell, and feed themselves and children . . . with skimmed cheese and skimmed milk and whey curds. [19]

Baxter was referring to the small tenant farmers, rather than the landless labourers or cottagers. But these remarks would apply *a fortiori* to all those lower in the social scale who had to sell the produce of their few acres.

Baxter was not himself a farmer but a puritan minister, originally from the west Midlands and later living in London. His sympathy for the common people, among whom he had been born and bred, was strong. In particular he had seen and understood the plight of the poor husbandmen – those at the lower end of Gregory King's category of farmers, with an average yearly income of £42 10s. 'The labour of these men is great, and circular or endless: insomuch that their bodies are almost in constant weariness and their minds in constant care or trouble. . . . They are put to go through rain and wet, through thick and thin, through heat and cold and oft want that which nature needeth.' They are so poor that they have no time for bible reading or family prayer. 'They come in weary from their labours, so that they are fitter to sleep than to read or pray.' What strikes the modern reader is the hardness and coarseness of this life, the lack of comfort in the home, aggravated by the damp and cold of the English climate. We may surmise that since the men and many of the women and children spent their time in outside tasks the cottage or farmhouse was little more than a place for sleeping and eating, although in the long winter evenings odd jobs were done in the home by the light of the fire. Baxter attributed the poverty of the husbandmen to rack-renting or what the economists call payment of an economic rent. Freeholders and copyholders whose rents could not be raised were more fortunate than those small tenant farmers, who with only small capital resources and wholly dependent on the produce of their holdings were unable to resist the landlords' demands for increase of rent equal or nearly equal to the full market value of the land. It is not easy to assess the number of copyholders or customary tenants subject to such pressures, but it is clear that they survived in considerable numbers into the eighteenth century.

Yet Baxter does not pity the husbandmen for their labour and coarse fare, for he thinks that their life generally is healthy and their plain food nutritious. His pity is reserved for their servile dependence on their landlords, and their poverty which prevents them from attending to spiritual matters. But we do not know whether this was how things appeared to the husbandman himself. His own view of his life and work, like the cottager's and labourer's, is entirely missing. Only at moments such as Ket's rebellion does the authentic voice of a labourer occasionally burst out: 'As sheepe or lambs are a prey to the wolfe or lion, so are the poor men to the rich men.'[20]

Similarly that minority of the common people who lived in towns and those engaged in industry, both rural and urban, have left little record of themselves. In Gregory King's table they are noticeably absent, although English manufacturing (mainly woollen cloth) had long been famous. Presumably the spinners are included under the categories of cottagers and labouring people, and the weavers and other textile workers under artisans and handicrafts. Some of the Yorkshire clothiers may be classed as farmers or lesser freeholders. At the end of the seventeenth century about a quarter of the total population lived in towns. Only one city, however, London, had the qualities of urbanism with which we are familiar today, when 80 per cent of the British people are urban dwellers. 'Town' for many generations of English folk meant simply London, which was in every way unique and much the largest city in Europe. With a population grown to half a million by 1700 London accounted for one-tenth of the total population. No other city came anywhere near this in size. Bristol, Norwich and York – the largest of the provincial cities – had between twenty-five and thirty thousand people each, and the ten next largest cities around eighteen thousand each. The remainder of the towns were very small indeed, anything from under a thousand to towns like Leicester with about five thousand. It is questionable how far towns with less than five thousand inhabitants offered much in the way of a distinctive urban experience. As in the Middle Ages all town life, except in London, retained many rural qualities. For example townsmen, like the peasantry, enjoyed rights of common and were therefore drawn into the struggle against enclosure. Conversely industry was not confined to the towns. Some craftsmen had always worked in the villages; and in Tudor and Stuart times parts of the countryside became increasingly involved in manufacturing and extractive industries. It is not easy to recapture the realities of labouring life from the pattern of sixteenth- and seventeenth-century economic development as sketched out by historians. But from the basic institutions of economic life and industrial organization we can draw certain conclusions about conditions of work.

The official view of labour relations was set out in the Statute of Artificers which was passed in 1563 and lasted with minor amendments until 1813. It was concerned first to secure stability in employment and check the mobility of labour, by listing a whole series of occupations in which hiring was to be for not less than one year and notice of termination of the contract not less than one quarter. Second, provision was made for an adequate labour supply in agriculture. All persons between the ages of twelve and sixty without other employment or a minimum amount of property as laid down in the Act could 'be compelled to be retained to serve in husbandry'. At times of hay or corn harvest 'all such artificers and persons as be meet to labour' could be obliged to work in the harvest fields if required. Third, a system of apprenticeship was laid down. No one was to exercise any 'art, mistery or manual occupation' without first serving a seven years' apprenticeship, and superior callings such as draper, goldsmith or merchant were to be limited to the sons of members and others with a minimum property qualification. In certain named crafts, including weaving, tailoring and shoemaking, there was to be at least one journeyman to the first three apprentices employed, and one extra journeyman for every apprentice above that number. Fourth, wages were to be assessed by the justices of the peace in the counties and by mayors and chief officers in the towns annually at the first general sessions after Easter. Penalties were to be imposed on both masters and servants who exceeded the rates fixed. Lastly the length of the working day was ordained. This clause is worth quoting, though it is probably more valuable as an expression of ruling-class views of what common men ought ideally to do than as a statement of what they actually did, since little is heard of it subsequently:

> All artificers and labourers being hired for wages by the day or week shall betwixt the midst of the months of March and September be at their work at or before 5 of the clock in the morning, and continue at work until betwixt 7 and 8 of the clock at night, except it be in the time of breakfast, dinner or drinking, the which times at the most shall not exceed above 2½ hours in the day . . . and all the said artificers and labourers between the midst of September and the midst of March shall be at their work from the spring of the day in the morning until the night of the same day, except it be in time afore appointed for breakfast and dinner, upon pain to forfeit one penny for every hour's absence to be deducted out of his wages.[21]

As with the Elizabethan Poor Law, the operation of the Statute of Artificers was superintended by the justices of the peace. Its ancestry can be traced back to the Statute of Labourers of 1351; but its more immediate origin was in the local gild and town regulations which it codified and extended on a national scale. The Statute of Artificers was intended to be a conservative and stabilizing force. It assumed a universal obligation to work, and sought to fix the status and regulate the working life of the labouring population.

In London and the larger provincial cities industry continued to be organized through the gilds. But the tendencies observable in the later Middle Ages developed further, particularly the division between the richer merchants and entrepreneurs organized in the London livery companies and the craft gilds of the smaller tradesmen, masters and journeymen. The craft gild was the form in which handicraft industry was institutionalized, and its heyday was in the fourteenth and fifteenth centuries. The journeymen's associations, which had earlier clashed with the masters' craft gilds, do not figure prominently again until the end of the seventeenth century, and the main struggle appears to have been between the small masters and the merchant capitalists. However, reliance on the ample records of the gilds and municipalities for the industrial history of the sixteenth and seventeenth centuries may give an exaggerated view of the importance of the gild in the lives of many working people. Not all town workers, even those who were craftsmen, were members of gilds; and for gildsmen and non-gildsmen alike the nature of their work was largely determined by other, more basic factors.

For instance it was generally assumed that industry and trade would be carried on in the home. The typical figure in this type of enterprise was a baker, working tailor or cobbler. He worked with his own hands, assisted by members of his family and perhaps by apprentices and journeymen. He dealt directly with the consumer, had only a limited amount of capital, and sometimes worked on material supplied by the customer. Such men were the familiar small tradesmen who have survived right down to our own day; and the word tradesman still retains its dual meaning of one who works at a trade or craft as well as one who buys and sells. The social setting for this type of work was the neighbourhood rather than the town.

Production in the home was also carried on under a less independent arrangement, the domestic or putting-out system. A middleman (or putter-out) supplied the raw material, collected the worked-up product, and organized the finishing processes and sale. The producing craftsman thereby became dependent on (in fact employed by) a capitalist. Tailoring, shoemaking and cabinet-making in the East End of London were ultimately organized on the domestic system; as also were the cutlery trades of Sheffield, the chain- and nail-makers of the Black Country, the lace and hosiery trades of Nottingham and Leicester, and many other midland industries. In the greatest of English industries at this time, woollen textiles, the domestic system had been developed in the later Middle Ages and continued until the Industrial Revolution. Because of gild restrictions in the towns there had been a movement of weavers into the country. In the two principal clothing areas of East Anglia and the West Country (Wiltshire, Gloucestershire, Somerset and Devon) the weaver had become a cottager who worked up the wool supplied by a clothier-capitalist. But in the West Riding of Yorkshire a large number of independent small masters survived into the nineteenth century. Daniel Defoe has left a memorable account of them in 1724:

... The nearer we came to Halifax, we found the houses thicker, and the villages greater in every bottom; and not only so, but the sides of the hills, which were very steep every way, were spread with houses, and that very thick; for the land being divided into small enclosures, that is to say, from two acres to six or seven acres each, seldom more; every three or four pieces of land had a house belonging to it. ...

[The] business is the clothing trade, for the convenience of which the houses are thus scattered and spread upon the sides of the hills. ... At every considerable house was a manufactury or work-house, and as they could not do their business without water, the little streams were so parted and guided by gutters or pipes, ... that none of those houses were without a river, ... running into and through their work-houses. ...

Then, as every clothier must keep a horse, perhaps two, to fetch and carry for the use of his manufacture, (viz.) to fetch home his wooll and his provisions from the market, to carry his yarn to the spinners, his manufacture to the fulling mill, and, when finished, to the market to be sold, and the like; so every manufacturer generally keeps a cow or two, or more, for his family, and this employs the two, or three, or four pieces of enclosed land about his house, for they scarce sow corn enough for their cocks and hens; and this feeding their grounds still adds by the dung of the cattle, to enrich the soil.

... Among the manufacturers houses are likewise scattered an infinite number of cottages or small dwellings, in which dwell the workmen which are employed, the women and children of whom, are always busy carding, spinning, etc. so that no hands being unemploy'd, all can gain their bread, even from the youngest to the antient; hardly any thing above four years old, but its hands are sufficient to it self.

This is the reason also why we saw so few people without doors; but if we knock'd at the door of any of the master manufacturers, we presently saw a house full of lusty fellows, some at the dye-vat, some dressing the cloths, some in the loom, some one thing, some another, all hard at work, and full employed upon the manufacture, and all seeming to have sufficient business. ...[22]

The close association of industry with agriculture is here nicely demonstrated. It was also present in other ways of making a living, some of which were far removed from domestic industry. Coal mining was, and still is, an industry set in the countryside. In medieval times coal pits were often worked by lords of manors or by husbandmen. But from the sixteenth century deeper pits, requiring pumping machinery and large capital expenditure, were opened in the Northeast and the Midlands. Other manufacturing enterprises such as saltworks, shipyards, ironworks and ordnance factories expanded in the sixteenth and seventeenth centuries. They all required capital and industrial organization on a much larger scale than the domestic system. They also needed larger workforces. By the late seventeenth century there were perhaps between twelve and fifteen thousand coal miners and this number increased to not less than fifty thousand in 1800. Pits seldom employed more than forty or fifty miners (often less than twenty) and even in the eighteenth century a coal mine employing one hundred colliers was considered a large undertaking. Working arrangements varied between regions. In the Northeast (the largest coalfield) the pitmen worked under the bond system, whereby they were hired for the year and effectively tied to one employer. Elsewhere, in south Yorkshire, Lancashire, the Midlands and Somerset, some form of gang system, working on a contract or piece rates, was usual. The same was true of the tin and copper miners in Cornwall and the lead miners in Derbyshire. Some of the largest units of industrial organization were the shipyards. In 1712 the four Kentish naval dockyards at Sheerness, Chatham, Deptford and Woolwich employed 2117 workmen and this number was liable to be doubled in times of war or crisis. The Plymouth and Portsmouth dockyards also had between one and two thousand men on the books. In addition there were private yards in Liverpool, Bristol and along the Thames. The workforces in these yards comprised skilled shipwrights and supporting sawyers, general carpenters, riggers, caulkers, ropemakers and labourers. Shipwrights worked in gangs or companies of fifteen to twenty men, under a foreman, the quarterman.

In enterprises such as these, and indeed wherever a substantial amount of capital was needed and production was carried on away from the home, the typical workman was a journeyman wage earner who was unlikely to be able to change his employee status. Within this category there were so many different occupations and crafts, so many variations between metropolitan and provincial workmen, and often such a large gap between the top and bottom ends of a trade, that generalization is impossible. Nevertheless certain observations about the experience of work in a fairly wide range of occupations before 1750 can be made. They tell us something of the attitudes and expectations of labouring people in their endeavours to make a living, though seldom in the words of the people themselves or before the late seventeenth and early eighteenth centuries.

First, employment was characteristically irregular. Almost all trades were subject to fluctuations caused by the seasons, bad weather, war and peace, fashion, the effect of falling demand in related industries, or overstocking of the trade. Building workers and house painters could not work in bad weather; wars closed overseas markets for the West Country clothiers; peace faced the naval dockyard workers with redundancy; and quality tailors, shoemakers and dressmakers in London complained that they had no work for several months in the year. The putting-out system created a pool of labour designed to meet the employers' needs at times of maximum demand. When trade fell off the domestic weavers and spinners found themselves without work – and those who were able to do so turned to agricultural jobs.

Second, when workers had work they did not pursue it in the same way as in a modern factory. Their rhythm of work was not steady and continuous, but alternate spurts of industriousness and idleness. In the home and small workshops the workman could control the pace and duration of his work. Payment by the piece facilitated irregular work patterns, which became sanctioned (indeed, sanctified) by custom. Thus in a great many trades Monday was taken as a holiday (Saint Monday), little work was done on Tuesday, and by Friday everyone was working furiously to complete the week's piece or assignment. According to Yorkshire tradition the beat of the handloom on Monday went slowly, *P l e n - ty of T i m e, P l e n - ty of T i m e*; on Thursday and Friday it had speeded up to *A day t'lat, A day t'lat*. A satirical comment on the irregularity of the working week comes from 1639:

You know that Munday is Sundayes brother;
Tuesday is such another;
Wednesday you must go to Church and pray;
Thursday is half-holiday;
On Friday it is too late to begin to spin;
The Saturday is half-holiday agen.[23]

Moreover workers did not always respond to changes in wages or piece rates in the way required by a market economy. Their acquisitive instincts were relatively undeveloped, and when given a choice many craft workers preferred more leisure to greater reward. William Hutton, who had been a framework knitter in the 1730s and 1740s, observed that 'if a man can support his family with three days labour, he will not work six'.[24]

Third, there was a widespread expectation of perquisites. 'Thou shalt not muzzle the ox when he treadeth out the corn' was a precept honoured in many trades. Weavers expected to keep the thrums or warp ends left on the loom when the cloth was cut off. Tailors had cabbage, which was the term for pieces of cloth not used after garments were cut out. Sawyers were allowed to keep sawdust. Colliers had a weekly coal allowance. In the royal dockyards shipwrights enjoyed the valuable right to chips or pieces of waste wood – a right which was originally intended to provide firewood but which became a private trade in timber. A whole vocabulary of terms for these perquisites is recorded in the 'dictionaries of the vulgar tongue' which were published in the late eighteenth and early nineteenth centuries. Perquisites were a constant source of friction, with workmen seeking to extend and employers trying to limit them. Accusations of exploitation from the one side and of embezzlement from the other were constant. The putting-out system, under which there could be no supervision of the work done on materials belonging to the supplier, provided many opportunities for fraud by workmen and short-changing by employers. Spinners, weavers and framework knitters knew of many ways in which to appropriate some of the raw material for themselves, concealing the deficit by damping or oiling the remainder. Shoemakers, clockmakers and nailers – in fact all out-workers using material not their own – were in a position to extend their perquisites by embezzlement. In the naval dockyards the practice of taking chips sometimes reached scandalous proportions, as in 1634 when it was alleged that the shipwrights took chips out of the yard three times a day, cut up large timber to make chips and built huts in which to store their plunder. Conversely from the workers' side came complaints of 'oppression' by the employers. This took several forms. Shipwrights and other workers in the naval dockyards normally had to wait many months, sometimes over a year, for payment of their wages. West Country weavers complained in the early eighteenth century that the clothiers forced them to accept truck, that is payment in kind. Another oppression was the employers' claim to deduct from (or 'bate') wages for faults or underweight. In 'The Clothier's Delight', a popular song of the late seventeenth century in which various methods of exploiting the weavers are gone through, the employers are made to say:

We'll make the poor Weavers work at a low rate,
We'll find fault where there's no fault, and so we will bate.[25]

For the Nottingham framework knitters there was the burden of frame rent. From the seventeenth century the practice developed of hosiers renting stocking frames to the knitters, who then had to pay rent whether there was work or not. In other occupations a middleman interposed between the employer and the worker and took a cut for himself, as with the London coal heavers who could not contract directly with the ships' masters for unloading coal but only through local publicans who acted as 'undertakers'.

The fourth aspect of work which is communicated strongly by the records of many different trades is the strength of workshop custom. A definite pattern of behaviour at work was expected and enforced in all the skilled crafts. Basically this was intended to preserve and strengthen the workman's control over his job and to limit the employer's prerogatives. It was in the workman's interest to be able to regulate the amount of work done and who should do it, as well as to control entry into the trade. In a printing house, for instance, the compositors selected one of their number to be the 'father of the chapel' and made him responsible for the observance by all of them of a body of agreed workshop practices. Work was apportioned collectively to each 'companionship' of three to six compositors under a leader or 'clicker'. Payment was usually by the number of pages and lines set, but there was also an entitlement for 'fat' such as titles and half-pages of print. Harmony and good work habits among the journeymen were maintained by the father, who could hold a trial and impose a fine on offenders. Detailed rules governed these proceedings. Drunkenness was not tolerated; but drink itself was intimately bound up with workshop rituals in most of the trades. Fines were generally used to buy drink. New apprentices and journeymen were obliged to pay 'footing' or 'maiden garnish', that is drink for their workmates. Initiation ceremonies into the mystery of the craft on the completion of apprenticeship, and the marriage of a workman, were occasions for drinking and sometimes coarse and brutal behaviour. Wages in the London building trades in the eighteenth century were often paid on Saturday nights in an alehouse.

Benjamin Franklin worked as a printer in London in 1725–6. He found that the house had an alehouse boy whose job was to supply the workmen with drink. Franklin's fellow-workman at the press 'drank every day a pint before breakfast, a pint at breakfast with his bread and cheese, a pint between breakfast and dinner, a pint at dinner, a pint in the afternoon about six o'clock, and another when he had done his day's work'.[26] Franklin was unpopular with his mates because he drank only water and refused to observe Saint Monday. When he moved from the press room to the composing room a new bienvenue (the printers' name for a maiden garnish) was demanded. Franklin refused, on the grounds that he had already paid one bienvenue on joining the house. He was then 'considered as an excommunicate, and had so many little pieces of private mischief done me, by mixing my sorts, transposing my pages, breaking my matter, etc, etc, if I were ever so little out of the room, and all ascribed to the chapel ghost' that after two or three weeks he was forced to pay.

Apprenticeship was a central part of workshop custom. It seems unlikely that the full rigours of the 1563 Statute of Artificers could ever have been universally enforced, but apprenticeship in various forms was too convenient an institution to be easily abandoned. For employers, especially small masters, it provided a cheap source of labour. Few if any trades required seven years for their learning, so that in the later stages of his apprenticeship (when he still received little or no remuneration) the apprentice did virtually a man's work for no wages. From the workers' side the restriction of entry to the trade to apprentices who had served their time together with the limitation of the number of apprentices per master or journeyman was an important check to overstocking the trade with too many workmen. Even when the apprentice did not live in his master's house as a member of the family but worked outdoors in a printing house or similar establishment, he still learned all the customs as well as the skills of his craft. By working alongside older men and being subject to their (often rough) discipline each succeeding generation of craftsmen imbibed the traditions and lore of the trade. They acquired the pride and skills and above all the independence that were the craftsman's most cherished possessions.

The realities of apprenticeship however did not always seem to the recipients quite so beneficial. In domestic industry the system could prove to be nothing short of a tyranny for the unlucky apprentice. William Hutton had the misfortune to serve not one but two apprenticeships.[27] First he served for seven years in a Derby silk mill, from the age of seven to fourteen, and then was bound for another seven years to his uncle, a Nottingham stockinger. The indenture, entered upon in 1737, stipulated that the apprentice was to receive only what he earned by 'overwork'. This meant that he had to earn 5s. 10d. each week for his master and could keep any earnings beyond this; but if his earnings did not reach 5s. 10d. he was in debt to the amount of the shortfall. He soon discovered that most apprentices were 'under the mark'. In addition to Hutton, his uncle regularly employed two or three other apprentices. By the end of the seven years' apprenticeship Hutton calculated that he had earned about £7 overwork (minus a debt of 30s. contracted to his uncle) which was just sufficient to keep him in clothes. His aunt was dominant, hypocritical and mean, and grudged him every bit of food he ate: 'It was considered by the mistress as almost a sin to eat.' He hated the work and after four years ran away, but returned to complete his apprenticeship and stayed on as journeyman with his uncle. 'I asked my uncle to permit me to set a frame in his work-room, paying the usual price; in which case I would hire one, and work for a warehouse. This would make me a master, though of the very lowest order. He cheerfully consented.' But a few days later, on the prompting of his wife, he refused. The next year his uncle died, and Hutton inherited the stocking frame. He found however that trade was dead and that the hosiers would not employ him, having scarcely enough work for their own frames. He therefore decided to leave the trade altogether and set up as bookseller.

Hutton's autobiography serves to remind us of the centrality of the family as a social unit. The extent to which everyday living and working were dependent upon family relationships comes out clearly in its pages. Through the eyes of one who was born and bred an artisan and who later prospered as an entrepreneur we can observe the life cycle of a family of small Midland tradesmen and domestic workers in the first half of the eighteenth century. Hutton's story unfolds round the great life experiences of birth, marriage and death, each of which was in the anthropological sense a crisis producing disturbance for the individual and the family. The complexities of growing up, making a living, becoming literate, finding sexual fulfilment, and passing into old age are all touched upon to a greater or lesser extent.

The Huttons were a family who worked in the textile trades. William Hutton's grandfather, born in 1659, was a flax-dresser of Derby, who never travelled 'more than twelve miles from home, and that but once; or more than thirty yards to procure a wife'. His son (William Hutton's father), born in 1691, was a woolcomber, who after serving his seven years' apprenticeship became a small master, and who in turn apprenticed his three sons, including William, as stocking-frame knitters with his brother in Nottingham. Births occurred frequently and regularly. In his grandfather's generation there were ten children, in his father's six, and Hutton himself was one of nine. Nevertheless the family unit was not large: a steady proportion of children died in infancy, others left home, as early as ten years old, to enter service, and some were fostered by childless uncles and aunts. The crisis caused by birth (and death which all too frequently accompanied it) was shown in 1733, when Hutton was nine. In March of that year his mother, aged forty-one, died after giving birth to her ninth child. Immediately the family was plunged into disorder. Even before this catastrophe they had been in dire want, as his father failed in business and was a poor provider. Woolcombing was traditionally thirsty work: 'His occupation taught him to drink, which he learned with willingness, while his family wanted bread.' He was now left with five children aged fourteen years to a few weeks (the other four having died), and according to his son virtually abdicated his parental responsibilities. He sold up his home, spent the money, and with the three younger children took lodgings with a widow who also had four young children. At this stage Hutton, aged ten, and his brother were working in a silk mill; and 'though my brother and I laboured daily, we experienced the want of bread, of apparel, and seemed little beings whom nobody owned'. The eldest child was already living and working with two maiden aunts at Swithland in Leicestershire, the new baby was put out to nurse with a couple at Mackworth for 1s. 6d. a week, and the remaining child died through neglect five months later.

The case of the Hutton family puts flesh and blood on the bare bones of the statistics of birth and death. In the first half of the eighteenth century birth rates were about 32 to 35 per thousand and death rates about 28 to 32 per thousand. This compares with 1968 figures of about 17 and 12 per thousand respectively. In other words, more children were born to the Huttons of the world than today but more died in infancy. According to Gregory King the expectation of life at birth in the 1690s was thirty-two years; today it is twice that figure. Recent studies, for example of the villagers of Colyton in Devon, show that between 1550 and 1750 a quarter to a third of all children died before the age of fifteen. In some London parishes the figures were worse: between 1730 and 1749 perhaps as many as three-quarters of children who were christened died before the age of five.

These figures prompt interesting speculations. The high mortality rates meant that everyone was more intimately acquainted with death than in the late twentieth century. Death came more frequently and at different times in the history of a family than is likely today, cutting off children and women in their prime as well as the aged. Did this in some way affect the emotional relationships between spouses or between parents and their children? Hutton records that his father grieved sorely over the death of his youngest daughter whom he loved after a fashion and yet neglected to look after. 'My Father had no violent love for any of his children, but the least of all for the last [a son], although deprived of the tenderness of a mother, which ought to have excited compassion.' He never kissed his children (except once when drunk) or showed any outward signs of endearment towards them or his wife. The family were Dissenters, but Hutton does not suggest that their faith inhibited public emotion or provided consolation in bereavement. When he burst into tears on hearing of his mother's death he was told, 'Don't cry, you will go yourself soon.' Hutton was uncertain whether his parents married 'from love or custom'. But in his own case he leaves us in no doubt that he loved his wife dearly and delighted in his children. Hutton remembered his father saying on the death of his wife, 'You have lost an excellent mother, and I a wife'; but within a few days he had gone to live with a widow. Autobiographies as evidence of personal emotions, however, have to be used with caution. In a labouring family the impact of death was often so closely associated with disruption and poverty that in later years the two had become inextricable in the mind of the writer.

High mortality rates had other implications. After the death of their mother, Hutton and his brothers and sisters were at the mercy of the widow Mary Sore, 'who was a fine figure, tolerably handsome and intolerably ignorant, completely vulgar and completely filthy'. She treated the children 'with the worst food that could be bought or begged, with lodging beneath that of a dog, and with punishment whenever she pleased'. She was in fact the classic evil step-mother of the fairy tale. A large number of children lost at least one parent before they were adult: in Bristol in the 1630s 34 per cent of the apprentices were fatherless, and in 1696 one-third of all children in the city were orphans; the records of first marriages in Manchester in the 1650s show that over half the brides and nearly half of the grooms had lost their fathers; and in 1688 in the village of Clayworth in Nottinghamshire 35·5 per cent of all the children were orphans. Such figures suggest that step-parenthood was a common experience; but what its psychological and emotional influence was on the lives of working people we can only guess. William Hutton was one who eventually overcame the material handicap it imposed, but a legacy of bitterness is traceable in his writing.

Another consequence of the early death of one or other spouse was that marriages were of relatively short duration. The marriage of Hutton's parents lasted for only fifteen years – which was probably about the average expectation in the period. Marriages today, despite a high divorce rate, last longer than in the seventeenth and eighteenth centuries, when they were broken by the death of the husband or wife. Indeed, it has been suggested that modern divorce may be little more than a functional substitute for death.[28] However, death could not always be relied on to secure release from an unhappy marriage and divorce was unobtainable. The problems caused by the indissolubility of marriage were brought home to Hutton by the position of his favourite sister, Catherine. She was in service in Leicestershire, and after being courted for thirteen years by a neighbouring tailor consented to marry him. Marriage proved distasteful to her and the union was unconsummated, and so the couple separated. She lived by herself in Nottingham and supported herself by spinning. The short duration of marriage was also the result of the fairly high age at which marriage took place. Hutton's father was twenty-seven when he married, and his wife was twenty-six; Hutton himself was thirty-two and his wife a little younger. His brothers and uncles seem to have married at about the same age. Apprenticeships and the need to become established in a trade before starting a family probably account for the custom of late marriage among artisans.

Unlike most self-educated autobiographers Hutton is fairly informative about courting and marriage. He does not of course refer directly to the most obvious sexual problem of late marriage, namely the ten or more years between puberty and wedlock. Adolescent sexuality, especially in London where there were large numbers of apprentices (forbidden to marry by their indentures), was a constant social preoccupation; but it had a personal side to it about which we hear very little. Sexual behaviour was guided by custom and religious restraint, which condemned and punished sex outside marriage. 'It is difficult for a young man to live without love,' admitted Hutton, and went on to record how at twenty-five, 'I was intimate with a young widow, but never touched upon the word Marriage.' However, 'she frequently dragged me to the test', and he had finally to decline marriage because he did not have a trade to live by. He 'kept company' with several other girls and regarded marriage as a matter primarily of love, not economics. When a young lady told him that she would never keep company with anyone without her father's consent, Hutton was dumb-founded. 'I consider a parent's consent requisite,' he explained, 'yet it is but a secondary step.' Nevertheless, when he decided to marry the niece of his next-door neighbour he bargained hard over the amount of settlement. He insisted in his autobiography that although he loved his fiancée most dearly, 'our courtship . . . was always a *day-light* courtship'. Hutton's marriage lasted forty-one years, but in this respect he was unusually fortunate. The high mortality of spouses made remarriage common; about a quarter of all marriages in the sixteenth and seventeenth centuries were remarriages for one of the partners. Hutton's father was married three times, in addition to living (unmarried) with a widow for ten years. His second and third wives were also widows. It seemed incredible to Hutton that women should wish to marry his father who was middle-aged, one-eyed, and a heavy drinker with five children.

About the final years of the artisan's life cycle the auto-biography is again informative. Hutton's picture of the latter days of members of his family is, as he put it, melancholy. 'The little good fortune experienced through life, if any, has vanished, their remaining moments have been embittered, and they have depar-ted in wretchedness, want and distress. Their weekly earnings being small, and consumed as soon as earned, nothing has remained for sickness, age or accident. Deprived of the benefits of their own labour, they have been dependent on the scanty succour of others.' His grandfather 'sustained a long decline', during which his wife and children were in great distress. His son (Hutton's father) during the last six years of his life 'groaned under the palsy, the stone, severe poverty, and the greater severity of a cruel wife'. Hutton's uncle George, with whom he had served his apprentice-ship, was ill for the last two years of his life and was deserted by his apprentices. He died at the age of fifty-one, 'and thus escaped the poverty which began to stare him in the face'. Hutton himself took comfort that he had been spared such misery: 'Where should I have been now', he wrote, 'if I had continued a stockinger? I must have been in the workhouse. They all go there when they cannot see to work.' This does not suggest anything in the way of peaceful and comfortable retirement following a withdrawal from work. The most to be expected was a gradual descent into non-productivity as physical powers declined, with some help from children. The total number of old people however was relatively small. Probably no more than 5 per cent of the total population in the late seventeenth and early eighteenth centuries were over sixty-five, compared with 12 per cent in the 1960s.

It is clear from Hutton's account that the family was expected to be mutually supportive, but that poverty and personalities sometimes limited its effectiveness. At crucial points in his career Hutton received help of this kind. In 1727 at the age of four he was boarded out for fifteen months among uncles and aunts in Leicestershire to relieve his parents. His apprenticeship, like that of his brothers, was with his uncle in Nottingham. When he wanted to leave framework knitting and set up as a bookseller it was his sister Catherine who encouraged him and lent him the vital £15 capital out of her savings. Nothing of this is very extraordinary. It is well within the experience of most of us to understand. Yet the outward familiarity of the family structure may be deceptive. It is not the formal family organization that has changed but the human relationships within it. The common people lived out their lives within the family, but it was a family which was demographically different from our own. The eternal cycle of birth, marriage and death was the same; but the crises came at different times, in different ways and with different results. In this chapter we have looked at some of the commonest, inescapable facts of life from the outside. We have next to look at them from the inside, to probe the values and beliefs which people held about their lives.

5. Attitudes and Beliefs

We all have what may be loosely termed a philosophy of life: a bundle of attitudes, beliefs and values with which we navigate our way through the pleasures and perils of everyday living. At any given moment the responses we make, the decisions we take, the things we do or do not do, are determined according to our notions about ourselves and the physical and social world. For much of the time this process is instinctive and automatic, and not subject to conscious reasoning. But on other occasions – as when people differ from us – we become aware that there are some things we believe and others which we do not. Beliefs are not held singly, but in clusters, organized in a structure and having behavioural consequences. 'A belief system may be defined as having represented within it, in some organized psychological but not necessarily logical form, each and every one of a person's countless beliefs about physical and social reality. By definition, we do not allow beliefs to exist outside the belief system for the same reason that the astronomer does not allow stars to remain outside the universe.'[1] Not all beliefs are of equal importance to us. Some are central, and reach down deep into our being. They concern basic truths about our own existence and the nature of the world in which we find ourselves. They are largely taken for granted, and to question them would cause a serious disruption in our lives. Other beliefs are not so central, and do not have the same taken-for-granted character. They are beliefs derived from the authority of family, class or religious group, and we recognize differences of opinion about them. Beyond these are beliefs which are no more than matters of taste, and which are inconsequential in their relation to our central or primary beliefs. Many questions arise as to the nature of such a belief system: whence comes the stimulus to formulate it; what elements are available for its construction; what are its functions? We have only to ask these questions to realize the formidable nature of any attempt to probe into the mental world of people in the past, especially people who have left few records of what they think and feel. Nor is there good reason to suppose that people who led apparently simple lives necessarily held simple beliefs. The ways of thinking of labouring men and women are as complicated and difficult to unravel as for the more educated classes. But we are less familiar with the problems involved.

Most of the evidence available to us is not directly about what people thought or believed but about what they did. They stayed away from church, produced illegitimate children, visited wise men and accused old women of being witches. From such behaviour we have to try to deduce the ideas, feelings and judgements which make up the mental states of the people concerned. We try to discover the basis on which people distinguish between good and bad, and between what is and what ought to be. Yet always we are looking from the outside at something which is interior. The problem of historical understanding is here at its most intractable. For the period 1500–1750 there are two main sources for the study of popular belief: religion and folk custom. From some of this material we may be able to recapture something of the outlook on life of labouring people.

As in the Middle Ages, the routine of daily life was set in the context of Christian belief and practice. The working year, for instance, was marked by feasts and festivals which were a mixture of Christian ritual and ancient pagan customs: Plough Monday, Candlemas, Shrovetide, Lady Day, Palm Sunday, Easter, Hocktide, May Day, Whitsuntide, Midsummer, Lammas, Michaelmas, Allhallows, Christmas. Intertwined with the church's calendar were local customs and usages determined by the needs of work and leisure. Rents were paid at Lady Day and Michaelmas; events were dated by reference to the nearest saint's day. The outward forms of religion were ubiquitous; and when statistics of church attendance become available (as they do for the seventeenth century), they show a high percentage of churchgoers. At Goodnestone in Kent 128 people out of a total population of 281 took communion at Easter 1676, and 200 out of 401 at Clayworth on the same date. At Cogenhoe, Northamptonshire, in 1612 the number of Easter communicants was 63, which was just over half of the qualified adults.[2] But there is at present no means of knowing how typical these figures are. Nor do we know what the church's teaching meant to labouring people. Even after the service was in English, as was the case from 1549, the popular apprehension of Christianity was not necessarily the same as the official expectation. In the early seventeenth century a man of sixty, who had been a regular church-attender all his life, was questioned on his deathbed:

> Being demanded what he thought of God, he answers that he was a good old man; and what of Christ, that he was a towardly young youth; and of his soul, that it was a great bone in his body; and what should become of his soul after he was dead, that if he had done well he should be put into a pleasant green meadow.[3]

Are these thoughts merely a simplified or garbled version of official teaching; or do they spring from something quite different, some relic of peasant culture now lost? We do not know.

This man was outwardly an orthodox believer. But there were other labouring men and women whose beliefs were condemned as heretical. They were loosely known as Lollards, and from the later fourteenth century to the 1530s their trials for heresy periodically punctuate the prevailing orthodoxy. Just as we can sometimes find in riots and rebellions the authentic voice of the common people, so it is possible to hear in the trials of religious dissenters the expression of some beliefs from below. The Lollards were never more than a small minority, but there is reason to suspect that some of their opinions were quite widely accepted. John Skilly, a miller of Flixton in Norfolk, declared in 1428 that he believed 'that confession should be made unto no priest, but only to God, for no priest hath the power to absolve a man of sin'; that 'no priest hath power to make Christ's body in the form of bread in the sacrament of the altar'; that 'consent of love between man and woman is [alone] sufficient for matrimony, without expression of words and . . . solemnisation in church'; 'every true man and woman being in charity is a priest'; 'the pope of Rome is antichrist and . . . hath no power to bind or loose'; 'it is lawful for priests to take wives and nuns to take husbands'; 'it is not lawful to swear in any case'; 'no pilgrimage ought to be done, nor no manner of worship ought to be done unto any images of the crucifix, of Our Lady, or of any other saints'; 'holy water hallowed by a priest is of no more effect than the water of the river or of a well'; 'it is not lawful [for] any man to fight or do battle for a realm or a country'; 'every man's prayer said in the field is as good as the prayer said in the church'.[4] These and other similar opinions, which he was forced to abjure, amounted to a radical rejection of the ministrations of the church.

Also among the sixty Norwich heresy trials of 1428–31 is the case of Margery Baxter, wife of William Baxter, a wright from Martham in Norfolk. She was accused of telling a friend that the true cross of Christ was not the crucifix in church, and 'the said Margery, stretching out her arms abroad, said . . . "This is the true cross of Christ, and this cross thou oughtest and mayest every day behold and worship in thine own house." ' She denied that the bread consecrated in the mass was the very body of Christ, 'for if every such sacrament were God, and the very body of Christ, there should be an infinite number of gods, because that a thousand priests and more do every day make a thousand such gods, and afterwards eat them, and void them out again in places where . . . you may find many such gods.' And she argued that the devils who fell from heaven with Lucifer 'entered into the images which stand in the churches . . . so that the people worshipping those images commit idolatry'.[5]

Historians have noted how these Lollard views anticipated the Protestantism of the Reformation, and their plebeian character has reinforced the argument of a popular base for the reforms of the sixteenth century. Among fifteenth-century peasants and weavers in the West Country and the Chilterns, and among tradesmen and artisans in London, Bristol, Coventry and York was nourished a strong anti-clericalism which was later to bear fruit. Lollardy and Lollard doctrines have been studied mainly as an early Protestant or late medieval heretical sect, and measured against the writings of Wycliffe. But it is possible to see in Lollardy something rather different. When Richard Fletcher of Beccles declared that 'every Christian man is a priest', that 'it is lawful . . . to do all bodily works on Sundays and other festival days', and that the 'common blessing that men use and make with their right hand, it availeth to nothing else but to scare away flies', he was doing more than differ from the bishop of Norwich on academic points of religious doctrine.[6] Fletcher's beliefs indicate a view of life which was different in certain important respects from that of his interrogators.

The elements of his belief system however remain tantalizingly obscure. We do not for England have anything like the marvellous detail of inquisitors' reports which have made possible the reconstruction of the mental and religious world of Domenico Scandella (called Menocchio), a sixteenth-century miller from Friuli in Italy.[7] The questions and answers in Lollard trials are largely stereotyped and to that extent represent the views of the prosecutors as much as the accused. We have only the recorded answers to a fairly narrow range of questions, which the prosecutors (but not necessarily the defendants) thought important. There is no record of wide-ranging discussion about the accused's life and habits and speculations as in Menocchio's case. The Lollard trials provide not a full picture of the accused's beliefs, but a partial account of particular heresies. Even so, there are occasional hints of other things. In 1453 a butcher and a labourer of Standon, Hertfordshire, were denounced for speaking against the need for baptism and the veneration of images and also for saying that there was no god except the sun and the moon. William Aylward, a smith from Henley, who abjured his Lollard views in 1426, admitted during his trial that he had previously used charms and spells to heal sick children. In 1507 John Pasmer, a Berkshire husbandman, abjured the usual Lollard beliefs and denied also saying the paternoster backwards – a practice which smacks of necromancy.[8] These are no more than hints; but they suggest at least the possibility of some wider spectrum of belief.

The majority of Lollards when brought to trial abjured; but not all. Some were burnt at the stake for their beliefs. John Badby, a tailor from Evesham, who was burned in a barrel at Smithfield in 1409, was one of the earliest of a succession of Lollard martyrs memorialized for later generations of humble readers in the gruesome illustrations to Foxe's *Book of Martyrs*. It is clear from John Foxe's great work (which in its full form, *The Acts and Monuments*, runs to eight volumes) that Lollards survived into the 1530s, and that most of them belonged to the common people: 'Few or none were learned, being simple labourers and artificers.' Tradesmen and craftsmen seem to have been more numerous than husbandmen, and there was a handful of merchants and professional men from the towns, especially London. Their social background was similar to the dissenters of the seventeenth century and indeed to reform groups later. Women were prominent among them. In 1511–12 a third of the seventy-four or so heretics who were accused at Lichfield were women. Among the seven martyrs burnt at Coventry in 1519 one was a widow, 'Mistress Smith'; four of the others were shoemakers, one was a glover, and one a hosier.

This is a grim page in the annals of the common people. Between 1401 and 1529 perhaps a hundred Lollards were burnt. Men and women do not go to the stake lightly, especially when (as with the Lollards) they are given every opportunity and encouragement to recant. Foxe records that even after the fire had been lighted around Badby and he cried out, the king's eldest son tried to persuade him to abjure and ordered the fire to be quenched; but Badby remained steadfast. Badby's offence was that he denied transubstantiation: 'After the consecration at the altar, there remaineth material bread, and the same bread which was before.' The Coventry martyrs were arrested and condemned principally for teaching their children and families the Lord's prayer and ten commandments in English. Lollards were commonly accused of denying the validity of the sacraments (baptism, confession, eucharist, confirmation, matrimony), ridiculing the veneration of images, and anti-clericalism. For the men and women who were burned these articles of religious faith were not intellectual speculation but central to their very being. Exactly why and how this was so in each individual case is far from clear. Between us and the victim is the barrier of the written record, which formalizes belief into acceptable theological categories. A veil is drawn across the anguish of mind which we sense was there. Once again we are on the outside looking in.

In the sixteenth and seventeenth centuries these questions of religious belief became even more urgent than in medieval England. What had been the heretical views and anti-clericalism of a minority swelled into a mighty movement for church reform, which in turn associated itself with the Reformation in Europe. The English Reformation was not, in its early stages, a movement from below, but a series of acts of state imposed by Henry VIII and his successors for dynastic and political reasons. The common people were the recipients, not the instigators of religious changes;

as usual they played no part in the high decisions but had to live with their results. Our concern therefore will be not so much with the history of the Reformation itself as with the impact of the changes brought by the Reformation upon the people.

Between 1529 and 1559 the English church was changed more rapidly and more drastically than at any other time in its history. First, under the compulsion of Henry VIII's desire for a divorce, papal supremacy was repudiated and the king was declared to be supreme head on earth of the Church of England. In 1536 and 1539 the monasteries were dissolved and their lands and wealth appropriated to the crown. The second phase of the Reformation in England was marked by the doctrinal changes of Edward VI's reign. The first English Prayer Book was issued in 1549, and until 1553 there was a steady advance of Protestant doctrines and practices. This was abruptly halted on the accession of Mary, and for the next five years England returned to the Roman Catholic fold. But under Elizabeth papal obedience was again repudiated, the crown assumed the governorship of the church, and a compromise settlement of contentious religious issues was attempted in the 1559 Act of Uniformity. This was the famous *via media*, or middle road which, it was claimed, the Church of England took between the papists on the one hand and the puritans on the other. In fact the church was Protestant, and the Elizabethan settlement did not end religious division. Not until 1662, after a century of conflict and a civil war, were the issues of the English Reformation settled in a national, established church and a strong dissenting minority outside it.

Probably the main events of the Henrician Reformation made little difference to the lives of the majority of labouring people. They were unlikely to have been much affected by papal supremacy, which was altogether too remote from them. The changes they noticed were those which had an impact on life at the parish level. The sale of confiscated monastic land by the crown involved the greatest change in landownership since the Norman Conquest; but the beneficiaries were the nobility and gentry, not the peasantry. For the tenant of monastic land it was only a change from one landowner to another. Nevertheless the dissolution of the monasteries provoked risings in Lincolnshire and Yorkshire in 1536 which were a mixture of feudal and peasant revolt. Although economic grievances figured among the complaints of these rebels in the Pilgrimage of Grace, Foxe had no doubt that it was a 'popish insurrection' and noted that the rebels carried banners with 'the five wounds [of Christ], the sign of the sacrament, and "Jesus" written in the midst'.[9] Yet it was not until the reforms of Edward VI's reign that changes in worship at the parish level appeared; and then they were greeted ambivalently. In Devon and Cornwall from June to August 1549 the rebels of the Western rising repudiated the English Prayer Book and demanded the restoration of the Roman Catholic mass and ceremonies. But Ket's revolt later in the same summer was noticeably anti-clerical and the new Prayer Book was used in the daily services on Mousehold Heath.

Protestantism's earliest strongholds were in London, the home counties, East Anglia and the southeast, as became evident in the persecution of Protestants under Mary. In the four years before 1558 nearly three hundred people were burnt for heresy, and the vast majority of them were tradesmen, artificers, servants and husbandmen. (By contrast the Marian exiles who fled to the continent on account of their Protestantism were overwhelmingly gentlemen, merchants, clerics and university students.) For what precise beliefs were these obscure men and women prepared to suffer a martyr's death? The following account of Edmund Allin of Frittenden, Kent, is perhaps as near as we are likely to get to an answer. Allin, like Menocchio, was a miller, and was accused of disseminating heretical opinions. 'Why didst thou teach the people, whom thou saidst thou didst feed both bodily and spiritually, being no priest?' he was asked. 'Because that we are all kings to rule our affections, priests to preach out the virtues and word of God,' he replied. Later in his interrogation by a priest, Martin Collins, before Sir John Baker, the miller was asked why he refused to worship the blessed sacrament of the altar:

ALLIN: It is an idol.
COLLINS: It is God's body.
ALLIN: It is not.
COLLINS: By the mass it is.
ALLIN: It is bread.
COLLINS: How provest thou that?

ALLIN: When Christ sat at his supper, and gave them bread to eat.

COLLINS: Bread, knave?

ALLIN: Yea bread, which you call Christ's body. Sat he still at the table, or was he both in their mouths, and at the table? If he were in their mouths, and at the table then had he two bodies, or else had a phantastical body; which is an absurdity to say it.

BAKER: Christ's body was glorified, and might be in more places than one.

ALLIN: Then had he more bodies than one, by your own placing of him.

COLLINS: Thou ignorant ass! the schoolmen say, that a glorified body may be everywhere.

ALLIN: If his body was not glorified till it rose again, then was it not glorified at his last supper; and therefore was not at the table, and in their mouths by your own reason.

COLLINS: A glorified body occupieth no place.

ALLIN: That which occupieth no place, is neither God, nor any thing else. But Christ's body, say you, occupieth no place; therefore it is neither God, nor any thing else. If it be nothing, then is your religion nothing. If it be God, then have we four in one Trinity, which is the person of the Father, the person of the Son, the person of the Holy Ghost, the human nature of Christ. If Christ be nothing, which you must needs confess, if he occupieth no place, then is our study in vain, our faith frustrate, and our hope without reward.

COLLINS: This rebel will believe nothing but Scripture.[10]

On 18 June 1557 Allin, together with his wife and five others, was burned at Maidstone.

Allin's familiarity with scripture was typical of many of Foxe's martyrs. It raises the interesting question of literacy among an important minority of the common people, and the implications of this for belief. There is general agreement that in medieval times very few labouring people could read or write: perhaps in the later Middle Ages out of the total population 10 per cent of men and 1 per cent of women were literate. In the fifteenth century there are signs that some of the common people were able to read. Lollards were accused of possessing translations of the scriptures and other books in English. In 1424 Richard Belward was accused before the bishop of Norwich of keeping a school of Lollardy in Ditchingham, 'and a certain parchment-maker bringeth him all the books containing that doctrine from London'. At Marlborough groups of weavers met for bible reading in the 1440s. Suspected heretics interrogated before the bishop of Lincoln between 1509 and 1518 were asked, among other things, whether they 'have been ever at any readings' of such as have been convicted of heresy. By the 1530s there is evidence of working people in London and elsewhere reading Protestant books and indulging in religious speculation; and the bible in the vernacular was for the first time legally available. The Lollards used the (officially prohibited) Wycliffite translations, but in 1539 the Great Bible, based on translations by William Tyndale and Miles Coverdale, was set up in all churches. Foxe's account of the Marian persecution fifteen years later contains suggestions of popular literacy. Among the Colchester martyrs of 1557, John Johnson, alias Aliker, a thirty-four-year-old labourer of Thorpe, Essex, 'can read a little'; and Robert Purcas, a fuller from Bocking, is described as 'lettered'.

Recent studies suggest that in the mid-seventeenth century about 30 per cent of adult males and 11 per cent of women were literate.[11] But these overall figures mask differences between classes; for while 65 per cent of yeomen and 56 per cent of tradesmen and craftsmen were literate, only 21 per cent of husbandmen and 15 per cent of labourers could write their names. Regional differences were also very considerable: overall literacy figures for London were 78 per cent, for Suffolk 55 per cent and for Nottinghamshire 24 per cent; and within counties the figures for individual parishes varied widely. Labourers and servants in London were 67 per cent literate, whereas the figure for their counterparts in East Anglia was only 8 per cent. Between different trades there was also significant variation: weavers and bakers were more literate than butchers, building workers and fishermen. These figures are based on ability to sign one's name as opposed to making a mark, and are derived from collections of signatures required for documents such as the protestation oath of 1642 when all adult males had to attest that they would 'maintain and defend the true Reformed Religion expressed in the Doctrine of the Church of England against all Poperie and Popish Innovations'. It is generally assumed that ability to sign one's name implies ability to read but not necessarily to write. The level of reading is somewhat speculative; but it seems safe to assume that the percentage of readers was not less – and may have been more – than the percentage of name-signers. There is also evidence of an increase in literacy in the seventeenth century. In the village of Terling, Essex, for example, in the period 1580–1609 literacy among yeomen and wealthy craftsmen was 44 per cent, among husbandmen and craftsmen 25 per cent, and among labourers and poor craftsmen 0 per cent. By 1670–99 these figures had risen to 83 per cent, 68 per cent and 36 per cent respectively.[12]

Literacy rates correspond roughly to opportunities for schooling. The children of labourers and small farmers who were put to work at the age of seven could not hope to attend school long enough to do more than learn to read. Those who stayed to the age of eight or older could probably write a little as well. The availability of a local school and ability or willingness of parents to pay for schooling were obviously crucial. Not all humble men in the 1630s were as fortunate as John Bunyan, whose father was a tinker who had a cottage and nine acres in Bedfordshire: 'Notwithstanding the meanness . . . of my Parents, it pleased God to put it into their heart to put me to School, to learn both to Read and Write.'[13] As Bunyan and others demonstrated, this limited educational opportunity did not prevent a few (perhaps exceptional) working men from attaining a high degree of literacy. Other rural workers however, after their year or two's schooling, were left with only elementary literary skills, perhaps sufficient to read slowly. Among craftsmen some degree of literacy seems to have been taken for granted by the early eighteenth century. William Hutton records that his father (born in 1691) 'was fond of reading but never purchased a book', and that his brother (born in 1722) 'was put to school, but had no need of being taught his book, for he seemed, by a kind of instinct, to learn without'.[14] This last remark perhaps hints at the possibility of informal instruction by parents or friends outside the normal educational structure. In the assessment of the extent of literacy it is also possible that the statistics based on name-signing may underestimate the total number able to read at an elementary level, and very probable that they underestimate the number of women who were literate.

The existence of literacy among sections of the common people raises interesting, if unresolved, questions about ideas and beliefs. In the Middle Ages popular culture was overwhelmingly oral. It was cut off from high or polite culture which was both literary and in a foreign tongue (Latin or Norman-French). But from the sixteenth century the relationship between the two cultures changed. The invention of printing made possible, and the Reformation imperative, the dissemination of books and pamphlets. The oral culture was now faced by the written word, and as literacy increased, the influence of book learning grew too. Eventually the written triumphed over the oral culture in the main areas of national life. But the victory was neither sudden nor complete, and for several hundred years the two co-existed as different cultural levels within the same society. Literate labouring people could, and did, derive their ideas and attitudes from either or both traditional oral culture and the literate culture. Even people who were essentially illiterate, like many agricultural labourers, could participate in some aspects of the literate culture. There was no dichotomy between literate and illiterate but rather an infinite grading of degrees of literacy, ranging from poor labourers who could not read or write, through those who could slowly spell out the message of a handbill or passage of scripture, to self-educated artisans who read the classics and wrote religious and political tracts.

Once sizeable sections of the common people were literate their culture was vulnerable to penetration by the values and beliefs of the dominant culture to an extent which was not possible before. In this process the spread of ideas was downwards from the affluent and educated classes to their poorer and less educated neighbours: 'The cast-off garments of the intellectuals of one age are found, albeit soiled and ragged, on the backs of the ignorant many in the next.'[15] Or so some historians of ideas have believed. But this is to oversimplify the relation between popular and dominant culture. It ignores the very real problem of how working people read texts, of how they interpreted the ideas from books. We know, for instance, that many thousands of labouring people in the eighteenth century sang hymns which enshrined the basic doctrines of Methodism. But we are not warranted in assuming that when humble Methodists sang of grace, salvation and the blood of the lamb, these words had the same meaning for them as for John Wesley (1703–91), or the same significance that theologians, psychologists and historians have attributed to them later. What historians have described as the simplification and distortion of ideas and concepts in the process of cultural diffusion may be seen in a different light – as the appropriation by working people in their own way and for their own purposes of such elements in the dominant culture as they deem useful. The traditional attitudes and assumptions of a largely oral culture may have been a screen or filter (sometimes a barrier) through which a husbandman or artisan received ideas from the printed word. If this were so it casts a new light on the complaints of the middle classes from Elizabethan times to the present about the resistance of the common people to accepting middle-class values and habits.

In one of the greatest and most influential of all the books of the English common people – Bunyan's *The Pilgrim's Progress* – the fusion of the two worlds of traditional and literate culture is most evident. Bunyan, in an autobiographical fragment, recalls his reading in his unregenerate youth: 'Give me a ballad, a news-book, George on horseback, or Bevis of Southampton; give me some book that teaches curious arts, that tells of old fables; but for the holy Scriptures I cared not.'[16] This is ballad and chapbook literature, much of which was based on traditional lore and legend. It is full of chivalrous romances, improbable adventures, princes and princesses, giants, dragons, lions, dungeons, wonders and horrors. Here is Bunyan's description of Apollyon: 'The Monster was hideous to behold, he was cloathed with scales like a Fish (and they are his pride) he had Wings like a Dragon, feet like a Bear, and out of his belly came Fire and Smoak, and his mouth was as the mouth of a Lion.'[17] Similarly the lions guarding the Palace Beautiful, the giants Pope and Pagan in their cave, and Giant Despair himself are from the world of folk heroes and popular culture, though the purpose of the book is to convey spiritual truths and the margins are filled with scriptural references.

The ballads, fables and books on the 'curious arts' to which the young Bunyan was addicted comprised the popular literature of the late sixteenth to the nineteenth centuries. It is evidence of what the people read and also a key to some aspects of what they

believed. But its use is not without problems. By popular literature we can mean either literature produced indigenously and
spontaneously by the people, or literature provided for the people
by other classes or interests. Both types could be read by un-
sophisticated readers for enjoyment or improvement; and the distinction presumably mattered little to them so long as they
derived pleasure from their reading. However, if this literature of
the streets and itinerant vendors (chapmen) is to be used as
evidence of popular beliefs one has to be aware of the difference.
Some of it, like ballads and legends, could be a printed version of
oral culture; other parts, like the almanacs, were a mixture of
traditional beliefs and popularized versions of standard works;
while others, like the religious tracts of the late eighteenth and
early nineteenth centuries, were an attempt by members of the
middle and upper classes to evangelize the lower orders. The
folklore which was first discovered and exposed to public view in
the sixteenth and seventeenth centuries had a remarkable
resilience and tenacity – as attested by the huge amount of
material collected in the last hundred years by enthusiastic
folklorists. Some of the constituents of this folklore, such as omens
and auguries, dreams and divinations, magic, witchcraft and
demons, indicate important areas of popular belief. Folklore is
notoriously vague in its chronology and context; cases of magic
and ritual, for example, may be culled from any period between
the sixteenth and nineteenth centuries and from any region of the
British Isles. After the late seventeenth century educated and
upper-class opinion turned against belief in magic, and increasingly came to condemn popular culture as vulgar, crude, ignorant
and superstitious. When the folklore collectors of the nineteenth
century discovered the continuing existence of magical and occult
beliefs they reported them as outsiders, not as believers, and their
findings have to be drawn upon with caution. Nevertheless with
this *caveat* the popular literature of almanacs, chapbooks and
street ballads may be taken as reflecting the values and interests of
labouring people.

The almanac was perhaps the most popular book in England for
over three and a half centuries, and together with the bible was the
work most likely to be found in a cottage home. *Moore's Almanac*, it
was noted in 1810 by an observer in Reading, 'may be found not

only in every house in the town but also in every one in the neighbourhood and partakes nearly of the same degree of belief in its prognostications as the bible itself'.[18] An almanac consisted of three parts: the calendar, which showed the days and weeks for each month and indicated the church festivals; the almanac proper, giving general astronomical information for the year and an ephemeris or tables showing the daily position of the stars; and the prognostication or forecast of events for the coming year. These were bound together, and there was also information about the tides, and lists of kings and queens. An anatomical diagram of a man's body (showing which parts were under the dominion of the different signs of the zodiac), a ready reckoner, snippets of miscellaneous information, and weather forecasts completed the volume. Sometimes blank sheets were interleaved or bound in at the end, the whole serving as a working guide and notebook. Another form was the sheet almanac, intended to be pinned on the wall like a modern calendar. The practical significance of the almanac is today obscured, for we forget the overwhelming importance of the weather for past generations. The lives of farmers – and of labourers, artisans and tradesmen who were close to them – were geared to the rhythm of the seasons. Most personal diaries and letters of the eighteenth and nineteenth centuries (and not only of people living on the land) contain constant observations about the weather. The almanac catered to the needs of a great part of the nation, and its peculiar form served to keep alive the ancient traditions of folk astrology.

It has been estimated that in the seventeenth century there were over two thousand separate almanacs published and more than two hundred authors were involved.[19] By the mid-eighteenth century the trade seems to have settled into the hands of such steady favourites as Partridge's *Merlinus Liberatus*, Moore's *Vox Stellarum*, Rider's *British Merlin*, Saunders's *English Apollo*, Season's *Speculum Anni Redivivum*, Poor Robin's *Almanack*, and others under the names of Tycho Wing, White, Pearse, Gadbury, Andrews and Coley. Eighty years later at least five of these were still going strong, with a sale of half a million copies – and in addition there was a huge sale of unstamped (and therefore illegal) almanacs. A newcomer in the field was *Raphael's Prophetic Messenger*, begun by Robert Cross Smith in 1826. This was a very complete almanac of up to one hundred and twenty pages, with a large coloured hieroglyphic full of mystical signs and apocalyptic figures. It was an attempt to provide something less crude and bucolic than the old almanacs, rather as Zadkiel's *Astrology* was intended for Victorian readers who wanted something more up-to-date than reprints of the seventeenth-century astrologers. The continuing popularity of almanacs in the nineteenth century is evidenced by the fierceness of the attacks on them and by the number of imitators. Almanacs were exhibitions of 'palpable imposture, impudent mendacity, vulgar ignorance, and low obscenity', thundered the *Athenaeum* in 1828. They 'have continued wholly unchanged; precisely of the same character that they held in the days when witches were burnt and horoscopes were drawn; utterly uninfluenced by any of the modes of thinking which have marked the emancipation of the present generation from ignorance and credulity'.[20] Yet so indigenous were they that the Society for the Diffusion of Useful Knowledge issued their counterpropaganda in the same form, *The British Almanac*. Others who wished to take their cause to the people – political radicals, Anti-Corn Law Leaguers, phrenologists – also adopted the form of the almanac. Only later in the century was the old popularity of the almanac eclipsed by newer publications.

Chapbooks (or penny histories, as they were sometimes called) had a wider variety of content than almanacs. They were sold by chapmen at a price of 1d. to 6d., and were small, paper-covered booklets, embellished with a crude and sometimes highly coloured woodcut illustration. The type was of all styles and sizes, the paper was thick and rough, and each production had a vigour and individuality of its own. The contents were seldom original, and as befitted folk art the authorship was anonymous. Romances, often of great antiquity, were always popular: *Guy of Warwick*, *The History of Valentine and Orson*, *Bevis of Southampton*; so also were lives and executions of criminals, song and jest books (often bawdy), and legendary histories. Other chapbooks dealt with dreams, fortune-telling, demonology, witchcraft, and the world of spirits. Little manuals on household and farm economy, sex and practical medicine, herbals, and advice for the young of both sexes were legion. Love in all its ramifications (seduction, elopement, separation), marriage and the family figured prominently. Sermons, prophecies, signs and wonders were printed and reprinted. Acquaintance with this literature began in childhood, and indeed such parts of it as have survived have done so as nursery tales. But until the mid-nineteenth century chapbooks and chapbook-style literature was the common reading of adults of all ages. In cities, especially London, street literature included all forms of the chapbook, as well as ballads, broadsheets and handbills. At this point urban and rural folklore were very close together.

Underlying this literature was a deep respect for the world of the unknown. Popular belief in the supernatural found expression in many forms. At its most general it was a simple, unintellectual type of neoplatonism: all forms of life are animated by a spirit, and there is an essential oneness of all God's creatures. Further, there is no clear distinction between matter and spirit: the earth is not an inanimate mass but is deemed to be alive, and the universe is peopled by a hierarchy of spirits. The cosmos is an organic unity, in which every part is related to the rest.[21] These things can be but dimly perceived, for the veil of the world obscures them. But occasionally the veil may be lifted, and men may glimpse something of the mysteries and occult qualities of nature, the virtues of plants, metals and minerals. Given these assumptions, other beliefs follow, and assume a plausibility which is otherwise difficult to appreciate today. Two such beliefs were in correspondences and signatures.

The doctrine of correspondences held that every part of the physical world corresponds to some aspect of the spiritual. This relationship is not only general but also particular; so that everything in nature has a spiritual meaning. There is an outward and inward significance to all things. Spiritual reality is mirrored in the homely, everyday events of life if we can but see it. Words – including the words of scripture – have an internal or spiritual meaning as well as their outward sense. Visions and dreams are to be interpreted spiritually by those competent to do so.

Similarly the doctrine of signatures, with its very practical applications, was a constant reminder of the reality of supernatural power. The resemblance in the shape of the root, leaf or fruit of any plant to a particular part of the human body was taken to indicate its possessing some beneficial or hurtful power over the corresponding part. For example a decoction of maidenhair fern was good for washing the head and making the hair grow. Balm and wood-sorrel, representing the heart in figure, were cardiacal. The walnut, which bore the signature of the whole head, was good for the brain and mental disease. 'Thus did Divine Providence, by natural hieroglyphics, read lectures to the rude wit of vulgar man.'[22]

In a world so thoroughly subject to invisible spiritual influences, the claims of conjurors, magicians and astrologers were entirely credible. After all, to conjure meant originally to compel the spirits of men and angels. Magic is the ancient occult science which once led its devotees, the magi, to follow a star which took them to the cradle at Bethlehem: 'We have seen his star in the east and are come to worship him.' Astrology is referred to many times in the scriptures, and in a universe so completely one and interdependent it was reasonable to assume that the stars might influence earthly bodies. Beliefs of this kind were not, however, part of acknowledged religion. But neither were they scientific or secular. Usually they are called superstitions, but perhaps it is more useful to classify them as popular (or people's) religion. Many such beliefs have existed for centuries, despite official disapproval and sometimes condemnation by the churches. Theologians separated 'religious' from 'superstitious' belief, though philosophically the distinction is by no means clear-cut, and all ceremonial religion contains some elements of magic. It is unlikely that popular religion would have survived so long unless it had a fairly powerful functional role. Untidy, confused and incomplete as this collection of beliefs was, it nevertheless provided a fabric which held together folk memories, the meaning of daily joys and suffering, the hopes and expectations for the future. For many labouring people in the eighteenth century the sense of the impossible had not yet been redrawn (as it had for some of the educated classes) to exclude belief in magic, divination and occult forces. Despite Newton, for many of his humbler fellow-countrymen, 'Nature and Nature's laws lay hid in night.' There is a danger in exaggerating the extent to which the Newtonian revolution in intellectual outlook involved changes in statements of religious belief. We do not know how many people, like William Blake, rejected 'Single vision and Newton's sleep'.[23] In the long run, and more immediately for intellectuals, the simple conception of the cosmos which had come from Aristotle and Aquinas had to be abandoned. But at the popular level heaven and the angels remained just above the sky, thunder was the voice of God, and Satan could be encountered in darkness and storm.

There is abundant evidence of the persistence of folk belief and popular religion in the nineteenth century, and that not only in rural areas. 'Those who are not in daily intercourse with the peasantry', it was reported from Lincolnshire in 1856, 'can hardly be made to believe or comprehend the hold that charms, witchcraft, wise men and other relics of heathendom have upon the people.'[24] The autobiographies of working men almost invariably refer to such beliefs in their childhood.[25] Thomas Cooper, whose home was in Gainsborough during the second decade of the nineteenth century, described how he acquired herbal lore from a friend whose father was a fisherman and herb-gatherer; and how a little later he was attracted to an old man, George White (known as the 'Wise Man of Retford'), who was an astrologer and devotee of the 'higher knowledge'. William Lovett, living at the same time in Cornwall, attested his firm belief in ghosts and recalled an old woman, Aunt Tammy, 'who was reputed to be a white witch, one who, from the ill she was believed able to inflict, was regarded by some with superstitious dread'. During the same period at Bramley, near Leeds, Joseph Barker noted many instances of magic and the use of charms. 'My parents were both believers in witchcraft and fairies, as well as in some other superstitions. They believed that some persons, especially certain women, had the power of causing diseases in men and cattle, and of harassing and injuring people in various other ways, by an evil wish, or by diabolical influence.' Interestingly, they had no difficulty in reconciling these beliefs with a strong attachment to Methodism: 'Though they were foolish enough to cling to the superstitions of their childhood, their religious belief was, in general, the great ruling principle of their lives.' The richest collection of folklore in these autobiographies, however, is Samuel Bamford's *Passages in the Life of a Radical*, in which he recalled his memories of Middleton, Lancashire. His friend and fellow-radical, George Plant of Blackley, 'was a firm believer in ghosts, witches, and hobgoblins; in the virtues of herbs under certain planetary influences; and in the occult mysteries of Culpeper and Sibly. He was entirely self-taught; had been a great reader, knew something of arithmetic, was a botanist, and a dreary minded wanderer in lonely dells, on moors and heaths; searching after herbs of surpassing virtue, of mysterious growth and concealment, and of wonderful and unaccountable power.' Another of Bamford's acquaintances was Limping Billy, a noted seer residing at Radcliffe Bridge. These accounts could be matched by other local reminiscences from all parts of Britain. The list is endless – for we are chronicling something which had once existed everywhere and which still existed perhaps more widely than any other set of beliefs.

Signs and wonders were a staple of this type of belief. Any instance in which the laws of nature appeared to have been set aside, any abnormal or inexplicable happening, any unusual behaviour in man or beast aroused widespread interest and speculation. It created wonder in itself, and prompted thoughts as to what it might portend as a 'sign of the times'. John Wesley had an insatiable curiosity about such things, and would always turn out of his way to see, for instance, a man born without arms, or a 'monster' at Bristol fair.

Even more widespread than signs and wonders was belief in the significance of dreams. From time immemorial it had been taken for granted that dreams were related to the world of the supernatural, and as long as the latter was accepted there was little reason to doubt the traditional view of dreams. It was believed that dreams must serve some special purpose, and that as a rule they predicted the future. The great diversity in the content of dreams and of their impact on the dreamer necessitated an elaborate system of classification and yet baffled attempts at formulating a coherent explanation of their nature. Most popular interest in dreams was directed towards their interpretation, for which two methods were employed. The first method was to see the dream as a whole and as symbolic of something else. Many dreams in the bible were treated in this manner; for example Joseph interpreted Pharaoh's dream of the seven fat and seven lean kine as symbolic of the seven years of famine in Egypt which would consume all the surplus produced in the seven years of plenty. Bunyan, when writing *The Pilgrim's Progress* 'in the similitude of a dream', was using this technique of interpretation. The second method was quite different. Instead of interpreting the dream in its entirety, individual items were interpreted separately. The dream was treated as a kind of secret code, to be translated by means of an established key. To decipher this code one had to consult a 'dream-book' or 'book of fate'. 'Hawkers and small shops sell a vast quantity of penny dream-books in Lancashire,' it was reported as late as 1867.[26] Typical of this type of popular literature was *Mother Shipton's Legacy* (York, 1797), subtitled 'a favourite Fortune-book, in which is given a pleasing interpretation of dreams, and a collection of prophetic verses, moral and entertaining'. In the chapter on dreams the reader is warned that interpretation is not always obvious, and may in fact be contrary to the content of the dream. Thus, to dream of joy denotes grief; of fine clothes, poverty; of sweetmeats, a whipping; of gold, death; of drinking water, good entertainment. And the moral is inescapable:

> Though plain and palpable each subject seems,
> Yet do not put your trust too much in dreams;
> Events may happen, which in dreams you see,
> And yet as often quite contrary be:
> This learned hint observe, for Shipton's sake –
> Dreams are but interludes which fancies make.

Nevertheless, once the old Lancashire adage had been grasped ('Dreams always go by contraries'), dreams were to be taken as omens. In folk culture, dispute was not about the validity but the interpretation of dreams.

Dreams, like signs and wonders, could always be interpreted on a do-it-yourself basis, with the aid of a chapbook, an almanac or a bit of rule-of-thumb advice from friends. But in difficult and serious cases, such as those concerned with love, death and disease, help of a more expert kind was required; and then the services of magicians, witches, astrologers and herbalists were in demand. 'A cunning man, or a cunning woman, as they are termed, is to be found near every town, and though the laws are occasionally put in force against them, still it is a gainful trade,' reported Robert Southey in 1807.[27] From all over the country in the nineteenth century detailed examples confirmed Southey's report. White witches, or wisemen, used their magic powers benevolently; whereas black witches were malicious, and devoted their art to evil ends. But in both cases they operated to control supernatural forces. Generally speaking, wisemen and cunning women provided a service in areas of life where people felt insecure, anxious, and at a loss to know what to do for the best. They were adjusters, protectors, providers of relief in time of misfortune. The wiseman had remedies for diseases of man and beast; he could detect thieves and recover stolen goods. The wisewoman could counteract spells laid by unknown enemies, could advise in affairs of the heart, and was skilled in midwifery and women's ailments. At the best, witches were useful depositories of folk knowledge who were trusted at times when no outsider's advice or help would be considered; at the worst they were miserable, poor old people, on whom all the hatred and frustration of the neighbourhood could be vented. Robert Burton, though he looked on all conjurors and magicians as agents of the devil, saw clearly how they were regarded by many people.

> Sourcerers are too common; cunning men, wizards, and white-witches, as they call them, are in every village, which if they be sought unto will help almost all infirmities of body and mind. . . . 'Tis a common practice of some men to go first to a witch and then to a physician; if one cannot the other shall. 'It matters not', saith Paracelsus, 'whether it be God or the devil, angels or unclean spirits cure him, so that he be eased.' If a man fall into a ditch . . . what matter is it whether a friend or an enemy help him out?[28]

This was written in 1621; but it was a practical sentiment that could still be echoed two hundred years later.

Such, however, was but a minimal claim on behalf of witchcraft: if it works, what harm can there be in it? John Wesley put the case on a higher plane: 'I cannot give up to all the Deists in Great Britain the existence of witchcraft till I give up the credit of all history, sacred and profane.'[29] The evidence in its favour, he argued, was too strong to allow of doubt. To those who asked him, 'Did you ever see an apparition yourself?' he replied: 'No; nor did I ever see a murder; yet I believe there is such a thing.' He regretted that most learned men 'have given up all accounts of witches and apparitions as mere old wives' fables'. But his belief in the reality of the world of spirits precluded any abandonment of witchcraft; and he added ominously, 'The giving up witchcraft is, in effect, giving up the bible.'

Many of the wiseman's clients came to him for predictions which could guide them in their business and personal affairs; and nothing enhanced the reputation of a wiseman more than prophecies that were fulfilled. Fortune-telling and crystal-gazing were unlikely to produce more than a local trade; but pronouncements about dearth and plenty, wars, plagues and the significance of comets could raise the status of a cunning man until he was looked upon as a prophet. It seems likely that some of the 'prophets' reported from time to time in local newspapers in the first half of the nineteenth century were of this order.

The more sophisticated wisemen were often also astrologers, known colloquially as 'planet rulers'. By the end of the seventeenth century astrology was seldom taken seriously by educated men, but it retained its hold among labouring people. It had an obvious practical utility, and intellectually the all-embracing nature of its claims made it attractive to men who had little opportunity for study. Even today we still use its vocabulary to describe temperaments (jovial, mercurial, saturnine), states of mind (lunacy), or diseases (influenza). Astrology is basically the study of the influence of the relative positions of the moon, sun and stars on human affairs. It is assumed that each of the celestial bodies has a special influence or quality, which varies according to its position in the heavens. By ascertaining the movements of the stars and drawing a map of their positions at a given time (casting a horoscope) the astrologer can study the situation and draw certain conclusions. Astrology had four main branches. First were nativities, or figures of the heavens at the moment of birth, from which could be calculated the character and fate of individuals. Second was mundane astrology, which was the art of foreseeing the 'circumstances of nations', meaning wars, pestilences and natural disasters of all kinds. Third, by means of atmospherical astrology the quality of the weather at any required time or place could be known. Fourth was horary astrology which enabled the astrologer to foresee the result of any circumstance or undertaking from the position of the heavens at the time of the query. The great names in English astrology – William Lilly, Nicholas Culpeper,

John Gadbury – belong to the seventeenth century, and their works were reprinted and used as textbooks in the eighteenth and nineteenth centuries. However, to emphasize the long continuance of popular belief in astrology it will be more useful to look briefly at a later example.

Ebenezer Sibly's *A Complete Illustration of the Celestial Science of Astrology* was published in London in 1784–8. Its four parts totalled 1128 pages, and it was a favourite textbook of wisemen. The details of Sibly's astrology follow his seventeenth-century masters. He described the qualities of the signs of the zodiac, the properties of the twelve houses of heaven, the characters and aspects of the planets, and the utility of horary astrology in resolving a great range of personal questions. His attempt to justify astrology to his contemporaries of the 1780s is significant. How – and why – could an apparently discredited system of belief be seriously put forward at this time? At the beginning Sibly is on the defensive: 'Sensible as I am of the rooted prejudices of the times against the venerable science of Astrology, and sensible also of the reproach and obloquy that will be levelled against me . . .', nevertheless he will seek to rehabilitate the science by arguments 'founded on the principles of religion and morality', showing that 'God is a God of order, and created nothing in vain'.[30] This is his starting point: the familiar eighteenth-century notion of God, the divine watchmaker. 'It would be derogatory to the attributes of the Deity, not to believe that the minutest events of this world were foreseen and provided for in that most perfect frame or model of nature, which . . . may be compared to the construction of a watch, consisting of many small wheels, regulated by one master-wheel, or first mover.' This great watch was wound up at the creation and has been unwinding ever since. Every man is as a little wheel within the great world, and yet is also a little world within himself, containing 'many thousands of wheels'. It follows from this 'that every occurrence of our lives, and all the various productions of nature, however strange or incomprehensible they may appear, are brought to pass by a regular and established means, decreed by the wisdom of God, at the beginning of the world'. The key to understanding these events is astrology, which 'comprehends every operation that proceeds out of the master-wheel or frame of nature, and furnishes us with a knowledge of the occult virtues of all earthly substances, and of the nature and end of every particle of God's creation'.

These were very large claims indeed. Yet their very comprehensiveness was in part the reason why astrology was attractive. There was literally nothing it could not explain. At the same time on its practical side it was not too difficult for any intelligent person to master. Sibly assured his readers that the mathematics required was quite minimal: 'Every person who can make use of a *Ready Reckoner* or *Trader's Sure Guide* may with equal ease understand all the tables calculated for this work.' Despite some problems of astral determinism (which he attempted to deal with), Sibly saw no need for conflict between astrology and Christian doctrine. He regarded theology as 'the sister science of astrology'; and found plenty of scriptural confirmation of the influence of the stars in human affairs. When the great watch was finally unwound, the signs of the last days were that the sun and moon would be darkened and 'the stars shall fall from heaven' (Matthew 24:29).

Astrology was also a necessary component of folk medicine. Particular parts of the body were thought to be under the rule of the different signs of the zodiac, and treatment of diseases was therefore directly linked to the stars. A favourable time for taking medicine, blood-letting or any other treatment could be found by consulting the almanac. The collection, preparation and administration of herbs was governed by similar considerations, for the occult properties of plants were under the influence of the heavens. 'More copies of Culpeper's *Herbal* and Sibly's *Astrology* are sold in Lancashire than all other works on the same subjects put together, and this principally on account of the planetary influence with which each disease and its antidote are connected,' discovered the folklorists in 1867.[31] In his later work, *A Key to Physic, and the Occult Sciences*, Sibly collected more material on popular medicine, which he mixed with astrology, physiology, animal magnetism, curious stories and sex.

An extreme – and to modern readers bizarre – expression of popular belief was the persecution of witches. At its centre was the idea of *maleficium* or the ability of a witch to cause harm to others. She (for most witches were female) was thought to be able to cause death, illness, accidents, quarrels, barrenness and impotency among her neighbours; to kill and injure their animals; to destroy crops; and to frustrate their efforts at butter and cheese making and the brewing of beer. 'Agnes Whilland of Dagenham, spinster, on 10 July 1590 at Dagenham, bewitched to death 1 sow valued at 10s. of the goods and chattels of Richard Foster . . .' declared an indictment at the Essex summer assizes of 1591; and again, more seriously, 'Susan Pickenden of Halden, spinster, wife of John Pickenden of Halden, labourer, on 28 October 1648 at Halden, bewitched Elizabeth Lowes, daughter of William Lowes, aged about 17 yrs., who languished until 8 March following, when she died. . . .'[32] In a thousand different ways witches could cause harm by exercising an evil influence through a touch, a look, a curse or ritualistic magic, such as sticking pins in a wax image of the victim, or burning a piece of paper with his name on it. The witch was assisted by her familiar spirit or imp, who took the form of a cat, dog, toad or other small animal. 'Mary Hockett of Ramsey, widow, . . . did entertain three evil spirits each in the likeness of a mouse, called "Littleman", "Prettyman", and "Daynty" ', it was alleged in 1645; and Bridget Mayers, of Holland, the wife of a seaman, at the same assizes was charged with entertaining 'an evil spirit in the likeness of a mouse called "Prickeares" .' These familiars carried out the orders of the witch and were rewarded by being allowed to suck drops of her blood from a pricked finger or a teat somewhere on her body, which the devil had provided specially for this purpose. Suspects were searched for any unusual protuberance or wart which could be pronounced as a teat and used as evidence of guilt. A witch was believed to carry somewhere on her body a spot or 'unnatural mark' as the sign of her allegiance to the devil. These marks were supposed to be insensitive and not to bleed when pricked. They were taken as sure tokens of a witch. Another proof of witchcraft was 'swimming', a last relic of the medieval legal ordeal by water. The witch was stripped, bound with right thumb to left toe and left thumb to right toe, and then thrown into a pond or river. If she sank she was innocent, but often drowned; if she swam (that is, floated) she was guilty – because the pure water (of baptism) rejected those who renounced it. A diarist from Coggeshall recorded:

> July 13, 1699. The widow Comon was put into the river to see if she would sink, because she was suspected to be a witch – and

she did not sink but swim. And she was tryed again July 19th, and then she swam again, and did not sink.

July 24, 1699. The widow Comon was tryed a third time by putting her into the river, and she swam and did not sink.

Dec 27, 1699. The widow Comon, that was counted a witch, was buried.

Belief in witchcraft is extremely ancient and widespread. It existed in England in the Middle Ages, but in the sixteenth and seventeeth centuries assumed larger proportions than at any other time. Between 1542 and 1736, when witchcraft was a capital offence, the total number of witches executed in England has been estimated at something under a thousand, the majority in the period 1563–1685. By European or even Scottish standards this figure is not high; but it nevertheless indicates a period of persecution and witch mania unequalled before or since. In some counties, notably Essex, prosecutions were particularly numerous. During the exceptional witch hunt led by the 'discoverer' of witches, Matthew Hopkins, in 1644–7, several hundred witches were executed in Essex and the eastern counties. From the records it is clear that the overwhelming majority of witches were poor and female; they are described as spinsters, widows or wives of tradesmen, husbandmen and labourers. Witch beliefs were not confined to the common people; but the victims were almost always from the bottom of the social hierarchy. The last witch to be hanged as such in England was Alice Molland at Exeter in 1685, and the last recorded trial for witchcraft was at Leicester in 1717. But accusations of witchcraft and sporadic community violence against alleged witches continued into the later nineteenth century. Witch beliefs remained very much alive long after the end of the seventeenth century; though they were no longer supported by the lawyers, clergymen and substantial freeholders who had previously put the weight of the judicial system behind witch prosecution.

The persistence of belief in witchcraft emphasizes the hazardous nature of the social environment for most people. Daily life was full of inexplicable misfortunes of one sort or another: the death of a child or animal, an accident at work in the fields or workshop, the failure, for no apparent reason, of some undertaking or relationship. In the absence of any other explanation the evil influence of a neighbour could be held to account for such ills. There was virtually no misfortune that could not be ascribed to supernatural forces. Labouring people were prone to the aches and pains associated with outdoor work in the English climate, and indoors in inadequately heated rooms: rheumatism, arthritis, bronchitis. Many diseases which today we recognize were imperfectly understood: strokes, creeping paralysis, tuberculosis (consumption), cancer and many kinds of infectious ailments. Witchcraft could be diagnosed when medical knowledge was not able to deal adequately with illness in men and animals. It has been observed that two elements were present in most witchcraft accusations:[33] first, some personal misfortune for which there was no immediate natural explanation; and second, an awareness by the victim of having given offence to a neighbour, as for example refusing food or alms to an old person who came to the door, evicting a widow from her cottage, neglecting to invite someone to a sheep-shearing or harvest home, or refusing the loan of some utensil or time to pay a debt. The remedy for witchcraft, apart from the courts or open violence, was recourse to a countercharm. White magic was used to break the evil spell put upon man or beast. For this purpose the victim's urine, blood, hair clippings and nail parings were used in a ritual boiling or burning, or put into a bottle which was hidden, buried or thrown into a river. Various herbs such as garlic, vervain and St John's wort, and also wood from the rowan tree and salt, were powerful antidotes. But the most effective remedy for personal bewitchment was scratching or 'scoring' the witch to draw blood as this would break her power.

It was perhaps from the awareness by labouring people that their world was both precarious and in large part unknown that many aspects of popular belief stemmed. From Christianity or folk custom they sought assurance, guidance, protection, and some explanation of the world as they experienced it. Whether most of them sought security rather than change we cannot tell. The idea of fate seems to underlie many common attitudes to experience, as is no doubt natural among people who do not have any very effective choice in their futures. Astrology reinforced the notion, since the moon and the planets were held to rule men's destinies. But post-Reformation Christian teaching also contributed along the same lines, with the assurance that the world was ruled not by chance but by God's providence. Everything in one's life had meaning and significance; and indeed was foreordained or (in Calvinist theology) predestined. The doctrine of grace became in practice fate freely accepted. However, belief in the will of God, in a divine omnipotence controlling everything, did not always result in complete and passive acceptance of the social order and the destinies of individuals. There was always room for conflicting interpretations and even scepticism. To some of this we shall turn in the next chapter.

6. The World Upset

Although the Reformation in England was accomplished by acts of state and the decisions were not made by the common people, the changes in religious thought and practice affected them in important ways. In particular there was brought into being a minority of dissenters, recruited heavily from the 'middle and poorer sort of people', meaning tradesmen, shopkeepers, craftsmen and small farmers. A majority of the common people no doubt continued after the Elizabethan settlement to attend (or not attend) the parish church; though they would now discover that the services were in English, the liturgy had been changed, the use of vestments modified, and images, paintings and stained glass removed or covered up – in short, everything was plainer and more 'Protestant'. But these changes did not satisfy all; there were puritans (who wanted further reforms) both within and without the Church of England. Attendance at church on Sunday was still commonly regarded as the normal sign of religious orthodoxy and participation in the affairs of the community; and fines were levied for absence. Nevertheless, many of the most serious, devout, thinking members of the common people in the seventeenth century deserted the Church of England and became dissenters and nonconformists. This dissenting tradition is nowhere more beautifully or powerfully expressed than in Bunyan's *The Pilgrim's Progress*.

'What shall I do to be saved?' Christian's desperate cry on the eve of his pilgrimage echoed for over two hundred years through the minds of successive generations of humble readers. *The Pilgrim's Progress* is essentially an allegory of the soul, a statement of spiritual experience which through its direct and homely language spoke to the needs and understanding of those readers. It became a favourite book because it is full of people and problems which all could recognize from their own experience of good and evil.

As I walked through the wilderness of this world, I lighted on a certain place, where was a den; and I laid me down in that place to sleep: and as I slept I dreamed a dream. I dreamed, and behold I saw a man clothed with rags, standing in a certain place, with his face from his own house, a book in his hand, and a great burden upon his back. I looked, and saw him open the book, and read therein; and as he read, he wept and trembled: and not being able longer to contain, he brake out with a lamentable cry; saying, 'What shall I do?'[1]

Who could not understand and sympathize with the plight of Christian, alone with his Bible and burden of sin – and with the domestic anguish which followed?

In this plight therefore he went home, and restrained himself as long as he could, that his wife and children should not perceive his distress; but he could not be silent long, because that his trouble increased: wherefore at length he brake his mind to his wife and children; and thus he began to talk to them: 'O my dear wife,' said he, 'and you the children of my bowels, I your dear friend am in myself undone, by reason of a burden that lieth hard upon me: moreover, I am for certain informed that this our city will be burned with fire from Heaven, in which fearful overthrow, both myself, with thee, my wife, and you my sweet babes, shall miserably come to ruin; except (the which yet I see not) some way of escape can be found, whereby we may be delivered.' At this his relations were sore amazed; not for that they believed that what he said to them was true, but because they thought that some frenzy distemper had got into his head: therefore, it drawing towards night, and they hoping that sleep might settle his brains, with all haste they got him to bed; but the night was as troublesome to him as the day: wherefore instead of sleeping, he spent it in sighs and tears. So when the morning was come, they would know how he did and he told them worse and worse. He also set to talking to them again, but they began to be hardened; they also thought to drive away his distemper by harsh and surly carriages to him: sometimes they would deride, sometimes they would chide, and sometimes they would quite neglect him: wherefore he began to retire himself to his chamber to pray for, and pity them; and also to condole his own misery: he would also walk solitarily in the fields, sometimes reading, and sometimes praying: and thus for some days he spent his time.

During one of these walks Christian met Evangelist who counselled him to 'fly from the wrath to come':

So I saw in my dream that the man began to run. Now he had not run far from his own door, but his wife and children perceiving it began to cry after him to return: but the man put his fingers in his ears, and ran on crying, 'Life, life, eternal life.' So he looked not behind him, but fled towards the middle of the plain.

The neighbours also came out to see him run, and as he ran some mocked, others threatened; and some cried after him to return.

In his pilgrimage Christian encounters a remarkable cross-section of society and many unlovely characters, among whom is Mr By-ends of the town of Fairspeech:

CHRISTIAN: Pray who are your kindred there, if a man may be so bold?

BY-ENDS: Almost the whole town; and in particular, my Lord Turn-about, my Lord Time-server, my Lord Fair-speech (from whose ancestors that town first took its name), also Mr Smooth-man, Mr Facing-bothways, Mr Any-thing, and the parson of our parish, Mr Two-tongues, was my mother's own brother by father's side: and to tell you the truth, I am become a gentleman of good quality; yet my great-grandfather was but a waterman, looking one way and rowing another: and I got most of my estate by the same occupation.

Previous to this encounter with By-ends, Christian and his companion, Faithful, had been arrested and imprisoned in Vanity-Fair and brought before the judge, Lord Hategood, on the grounds 'that they were enemies to, and disturbers of their trade; that they had made commotions and divisions in the town, and had won a party to their own most dangerous opinions, in contempt of the law of their prince'. The judge showed little concern for justice:

> JUDGE: Thou runagate, heretic, and traitor, hast thou heard what these honest gentlemen have witnessed against thee?
> FAITHFUL: May I speak a few words in my own defence?
> JUDGE: Sirrah, sirrah, thou deservest to live no longer, but to be slain immediately . . .; yet that all men may see our gentleness towards thee, let us hear what thou hast to say.

But there was no hope of mercy from a jury made up of Mr Blind-man, Mr No-good, Mr Malice, Mr Love-lust, Mr Live-loose, Mr Heady, Mr High-mind, Mr Enmity, Mr Liar, Mr Cruelty, Mr Hate-light and Mr Implacable. Faithful was condemned, and suffered a cruel martyr's death.

Bunyan had good cause to know what he wrote about. *The Pilgrim's Progress* was written in part during his twelve-year (1660–72) and six-month (1677) imprisonments in Bedford gaol for unauthorized preaching. He experienced at first hand the nature of English justice as it applied to 'mechanick' preachers. To try to secure his release, his wife Elizabeth in August 1661 pleaded with the justices:[2] 'My Lord,' she said to Judge Hales, 'I make bold to come once again to your Lordship to know what may be done with my husband.'

> JUDGE HALES: Woman, I told thee before I could do thee no good; because they have taken that for a conviction which thy husband spoke at the sessions.
> WOMAN: My Lord, he is kept unlawfully in prison, they clap'd him up before there were any proclamation against the meetings; the indictment also is false . . .
> JUDGE TWISDON: (very angrily): What, you think we can do what we list; your husband is a breaker of the peace, and is convicted by the law.
> WOMAN: But my Lord, he was not lawfully convicted.
> JUSTICE CHESTER: But it is recorded, woman, it is recorded. (With which words he often endeavoured to stop her mouth, having no other argument to convince her, but it is recorded, it is recorded.)

Chester opined that Bunyan was 'a pestilent fellow' and Twisdon asked if he would stop preaching; to which Elizabeth replied, 'My Lord, he dares not leave preaching as long as he can speak,' but assured them 'that he desired to live peaceably, and to follow his calling, that his family might be maintained'. There then ensued the following exchange:

> WOMAN: My Lord, I have four small children, that cannot help themselves, of which one is blind, and have nothing to live upon, but the charity of good people.
>
> HALES: Hast thou four children?; thou art but a young woman to have four children.
>
> WOMAN: My Lord, I am but mother-in-law [step-mother] to them, having not been married to him yet full two years. Indeed I was with child when my husband was first apprehended. But being young and unaccustomed to such things, I being smayed [dismayed] at the news, fell into labour, and so continued for eight days, and then was delivered, but my child died.
>
> HALES: Alas poor woman!

But Twisdon told her that 'she made poverty her cloak' and understood that Bunyan 'was maintained better by running up and down a-preaching than by following [his] calling'.

> HALES: What is his calling?
>
> ANSWER: A Tinker, my Lord.
>
> WOMAN: Yes, and because he is a Tinker, and a poor man, therefore he is despised, and cannot have justice.

Bunyan and *The Pilgrim's Progress* are quoted at some length because they are representative statements about dissent in the seventeenth century and later. They focus on the experiences of an important section of the common people, the puritans – men and women who took the bible to be their guide for daily living and who subjected all matters of faith and worship to the test of scriptural warrant. Individual conscience, not the tradition of the church, was for them the supreme authority. They cared very little for outward forms and ceremonies, and very much for spiritual rebirth and the building of a godly community living under godly discipline. Until the civil war most of them remained within the Church of England, but from the 1640s increasing numbers broke away and formed separate congregations. Independency, or congregationalism, asserted the right of each local congregation to control its own affairs under leaders (pastors and elders) of its own choosing. Bunyan became a member of such an independent congregation in Bedford in 1653; and from 1656 began to preach in public. Puritanism emphasized the duty of those who had through God's grace gained assurance of salvation (the elect) to preach the word of God to all and sundry. The idea of labouring men (and also women) preaching was deeply offensive to the ruling classes, as Judge Twisdon's scornful remarks indicated. Elizabeth Bunyan was perfectly sincere when she said that her husband desired only to live peaceably with his neighbours. But to the justices he appeared to be a dangerous and pernicious fellow who, like Paul at Thessalonica, sought to turn the world upside down.

For that was indeed the social implication of puritan sectarianism, particularly of the more extreme kind that flourished among some tradesmen and artisans. The claim of ordinary men and women to be guided solely by the light of Christ within them and manifested in the individual conscience was profoundly disturbing, for it struck at the roots of established religion and social order. In a society dominated by an aristocratic and Anglican establishment — as England was from the seventeenth to the nineteenth centuries — any movement outside its paternalistic control was a radical departure, a potential threat to that deference, respect and subordination which was held to be necessary for social stability. The very existence of ideas and voluntary associations independent of traditional institutions and leaders was suspect. It was not necessary to profess liberal opinions to be branded as a subversive: the suspicion of being tainted with any form of religious deviance was taken to imply sympathy with upsetting the status quo. And this was as true for Methodists in the eighteenth and nineteenth centuries as for Bunyan and the sectaries in the seventeenth.

Bunyan as a young man had been a soldier in the parliamentary army; and it was in the crucible of civil war that popular puritanism came to the fore. For twenty years between 1640 and 1660 the country underwent a series of changes which historians have labelled the English Revolution, comparable in many respects to the French and Russian revolutions later. In 1640, after eleven years of personal rule, Charles I was compelled to summon parliament because he needed money. His attempts to impose episcopacy and a Prayer Book on Scotland had driven the Scots to armed resistance, and he was unable to subdue them without funds for an army. When parliament met it pressed home a long list of grievances against the king and his ministers. Two years later there followed a series of momentous events without parallel in the national history: civil war from 1642 to 1646 and renewed fighting in 1648–9; the execution of Charles I in 1649; a republican commonwealth from 1649 to 1660; and the restoration of the monarchy in 1660. As a coda, or delayed completion of the English Revolution, should be added the deposition of another king, James II, and the Glorious Revolution of 1688.

It is a moot point as to how much the common people were involved in the basic issues over which the civil war was fought. The view that the war was really only between rival sections of the ruling class (declining feudal order versus rising bourgeoisie, for instance) with the common people used simply as cannon-fodder is now generally regarded as too simplistic; and in any case does little to illuminate the problem from below. Class alignments were anything but clear-cut and, as in all civil wars, families were divided among themselves and localities acted in accordance with their own special needs and grievances. Nevertheless, Cavalier (meaning gentleman) and Roundhead (citizen with short hair) were terms of class as well as abuse when they were first used in 1641; and the nature of the division between royalists and parliamentarians is relevant to the role played, or not played, by the common people. A few broad generalizations may be helpful.

First, the country was divided geographically between the royalist north and west and the parliamentarian east and south. London, the main seaports, the industrial (clothing) areas, and the eastern counties were for parliament. The king drew support from the West Country, Wales, the still-Catholic areas of Lancashire, and some parts of the west Midlands including Oxford, which he made his headquarters. Second, the nobility and gentry were divided, some supporting parliament, and others (possibly a majority) the king. But whereas parliament could rely on the support of the industrial and merchant communities, the king was more dependent on the wealth and local power of the larger landlords who recruited and maintained his armies. Third, religious divisions were everywhere apparent, both between royalists and parliamentarians and also within the two rival camps. Puritans, for instance, were much divided among themselves: well-to-do Presbyterians (who wanted a hierarchical church organization based on presbyteries and synods, instead of on bishops) were contemptuous of the Independents who would not compromise the autonomy of each local congregation. Richard Baxter, who served as a chaplain in a parliamentary regiment, observed later that

> though it must be confessed that the public safety and liberty wrought very much with most, especially with the nobility and gentry who adhered to parliament, yet it was principally the differences about religious matters that filled up the parliament's armies and put resolution and valour into their soldiers, which carried them on in another manner than mercenary soldiers are carried on.

And he offered a puritan analysis of the two sides:

> The generality of the people . . . who were then called Puritans . . . that used to talk of God, and heaven, and Scripture, and holiness . . . adhered to the parliament. And on the other side, the gentry that were not so precise and strict against an oath, or gaming, or plays, or drinking, nor troubled themselves so much about the matters of God and the world to come, and the ministers and people that were for . . . dancing and recreations on the Lord's days, and those that made not so great a matter of every sin, but went to church and heard Common Prayer, and were glad to hear a sermon which lashed the Puritans. . . .[3]

Unfortunately we have no means of knowing how widely such a view was held among the rank-and-file supporters on either side, let alone among those who were uncommitted. There is evidence of popular support for the royalist cause. Baxter himself describes an incident in Kidderminster when the churchwarden tried to take down a crucifix from a cross in the churchyard and thereby attracted 'a crew of the drunken riotous party of the town (poor journeymen and servants) [who] took the alarm and ran altogether with weapons to defend the crucifix and the church images'. In royalist rural areas labourers and cottagers who had not the means to be independent would have little choice but to show their expected deference by supporting the king. For the parliamentary side there is more evidence to show the sort of people who were its supporters below the rank of gentry: they were, in general, small farmers, tradesmen, craftsmen and apprentices, in short the middle sort of people. They were small men with a measure of independence and the grievances common to this type of producer. Their puritanism and sense of godly discipline distinguished them from the rich above and the poor below them. Typically, the backbone of Baxter's puritan congregation in Kidderminster were the master weavers, who, he says, 'were not rich', but whose trade 'allowed them time enough to read or talk of holy things . . . and as they stand in their loom they can set a book before them or edify one another . . .' – very different from the journeymen and servants who had rioted in the churchyard.

Popular support for the parliamentary cause sprang from several different types of grievance and perception.[4] Agrarian discontent became anti-royalist when peasant farmers found themselves in conflict with large landowners who were backed up by the king and House of Lords. Such was the case in the fenlands of Lincolnshire, Cambridgeshire and Huntingdonshire, where drainage and the enclosure of commons and wastes provoked rural rebellion in 1641–2. Cromwell's sympathy for the tenants in their struggle doubtless stood him in good stead when he needed recruits for his regiments. Elsewhere similar disputes with the king or royalist landlords over enclosures, security of tenure and increases in rents and fines convinced small farmers that their best interests might not necessarily be served by a royalist victory. Taxation is always felt as a grievance, but particularly so by the small producer who suspects, often rightly, that he pays more than the rich. Charles I had already incurred much odium by his system of taxation, including the levying of shipmoney. Tithes were also particularly resented by the rural community, especially where, as a result of the dissolution of the monasteries, they had been impropriated and were owned by laymen to whom the payment was due. Nothing was better calculated to nurture anti-clericalism and to combine economic grievance with religious radicalism. King, lords and bishops were perceived as parts of a single establishment which oppressed the people at many different points.

Small men in the towns had even stronger reasons for siding with parliament. It was crown policy under the early Stuarts to support the urban oligarchies of wealthy merchants in their attempts to control the lesser merchants, tradesmen and craftsmen. In the cloth industry this took the form of a monopoly of the export trade by a small number of big London merchants organized as the Company of Merchant Adventurers. At Newcastle-upon-Tyne the Company of Hostmen monopolized the export of coal and thereby controlled the industry. In Shrewsbury, Chester and Leeds small cliques of wealthy merchants, with the assistance of the crown, dominated the municipal government and exploited their monopoly position at the expense of smaller merchants and producers. There thus developed a struggle of the smaller traders and craftsmen against the merchant oligarchy. The crown was clearly identified with the policy of the latter; only from parliament could the craftsmen as well as the clothiers and smaller provincial merchants hope for some favour. A democratic movement to give craftsmen a vote in the election of the officers of their livery companies and municipalities developed in the 1640s and 1650s, and this in turn led to radical political demands.

The growth of radicalism, political and religious, advanced fastest in London. From the very beginning of the crisis in 1641 the common people of the metropolis, led and encouraged by a small group of parliamentary puritans, had asserted themselves in no uncertain way. Complaints about the number of separatist religious congregations in London and the hordes of 'mechanic fellows' turned preacher are heard at this time; and their suppression was a frequently declared aim of royalist policy. The intervention of the people in politics was decisive in December 1641. Crowds of Londoners, mainly 'the lower sort of citizens' and apprentices, demonstrated against the king and in support of the commons, with demands for the abolition of bishops and the elimination of papists. When the time came for something more than mob action it was the common people of London who formed the rank and file of the parliamentary army. Several thousand citizens and apprentices enlisted under the earl of Essex in the summer of 1642, and it was they who, at Turnham Green in November, prevented Prince Rupert and the royalist cavalry from taking London and winning a quick victory for the king.

The most remarkable manifestation of radicalism however came a little later and from a different quarter. Although citizens organized in the trained bands were able to stem the initial royalist advance, local forces could not be relied on for long-term campaigning, and the parliamentary force which finally defeated the king was the New Model army under the command of Sir Thomas Fairfax and Oliver Cromwell. This famous army of eleven regiments of horse and twelve regiments of foot, formed in 1645, became an independent force, treated with both king and parliament, and was ultimately (after 1649) the supreme power in the land. It was at first recruited from both volunteers and pressed men, but after 1651 from volunteers only. The cavalry were usually superior to the infantry in education and social standing: they were paid more, and had to provide their own horses and accoutrements. They may not all have been like the men Cromwell recruited into his own regiment, who 'had the fear of God before them and made some conscience of what they did'. But in the political movements of 1647 and subsequently it is noticeable that the troopers of the cavalry took the lead. Within the New Model army promotion from the ranks to a commission was possible, and some of the men's leaders later became officers. Cromwell himself (in a famous phrase) preferred 'the plain russet-coated captain that knows what he fights for and loves what he knows' to 'that which you call a gentleman and is nothing else'. The eruption of radical sentiment came in 1647 as a result of grievances over arrears of pay and the attempt by a Presbyterian parliament to remove the threat to its own power by disbanding the army and sending several regiments to serve in Ireland. An extraordinary political ferment in the army was then revealed. The rank and file elected 'agitators' (agents) representing each troop, company and regiment, and set up a democratic organization to voice their demands. That the independents and sectaries were a strong and zealous element in the army was well known. To their radical

194

religious principles was now added social and political democracy. These views were set forth in the programme of the Levellers.

A good deal of attention (some historians would argue too much) has been paid to the Levellers in recent years. They have been lauded as pioneers of modern democracy and anticipators of the American constitution. There has been argument as to their social origins and doubt expressed whether their democratic programme for the franchise included servants and wage labourers (it certainly excluded women). The extent of their support among the rank-and-file has also been questioned; and it has been pointed out that the Levellers originated outside the army, among London artisans, and drew many of their ideas from John Lilburne. Nevertheless, with all these qualifications the Levellers stand out as a unique expression of ideas from the ranks of the parliamentary army which was their stronghold. Once again we have one of those rare moments when we can hear the voices of those who are normally inarticulate. We do not know (and in a sense it is of secondary importance) whether they were typical or representative of a majority of the rank-and-file. The significant point is that sentiments of equality and perceptions of conflict in society should have been made in the 1640s – as they had been in the Peasants' Revolt and were to be again later in the Chartist movement.

In the debates of the General Council of the army held in the church at Putney during October and November 1647 we have a remarkable record of the radical views of the troops and some of their officers. The speeches were taken down in shorthand and written up later. They are perhaps the nearest we shall ever get to oral history of the seventeenth century and have that spontaneous quality of men speaking their minds about the things they hold dear, not for effect or for posterity, but to achieve immediate ends. Generals Cromwell and Ireton are arguing with the agitators and Levellers about their proposals for democratic rights put forward in *An Agreement of the People*. The crux comes over the demand for an extension of the franchise.

MAXIMILIAN PETTY (a Leveller and civilian): We judge that all inhabitants that have not lost their birthright should have an equal voice in elections.

COLONEL THOMAS RAINBOROUGH (or Rainborow(e), commander of a regiment of foot): I think that the poorest he that is in England hath a life to live, as the greatest he; and therefore truly, sir, I think it's clear, that every man that is to live under a government ought first by his own consent to put himself under that government; and I do think that the poorest man in England is not at all bound in a strict sense to that government that he hath not had a voice to put himself under.

LIEUTENANT-GENERAL HENRY IRETON (Cromwell's son-in-law and right-hand man): I think that no person hath a right to an interest or share in the disposing of the affairs of the kingdom, and in determining or choosing those that shall determine what laws we shall be ruled by here – no person hath a right to this, that hath not a permanent fixed interest in this kingdom. . . . All the main thing that I speak for, is because I would have an eye to property.

Later in the debate he argued:

If there be anything at all that is a foundation of liberty it is this, that those who shall choose the law-makers shall be men freed from dependence upon others.

SERGEANT EDWARD SEXBY (a Suffolk man who had served as a trooper in Cromwell's regiment and was later promoted to Lt-Colonel): We have engaged in this kingdom and ventured our lives . . . to recover our birthrights and privileges as Englishmen. . . . There are many thousands of us soldiers that have ventured our lives; we have had little propriety in the kingdom as to our estates, yet we have had a birthright. But it seems now, except a man hath a fixed estate in this kingdom, he hath no right in this kingdom. I wonder we were so much deceived. If we had not a right to the kingdom, we were mercenary soldiers.

RAINBOROUGH (to Ireton): There is a great deal of difference between us two. If a man hath all he doth desire, he may wish to sit still; but if I think I have nothing at all of what I fought for, I do not think the argument holds that I must desist as well as he.[5]

The clash between two opposing interests and ideologies could not be clearer. On the one hand were the soldiers, claiming a right to the suffrage for every freeborn Englishman, a right which they had recently asserted by fighting for freedom; on the other Ireton and Cromwell arguing that the suffrage was based on property, not natural right. Beneath the surface were other attitudes and assumptions about class divisions and the struggle of the 'Plaine Men of England against the Rich and Mightie'. These issues and arguments were not resolved, but were to be repeated continuously for the next 250 years. The Putney debates however were but one dramatic incident in an unprecedented ferment of argument which poured forth in manifestoes, petitions, remonstrances, broadsides, pamphlets, journals, books and sermons in the 1640s and 1650s. The famous Thomason collection of such material (now in the British Library), formed between 1640 and 1661 by George Thomason, a London bookseller, contains over 22,000 items, including 15,000 pamphlets. In this 'teeming freedom', as one contemporary described it, the Levellers put forward the demands and voiced the sentiments of a thoroughgoing radicalism.

None of the Levellers' demands was met in their own day, and their practical achievements were negligible. We do not however need to resort to the historian's familiar and largely meaningless cliché that they were 'ahead of their time' to assess their significance. Although the Levellers were not strong enough to carry out their programme, the perceptions on which it was based were for them, and perhaps for others, a valid way of looking at the world. Their attempts to change society, even though unsuccessful, are part of the history of the common people; for history (particularly popular history) is more than simply a record of what succeeded.

For the Levellers the basic conflict in society was between rich and poor. In the first category they included aristocrats, landowners, merchants and all who did not have to perform manual labour; by the poor they meant small traders, farmers and craftsmen, all of whom had to work with their hands. Hatred of the rich came not so much from envy of their possessions as from the observation that the rich were also able to exercise power in all its forms to exploit other men. The poor were not pitied for their poverty but because they were weak, and ultimately therefore unfree. The Levellers subscribed to a simple labour theory based on the natural right of every man to the fruits of his own labour; with the corollary that to take it away was theft. Freedom was essentially the right to the property in a man's own labour, which secured his independence. To account for the prevailing lack of freedom the Levellers had recourse to history and developed the theory of the Norman yoke: 'The history of our forefathers since they were conquered by the Normans, doth manifest that this nation hath been held in bondage all along ever since by the policies and force of the officers of trust in the Commonwealth, amongst whom, we always esteemed kings the chiefest. . . .'[6] William the Conqueror stole the land from the people to give to his barons, which was the origin and only basis of the aristocratic system of titles and landholding: 'Hence come landlord, tenant, holds, tenures, etc. which are slavish ties and badges upon men, grounded originally on conquest and power.' The recent civil war had been fought to recover the lost liberties of the people of England: the freeborn Englishmen ('with our swords in our hands') had asserted their birthright. A rough equalitarianism accompanied these sentiments: 'For as God created every man free in Adam: so by nature are all alike freemen born. . . .'

These were the perceptions of the 'plain men', the middle sort of people, and those whom John Lilburne described as 'the hobnails, clouted shoes, the private soldiers, the leather and woollen aprons and the laborious and industrious people . . .'[7] They scorned and resented the classes above them who did not work but who arranged the world for their own convenience and profit. Socially they were the small men; economically they were the typical independent producers; and the Leveller programme faithfully mirrored their interests. They wanted an effective say in the making of decisions which closely affected them, and they saw that they would never achieve that without political power. Hence their concern for democratic government at the local and national levels. Kings, lords and bishops should all be abolished, and supreme power vested in a parliament elected by, and directly responsible to the people. Lawyers, priests and merchants were enemies of the people. The law should be simplified and purged of Latin and French phraseology (another imposition of the Norman Conquest), so that the people could handle their own legal affairs without the need for lawyers. There should be no more imprisonment for debt. The monopoly of the Merchant Adventurers was to be broken, and the merchant oligarchies everywhere were to be superseded by elected officials. Bishops and priests were exercisers of a similar oligarchic and monopoly power which served only to enslave the people. Rural grievances were also on the agenda. Tithes were to be abolished, and there was to be an end to the enclosure of commons and wastes.

None of these demands today seems outrageous; but they did to the governing classes in the seventeenth century. Altogether the implications of the programme were revolutionary: they amounted to nothing less than the triumph of all the 'plain and mean people throughout the land'. The world would indeed be turned upside down. Some Leveller leaders would have denied this. Lilburne for instance declared that the Levellers 'have been the truest and constantest asserters of liberty and propriety (which are quite opposite to communitie and levelling) that have been in the whole land'.[8] But the True Levellers, or Diggers, thought otherwise.

On 1 April 1649 a small group of about thirty or forty people began to dig and plant the common land on St George's Hill in Surrey. They were mainly labouring men and their families, and they confidently hoped that five thousand others would join them. Their leaders were William Everard, a soldier who had been cashiered from the New Model army on account of his radicalism, and Gerrard Winstanley, a small cloth merchant from London who had been ruined by the economic depression of the early 1640s and who was then living at nearby Cobham. The intention was to cultivate the land communally, to make the earth (in Winstanley's favourite phrase) 'a common treasury', which God had intended it to be. 'The work we are going about is this,' declared *The True Levellers' Standard Advanced*: 'to dig up George's Hill and the waste ground thereabouts, and to sow corn, and to eat our bread together by the sweat of our brows.'[9] But the local inhabitants were bitterly opposed to the Diggers and set about harassing them. They were repeatedly attacked and beaten; their crops were uprooted, their tools destroyed, and their rough houses were burned. In July they were arrested and taken before the local magistrates. Heavy fines were imposed; and in execution of the sentence bailiffs were sent to take away Winstanley's few cattle. The persecution of the Diggers continued, urged on by the lord of the manor and the local parson; and after struggling on for a year the little colony was broken up. The Diggers planned to extend their colonies throughout the country. The poor, they said, could right their condition only by cultivating the commons and wastes, which were their rightful possession and from which they had been disinherited by 'the Norman Bastard' and his followers. Colonies were begun at Cobham (in addition to St George's Hill) in Surrey, Wellingborough (Northamptonshire), Cox Hall (Kent), Iver (Buckinghamshire), and perhaps in other places too. But none of these seems to have lasted very long, and after 1650 the Digger movement was effectively dead.

Winstanley has an honoured place in the pantheon of the Left as a pioneer communist. In the history of the common people he is also representative of that other minority tradition of popular religious radicalism, which, although it reached a crescendo during the Interregnum, had existed since the Middle Ages and was to continue into modern times. Totally opposed to the established church and also separate from (yet at times overlapping) orthodox puritanism, was a third culture which was lower-class and heretical. At its centre was a belief in the direct relationship between God and man, without the need of any institution or formal rites. Emphasis was on an inner spiritual experience and obedience to the voice of God within each man and woman. This inner-light religion appeared in many different sects, though the best known and longest lived were the Quakers. In a more extreme form the doctrine of the 'free spirit', as expressed by the Ranters in their pursuit of total emancipation, led to self-deification. They argued that man became God and in God's name could act with the freedom and self-justification with which God acted. In this obliteration of the difference between God and man, the infinite and the finite, they slipped into antinomianism and the Pelagian heresy; and at this point were close to the popular neoplatonism described in the last chapter. Amidst the turmoil of civil war and the shock of the king's execution such ideas flourished, popular prophets multiplied and millenarian hopes were rife. Winstanley was not alone in his conviction that the old world was 'running up like parchment in the fire and wearing away'. Among soldiers in the army and artisans and labouring people in London were many who felt that the prophecies of Daniel and Revelation were about to be fulfilled, that the last days had come, and that the vials of wrath were about to be poured out. Daniel's vision of the rise and fall of four successive empires, after which would come a kingdom that would last for ever, inspired the formation of a sect of Fifth Monarchy Men, drawn mainly from the Baptists and Independents.

Across this religious landscape wandered many colourful sectarian leaders. George Fox, a shoemaker and grazier from Leicestershire and founder of the Quakers, walking barefoot through Lichfield market place crying, 'Woe unto the bloody city of Lichfield,' saw in a vision that 'there ran like a channel of blood down the streets, and the market place was like a pool of blood'. But no one stopped him, and his friends merely said, 'Alack George! where are thy shoes?'[10] James Nayler was a yeoman farmer from Yorkshire who had served as quartermaster in a parliamentary cavalry regiment and was a friend of Fox. In October 1656 he rode into Bristol like the messiah, with women disciples strewing their garments before him and crying, 'Holy, Holy, Holy.' For this blasphemy poor Nayler was by order of parliament so cruelly punished with whipping, mutilation and imprisonment that he died three years later. From 1652 dates the 'commission' of a London tailor, Lodowick Muggleton, and his cousin John Reeve, to proclaim themselves as the Two Witnesses of Revelation 11. They were the Lord's last messengers before the second coming, mandated to declare a new system of faith and empowered to pronounce eternal life or death on individuals: 'God hath chosen us two only, and hath put the two-edged sword of the Spirit into our mouths . . ., that whom we are made to pronounce blessed, are blessed to eternity, and whom we are made to pronounce cursed, are cursed to eternity.'[11] They made full use of this authority by damning and blessing their contemporaries. And so one could multiply the number of bizarre doings and unorthodox beliefs of Seekers, Anabaptists, Socinians, Brownists, Familists and Ranters. These were the people who kept their hats on before magistrates and superior officials, refused to swear oaths, whose pacifism made them reject military service, and who were familiar with the gaols of every county in the land.

It has usually been assumed that most of the sects either disappeared at the end of the seventeenth century or toned themselves down in the eighteenth century into respectable, middle-class dissenting minorities like the Quakers, [Ana]Baptists and Congregationalists. But there is some evidence that the tradition of mystical religion, millenarianism and antinomianism continued at the popular level throughout the eighteenth century and surfaced again in the 1790s. Ranterism did not completely die out – as John Wesley discovered in the 1740s; humble prophets and prophetesses continued to appear throughout the eighteenth and nineteenth centuries; and the last known member of the tiny sect of Muggletonians died only in the 1970s.

George Fox in his *Journal* records how in 1651, before the battle of Worcester, attempts were made, unsuccessfully, to press him for a soldier. This may serve to remind us that it was the civil war as much as the issues of religious radicalism that probably occupied the minds of numbers of ordinary people. How to assess the impact of the war is not by any means obvious. There is a lack of quantifiable evidence about the actual behaviour of the common people in the civil war, and very few accounts of army life or of the fighting by soldiers in the ranks. The problem is to find out just what the civil war meant to the majority of the population, both those who took an active part in it and those who did not. By no means every man of eligible age 'went for a soldier', either voluntarily or by impressment. At the height of the conflict each side had about 60 to 70,000 armed troops, but the numbers engaged in the major battles were less than this. At Marston Moor in the summer of 1644 the royalist army numbered about 18,000 men and the parliamentary forces about 26,000. Some 4150 royalists were killed and 1500 taken prisoner. The victorious parliamentarians lost no more than 300 killed, although many more were wounded. At Naseby the following year the royalist army of 9000 men was defeated by the New Model numbering about 14,000. The royalist casualties were 400 to 1000 killed and 4500 taken prisoner; the parliamentary army lost no more than 150 killed. By modern, and even by contemporary continental standards, these numbers are small; though to the men involved they were probably larger than any other assembly (except possibly a London crowd) that they had taken part in.

One might have expected that for these men the army and especially the experience of battle would have left an indelible mark on their lives; but if it were so it has left no trace. The civil war from below remains hidden. No common soldier or non-commissioned officer has left an account of what it was actually like to stand behind a pike facing Prince Rupert's or Cromwell's charging cavalry. We know from recent research that the common soldier's view of his involvement in a battle is very different from his commander's or later historians' concepts of winning and losing. The soldier has no well-ordered idea of what is going on, but only a frightening and very immediate physical experience in the company of a little band of comrades. To the civilian and quite inexperienced soldiers who made up the bulk of the armies on both sides in 1642 (and later) the bewilderment must have been total. From the few chronicles that survive we learn a little about army life but nothing about the soldier's own perception of battle.

Nehemiah Wharton, a London apprentice, became a sergeant in the London volunteers under the earl of Essex in the summer and autumn of 1642, and wrote an account of his adventures in a series of letters to his former master.[12] The highlights of his army career seem to have been poaching the deer of a royalist squire to feast his officers, defacing 'popish' churches and burning their communion rails, and listening to godly sermons from his favourite preachers. He has little to say about actually fighting the cavaliers (despite boasting that 'our soldiers . . . were crying out for a dish of Cavaliers to supper'), but much upon the discomforts of marching in wet weather and the difficulty of finding quarters. The war for him was made up of innumerable daily happenings – some exciting, some boring – which contrasted with his normal civilian life. More of the perils of civil war is conveyed by another sergeant, Henry Foster, who served with the London trained bands in 1643. He describes how the enemy pursued and attacked them in a narrow lane near Aldermaston in Berkshire:[13]

they came upon us with a great body of foot and horse: our London brigade marched in the rear, and a forlorn hope [i.e. picked troops for attack] of six hundred musketiers in the rear of them, besides a great number of our horse: but our horse which brought up our rear, durst not stand to charge the enemy, but

fled, running into the narrow lane, routed our own foot, tram-
pling many of them under their horse feet, crying out to them,
'Away, away, every man shift for his life, you are all dead men';
which caused a most strange confusion amongst us. We fired ten
or twelve drakes [i.e. small cannon] at the enemy, but they came
upon us very fiercely, having their foot on the other side of the
hedges; many of our waggons were overthrowne and broken:
others cut their traces and horse-harnesse, and run away with
their horses, leaving their waggons and carriages behind them:
our foot fired upon the enemy's horse very bravely, and slew
many of them; some report above one hundred, and not ten of
ours: some that we took prisoners our men were so enraged at
them that they knocked out their brains with the butt end of
their muskets.

Foster was also in the thick of the fighting at the second battle of
Newbury. His regiment of the London trained bands suffered
heavily from the royalist artillery: 'They did some execution
amongst us at first, and were somewhat dreadful when men's
bowels and brains flew in our faces.' But, he adds, 'Blessed be God
that gave us courage, so that we kept our ground, and after a while
feared them not.' The next day he viewed the dead:

> there lay about one hundred stript naked in that field where our
> two regiments stood in battalia. This night the enemy conveyed
> away about thirty cart load of maimed and dead men, as the
> town-people credibly reported to us, and I think they might
> have carried away twenty cart load more of their dead men the
> next morning, they buried thirty in one pit. Fourteen lay dead in
> one ditch.

The horror and tragedy of the war was not limited to the
combatants. Any town that resisted either army could expect to be
burned and plundered when the attackers were successful. Such
was the fate of Birmingham in 1643 and Leicester in 1645 when
they tried to hold out against Prince Rupert and his troops. Lawful
plunder was allowed the parliamentarian troops when they
stormed Dundee in 1651 and at the capture of Sherborne Castle
and Basing House in 1645. In the seventeenth century there was

widespread fear of soldiers, whether hostile or friendly, because they were known to be cruel, lawless and licentious. The failure to pay or provision the troops adequately, especially the royal armies, forced them to live off the land, that is at the expense of the local inhabitants. Free quarter was particularly resented. Under this system householders were compelled to provide food and lodging for a given number of soldiers at a fixed rate, and were given a ticket as a claim for future payment. Supplies of food, horses and all kinds of provisions for the troops in any district were also requisitioned under promise that they would be paid for later. Each side imposed levies on the areas under its control to pay for the garrisons, and in disputed areas like the west Midlands the unfortunate inhabitants had to maintain both royalist and parliamentary forces. A midland farmer wrote:

> I had eleven horses taken away by the King's soldiers and four of the eleven were worth £40 . . . the soldiers took the other nine away and I could never have them more. . . . Since again . . . going to market with a load of corn, the Earl of Manchester's soldiers [i.e. parliamentary] met with my men and took away my whole team of horses . . . the King's soldiers call me Roundhead . . . and the Parliament soldiers tell me I pay rent to Worcester [in royalist hands].[14]

In such cases resentment at having to pay the cost of the war may well have been stronger than allegiance to one side or the other, and led naturally to an attitude of 'a plague on both your houses'.

Indifference to the issues of the war among the common people was noted by contemporary observers. 'There were few of the common people that cared much for either of the causes, but would have taken either side for pay or plunder,' commented the royalist philosopher, Thomas Hobbes. After the surrender of royal garrisons in 1645–7 numbers of the king's soldiers had no objection to enlisting in the New Model army. But deeper and more widespread than this was a desire to be left alone in peace to get on with the task of making a living. Lord Clarendon, a loyal supporter of the king, admitted that 'the number of those who desired to sit still was greater than those who desired to engage in either party'. At the beginning of the war there was no lack of volunteers on either side, but from 1643 impressment had to be used. Desertion was very common, and commanders were always complaining that after a battle their troops wanted to do nothing but go home. An invincible localism pervaded many of the parliamentary units; once the royalist threat in their neighbourhood had been removed the troops saw no reason to stay in the army, but expected to return to their farms and looms. In some parts of the country there was evidence of active neutralism. Large areas of the south and west were affected in 1645 by armed risings of the Clubmen. They were associations of local inhabitants who combined to resist invasion of their area by external, plundering armies. Their existence suggests that in Dorset, Wiltshire, Berkshire, Glamorgan, Somerset, Shropshire, Herefordshire and other counties, the common people desired peace, neutrality and as little involvement in the issues of the civil war as possible. When they had to make decisions between one side and the other they were made in the light of traditional, provincial interests, remote from the national conflict between king and parliament.

To what extent then were the common people affected by the civil war? A general assessment would be that, first, a minority consciously and deliberately supported, for various reasons, either the king or parliament; a small percentage of the adult male population was actively engaged in the fighting – many of them not by choice; but in rural areas, whether controlled by royalists or parliamentarians, habits and expectations of deference made it difficult for ordinary people not to follow the preference of their social superiors and become involved in the war. Second, the cost of the war fell heavily and directly on a wide section of the people, who universally resented it. Third, there was a widespread desire and determination not to take sides if at all possible. From the perspective of the common people the civil war may not be quite as central as traditional histories supposed. Catastrophic as the war could be for individual towns and agricultural areas, it may have been little worse than the natural hazards of fire, plague and harvest failure which were endemic to seventeenth-century society. It is possible that 100,000 people (out of a total population of about 5 million) were killed in the whole of the civil war. This is about the same as the total deaths in London during 1665, the year of the Great Plague – and the visitations of plague in 1603 and 1625 had also been very severe. No single disaster in the civil war could have been worse than the experience of a labouring man or woman who lived through the horrors of the Great Plague and then the inferno of the Great Fire the following year, when 88 churches, 13,200 houses and two-thirds of the metropolis were destroyed in four days. This is not to minimize the impact of the civil war, but to set it against the hazards of daily life in a society only too prone to disaster involving the common people in want and hardship. Despite the fears of conservatives and the hopes of radicals, the English revolution and civil war did not turn the world upside down. But they helped to release ideas which later did just that.

PART III

The Working Class (1780–1880)

7. The Emergence of the Working Class

Numerous and far-reaching as were all the changes in the history of the common people since 1066, they are completely eclipsed by the magnitude of the changes that we have now to consider. Possibly the only time parallel to the events of 1760–1830 is to be found in the Neolithic Age when man discovered how to become a settled agriculturist and herdsman instead of a hunter and nomad. Within the short span of one man's lifetime England changed more fundamentally than it had for hundreds of years before. And the process then begun is continuing today, not only in England but in the rest of the world. To these momentous changes historians have given the name Industrial Revolution.

Essentially the Industrial Revolution created the kind of society with which we are familiar. There is for most of us an indescribable but inescapable feeling of remoteness about all pre-industrial societies, be they ancient, medieval or early modern. We are conscious of certain barriers to understanding, and these barriers are not primarily ignorance of the material facts of life in the past (for we can easily read books and look at pictures of our ancestors at work and play) but lack of sympathy for their fundamental ideas and attitudes. Only from the second half of the nineteenth century do we begin to recognize values and concerns that seem akin to our own. The Industrial Revolution was the great watershed in recent history, dividing what we know as modern England from all previous types of society. This transformation was more than a series of technological innovations and economic changes. It offered to men, for the first time in human history, the way toward controlling their environment instead of being at its mercy. The possibility of material abundance for all was no longer an idle dream, although it took time before the full implications of this change were grasped by any large number of people. With the appearance of these new practical possibilities men's ideas and assumptions also changed. The Industrial Revolution was a new way in which men looked at themselves, at society, and at the world at large. Ultimately, it offered a new dimension of freedom; though its immediate effect for large numbers of labouring people was quite the reverse.

There can be no mistaking the main areas of change. Before about 1760 England was basically an agricultural country, with a small population, a low standard of living for the majority of the people, a hierarchical social system, and an aristocratic oligarchy in political control. As a result of the Industrial Revolution she became a nation dependent on her manufacturing and extractive industries, with a large population, great urban centres, vastly increased wealth (some of which slowly percolated down to the lower classes), an increasing degree of social mobility, and political democracy. It can be said without exaggeration that virtually no institution or aspect of life was unaffected by these changes. Much of the very face of England that we see today did not exist two hundred years ago, so thickly lies the blanket of industrialism.

It is nowadays taken for granted that if a nation is to become prosperous and powerful it must have an industrial revolution. Following the British lead, most Western and some Eastern societies industrialized in the nineteenth and twentieth centuries, and the idea of an industrial revolution is now accepted as a definite phase in the life of modern nations. Everywhere the main characteristics of industrialization have been the same, although the details have varied according to the time and local context. The British Industrial Revolution, however, was unique in that it was the first. Unlike all succeeding industrial revolutions, it was endogenous; that is, it developed spontaneously and internally, without any significant stimulus from outside and without any model to copy. Once it had happened it was irreversible. It was not deliberately planned, nor did its pioneers have any star to guide them. Just why the first industrial revolution should have occurred in England (rather than in, say, Holland or France) and at the particular time in the eighteenth century that it did continues to puzzle historians. But they are agreed that the Industrial Revolution was a complex and interlocking series of changes which defy any single-cause explanation.

Labouring men, however, were not aware of living through the world's first industrial revolution. Contemporaries did not use the term Industrial Revolution (which was introduced only in 1884) but talked rather of progress and machinery. Nevertheless they were aware of great and sudden changes affecting their mode of living; and they reacted in various ways, depending upon their position in the social structure. But if Industrial Revolution suggests that a series of inventions in the textile, iron and engineering industries transformed the whole of English economic and social life as suddenly and as completely as political change was effected by the American or French revolutions, it is somewhat misleading. While men and women who lived between 1760 and 1830 were constantly amazed at the pace of the changes going on around them, in fact the changes were largely confined to certain sectors of the economy, though these tended to be the pace-setters for the rest. Industrialization was a process, or series of modifications of traditional society, which during the past two hundred years has steadily shrunk in relation to industrial England. In this process the common people were transformed from the labouring poor into the working class. The first and most acute phase of this transition was between 1760 and 1830.

Most accounts of the Industrial Revolution nowadays start with population. The number of people in a country is a crucial factor in determining what sort of lives they are likely to be living. Leaving aside other variables, an England of 2 to 3 million people, as in the Middle Ages, will be a vastly different society from modern Britain with over 55 million, by sheer virtue of the difference in numbers; for the quantitative difference means also a difference in quality and sets the bounds for the potentialities and limits of human achievement. The size of the population in the early eighteenth century was between 5·5 and 6 million for England and Wales; with a high birth rate (35 or more live births per 1000 of population per annum) and a death rate only slightly less, so that the rate of natural increase was low. But beginning about 1740 the population began to grow, and it continued to do so throughout the nineteenth and twentieth centuries. Each decade there were, and are, more people than ever before; the same was true of the other nations of Western Europe. The first census, taken in 1801, showed that the population of England and Wales had grown to 9 million; by 1831 it was 14 million; and at the end of the century

32·5 million. From 1750 the rate of growth accelerated each decade, until it reached a peak in the period 1811–21.

The massive facts of population growth are not in dispute. What is arguable is the explanation of how and why this increase came about. Without entering into the niceties of this debate, it will be obvious that a rise in population can be caused by several factors: an increase in the birth rate, a decrease in mortality (death rate), and immigration. Any of these, if on a sufficient scale, could affect the rate of population growth, and a combination of two or more would be decisive. Until 1740 mortality was high, especially in London. Thereafter the death rate declined steadily, from about 33·5 to 21 per 1000 in the 1820s. Contrary to older opinions, this decline in mortality is not to be attributed to progress in medical knowledge or techniques, but rather to a general improvement in standards of living, which strengthened people's resistance to disease and mitigated some of the worst harshness of life. In particular there was some improvement in infant mortality, which was where the greatest waste of human life occurred. The incidence of mortality, however, was not uniform between different social classes, and the mean chances of life differed accordingly. In the 1840s the average age of death among gentlemen and professional men in Leeds was forty-four; among tradesmen and farmers, twenty-seven; and among operatives, nineteen.

The population explosion created the basis of the new labour force required for the Industrial Revolution, but this was not how the common people perceived their new role. They were aware only that the conditions of their daily labour were changing, sometimes suddenly and drastically, more often subtly and gradually. To labouring people, as to other classes, it was soon borne in that the new population would result in a new kind of society, and that discussion of population problems was really about the whole future of society. How far an increasing population was responsible for an increase in economic output and how far economic growth encouraged a rise in population are hard to determine. But it is clear that the combination of unprecedented growth of both economic wealth and population was the basis of the Industrial Revolution.

Economic growth can be documented in various ways, as for instance by the increase in average real income per head which rose sevenfold between 1688 and 1959; but we do not know how much of this was enjoyed by the common people. For them economic growth resulted in the creation of new kinds of work and the modification or destruction of existing jobs. New types of worker were called into existence and traditional workers had to adapt to new modes of production. These changes can be seen most clearly if we look at one particular industry – textiles – although it should be emphasized that the same basic methods and organization were found in other trades too. We have seen earlier how the woollen industry was widely dispersed throughout all parts of the country, but by the eighteenth century three regions were pre-eminent: the West Riding of Yorkshire, East Anglia, and the West Country. Under the domestic system the Yorkshire clothiers were still independent producers, but elsewhere the weavers had become virtually employees of middlemen or merchants. In the hosiery branch of textiles, centred in Leicester and Nottingham, the stocking knitters paid a rent for the knitting frames which belonged wholly to the master stockingers.

However, it was not in wool or hosiery that the breakthrough in economic expansion that powered the Industrial Revolution first came, but in the newer and smaller branch of textiles: cotton. Localized mainly in Lancashire and parts of lowland Scotland, the cotton industry was organized similarly to other textiles, with merchants and a putting-out system. Samuel Bamford, a weaver from Middleton, Lancashire, described the system as he remembered it around the turn of the century. The following account is from his autobiography, *Early Days* (1849):

> My uncle's domicile, like all the others, consisted of one principal room called 'the house'; on the same floor with this was a loom-shop capable of containing four looms, and in the rear of the house on the same floor, were a small kitchen and a buttery.

Bamford then describes how he accompanied his uncle to Manchester, carrying the woven cloth and returning with fresh material for the following week's work:

The family were, at that time, chiefly employed by Messrs. Samuel and James Broadbent, of Cannon Street, and as the work was for the most part 'pollicat' and 'romoll' handkerchiefs, with a finer reed, occasionally, of silk and cotton 'garments', or handkerchiefs, the 'bearing-home wallet' was often both bulky and heavy; and when it happened to be too much so for one person to carry, a neighbour's wallet would be borrowed, the burden divided into two, and I would go with one part over my shoulder, behind or before my uncle. . . .

The warehouse of Messrs. Broadbent was nearly at the top of Cannon Street, on the right-hand side. We mounted some steps, went along a covered passage, and up a height or two of stairs, to a landing place, one side of which was railed off by the bannister, and the other furnished with a seat for weavers to rest upon when they arrived. Here we should probably find some half-dozen weavers and winders, waiting for their turn to deliver in their work and to receive fresh material; and the business betwixt workman and putter-out was generally done in an amicable, reasonable way. . . .

It would sometimes happen that warp or weft would not be ready until after dinner, and on such occasions, my uncle having left his wallet in care of the putter-out, would go downstairs and get paid at the counting-house, and from thence go to the public-house where we lunched on bread and cheese, or cold meat and bread, with ale, to which my uncle added his ever-favourite pipe of tobacco. This house, which was the 'Hope and Anchor', in the old churchyard, was also frequented by other weavers; the putter-out at Broadbents generally dined there in the parlour, and when he had dined he would come and take a glass of ale, smoke his pipe, and chat with the weavers. . . .[1]

By Bamford's time the domestic system had been undermined, for his uncle was in effect simply an out-worker for a Manchester firm. This undermining came about through a series of inventions in the textile industry that enabled it greatly to increase its output, and thereby started a chain reaction that set in motion further changes in the rest of the economy. The first of these major inventions in textiles was John Kay's flying shuttle, perfected in 1733 and widely adopted in cotton by the 1760s. It enabled the weaver to produce both more and broader cloth, thus increasing still further the imbalance between the spinning and weaving sectors of the trade. Consequently, the next inventions were in spinning: James Hargreaves's spinning jenny of the 1760s, which could spin many threads at once – at first it had eight, later 120 spindles; Richard Arkwright's waterframe (patented in 1769), to produce stronger cotton yarn suitable for warp (hitherto linen had been used); and Samuel Crompton's mule (1779), which combined the jenny and the waterframe. The weavers were now assured of a plentiful supply of yarn, and the 1790s became the golden age of handloom weaving, when work was plentiful and wages high. This period of prosperity, however, did not last long, for in the 1780s the first powerloom was developed, and although its adoption was slow for some years, by 1820 there were 14,000 powerlooms in Britain, and by 1833, 100,000.

Judged by today's standards, the early textile machines seem relatively simple. Yet it was not the new technology alone, but the new industrial system which it implied, that was revolutionary. The new machines required power to drive them, and so could not be housed in the homes of the people but only in what contemporaries called 'manufactories'. Water provided the motive power, and the early cotton factories or mills of the 1770s and 1780s were therefore located in remote areas of the Pennines and the Derbyshire hills where there was a plentiful supply of swift-flowing water. The new industry was initially based in country factories. This stage of the Industrial Revolution soon proved to be a false dawn, for in the 1780s the steam engine was perfected and immediately applied to driving textile machinery. Cotton spinners were thus freed from their dependence on water power, and further development of factories thence took place in urban areas where labour was more plentiful and coal supplies not far away. The basic elements in the pattern of modern British industrialism had begun to emerge: steam-powered machine production in urban factories. Manchester, which more than any other city was the symbol of the new industrial age, accurately reflected these changes. In 1773, with a population of 27,000, Manchester had not a single spinning mill; by 1802 the population was 95,000 and there were fifty-two cotton mills.

In the early stages of the Industrial Revolution the employers' desire for cheap labour and the need to locate the early water-driven mills in isolated places where there was little local supply of labour led to some of the worst practices of early industrialism, such as the employment of children. To overcome the labour shortage, pauper children from London workhouses were bound apprentice to northern mill-owners who worked them long hours and boarded them in dormitories (apprentice houses). In one notorious case, reported to the House of Commons in 1815, a Lancashire mill-owner agreed to take one idiot with every twenty normal children supplied by a London parish. The system of pauper apprenticeship in factories declined after legislation against it in 1816, but children continued to be employed as wage earners, and their working life differed little from the previous conditions. The following passage describes the experiences of a ten-year-old parish apprentice at Litton Mill in Derbyshire in 1815–16:

[The 'Prentice House] was a large stone house surrounded by a wall from two to three yards high with but one door, which was kept locked. It was capable of lodging about one hundred and fifty prentices. . . .

We went to the mill at five o'clock without breakfast, and worked till about eight or nine, when they brought us our breakfast, which consisted of water porridge with oat-cake in it and onions to savour it with, in a tin can. This we ate as best we could, the wheel never stopping. We worked on till dinner time, which was not regular, sometimes half-past twelve, sometimes one. Our dinner was thus served to us. Across the door way of the room was a cross-bar like a police bar, and on the inside of the bar stood an old man with a stick to guard the provisions. These consisted of Derbyshire oat-cakes cut into four pieces, and ranged in two stacks. The one was buttered and the other treacled. By the side of the oat-cake were cans of milk piled up – butter-milk and sweet-milk. As we came up to the bar one by one the old man called out 'Which'll 'ta have, butter or treacle, sweet or sour?' We then made our choice, drank down the milk and ran back to the mill with the oat-cake in our hand, without ever sitting-down. We then worked on till nine or ten at night without bite or sup.[2]

King Cotton powered the first industrial revolution and its most distinctive form of organization was the factory system. Objectively this was simply a system of concentrated large-scale production, using power machinery and large numbers of operatives, together with the correspondingly necessary social institutions. Until 1850 the factory system was still mainly confined to the textile industries. The Factory Acts were designed to regulate working conditions in cotton and woollen mills, and the home of the factory system was assumed to be Lancashire, the West Riding of Yorkshire, and parts of Scotland.

The factory operatives represented for most observers the heart of the new industrial civilization, about whose benefits or iniquities there was much argument. As always, investigators tended to find what they were looking for: the lot of the factory operative was presented both as a state of continual misery and as a life of modest comfort and respectability. Here are two contrasting examples. The first is a rosy description of the homes of the operatives near Messrs Ashworth's model cotton mill at Turton, near Bolton, Lancashire. It was written by William Cooke Taylor in his *Notes of a Tour in the Manufacturing Districts* (1842):

The situation [of Banktop, the operatives' village], though open and airy, is not unsheltered; the cottages are built of stone, and contain from four to six rooms each; back-premises with suitable conveniences are attached to them all. . . . I visited the interior of nearly every cottage; I found all well, and very many respectably, furnished: there were generally a mahogany table and chest of drawers. Daughters from most of the houses, but wives, as far as I could learn, from none, worked in the factory. Many of the women were not a little proud of their housewifery, and exhibited the Sunday wardrobes of their husbands, the stock of neatly folded shirts, etc.; . . . I found that there were some processes connected with the cotton manufacture which the women were permitted to execute in their own houses. 'The pay', said one of the women, 'is not much, but it helps to boil the pot.' . . . I was informed by the operatives that permission to rent one of the cottages was regarded as a privilege and favour, that it was in fact a reward reserved for honesty, industry and sobriety. . . . All were not merely contented with their situation, but proud of it. . . . It is not easy to fix upon a statistical test for measuring the intelligence of the adult operatives. I found clocks and small collections of books in all their dwellings; several had wheel-barometers. . . . I have more than once gone down in the evening to Turton Mills, to see the operatives coming from work. . . . The boys were as merry as crickets: there was not one of the girls who looked as if she would refuse an invitation to a dance.[3]

A very different impression is left by William Dodd's account in his *The Factory System Illustrated* (1842) of a young girl factory worker in Manchester in 1841. After the watchman has knocked on the window at 4.30 in the morning, the girl's mother

rouses the unwilling girl to another day of toil. At length you hear her on the floor; the clock is striking five. Then, for the first time, the girl becomes conscious of the necessity for haste; and having slipped on her clothes, and (if she thinks there is time) washed herself, she takes a drink of cold coffee, which has been left standing in the fireplace, a mouthful of bread (if she can eat it), and having packed up her breakfast in her handkerchief, hastens to the factory. The bell rings as she leaves the threshold of her home. Five minutes more, and she is in the factory, stripped and ready for work. The clock strikes half-past five; the engine starts, and her day's work commences.

At half-past seven . . . the engine slacks its pace (seldom stopping) for a short time till the hands have cleaned the machinery and swallowed a little food. It then goes on again, and continues at full speed till twelve o'clock when it stops for dinner. Previously to leaving the factory, and in her dinner-hour, she has her machine to clean. The distance of the factory is about five minutes' walk from her home. I noticed every day that she came in at half-past twelve, or within a minute or two, and once she was over the half hour; the first thing she did was to wash herself, then get her dinner (which she was seldom able to eat), and pack up her drinking for the afternoon. This done, it was time to be on her way to work again, where she remains, without one minute's relaxation, till seven o'clock. She then comes home, and throws herself into a chair exhausted. This [is] repeated six days in the week (save that on Saturdays she may get back a little earlier, say, an hour or two). . . . This young woman looks very pale and delicate, and has every appearance of an approaching decline. I was asked to guess her age; I said, perhaps fifteen. . . . Her mother . . . told me she was going nineteen. . . . She is a fair specimen of a great proportion of factory girls in Manchester.[4]

By the 1840s the term 'factory system' had ceased to be an objective description of a certain type of economic and social organization and had become a slogan or a convenient label for a complex of social attitudes and assumptions. This is not hard to appreciate, for the changes demanded by the new order were terrifyingly fundamental and aroused men's deepest responses. The factory integrated men and machines in a way that had never before been attempted. 'Whilst the engine runs, the people must work – men, women and children are yoked together with iron and steam. The animal machine . . . is chained fast to the iron machine, which knows no suffering and no weariness,' wrote James Kay Shuttleworth in 1832. Reactions to this phenomenon varied according to a man's position in life and his social and temperamental attitudes. To some the factory system was the practical application of Adam Smith's principle of the division of labour; others saw it as a system of gross immorality in which sexual appetite and precociousness were fostered by the over-heated atmosphere of mills; working men complained that too often it meant the introduction of machines that put them out of work; and reformers denounced it as a system of child slavery. The factory system was all of these things, but was not bounded by any one of them. It was more than simply an aggregate of individual factories; it was a new order, a completely new way of life.

Within the textile industry, where most of the factory operatives were to be found, wages and working conditions were affected by a number of factors. The particular branch of the industry (cotton, wool, worsted, flax, silk), the constant replacement of one machine or process by another, the relative use of women and children instead of men, and the vagaries of unemployment, all helped to determine the fortunes of any one group of operatives. In general, however, a male factory hand in Yorkshire or Lancashire (employed, say, as a third-grade spinner) could hope to earn between 14s. and 22s. a week. If to this could be added the earnings of his wife and children the weekly family income would be raised to 30s. or more, depending on the age and number of the children. The women were employed as throstle spinners (in cotton) and as powerloom weavers, and their wages were 5s. to 10s. a week. Children were frequently used as piecers and paid 2s. 6d. to 5s. weekly. In Leeds in 1839 male cloth-pressers averaged 20s. a week, cloth-drawers 24s. 6d., slubbers 24s. and wool-sorters 21s. – which compared favourably with 16s. for tailors and 14s. for shoe-makers.[5] It was characteristic of the factory operatives, as of some other sections of the labouring poor, that the unit of earning was the family, not a single breadwinner. No aspect of the factory system aroused more controversy than this, and the employment of women and children became a focus for agitation and legislation in the 1830s and 1840s.

As the textile mill operative was felt to be the representative type of worker in the machine age, so the handloom weaver was the representative figure from the past. The golden age of handloom weaving came to an end before the conclusion of the Napoleonic Wars, but the craft remained attractive despite a fall in earnings. It was an occupation which was pursued in the worker's own home surrounded (and also assisted) by his wife and family. He could, and did, work at his own pace and to suit his own convenience. If he wished to work hard for four days and loaf for three, he was at liberty to do so. He was free from the irksome discipline of the factory, and if most yardage weaving was monotonous he could always break off for a smoke or a drink when he felt inclined. Handloom weaving was popular because of its freedom and because it satisfied the old artisan craving for independence. Unfortunately it was also, at least in its plain and coarser departments, a skill which was easily acquired. Little capital was necessary: a loom and lodgings could be hired in Burnley and Colne for a shilling a week. There were no restrictive apprenticeship regulations, and much of the work could be done by women and children. An assistant commissioner who inquired into the state of the industry in 1838–9 reported that in Barnsley thirty Irishmen entered the town one morning and set up as handloom weavers, though they had never done any weaving before. From 1815 to the 1830s the handweaver's earnings were reduced drastically, and he was forced to work longer and longer hours and accept more onerous conditions for the privilege of getting work. By 1838–9 in Manchester the total family earnings of weavers of coarse fabrics averaged only 8s. a week, and similar figures were reported from Glasgow and Barnsley. Although there were important differences between cotton weavers in Lancashire, woollen and worsted weavers in Yorkshire, and silk weavers in London and Coventry, the trend was everywhere the same. Selected groups of weavers who did extra fine or specialized work were able to make up to 16s. a week. But such earnings were a sad reward for a once-proud craft.

The 'distress' of the handloom weavers in the 1830s and 1840s received a good deal of publicity, though little constructive help. They were, after the agricultural workers and domestic servants, the largest occupational group in the country, numbering with their families over 800,000 persons. Their reduction in status from respectable artisans to workers on the edge of starvation represented an important cultural shift within a significantly large section of the labouring population. It is easy to write them off simply as unfortunate casualties of the Industrial Revolution, outmoded handworkers who were unable to compete with the machine. But this is by no means the whole story, and obscures the essential nature of the impact of industrialism on the labouring poor. Only in the 1830s in the cotton, and in the 1840s in the woollen, industries did powerlooms in the factories compete fully and directly with handlooms. Until that time the two existed side by side, with the handloom weaver reduced to being an auxiliary of the factory, but not yet driven out of existence by competition. His role was to take up the slack in busy times, and to bear the first brunt of a recession. He also acted as a check on the wages of powerloom operators, most of whom were women. The plight of the weavers was a vivid illustration of how helpless a section of labouring men could be when caught between the relics of the domestic system and the full force of competitive industrial capitalism. In classical economic theory the handloom weaver should no doubt, under the stress of severe competition, have transferred his labour to some other sector of the economy. But in fact this did not happen. Weavers for the most part would not, and could not, find other employment. 'Too great attachment to the occupation is the bane of the trade,' commented Dr Mitchell, one of the assistant handloom weavers' commissioners, in the 1841 Report. Quite apart from their strong desire to cling to an occupation which enabled them to preserve something of their traditional way of life, their opportunities of alternative jobs were strictly limited. They were barred from entering, or apprenticing their children to, skilled handicrafts by the trade societies; they were not required in the mills, where powerloom weavers were usually women and girls; and they seldom had the physique or strength for an outdoor labouring job. Their occupation, protected neither by unions nor trade customs, was wide open to anyone who wished to take it up; and the supply of weavers was always in excess of the demand for their labour. At the same time, as earnings and conditions of work deteriorated, more people became weavers; for poor as the remuneration was, it was better than starvation, and for some sections of the labouring poor this was the choice in the 1830s.

Other out-workers, such as the framework knitters in the hosiery industry, suffered similar though not identical experiences. From the early nineteenth century two factors had combined to undermine the independence of the stockinger – the system of frame-letting and the growth of middlemen. Although in the eighteenth century some stockingers (like William Hutton's uncle mentioned in Chapter 4) had owned their own frames, by the 1830s this independence had disappeared, and virtually all frames were hired. The owners of the frames were of three different types – hosiers (or manufacturers), middlemen (bagmen), and persons not connected with the trade who let the frames solely for the profits of their rents. Among the varieties of middlemen it was not always possible to categorize exactly. But in addition to the 'putter-out' who simply gave out the yarn for the hosier and collected the hose when it had been made, there were two types of genuine contractor. The undertaker, or master stockinger, contracted with the larger hosiers to supply hose, and then put out the work to a number of framework knitters. Similar to, and often indistinguishable from, this type was the bagman or bag hosier. He flourished particularly in certain country districts, and manufactured on his own account. It was from the twin institutions of frame-letting and middlemen that most of the grievances of the framework knitters stemmed.

Frame rents were by no means the only grievance, but the

struggle for their abolition became synonymous with, and symbolic of, the general struggle to improve the stockinger's lot. Traditionally the rent for a frame was 9d. per week, but with the introduction of the new wider frames the rent went up. A constant complaint of the stockingers was the uncertainty and variability of frame rents. A full week's rent was paid whether or not there was a full week's work, and it was paid whether the frame was in the stockinger's home or in the employer's shop. In the latter case an additional charge for standing room was also made, together with charges for light, fuel and needles. Thus it was not uncommon in 1844 for 3s. in charges to be deducted from weekly earnings of 10s.; and there were cases where men who had work for only two or three days in the week found that they had worked for nothing else than the frame rent.

But, as Thomas Cooper discovered:

. . . it was by a number of petty and vexatious grindings, in addition to the obnoxious 'frame rent', that the poor framework knitter was worn down, till you might have known him by his peculiar air of misery and dejection, if you had met him a hundred miles from Leicester. He had to pay, not only 'frame rent', but so much per week for the 'standing' of the frame in the shop of the 'master', for the frames were grouped together in the shops, generally, though you would often find a single frame in a weaver's cottage. The man had also to pay threepence per dozen to the 'master' for 'giving out' of the work. He had also to pay so much per dozen to the female 'seamer' of the hose. And he had also oil to buy for his machine, and lights to pay for in the darker half of the year. All the deductions brought the average earnings of the stocking-weaver to four and sixpence per week. I found this to be a truth confirmed on every hand.

And when he was 'in work', the man was evermore experiencing some new attempt at grinding him down to a lower sum per dozen for the weaving, or at 'docking' him so much per dozen for alleged faults in his work; while sometimes – and even for several weeks altogether – he experienced the most grievous wrong of all. The 'master' not being able to obtain full employment for all the frames he rented of the manufacturer, but perhaps only half employ for them – distributed, or 'spread' the work over all the frames. . . . But the foul grievance was this: each man had to pay a whole week's frame rent, though he had only half a week's work! Thus while the poor miserable weaver knew that this half-week's work, after all the deductions, would produce him such a mere pittance that he could only secure a scant share of the meanest food, he remembered that the owner of the frame had the full rent per week, and the middleman or 'master' had also his weekly pickings secured to him. Again, a kind of hose would be demanded for which the frame needed a deal of troublesome and tedious altering. But the poor weaver was expected to make all the alterations himself. And sometimes he would not begin his week's weaving until a day, or a day and a half, had been spent in making the necessary alterations. Delay was also a custom on Monday mornings. The working man must call again. He was too early. And, finally, all the work was ended. The warehouses were glutted, and the hosiery firms had no orders. This came again and again, in Leicester and Loughborough and Hinckley, and the framework knitting villages of the county, until, when a little prosperity returned, no one expected it to continue.[6]

Textiles, having powered the take-off of the Industrial Revolution in the eighteenth century, dominated and set the pace of the industrial life of the nation for the next century. The numbers employed in the main branches of the trade were large: probably about 1,100,000, excluding hosiery and lace, in 1851. But of almost equal importance were technological developments in the iron and engineering industries and the expansion in output of coal. For the Victorians the spinning jenny and the steam engine were twin symbols of the basis of British prosperity. Yet working life in the Workshop of the World was by no means limited to the factory and the foundry. The basic sector of the economy (sometimes called the Great Industry) comprising manufacturing and mining probably did not employ more than 1,700,000 workers. This was less than a quarter of the occupied persons listed in 1851, and only a fraction of the total population of 21 million. Yet it provided the main motive force for the economy.

Industrialism was closely associated in men's minds with another great change: urbanization. The census of 1851 showed that for the first time in history just over half the population of England and Wales was living in urban areas. The path to the present day, when over 80 per cent of the British people are urbanized, was established. The period of fastest urban growth was the decade 1821–31, but the increase was not much less during the succeeding twenty years. Most of what are now the principal cities of modern Britain grew rapidly between 1801 and 1851: Manchester from 95,000 to 303,000, Leeds from 53,000 to 172,000, to cite but two examples. Bradford, the fastest growing town in this period of the Industrial Revolution, had 13,000 inhabitants in 1801, 26,000 in 1821, and 104,000 by 1851. At the beginning of the century London (with nearly a million) was the only city with more than 100,000 population; by 1851 there were nine. This massive growth had come from both natural increase and immigration, the proportion differing considerably from town to town. In 1851 a half or more of the adult inhabitants of Leeds, Sheffield and Norwich had been born in the town; in Manchester, Bradford and Glasgow just over a quarter were natives; and in Liverpool the proportion was even less.

The great changes in industrial growth were accompanied by changes on the land. Agriculture was presented in the eighteenth century with challenges that, if they had not been successfully met, would have seriously retarded industrial progress. In the building of the first industrial society, agriculture was vital in three respects. It provided the food for a growing population, especially the urban workers; it contributed substantially to the capital required for early industrialization; and it produced a surplus from the agricultural population that helped to swell the ranks of the industrial proletariat. In view of the essentially slow nature of agricultural change, it is perhaps misleading to speak of an agricultural revolution; but the actual achievements in increased agricultural output by the end of the eighteenth century were totally unprecedented.

In 1820 the population of England and Wales was more than double what it had been in 1750, but the proportion of families engaged in agriculture was less. Moreover, only a very small percentage of the food consumed was imported, and that happened usually in times of bad harvest. More food was produced by proportionately fewer workers; in other words, the efficiency of

227

agriculture increased. Had this not come about, Britain would have had to import food for her growing population at the expense of the raw materials (cotton, iron ore, wool) required for the new industries, since she would not have been able to afford both. As it was, agriculture responded to the demands put on it and thus made possible the curious pattern of an industrial revolution in a country that had very few of the necessary raw materials (except coal) and that had therefore to rely on imports. The success of the agriculturists brought them increased incomes, which in turn stimulated the demand for the products of the new industry and also provided some surplus capital for investment in industry.

Unlike industry, the increase in agricultural productivity was not dependent to any significant extent on mechanical inventions. Jethro Tull's seed drill, which he publicized in the 1730s, was not widely used until the nineteenth century. Improved types of plough, which permitted the use of two horses instead of the traditional team of from four to eight oxen, were available after 1730; and the first threshing machines appeared in the 1780s. Nevertheless most threshing was done with a flail until the 1830s, and hay and grain were mown and reaped by hand (with scythe and sickle) for many years after that. Although there was some reduction in manual labour, farming remained predominantly an occupation requiring a great amount of sheer, hard muscle-power. The increase in agricultural output was the result of new techniques of production rather than technological innovation. By a combination of new types of crop, new rotation systems, and improved breeds of stock (sometimes collectively referred to as the Norfolk system because a number of 'improving' landlords and farmers were concentrated there), an overall increase in agricultural output in the region of 40 to 50 per cent was achieved during the eighteenth century.

Before the new techniques of production could be fully employed, however, certain weaknesses in the traditional agricultural system had to be eliminated. At the beginning of the eighteenth century about half the arable land was still cultivated on the open-field system. By 1820 there were only a few counties where this system remained, and by the 1830s it had virtually disappeared. This dramatic transformation of the face of the country was effected by enclosure, which, as in the sixteenth century, again became a slogan in the period 1760 to 1820. It will be recalled that enclosure could be of three types: the enclosure of arable land to convert it to pasture for sheep; the consolidation of scattered arable strips into one compact holding; and the enclosure of common land or waste that had previously been uncultivated. The first type of enclosure had been carried out mainly in the sixteenth century. The second had proceeded spasmodically and slowly for many generations, as individuals made private arrangements to reorganize or enlarge their holdings; and there had also been incorporation of new land from the waste that was usually enclosed. Until about 1760 these developments had been slow and fairly steady. Thereafter, the pressure of increasing population and urbanization, with the consequent rise in food prices, greatly accelerated the rate of change.

The reasons for enclosure arose, in one form or another, from frustration with the conservatism and rigidities of the open-field system. An improving farmer or landlord found it extremely difficult to institute new crops and rotations or a new drainage system if his neighbours refused to cooperate, since cultivation (and indeed the whole life of the village) was governed by the rule of custom. In a communal system there is little scope for individual deviation or experiment. A compact, enclosed farm was easier to work and enabled an enterprising farmer to try out the new farming techniques. The enclosure of commons and wastes made them available for commercially profitable use and increased the total amount of land under cultivation. In general, enclosure strengthened a trend toward larger units and a more capitalist-minded approach to agriculture.

Before 1760 most enclosure was by private agreement among the owners of the land concerned. Where the number of owners was small or where they were prepared to sell out their rights, no problem was presented. But where there was opposition, the only way to overcome it was by a special act of parliament ordering the enclosure of that particular parish or manor. In the sixty years before 1760 slightly more than 200 such Enclosure Acts were passed; between 1761 and 1801 there were about 2000; and another 2000 were enacted between 1802 and 1844. The total area of land affected by these enclosures was over 6 million acres, or about a quarter of all the land in cultivation.

Contemporaries, like historians later, were divided in their views of the effects and desirability of enclosures. Not surprisingly, the landlords and larger farmers fared best, and the poorer villagers fared worst. The enclosure commissioners, who were responsible for dividing up the land after an Enclosure Act had been passed, respected the rights of all who had a legal title to land, but usually disregarded claims based on custom or tenancy. This meant that small farmers and cottagers, who had customarily used the commons for grazing a cow and for cutting fuel, received no share of the land when it was divided, and were thus deprived of their former rights. Previously, they had been able to eke out a living from their combined resources of wage labour, a small-holding, and common rights. Enclosure took away a vital element in this economy and reduced many of them to simple wage labourers. The same fate was even more likely for the squatters, a class of labourers who lived in hovels on the edge of the commons and who had no legal claim to land or common rights; on enclosure their homes were simply pulled down. Even when small farmers and cottagers had enforceable claims, they were faced with the problem of how to pay their share of the legal costs of enclosure (which were heavy) and the cost of fencing. At such times the temptation to sell out to a richer neighbour was great.

It is unlikely that enclosures were responsible for all the social evils that were once ascribed to them, although the loss of the commons was an important step toward the pauperization of the rural poor in the early nineteenth century. William Cobbett, the most consistent spokesman for the agricultural labourers, was convinced that the rural poor were worse off in 1806 than when he was born in 1763, and he regarded enclosure as a main cause of their degradation. John Clare, the peasant-poet and son of a cottage farmer in Helpstone, Northamptonshire, is perhaps the only voice of an actual victim of enclosure. Helpstone was enclosed by an Act of 1809 when Clare was sixteen. He was in no doubt about its results:

> Enclosure came, and trampled on the grave
> Of labour's rights, and left the poor a slave.[7]

Arthur Young, an agricultural journalist and advocate of scientific

farming, at first welcomed enclosure but later had second
thoughts:

> Go to an ale-house kitchen of an old enclosed country, and there
> you will see the origin of poverty and poor-rates. For whom are
> they to be sober? For whom are they to save? For the parish? If I
> am diligent, shall I have leave to build a cottage? If I am sober,
> shall I have land for a cow? If I am frugal, shall I have half an
> acre of potatoes? You offer no motives; you have nothing but a
> parish officer and a workhouse! – Bring me another pot.[8]

Enclosure extended and accelerated a process that had been going
on for two hundred years previously. The number of small landowners had begun to decline before the period 1760–1820, and the
rural poverty and unrest of the early nineteenth century was the
result of low wages and unemployment as much as enclosure.
Nevertheless, when a village was enclosed it was a visible sign and
symbol that a great change in the community had come about.
The balance of village life had been altered – almost always to the
disadvantage of its poorest members. In particular the position of
the agricultural labourer was different: 'Before enclosure the
cottager was a labourer with land, after enclosure he was a
labourer without land.'[9] The three-tier system (peculiar to English
agriculture) of landlord, tenant farmer and landless wage
labourer, had come into being, and the relics of peasant farming
were swept away in the main farming areas. In the new industrial
society agriculture had ultimately to conform to the same pattern
of capitalist development as manufacturing and commerce.

The changes brought by the combination of population growth,
industrialism and enclosure between 1760 and 1830 were so
fundamental that the rest of this book is in effect simply the
working out of the logic of those changes in the lives of the common
people. The very identity of the common people changed: they
perceived themselves, and were perceived by others, in a new way.
This was expressed in various forms, but in none more tellingly
than by the creation of a new vocabulary. In the 1780s men still
used the language of ranks and orders, as they had done in the days
of Gregory King. The common people were referred to as the
lower orders or the labouring poor. But thereafter this usage was

A Map of Society in 1814

	Heads of Families	Total persons, comprising their Families
HIGHEST ORDERS		
1st. The Royal Family, the Lords Spiritual and Temporal, the Great Officers of State, and all above the degree of a Baronet, with their families	576	2,880
SECOND CLASS		
2d. Baronets, Knights, Country Gentlemen, and others having large incomes, with their families	46,861	234,305
THIRD CLASS		
3d. Dignified Clergy, Persons holding considerable employments in the State, elevated situations in the Law, eminent Practitioners in Physic, considerable Merchants, Manufacturers upon a large scale, and Bankers of the first order, with their families	12,200	61,000
Carried forward	59,637	298,185
FOURTH CLASS		
4th. Persons holding inferior situations in Church and State, respectable Clergymen of different persuasions, Practitioners in Law and Physic, Teachers of Youth of the superior order, respectable Freeholders, Ship Owners, Merchants and Manufacturers of the second class, Warehousemen and respectable Shopkeepers, Artists, respectable Builders, Mechanics, and Persons living on moderate incomes, with their families	233,650	1,168,250
FIFTH CLASS		
5th. Lesser Freeholders, Shopkeepers of the second order, Inn-keepers, Publicans, and Persons engaged in miscellaneous occupations or living on moderate incomes, with their families	564,799	2,798,475

SIXTH CLASS

6th. Working Mechanics, Artisans, Handicrafts, Agricultural Labourers, and others who subsist by labour in various employments, with their families 2,126,095   8,792,800

Menial Servants 1,279,923

SEVENTH, OR LOWEST CLASS

7th. Paupers and their families, Vagrants, Gipsies, Rogues, Vagabonds, and idle and disorderly persons, supported by criminal delinquency 387,100   1,828,170

3,371,281   16,165,803

THE ARMY AND NAVY

Officers of the Army, Navy, and Marines, including all Officers on half-pay and superannuated, with their families 10,500   69,000

Non-commissioned Officers in the Army, Navy, and Marines, Soldiers, Seamen, and Marines, including Pensioners of the Army, Navy, etc. and their families 120,000   862,000

Total   3,501,781   17,096,803

Productive Labourers, by whose exertions a new Property is created every year.

	Families	Persons	Income
Agriculture, Mines, &c.	1,302,151	6,129,142	£107,246,795
Foreign Commerce, Shipping, Trade, Manufactures, Fisheries, &c.	1,506,774	7,071,989	183,908,352
Fine Arts	5,000	25,000	1,400,000
Total.........	2,813,925	13,226,131	£292,555,147

Unproductive Labourers, whose exertions do not create any new Property.

	Families	Persons	Income
Royalty Nobility Gentry	47,437	416,835	£58,923,590

State and Revenue			
Army			
Navy	152,000	1,056,000	34,036,280
Half-pay			
Pensioners			
Clergy			
Law	56,000	281,500	17,580,000
Physic			
Universities			
Schools	45,319	567,937	17,555,355
Miscellaneous			
Paupers	387,100	1,548,400	9,871,000
Total.........	687,856	3,870,672	£137,966,225

From Patrick Colquhoun, *A Treatise on the Wealth, Power, and Resources of the British Empire* (1814).

---

increasingly replaced by the language of class, and by the 1830s it was common to refer to the working classes and the middle classes. This shift in language was a recognition of new interests and divisions in society. Patrick Colquhoun's map of society in 1814 (as he called the table on the previous pages) represents a transition between Gregory King's categories and the nineteenth-century concept of class stratification. Colquhoun's sixth class of some 10 million people contains most of those who a few years later were to appear as the working classes. Contemporaries were aware of the Industrial Revolution as a massive disruption and discontinuity, which not only created new social classes but also changed the nature of the relationship between classes. Thomas Carlyle, the prophet of the Victorian age, wrote of the 'cash nexus' which by the 1830s had come to dominate all social relationships, to the exclusion of older ties of mutual obligation.

The change as it affected the common people, however, was more than a change in the social structure. Class has a dual meaning: it can be used either as a description of social strata or in the sense of class consciousness. The working class (or classes) was a socio-economic group separated from other groups such as the middle class by differences of income and power. But the working class was also distinguished by a sense of its own identity, an awareness or perception of itself – in fact, a class consciousness. The exact nature of that consciousness, how and when it emerged, and what significance to place upon it, have been subjects of argument among historians. Perhaps the best guide through this complex and thorny field is to follow the advice of E.P. Thompson to think always of class as a relationship, not a thing.[10] Certainly it is in this sense that the leaders of the working class in the 1830s and 1840s defined their class interests and identity.

As an example of the common people's experience in the sharpening of class relationships we may take the case of the changes in the Poor Laws. The Elizabethan Poor Law Act, which was still in operation, provided overseers of the poor who were to levy a poor-rate for the relief of the sick, aged and unemployed. With the spread of enclosures after 1760 and the rise in food prices during the French wars, the number of poor to be relieved increased rapidly, and the poor-rates jumped accordingly. In 1775 they had amounted to less than £2 million, by 1801 they had doubled, and in 1831 they were nearly £7 million – provoking loud protestations from the rate-payers. In many districts the practice of granting outdoor relief to employed as well as unemployed labourers had grown up, and in 1795 this became semi-regularized as the 'Speenhamland system'. It was the intention of the Berkshire justices, meeting at the village of Speenhamland, to help the poor by ensuring that each family had a minimum income calculated according to the price of bread and number of dependants, but the effect was to subsidize low wages out of poor-rates. The system was adopted widely in the southern counties and was held by orthodox political economists to be largely responsible for rural pauperization. For over forty years the problem of how to reduce the growing burden of poor-rates (which fell mainly on the farmers in the countryside and the middle classes in the towns) had been debated, without any conclusive result. But in the early 1830s the pressure to do away with the Old Poor Law and to create a free labour market in accordance with the principles of political economy was sufficiently strong to overcome working-class radical and Tory opposition. A royal commission on the Poor Laws was appointed, and its Report provided the basis for a New Poor Law, enacted in 1834.

The new law, like the old, accepted the principle that every necessitous person had a claim to relief; but the relief was to be given only under new and stricter conditions. First, outdoor relief was to be abolished and all recipients made to enter the workhouse. Second, conditions in the workhouse were made 'less eligible' (that is, more miserable) than the condition of the lowest-paid worker outside. A rigorous workhouse test was thus applied to all applicants for relief, the intention being to deter all but the really 'deserving' (that is, desperate) cases. To carry out this sweeping reform of the Old Poor Law system, a centralized administration was established, consisting of a board of three commissioners, who in turn appointed regional assistant commissioners. The old parish workhouses were abolished and the parishes grouped together in unions, each with one large central workhouse. Boards of guardians were elected by the rate-payers in each Poor Law union and were responsible for carrying out the regulations imposed by the commissioners.

The rationale of the New Poor Law lay in the doctrines of orthodox political economy. Anything that interfered with the working of the 'natural' laws of supply and demand was felt to be undesirable. By this test trade unions, factory regulations, and poor relief stood alike condemned. The widespread acceptance among the educated classes of a *laissez-faire* philosophy, coupled with the desire to reduce the poor-rates, ensured a sympathetic response to the Poor Law Report and support for the government's Act of 1834. Edwin Chadwick, the first secretary of the central board and drafter of the Report, was a disciple of Jeremy Bentham, the philosopher who questioned the value of all institutions and customs by the test of whether they contributed to 'the greatest happiness of the greatest number'. Benthamism led to positive action by the state in the furtherance of administrative reform – which conflicted to some extent with the doctrines of the classical political economists, who advocated strictly limiting the role of government in social and economic affairs. Nassau Senior, Chadwick's colleague and professor of political economy at Oxford, favoured doing away with the Poor Laws altogether. Between them they concocted a drastic revision of English social policy. Ramshackle and inefficient as the Old Poor Law had been, it nevertheless provided the rudiments of a system of social welfare: income maintenance for the poorest workers, unemployment compensation, and family endowment. This was now to be swept away, on the grounds that public charity was incompatible with the principles of the economists.

Critics, however, saw the matter differently. To Thomas Carlyle, it was not the application of natural, scientific or immutable laws of political economy but the application of a very simple and brutal axiom: 'If paupers are made miserable, paupers will needs decline in multitude. It is a secret known to all rat-catchers.' And he sarcastically suggested that poisoning paupers, like rats, with arsenic would be even more efficient. The 'social principle' of the New Poor Law was no principle at all, he argued, but simply an attempt to sweep the problems of the poor and luckless out of sight. In one sense Carlyle was right: the New Poor Law was an attempt to deal not with the fundamental causes of destitution but only with its symptoms as expressed in the demand for relief. In other respects, however, the 1834 Act was a basic measure, for it defined the social policy of the state, as it affected a majority of the population, in a new way. The issue was more than the replacement of a lenient by a severe administration of the laws governing relief; it was the announcement that henceforth the labouring poor must abandon many of their traditional attitudes and expectations and conform to new standards of social and economic rectitude.

The new measures were greeted with bitter opposition from working people. Inevitably, the Poor Laws affected the life of a labouring man at its most tender spots. In times of distress caused by unemployment, sickness, old age and death, he and his family were under strain and most in need of sympathetic help and consideration. Yet this was the last thing to be expected under the new regime. As they watched the building of the great, grim new workhouses and heard the rumours of the prisonlike discipline enforced behind the high walls, the working classes were seized with a great and sudden fear. On the outskirts of every medium-sized town and at remote crossroads in country districts, the new, raw redbrick buildings appeared. They looked like prisons and were called the 'bastilles'. Inside them, life was made as dreary and comfortless as was possible without actually endangering health. When a pauper family presented itself for relief at the gates of the workhouse it was immediately broken up, men, women and children being housed in separate parts of the building and forbidden to reunite as long as they remained. Able-bodied men were set to work at breaking stone, grinding corn or picking oakum. Food was plain and monotonous: mainly bread and gruel, with a small allowance of meat and cheese. Until 1842 all meals were eaten in silence, and smoking was forbidden. A special workhouse dress was worn, and the master of the workhouse was enjoined 'to enforce industry, order, punctuality, and cleanliness' at all times. Visitors were allowed infrequently and only in the presence of the master or matron. The commissioners (and usually also the guardians) were especially keen that the greatest economy should be exercised; any little comfort that might be considered a luxury was carefully excluded: an occasional cup of tea for the old folks or a few extra delicacies for Christmas dinner (although paid for by a private benefactor) were considered exceedingly dubious relaxations of the regulations.

Such a system would have been sufficiently terrifying had all the masters and matrons, overseers and guardians been humane and honest. But given the normal incidence of sadism, greed and petty-mindedness among mankind, and the credulity with which reports of abuses are received, it was inevitable that the horror of the new workhouses would be magnified further. There were in any event sufficient bad cases to nourish the worst of contemporary fears and rumours. Most notorious was the scandal in the Andover workhouse, where the paupers were so hungry that they fought among themselves for bits of gristle and marrow among the old bones they were set to crush. Typical of the insensitivity of the commissioners was the attempt in 1836 to save the cost of tolling the bell at pauper funerals. The desire for a respectable burial was (and long remained) deeply ingrained in the English poor, and Chadwick's circular was an outrage upon their feelings of common decency. The New Poor Law was by its very nature a piece of class legislation, in that decisions affecting one class (the poor) were made by another. Even so, it was unusually blatant in the way it trampled on so much that the labouring poor held dear.

Charles Shaw was the son of a working potter. In 1842 his

father was victimized after a strike, and the family had to go into the workhouse at Chell, near Tunstall:

> Early in the morning we left home without a morsel of food. We called on a relative who had kindly provided breakfast for us, and yet it was a wretched meal for my parents. I remember the choking sobs . . . I remember, too, how the food seemed to choke as much as the sobs, and the vain entreaties to 'eat a little more'. We went by the field road to Chell, so as to escape as much observation as possible. One child had to be carried as she was too young to walk.

Their reception at the 'Bastille' was chilly:

> Everybody we saw and spoke to looked metallic, as if worked from within by a hidden machinery. Their voices were metallic, and sounded harsh and imperative. The younger ones huddled more closely to their parents, as if from fear of these stern officials. Doors were unlocked by keys belonging to bunches, and the sound of keys and locks and bars, and doors banging, froze the blood within us. It was all so unusual and strange, and so unhomelike. . . . We youngsters were roughly disrobed, roughly and coldly washed, and roughly attired in rough clothes, our under garments being all covered up by a rough linen pinafore. Then we parted amid bitter cries, the young ones being taken one way and the parents (separated too) taken as well to different regions . . .[11]

The meagre meals were always preceded by prayers ('a fine piece of mockery') and the main diet was bread and skilly. Shaw had heard of workhouse skilly (soup made of oatmeal and water) but had never before seen it. He discovered that it was 'the vilest compound I have ever tasted . . . a malignant mockery of food'. At night the bedroom, with its long rows of beds, was the scene of bullying, cruelty and obscenity. A wide, shallow tub served as a lavatory and had to be carried down the stairs every morning before breakfast by two small boys in turn. 'Discipline' was maintained by a daily routine of cuts, slashes and cuffs, administered by the schoolmaster. For 'extreme' cases, such as an attempt to run away, there was ritual flogging before the governor, officials and inmates.

The New Poor Law was basically an attempt to deal with pauperism rather than poverty. Applied first to the southern counties, where rural pauperism was worst, and helped by two good harvests and the demand for labour to build railways, the abuses of the allowance (or Speenhamland) system were speedily removed, and the old evil of underemployment in agriculture largely disappeared. To this extent the New Poor Law succeeded in its aim of restoring the labourer to something like a condition of formal independence. The social disease of pauperism, it was argued, had been cured by the drastic but necessary surgery of cutting off outdoor relief. In fact, the guardians in rural areas had to continue outdoor relief for the able-bodied in cases of urgency as well as for some of the aged and infirm. When the commissioners turned their attention to the industrial districts in 1837, they found even less possibility of a blanket application of the new regulations to all and sundry. The needs of industrial workers were not the same as for agricultural labourers, and moreover they were on the brink of the worst economic depression of the nineteenth century. Factory operatives and handworkers were not suffering the effects of an allowance system that artificially depressed wages; they required short-term relief to tide them over periods of temporary unemployment until good times returned. They regarded the idea of having to enter the workhouse in order to get relief as monstrous and totally irrelevant to their real needs. The resistance to the New Poor Law in the northern towns delayed its introduction for many months, but by 1840 Poor Law unions were established throughout the country. It proved impossible to implement all the principles of the 'harsh but salutary Act': outdoor relief simply could not be completely abolished, nor did the mixed workhouse (catering to all types of indigent poor from orphans to old people, able-bodied and sick), which had been condemned in the 1834 Report, disappear. The principle of less eligibility, however, was sufficiently enforced to make the workhouse a terror and shame to ordinary people. Henceforth its shadow fell across the lives of labouring men, reminding them always of the price of indigency.

The only way in which the Industrial Revolution and its social consequences could have been justified or made acceptable to the common people was if they had benefited from it materially. In fact the first results were economic and social misery on a scale never before experienced. The writers of the time were divided between those who took an optimistic view of the new industrial civilization and those whose verdict was pessimistic, and historians later have debated likewise. More recently the issues have been narrowed down to an argument as to whether the standard of living of the working classes improved or deteriorated between 1780 and 1850. No very clear conclusion has so far emerged, perhaps because of failure to agree on standards of measurement. Statistics of earnings and prices, unemployment, patterns of consumption (including food), and population growth have all been introduced as variables in assessing changes in working-class living standards. Even more difficult to ascertain is firm information about the qualitative aspects of life of the labouring poor; for here there is almost no escape from personal judgements, whether by contemporaries or historians. If a general statement about the material condition of the working classes during the Industrial Revolution were to be hazarded, it would be that the real income of skilled artisans increased, the lot of the domestic workers deteriorated, and the living standards of the majority of the labouring poor remained stationary or at best improved slightly. During the crucial second quarter of the nineteenth century even this cautious evaluation may be disputed. So fluctuating was the economy in booms and slumps, and so widespread was the incidence of unemployment, that generalization becomes meaningless. It is clear that large numbers, possibly a majority, of the labouring poor suffered an absolute decline in living standards during the 1830s and 1840s, and that the working class as a whole declined relative to other groups in their share of the national income. From the late 1840s improvement began, and continued until late in the century.

There is a tendency in some accounts of the Industrial Revolution to regard the common people mainly as victims. In some ways of course they were the unfortunate participants in a process of change which they could neither escape nor control. The working class came into being as a reaction to the exploitation of industrial capitalism. But this is not the whole story. The working people were not content with a purely passive role in the transformation of

English society, nor had their history prepared them for such docility. They struggled and resisted and adapted to suit their needs as and when they could. From these experiences they emerged as a working class. As E.P. Thompson has put it, the English working class was present at its own making.

8. Protest and Revolt

The Industrial Revolution set in motion a train of changes which during the last two hundred years have altered fundamentally the position of the common people in society. In pre-industrial England the labouring poor could safely be ignored or taken for granted by the educated classes for most of the time. Only occasionally did they actively intervene in the affairs of the nation, and such eruptions soon subsided. They were not directly or continuously involved in important decisions; their views were neither sought nor heeded; and popular unrest was regarded as unfortunate but transitory. From the later eighteenth century this state of affairs began to change. By the 1830s the working classes were no longer largely invisible and could not safely be ignored. The middle classes became aware of the 'bitter discontent grown fierce and mad' which Thomas Carlyle characterized as the condition-of-England question. It was not that conflict was absent in traditional society, as we have seen earlier. But it had existed in different forms and for different purposes. The emergence of the working class was associated with new types of protest – more highly organized, sustained, political and, above all, class-conscious. As always, the change from one type of social action to another was not sudden and complete: old and new forms continued side by side. Nevertheless in these struggles the working class became a presence in its own right which could not be ignored.

Popular protest traditionally took the form of riot. A crowd of people assembled and demanded that certain specific grievances be remedied: that enclosures be pulled down, the price of bread reduced, or unpopular politicians dismissed. If they did not obtain satisfaction they took matters into their own hands. The commonest example in the eighteenth century was the food riot, but there were other varieties: no-popery, as in the Gordon riots of

1780 when London was in the hands of the rioters for a week; 'church and king' mobs who attacked the homes of dissenters and republicans like Joseph Priestley and William Hutton in the 1790s; and rural incendiaries protesting the poverty of agricultural labourers. An older generation of historians accepted the view of hostile observers that the 'mob' or the 'rabble' was primarily a problem of law and order. All crowd action was lumped together as proof of the instability and unreliability of the common people, who were prone to rumours and easily misled by agitators from outside. 'Discontent' would disappear when a few ringleaders had been apprehended and the rest mollified by promises that something would be done. A more sympathetic approach however now presents crowd action in a somewhat different light. Instead of aggregating different types of riot and assuming a crude motivation of hunger, envy or prejudice, we can listen to what the rioters actually said and examine carefully what they did. From such studies it becomes plain that the common people had certain strongly held notions of justice, and when these were grossly offended direct action followed.

Two concepts have proved useful in this new approach. First is the notion of a moral economy of the poor. Underlying the demands and actions of the rioters was a traditional view of society, in which everyone, rich and poor alike, had a proper function to perform in the community. 'An outrage to these moral assumptions, quite as much as actual deprivation, was the usual occasion for direct action.'[1] Second, and following from this, is the idea of legitimation. The participants in crowd action believed that they were only claiming what was traditionally right, and that in this defence of custom they had the support of the community at large. They assumed (with some justification) a consensus endorsed by the authorities in the community, a tacit understanding that the justices of the peace and the landowners would, or should, see the issues in the same light as themselves, as against others such as middlemen. This was the reverse side of paternalism. The foot riot was the commonest, and perhaps the clearest example of popular action based on this sense of legitimation. Since a very high percentage of a labourer's budget was spent on bread, a rise in bread prices (for whatever reason) was always likely to provoke protest. The object was to secure bread at the normal, socially accepted price, and the action of the crowd (often largely women) was directed at the millers, bakers and middlemen. Usually the rioters did little violence against persons, but sought by their demonstration to coerce the suppliers or the authorities into releasing bread at a lower price. This was a form of consumers' protest. But riot could also, in the absence of trade union organization, be extended into industrial relations, and become a form of collective bargaining.

Such was the case of Luddism. In 1811 the first threatening letters from the mysterious (General) Ned Ludd appeared in Nottingham. Bands of framework knitters assembled at night and broke the frames of selected employers. The action spread throughout the hosiery and lace-making districts of Nottinghamshire and parts of Leicestershire and Derbyshire during 1812, and then died down; but there were further outbreaks in 1814 and 1816. In the West Riding of Yorkshire the croppers engaged in the process of woollen cloth finishing destroyed the new shearing frames during 1812. In Lancashire in the same year rioters attacked cotton mills using new steam-powered looms. Although the events between 1811 and 1816 were all manifestations of machine-breaking, and have been given the generic name Luddism, on closer examination the three areas show considerable differences in aims and organization. The grievances of the Nottingham stockingers were over wage reductions, frame rents, truck payments, the use of colts (unapprenticed workmen) and the production of cut-ups (inferior hose made from broad pieces of knitwear). Frames were broken because they belonged to an employer who was held to be guilty of these practices, not because new machines were putting men out of work. But in Yorkshire Luddism was much more clearly a protest against machinery which caused unemployment. Here the croppers, a small and highly skilled group of cloth finishers, feared that the introduction of the gig-mill and shearing frame would put them out of work and destroy their privileged position as the aristocracy of the West Riding woollen workers. For the previous twenty years they had battled against the use of these machines. In Lancashire the position was different again. Luddism there was mainly among handloom weavers but the riots were supported by colliers and other workers. It is unlikely that most of the low wages and unemployment among handloom weavers in the cotton industry in 1812 were caused directly by competition from steam-power looms, which were not introduced widely until the 1820s. Nevertheless, factories using the new powerlooms were attacked, being held responsible or symbolical in some way for the distress.

Moreover the whole subject is shrouded in mystery and obscurity to such a degree that it almost seems as if deliberate measures were taken to make it so. In other words, the opaqueness of working-class culture at this point was the result of the need for secrecy in what may have been, for a few of its participants, something more than simply a movement with economic aims. Speculation about the political objectives of Luddism, and in particular the extent of secret revolutionary groups, has distinguished the movement from earlier (eighteenth-century) episodes of machine-breaking. At present the evidence is inconclusive. On the one hand, the government would hardly have stationed more than 12,000 troops (more than Wellington had in the Peninsula) in the disturbed districts during the summer of 1812 unless they had genuinely feared some form of insurrection; on the other, hard evidence about the 'Army of Redressers', despite some blood-curdling letters and the colourful imagination of spies and informers, has never amounted to more than a few conspiratorial groups which did not pose a formidable threat of revolution.

Luddism appears most clearly as a traditional form of collective bargaining, a practical attempt to prevent unemployment and maintain customary standards and modes of living in the face of *laissez faire* and the imposition of a market economy. A typical letter to a Huddersfield manufacturer in 1812 runs:

Sir. Information has just been given in that you are a holder of those detestable Shearing Frames, and I was desired by my Men to write to you and give you fair Warning to pull them down, and for that purpose I desire you will now understand I am now writing to you. You will take Notice that if they are not taken down by the end of next week, I will detach one of my Lieutenants with at least 300 Men to destroy them and furthermore take Notice that if you give us the Trouble of coming so far we will increase your misfortune by burning your Buildings down to Ashes and if you have Impudence to fire upon any of my Men, they have orders to murder you, & burn all your Housing, you will have the Goodness to your Neighbours to inform them that the same fate awaits them if their Frames are not speedily taken down as I understand their are several in your Neighbourhood, Frame holders . . .

Signed by the General of the Army of Redressers
Ned Ludd['s] Clerk
Redressers for ever Amen,
You may make this Public March 9th or 10th[2]

In the history of the common people the Yorkshire Luddites especially have a legendary place. The midnight drillings, raids for arms, and the plotting in local inns were recounted in many a story later. Careful planning and a high degree of organization were apparent in the Luddites' nightly forays. The attacking party was divided into armed guards and smashers, the latter carrying heavy sledgehammers called 'Enochs', as in the cropper's song:

> Come, cropper lads of high renown,
> Who love to drink good ale that's brown,
> And strike each haughty tyrant down,
>   With hatchet, pike, and gun!
> Oh, the cropper lads for me,
> The gallant lads for me,
> Who with lusty stroke,
> The shear frames broke,
> The cropper lads for me!
>
> Great Enoch still shall lead the van.
> Stop him who dare! stop him who can!
> Press forward every gallant man
>   With hatchet, pike, and gun!
> Oh, the cropper lads for me . . .[3]

Of all the Luddite incidents the most celebrated (thanks to Charlotte Brontë's account in *Shirley*) is the attack upon William Cartwright's mill at Rawfolds, near Cleckheaton, in April 1812. The Luddites met with determined opposition from Cartwright, who had fortified the mill and defended it with armed workmen and soldiers. The action had all the ingredients of high drama: two Luddites mortally wounded and left dying in the millyard; the unsuccessful attempt to obtain confessions from the dying men; the flogging in the millyard, later, of one of the soldiers who had refused to fire on the rioters; the attempted murder of Cartwright subsequently and the successful murder of William Horsfall, another owner of shearing frames; and the hunting down of suspected Luddites for many weeks during the summer. All this is the stuff from which popular legend is woven, and the folklore of the West Riding is rich in stories of the Luddite days.

That the Luddites enjoyed the tacit support of the community at large there can be little doubt. Probably 150 men took part in the attack on Cartwright's mill, and many more must have known or suspected what was going on. Yet the authorities had great difficulty in tracking down the rioters, and it was only when certain Luddites turned king's evidence that the leaders could be brought to trial. About a hundred suspects were rounded up and lodged in York gaol, and sixty-four were indicted. Nearly half of these were discharged without trial, officially as an act of clemency but really from lack of evidence. The three leaders convicted for the murder of Horsfall were executed within two days of their trial. For the attack on Rawfolds mill fourteen were executed, and seven were transported for seven years. The condemned men were hanged in two batches in the yard of York castle, and the first seven went to the scaffold singing the Methodist hymn:

> Behold the Saviour of mankind
> Nail'd to the shameful tree;
> How vast the love that him inclined
> To bleed and die for me.[4]

This was early in January 1813. A similar gruesome end had earlier awaited the Lancashire Luddites in May–June 1812: twenty-eight convictions (including eight sentenced to death and thirteen to transportation) at Lancaster; and a further twenty-nine convictions (fifteen sentenced to death and eight to transportation) at Chester. To those Luddites for whom there was sufficient evidence for a conviction, little mercy was shown. As the judge, Baron Thomson, told the prisoners at York:

You have been guilty of one of the greatest outrages that ever was committed in a civilized country. . . . It is of infinite importance . . . that no mercy should be shown to any of you . . . [and] that the sentence of the law . . . should be very speedily executed.[5]

The last large-scale protest of the traditional type was in 1830: the Swing riots. For the previous twenty years and more the condition of the agricultural labourers, especially in the southern counties, had deteriorated. Wages were forced down to as low as 6s. to 7s. a week in Wiltshire, 7s. to 9s. in Berkshire, and 8s. in Hampshire. Unemployed workers were mobilized by the parish authorities into gangs to work on the roads like common criminals; in some villages men and women were harnessed to the parish cart; and labourers on relief were humiliated in every possible way. It was reported in the House of Lords that four harvest labourers in the summer of 1830 had been found dead of starvation in a ditch, having had only roots and sorrel to fill their bellies. The riots began in Kent. At Hardres on 29 August 1830 400 labourers destroyed some threshing machines and later fired the ricks of an unpopular magistrate and a farmer. Rapidly similar action spread to other areas in the county and then across the border into Sussex and on into Hampshire, Wiltshire and Dorset. From there the riots spread to Berkshire, Oxfordshire, Buckinghamshire and Bedfordshire; and there were outbreaks (largely independent) in East Anglia and adjoining counties. Despite the best efforts of the authorities (and historians) to uncover some organized movement, the riots seem to have been essentially local affairs, triggered by news of what was happening in neighbouring villages, and spreading like a series of ripples. In many places the riots lasted only a few days; but in some villages in Kent and east Sussex the disturbances continued for several weeks.

Basically Swing was a labourers' movement for economic ends. A typical demand from east Sussex ran:

Now gentlemen this is wat we intend to have for a maried man to have 2s. and 3d. per Day and all over two children 1s. 6d. per head a week and if a Man has got any boys or girls over age for to have employ that they may live by there Labour and likewise all single men to have 1s. 9d. a day per head and we intend to have the rents lowered likewise and this is what we intend to have before we leave the place and if ther is no alteration we shall proceed further about it. For we are all at one and we will keep to each other.[6]

The object in most places was to obtain an agreement from the farmers to raise wages by a small amount, and also, if threshing machines were used, to abolish them:

Sir

This is to acquaint you that if your thrashing machines are not destroyed by you directly we shall commence our labours signed on behalf
of the whole
    Swing[7]

Threshing by hand with a flail was an important source of employment. It was labour-intensive and provided work during the slack season of the agricultural year. The introduction of the threshing machine reduced the need for such labour and deprived the agricultural worker of the one opportunity during the winter to increase his income above starvation level.

Once the movement was under way the labourers took advantage of the rising to seek redress of other grievances. A tyrannical overseer was compelled to get into the hated village cart (which he had introduced) and escorted out of the village; bands of rioters visited the houses of local magistrates, clergy and farmers demanding food, drink or money; in Hampshire two workhouses were demolished; and everywhere threatening letters were received from Captain Swing:

Sir

Your name is down amongst the Black hearts in the Black Book and this is to advise you and the like of you, who are Parson Justasses, to make your Wills. Ye have been the Blackguard Enemies of the People on all occasions,
Ye have not yet done
as ye ought
    Swing[8]

Who or what Swing was we do not know. He remains as obscure as the equally mythical Ned Ludd or Rebecca (of Rebecca's Daughters in the Welsh anti-tollgate riots of 1842) – perhaps part of that secret, opaque society into which the early nineteenth-century working class retreated when they had recourse to direct action.

Inevitably some actions of the Swing rioters, such as arson, were best conducted in secret, with blackened faces and at night. But the meetings with farmers about wages and the attacks on justices and overseers were in daylight, with the rioters sometimes in their Sunday best and carrying banners and emblems. Not all the rioters were labourers. Among those subsequently punished, between a quarter and a sixth were rural artisans: carpenters, wheelwrights, blacksmiths, bricklayers, shoemakers and cobblers – as well as the odd pedlar, beerhouse keeper and horse dealer. Some small farmers were also involved, perhaps because they too had an interest in preventing the use of threshing machines, which were costly and to the advantage of their wealthier neighbours. Paradoxically Swing was intensely local in its form; but it scared the authorities into repressing it as if it had been a national rising.

The retribution which followed the Swing riots was harsh in the extreme. It was much more severe than the treatment of the Chartists a few years later, although politically Chartism was an infinitely more dangerous movement than Swing. Probably the government overreacted through fear of the unprecedented scale of this type of protest and the enormity of the very idea that such a deferential creature as Hodge should dare to rebel. To teach him a lesson he would not easily forget was regarded as imperative by the government of the day. Special Commissions were set up to collect evidence and bring charges in all the counties affected. Nearly 2000 prisoners were brought to trial in 1830–1. Of these 252 were sentenced to death and 19 were actually executed; 481 were transported to penal colonies in Australia; a further 644 were imprisoned; 7 were fined; one was whipped; and 800 were acquitted or bound over. Yet the only person killed in the riots was one of the rioters, and that by the action of either a soldier or a farmer: no one on the other side had been killed or seriously wounded. In passing sentence of transportation on three of the rioters, one of whom was an eighteen-year-old shepherd boy and another a bricklayer's labourer of nineteen, Mr Justice Alderson commented:

> I hope that your fate will be a warning to others. You will leave the country, all of you: you will see your friends and relatives no more; for though you will be transported for seven years only, it is not likely that at the expiration of that term you will find yourselves in a situation to return. You will be in a distant land at the expiration of your sentence. The land which you have disgraced will see you no more: the friends with whom you are connected will be parted from you for ever in this world.[9]

To press home the lessons of English justice for the poor, the convicted prisoners were compelled to watch the execution of their comrades. *The Times* correspondent described the occasion:

> At this moment I cast my eyes down into the felons' yard, and saw many of the convicts weeping bitterly, some burying their faces in their smock frocks, others wringing their hands convulsively, and others leaning for support against the wall of the yard and unable to cast their eyes upwards.[10]

The crushing effect of the sentences was catastrophic. Many of the prisoners were young men: the average age of those transported was between twenty-seven and thirty, and most were married. They were now torn from their families, who were left destitute and in despair. In Wiltshire and Hampshire there were whole villages that for a generation suffered from this loss. Eighty years later the memory of the tragic events was still alive in villages on the Wiltshire downs. For the 481 wretched men and boys transported there were all the brutalities of convict life: ironing (i.e. shackling with chains); collection in the hulks (old and rotting ships that served as floating dungeons); weeks below deck on the 12,000-mile sea voyage; and finally assignment as semi-slave labour in the penal colonies of New South Wales and Van Diemen's Land. Although most of the prisoners were pardoned later, no free passages were granted and very few ever returned. Whatever they made of their lives subsequently in Australia (and some prospered), as far as England was concerned they had simply disappeared and the land they had 'disgraced' saw them no more. As their epitaph we may quote the petition for release of a Hampshire farm labourer in 1838:

To D. Thompson, Secretary, Sydney.
Mr Thompson, Sir, pardon me for taking the Liberty of a Drass you but mi torobles calls me to do so. I rived by the Ship Captain Cook in the Year 1833 Santanse Life for Riating & Meshan Braking. I saw the newspaper with menn that was triad with me the have goot ther Liberty. I have been in no troble since mi arivale. I hope you will be so kind as to in form me if theires anthing aganst me mi name Is Jacob Wilsher and it so far up the contry I have no ways of guting Down to make in qury I have a sined Sarvent to Mr Thos BEATTS of Paramatta and is at Molong[y?] in the Districk of Willington . . .
   Your humble sarvent &&
     Jacob Wiltsher.[11]

Rural protest did not disappear after the Swing riots. Rick-burning and anti-Poor Law disturbances continued until later in the century, but were scattered and sporadic. More in tune with the tempo of the age were the Tolpuddle martyrs – six Dorsetshire agricultural labourers who were sentenced in 1834 to seven years' transportation for administering an illegal oath in their newly formed trade union lodge. As industrial society developed so popular protest changed from the traditional form of riot into political organization and the demand for democratic rights. The tradition of the true-born Englishman and the seventeenth-century legacy of popular rights surfaced from time to time in the eighteenth century, as during the Wilkite riots of 1768 and among the sympathizers with the American revolution in 1776–83. But it was the French revolution beginning in 1789 which galvanized groups of working men to organize political Corresponding Societies in London and the main provincial towns:

as Providence has kindly furnished men in every station, with faculties necessary for judging of what concerns themselves, shall we the multitude suffer a few, with no better right than ourselves to usurp the power of governing us without control? Surely not! Let us rather unite in one common cause, to cast away our bondage . . .[12]

Their bible was Thomas Paine's *Rights of Man* (1792) and their programme was for full political reform: universal male suffrage, annual parliaments and secret ballot.

Before working men could hope to exercise any degree of political power they had to secure a reform of the system. The complexities and anomalies in the franchise and size of the electorate made possible a system of proprietary politics. By means of bribery, corruption and the exertion of 'influence', rich men were able to control the election of members to parliament. This, when combined with a system of patronage, formed the basis of the eighteenth-century practice of government. In the counties everyone who owned freehold land to the value of 40s. a year was entitled to vote. Because of the fall in the value of money since 1430 (when the qualification was fixed) and the liberal interpretation of the term freehold, the electorate was fairly wide, although the two county members might be elected by a mere 600 voters in the smallest county, Rutland, or by 15,000 in the largest, Yorkshire. In the boroughs the franchise was more complicated. At one extreme were a few boroughs with virtually universal suffrage; at the other were the 'close', 'rotten' or 'pocket' boroughs in which there might be as few as ten or a dozen electors. Westminster in 1761 had 9000 voters and London 6000: but only 22 of the 203 English boroughs had electorates of 1000 or more, and 72 per cent of the borough members were returned by electorates of 500 or less. Cornwall and the southwestern counties were particularly rich in rotten boroughs, often small, decayed seaports. In Cornwall 42 members were returned by 21 boroughs with a total electorate of less than 1400. Yet towns like Manchester, Leeds and Birmingham returned no members. Voting was in public and so pressure could be exerted on most of the electors. The defects and abuses of the system stemmed mainly from the retention of institutions and practices that were completely out of date. 'England', observed the French historian, Elie Halévy, 'was a museum of constitutional archaeology where the relics of past ages accumulated.'

Politically minded artisans, journeymen and shopkeepers had

little use for such relics in the excitement of the early 1790s. They met in their 'Jacobin' clubs, addressed each other as 'Citizen' and debated the issues of the people versus the privileged: 'The usual mode of proceeding at these weekly meetings', wrote Francis Place (at this time a young leather-breeches maker and later famous as 'the radical tailor of Charing Cross'), 'was this. The Chairman (each man was chairman in rotation) read from some book . . . and the persons present were invited to make remarks thereon, as many as chose did so, but without rising. Then another portion was read and a second invitation given. Then the remainder was read and a third invitation was given. . . . Then there was a general discussion.'[13] In reply to Edmund Burke's condemnation of the French revolutionaries and his contempt for the 'swinish multitude' appeared *Hog's Wash* (1793) and similar democratic political journals. A spate of radical pamphlets poured out (unequalled since the days of the Commonwealth), together with cheap additions of the works of Paine, Volney, the French deists, and the millenarian prophecies of Richard Brothers. The government became alarmed (after all, the country was at war with revolutionary France) and instituted a policy of repression. Radicals were put on trial, patriotic 'church and king' mobs terrorized Jacobin sympathizers, and the little groups of reformers were driven underground.

The second phase of the reform agitation, from 1816 to 1822, was closely associated with the economic distress that followed the ending of the war with France. Working-class radicalism during these years was extraordinarily complex and was not confined to peaceful demands for political reform. Luddism broke out again in 1816–17. At the end of 1816 a mass meeting at Spa Fields in London turned into a riot, and the following month an attempt was made on the life of the prince regent. The year 1817 also saw the march of the Blanketeers – unemployed weavers who set out from Manchester for London; and in Derbyshire at Pentridge there was an attempt at armed insurrection. The response of the Tory government was repression: suspension of habeas corpus (1817), trials for blasphemy and sedition, imprisonment and execution of the leaders. Spies and *agents provocateurs* infiltrated the radical movement, and a general air of panic spread throughout the God-fearing and propertied classes. The campaign for parliamentary reform was carried on through Hampden clubs (initiated by the veteran radical, Major Cartwright) and mass demonstrations addressed by Henry (Orator) Hunt and other popular heroes. A flourishing radical press, inspired by the success of Cobbett's *Political Register*, added such titles as the *Black Dwarf*, the *Gorgon* and the *Republican*. Throughout the country this activity accelerated, reaching a climax at Peterloo in 1819.

The massacre at what was derisively dubbed 'Peterloo' took place in St Peter's Fields, Manchester, on 16 August. It had been intended as a massive culmination of the northern reform campaign and as a follow-up to similar meetings at Birmingham and elsewhere. Some 60,000 men and women had peaceably assembled and were about to listen to Orator Hunt, when the magistrates ordered the yeomanry (local, part-time cavalry) to arrest the speaker, and in their efforts to do so the yeomanry set about the crowd with their swords. What then happened is vividly described by Samuel Bamford, the weaver, who was present:

> On the cavalry drawing up they were received with a shout of good-will, as I understood it. They shouted again, waving their sabres over their heads; and then, slackening rein, and striking spur into their steeds, they dashed forward and began cutting the people.
>
> 'Stand fast,' I said, 'they are riding upon us; stand fast.' And there was a general cry in our quarter of 'Stand fast.' The cavalry were in confusion: they evidently could not, with all the weight of man and horse, penetrate that compact mass of human beings; and their sabres were plied to hew a way through naked held-up hands and defenceless heads; and then chopped limbs and wound-gaping skulls were seen; and groans and cries were mingled with the din of that horrid confusion. 'Ah! ah!' 'for shame! for shame!' was shouted. Then, 'Break! break! they are killing them in front, and they cannot get away;' and there was a general cry of 'break! break.' For a moment the crowd held back as in a pause; then was a rush, heavy and resistless as a headlong sea, and a sound like low thunder, with screams, prayers, and imprecations from the crowd-moiled and sabre-doomed who could not escape. . . .
>
> In ten minutes from the commencement of the havoc the field

was an open and almost deserted space. The sun looked down through a sultry and motionless air. The curtains and blinds of the windows within view were all closed. A gentleman or two might occasionally be seen looking out from one of the new houses before mentioned, near the door of which a group of persons (special constables) were collected, and apparently in conversation; others were assisting the wounded or carrying off the dead. The hustings remained, with a few broken and hewed flag-staves erect, and a torn and gashed banner or two drooping; whilst over the whole field were strewed caps, bonnets, hats, shawls, and shoes, and other parts of male and female dress, trampled, torn, and bloody. The yeomanry had dismounted – some were easing their horses' girths, others adjusting their accoutrements, and some were wiping their sabres. Several mounds of human beings still remained where they had fallen, crushed down and smothered. Some of these were still groaning, others with staring eyes, were gasping for breath, and others would never breathe more. All was silent save those low sounds, and the occasional snorting and pawing of steeds.[14]

Altogether eleven people were killed and over four hundred wounded. The outcry from liberals and reformers of every shade was immediate. The government equally promptly congratulated the magistrates and within a matter of weeks rushed through the notorious Six Acts, aimed at curbing radical journals and meetings as well as the danger of armed insurrection. Peterloo became a symbol: it was condemned at mass meetings throughout the country, and was commemorated at radical gatherings for many years afterwards. 'Remember the Bloody Deeds of Peterloo,' proclaimed the Chartist banners twenty years later.

With an improvement in economic conditions in 1820, the ferment for reform declined. A plot to murder the members of the cabinet (the Cato Street Conspiracy) was exposed in 1820; it was perhaps a last fling of the insurrectionary Jacobinism of the 1790s. But although the momentum of the political reform movement slowed down in the 1820s, the memories of recent struggles, especially Peterloo, remained. When the movement entered its third and final phase, it did so with renewed determination born of past organizational experience and with a consciousness of belonging to a great radical tradition.

The dynamics of the third phase, from 1830 to 1832, were different from earlier stages of the reform struggle in important respects. Essentially the Reform Bill of 1832 was a party measure, carried by one section of the ruling elite, the Whigs, against the other, the Tories, amid a great popular agitation throughout the country. The extra-parliamentary agitation was fierce and more widespread than ever before, but in addition battle was now joined in earnest in parliament. Reform was made the central issue between the contending political parties once the long period of Tory dominance was ended. For almost fifty years before 1830 the Tories had formed the government, and their home policy – at best conservative and at the worst repressive – was opposed to any significant parliamentary reform. The working classes were caught up in the 1830–2 struggles in various ways. Through local Parliamentary Reform Associations and Political Unions, they supported the middle-class agitation for reform; while at the same time preserving their separate identity in such bodies as the National Union of the Working Classes formed in 1831 by William Lovett, a cabinet-maker, for 'the Protection of Working Men; the Free Disposal of the Produce of Labour; an Effectual Reform of the Commons' House of Parliament; the Repeal of all Bad Laws; the Enactment of a Wise and Comprehensive Code of Laws; and to collect and organize a peaceful expression of public opinion'.[15]

At a different level of political consciousness the common people also demonstrated their feelings in the reform riots of 1831 at Nottingham (where the castle was burned down), Derby, Worcester, Bath and (most severely) Bristol. Despite warnings from some radical papers like the *Poor Man's Guardian* that the bill was a class measure for the benefit of the middle and not the working classes, great popular excitement and extravagant hopes were raised. Cobbett was sure that much would be gained:

> It may be asked, Will a reform of the Parliament give the labouring man a cow or a pig; will it put bread and cheese into his satchell instead of infernal cold potatoes; will it give him a bottle of beer to carry to the field instead of making him lie down upon his belly to drink out of the brook; will it put upon his back

a Sunday coat and send him to church, instead of leaving him to stand lounging about shivering with an unshaven face and a carcass half covered with a ragged smock frock, with a filthy cotton shirt beneath it as yellow as a kite's foot? Will parliamentary reform put an end to the harnessing of men and women by a hired overseer to draw carts like beasts of burden; . . . will it put an end to the system which caused the honest labourer to be fed worse than the felons in the jails; . . . will parliamentary reform put an end to . . . the basest acts which the Roman tyrants committed towards their slaves? The enemies of reform jeeringly ask us, whether reform would do these things for us; and I answer distinctly that IT WOULD DO THEM ALL![16]

But after the passing of the bill, and when the celebratory banquets, bonfires and ringing of church bells were over, it was apparent that only very modest gains had been achieved for the working classes. In the counties the 40s. freeholders continued to vote, but to them were added tenant farmers who paid at least £50 a year in rent. In the boroughs a new basic qualification for voting was introduced: occupation of premises of an annual value of £10. The enfranchisement of the £10 householders worked unevenly in different parts of the country. Where rents were low, as in Leeds, few working men had the vote; but where rents were higher, as in Manchester and London, some respectable working-class householders were enfranchised. 'Ancient right' voters (that is, those who had the vote before 1832) were allowed to continue to vote provided they remained resident in their old borough. In general, the new dispensation brought into the electoral system the tenant farmers of the counties, and held the line at the level of the lower middle and some respectable working classes in the towns. There was also a redistribution of seats. The rotten boroughs were swept away and representation was given to the new large towns like Manchester, Leeds and Birmingham. The overall effect of the Reform Act was to increase the number of voters by about 50 per cent: it added some 217,000 to an electorate of 435,000 in England and Wales. But 650,000 electors in a population of 14 million were a small minority. Most Englishmen, and all Englishwomen, were still without the vote, and were to remain so until much later.

The forms of social and political protest between 1815 and 1850 were legion: political reform, Chartism, trade unionism, factory reform, Owenite socialism, cooperation, anti-Poor Law agitation, secularism, the struggle for an unstamped press – to name only the most obvious. If we dip anywhere into these movements we uncover evidence of class conflict and struggle. Here for instance is Joseph Swann, a radical hatter from Macclesfield, imprisoned for selling illegal, unstamped newspapers:

BENCH: What have you to say in your defence?
DEFENDANT: Well, sir, I have been out of employment for some time; neither can I obtain work; my family are all starving. . . . And for another reason, the weightiest of all; I sell them for the good of my fellow countrymen; to let them see how they are misrepresented in parliament. . . . I wish to let the people know how they are humbugged . . .
BENCH: Hold your tongue a moment.
DEFENDANT: I shall not! for I wish every man to read those publications.
BENCH: You are very insolent, therefore you are committed to three months' imprisonment in Knutsford House of Correction, to hard labour.
DEFENDANT: I've nothing to thank you for; and whenever I come out I'll hawk them again. And mind you, the first that I hawk shall be to your house . . .[17]

The strategy of the struggle against the newspaper stamp duties ('taxes on knowledge'), which made papers expensive and therefore beyond the reach of working people, was for radicals to publish unstamped papers openly and defiantly. The publishers and sellers were then prosecuted and gaoled: between 1830 and 1836 over 700 people were prosecuted for selling unstamped papers, 219 of them in 1835. On another front a campaign to reduce the hours and conditions of labour in factories, first for children and then for adults, was mounted. Short Time Committees appeared in the northern factory districts in 1830–1 and linked up with Tory-Radicals to agitate for a Ten Hours Bill in parliament. Trade union activity, culminating in the Grand National Consolidated Trades Union of 1833–4 which claimed to have a million members, was directed into cooperative and syndicalist channels. Organized and bitter opposition to the New Poor Law was widespread in the northern towns in 1837–8. Throughout the 1830s and early 1840s there was intense and sustained protest by working people against the new industrial society which gripped them in its iron fist. The climax of their endeavours was Chartism, which in its most vigorous years (1837–42) seemed to swallow up lesser movements and incorporate their demands with its own.

A combination of disillusionment with the Reform Act of 1832 and a continuing belief in the possibility and efficacy of reform provided the immediate enthusiasm for the greatest of all the popular movements, Chartism. For nearly twenty years after 1837, Chartism was a name to evoke the wildest hopes and the worst fears, like Bolshevism in a later age. Some historians have seen Chartism as a forerunner of the Labour Party and the modern labour movement, which in a sense it was. Certainly no other movement before the rise of modern labour and socialism at the end of the century had anything like the mass following of Chartism. It was the first attempt to build an independent political party representing the interests of the labouring and unprivileged sections of the nation. Contemporaries noted that for many of its followers Chartism was basically 'a knife and fork question'. Yet its programme was a series of political demands. This has puzzled historians, who have concluded that one of the main reasons for Chartism's lack of success was its contradiction in seeking political remedies for economic grievances. In fact the Chartists' tactics made a good deal of sense at that time, and their analysis of what we should now call the power structure was evidently shrewder than the historians'. The link between economic ills and political representation was constantly elaborated in Chartist pamphlets and oratory; how, it was asked, could a 'rotten House of Commons', representing the interests of landholders, speculators, manufacturers and capitalists, be expected to do anything but uphold an economic system in which the poor were ground down and oppressed? Given the options open to them in the 1830s, and the experience of alternative paths which they had pursued and found blocked, the Chartists' programme for social advance through political power was perfectly sound. It was also the method adopted, though with more success, by the middle classes; and this lesson was by no means lost upon the Chartists. If

Chartism did not gain its objectives, the reasons have to be sought elsewhere than in the apparent paradox of economic ends through political means.

The Chartists were so named because they formulated their demands in a six-point charter: universal (manhood) suffrage, annual parliaments, vote by (secret) ballot, abolition of the property qualification for MPs, payment of MPs, and equal electoral districts. The object was to make the charter the law of the land, by legal, constitutional means if possible, or by force if necessary – or by a mixture of both. Most Chartist leaders were reluctant to be labelled as 'moral force' or 'physical force' men. 'We will have the charter,' they declared, 'peaceably if we can, forcibly if we must.' Great efforts were made to collect support for a petition to the House of Commons on behalf of the charter; but on each occasion that it was presented the House rejected its demands. Alternative methods were therefore bound to be advocated. There were plans for making the central body of Chartist delegates, the national convention, a people's parliament to bypass Westminster; a general strike ('national holiday') was attempted in August 1839; and local riots, and perhaps an abortive insurrection (in November 1839), showed that physical force might not be ruled out. But the Chartists were unable to repeat the tactics of 1830–2, when the Reform Bill was carried by a combination of support in parliament and the threat of force outside.

There was little that was new in the six points of the charter. They were drawn up by William Lovett and his friends in the London Working Men's Association in 1837, though the People's Charter was not officially published until the following year. Politically Chartism was in the central tradition of British radicalism, stretching back to the Corresponding Societies of 1792–3, and the Chartists were proud of their heritage. It was a tradition of mass meetings, imprisonments and conflicts with authority. In the provinces Working Men's Associations were formed on the London model in 1837, in each case building on the remains of earlier radical reform organizations, such as the Political Unions which had carried on the popular struggle for the Reform Bill.

The origins of Chartism, however, were more complex than a simple development from the London Working Men's Association. In Birmingham the movement at first was closely allied with middle-class radicals and currency reformers. In Leeds, Owenite socialists combined with middle-class radicals and physical-force militants to launch the Leeds Working Men's Association. And in other towns of the West Riding and the industrial North and Northeast local movements and grievances provided a basis for Chartism. Thus right from the start Chartism was not a national movement with its central headquarters in London, but a series of local and regional movements loosely federated together. This posed a problem of concerted action which was never solved. Attempts to build a national organization repeatedly fell apart; and the most effective link between Chartists was not their system of delegates to a national convention, but the widely read Chartist newspaper, the *Northern Star*. The geography of Chartism highlights a characteristic which is found in other contemporary movements, such as the Anti-Corn Law League, namely, the strength of provincial roots and the relative isolation of London. A clue to the reasons for this can be found in the economic and social pattern.

The point has been made that the British economy in the period 1830–50 was only partly industrialized, and that machinery and factory organization had been introduced unevenly between different industries and between different sectors of the same industry. Levels of wages, employment opportunities, social relationships, and general working conditions varied between industries and localities, creating different types and intensities of grievance. Within the labouring population divisions were created by differences of skill and earnings. Chartism was directly related to these varieties within the labour force, and faithfully reflected them in its regional peculiarities. Wherever there was a substantial number of skilled artisans, especially shoemakers, printers, tailors and cabinet-makers, a Chartist organization on the lines of the Working Men's Associations was to be expected, with an emphasis on self-help, independence and propaganda for universal suffrage. Such was the movement in London or Birmingham. But in areas where there were substantial numbers of distressed handloom weavers, as in Lancashire and the West Riding, Chartism assumed an altogether fiercer visage and adopted a more strident tone. The idol of the northern Chartists was not the reasoned, respectable artisan, William Lovett, with his appeal to 'the most intelligent and influential portion of the working classes', but the flamboyant Irish orator, Feargus O'Connor, who claimed to be the champion of the 'unshorn chins, blistered hands, and fustian jackets'. In Leicestershire and the east Midlands the backbone of the Chartist movement were the framework knitters – another group of domestic workers labouring, like the handloom weavers, in an overstocked trade. There was a close correlation between the distribution of knitting frames and the strength of Chartism; Leicester, Loughborough and Hinckley were centres of the hosiery industry and also Chartist strongholds; in the eastern half of Leicestershire, where there were practically no frames, Chartism did not develop. Leeds and Sheffield in the 1840s produced another type of Chartism, based on lower-middle-class radicalism and artisan support. The Chartists in these towns elected their own candidates to the Town Council and concerned themselves with local issues of importance to shopkeepers and tradesmen.

Just as the local variations of Chartism were related to the structure of the economy, so the chronology of the movement reflected the cycle of booms and slumps between 1836 and 1851. The first climax of Chartism came in the winter of 1839, at the height of the trade depression. In 1842 a second peak of Chartist activity was reached with the Plug riots, arising out of mass unemployment in the northern towns. And the last great flare-up of Chartism came in 1848, following a winter of economic recession and inspired by revolutions on the continent. In periods of relative prosperity (1843–7 and after 1848) Chartism lost its mass support. It then became a movement promoting education, temperance, municipal reforms and settlement on the land – while never losing faith that universal suffrage would some day, somehow, be won. After 1848, as a tantalizing sort of epilogue, a group of Chartists tried to steer the movement towards socialism and the international working-class movement of Marx and Engels.

If, as has been stressed, Chartism was in many ways a logical development within the tradition of radical reform, in what sense was it a distinctive movement, and in what lay its significance as a vehicle for social change in the 1830s and 1840s? Two characteristics seem to stand out from the Chartist record, especially in its early phase; first, its class-conscious tone and temper; second, its mass size. There are not many points in modern British history at which the historian can profitably speculate whether a revolutionary situation might have developed but did not. Among the dates for consideration, however, would have to be included the winter of 1839 and the spring and summer of 1848. At both these times Chartism seemed, to many contemporaries, to pose the threat of the barricades.

Chartists of many shades of opinion emphasized that their movement was concerned to promote the interests of working men as a class. The artisans of the Working Men's Associations no less than the distressed handworkers of the North assumed the need for class solidarity, and their leaders talked the language of class struggle. They denounced the Reform Act of 1832 as a middle-class measure, complained that the working classes had been deliberately duped, and argued that Whigs and Tories alike were enemies of the people. An old Chartist writing at the end of the century commented:

> People who have not shared in the hopes of the Chartists, who have no personal knowledge of the deep and intense feelings which animated them, can have little conception of the difference between our own times and those of fifty or sixty years ago. The whole governing classes – Whigs even more than Tories – were not only disliked, they were positively hated by the working population. Nor was this hostility to their own countrymen less manifest on the side of the 'better orders'.[18]

The picture of society here presented is very far from the comfortable, upper-class ideal of stability and a modest degree of sanctioned change. By its appeal to smouldering social antagonisms and its articulation of class consciousness, Chartism struck at the roots of deference – which helps to account for the support it received from other non-deferential groups such as some members of the radical lower middle classes. So strong was the feeling of working-class identification in Chartism that it defeated all attempts to form an alliance with middle-class reformers in the Anti-Corn Law League or the Complete Suffrage Union. Even in Birmingham, where such an alliance had the greatest hope of success, the proposal to drop the name Charter in favour of some new organization was sufficient to unite in opposition the mutually antagonistic Chartist leaders, Lovett and O'Connor. When this working-class consciousness was matched by an even stronger middle-class consciousness, as was the case in the 1830s and 1840s, the possibility of social conflict was enhanced.

The fear of Chartism by the opulent classes was inspired by the very large number of followers who appeared to be sympathetic to its militant tactics. Membership of popular movements in the nineteenth century is difficult to assess, and accounts of numbers at meetings are notoriously divergent between one newspaper and another. Contemporaries, however, were agreed that attendances at Chartist meetings were greater than anything they could remember previously. Something of the tone of these rallies is conveyed by R.G. Gammage, the only Chartist to attempt a history of the movement. He is describing the torchlight meetings held on the Lancashire moors in the autumn of 1838:

for a short period the factory districts presented a series of such imposing popular demonstrations, as were perhaps never witnessed in any previous agitation. Bolton, Stockport, Ashton, Hyde, Staleybridge, Leigh, and various other places, large and small, were the scenes of these magnificent gatherings. At the whole of them the working people met in their thousands and tens of thousands to swear devotion to the common cause. It is almost impossible to imagine the excitement caused by these manifestations. . . . The people did not go singly to the place of meeting, but met in a body at a starting point, from whence, at a given time, they issued in huge numbers, formed into procession, traversing the principal streets, making the heavens echo with the thunder of their cheers on recognizing the idols of their worship in the men who were to address them, and sending forth volleys of the most hideous groans on passing the office of some hostile newspaper, or the house of some obnoxious magistrate or employer. The banners containing the more formidable devices, viewed by the red light of the glaring torches, presented a scene of awful grandeur. The death's heads represented on some of them grinned like ghostly spectres, and served to remind many a mammon-worshipper of his expected doom. The uncouth appearance of thousands of artisans who had not time from leaving the factory to go home and attend to the ordinary duties of cleanliness, and whose faces were therefore begrimed with sweat and dirt, added to the strange aspect of the scene. The processions were frequently of immense length, sometimes containing as many as fifty thousand people; and along the whole line there blazed a stream of light, illuminating the lofty sky, like the reflection from a large city in a general conflagration. The meetings themselves were of a still more terrific character. The very appearance of such a vast number of blazing torches only seemed more effectually to inflame the minds alike of speaker and hearers.[19]

Another, and less inflammatory, type of Chartist meeting was the great open-air rally held on a public holiday. Contingents would march, with bands and banners, from surrounding towns and villages to a central meeting place, where they would listen to speeches from local and national leaders. Booths and stalls were set up, and the marchers were accompanied by their sweethearts, wives and children, so that the whole gathering had some of the atmosphere of a fair. In the West Riding, for example, such Chartist rallies were held at Peep Green, a natural amphitheatre in the hills and equally accessible from all the main industrial towns of the region. Ben Wilson, the Halifax Chartist, estimated that 200,000 people were present at the meeting there on Whit Monday 1839.

Chartism made a deep impression on the labouring poor and assisted their transformation into a working class. The events of 1837–48 lived long in popular memory: the ghostly torchlight meetings, the skirmishes with police and troops, the drilling with pikes, the moulding of bullets in the cellar, arrest and imprisonment of local leaders, the escape to America when things got too hot at home – all served to add another chapter to the tradition of radical struggle. There was a strong romantic strain in all this: Chartist oratory and poetry was rich in denunciation of tyrants and proclamation of the glories of freedom; every imprisoned Chartist was portrayed as a noble martyr languishing in a dungeon. But the general result was a heightening of class awareness, a strengthening of the conviction that the working classes as such had special and separate interests, to which other classes were hostile or indifferent. The development of this class consciousness was an essential part of the making of the English working class. At the same time Chartism was also rooted in an older and indigenous folk culture. It was a movement in the true sense of the word, and not just an organization. Like other British reformers, the Chartists frequently appealed to ancient liberties, and presented their new demands as the restoration of traditional rights. While they called for class solidarity (or 'union of sentiment', as they put it), they also saw themselves as freeborn Englishmen.

They also drew upon other sources for ideas. The most fruitful of these was Owenite socialism. Robert Owen, a successful industrialist who made a fortune in cotton spinning, elaborated his plans for social reconstruction in the years after the Napoleonic Wars. His first followers were mainly radical philanthropists, but in the late 1820s Owenism attracted support among working men. The trade union ferment of 1829–34 was dominated by Owenite theories, and for a few months in 1833–4 Owen was the acknowledged leader of the working classes. After the collapse of the Grand National Consolidated Trades Union, the Owenites developed a national organization of agents and branches which carried on propaganda and social activities until about 1845. The institutions of Owenism, however, were never as influential as its social theories. Many working-class leaders, who criticized Owen and the Owenites in the 1830s, nevertheless acknowledged their debt to Owenite socialism. Owenism provided a kind of reservoir from which different groups and individuals drew ideas and inspiration which they then applied as they chose.

Essentially Owenism was the main British variety of what Marx and Engels called utopian socialism, but which is more usefully described as communitarianism. The Owenites believed that society could be radically transformed by means of experimental communities, in which property was held in common, and social and economic activity was organized on a cooperative basis. This was a method of effecting social change which was radical, peaceful and immediate. Between 1825 and 1847 seven Owenite communities were founded in Britain, the largest being at Orbiston in Scotland and at East Tytherly, Hampshire. But attractive as the sectarian ideal of withdrawal from society in order to get on with building the 'new moral world' might appear in the grim years of the 1830s and 1840s, the communities did not flourish as had been hoped. Other Owenite institutions for changing society were scarcely more successful. Labour exchanges, where artisans could exchange the products of their labour through the medium of labour notes, did not spread beyond London and Birmingham. Only the cooperative trading stores, some of which were established by working men to accumulate funds for starting a community, proved eventually to be viable; and the continuous history of the modern cooperative movement is usually traced from the foundation of an Owenite store in Rochdale in 1844.

If Owenism did not produce strong and stable institutions, it did provide a yeast of ideas which found their way into other movements. Communitarianism was a challenge to a society in which community values had been weakened by emphasis on individual enterprise, self-help and competition. The Owenites called themselves socialists from the mid-1830s because they wished to emphasize a social, as opposed to an individual, approach in all fields of human endeavour, including economic organization. They formulated a critique of capitalism and an alternative theory to orthodox political economy which were echoed by many working-class leaders. The basis of the Owenite 'economy of cooperation' was a general labour theory of value, derived partly from a doctrine of natural right (as found in the works of John Locke) and partly from the economic arguments of the contemporary political economist, David Ricardo. If, as the Owenites maintained, labour is the source of all wealth, and men exchange their products according to the amount of labour embodied in them, it needed little theory to convince working men that they had a right to the whole produce of their labour – and, as a corollary, that if they were poor it must be because they were not receiving the full value of what they produced. In the bargain between capital and labour, it was argued, labour received only a part of the wealth to which it was entitled. Further, competitive commercial society was fettered by inadequate demand; the depression of wages to subsistence level destroyed incentive to higher production by labouring men, and the low level of their consumption caused by inadequate purchasing power put a ceiling on production. In its emphasis on the contrast between 'wealth and misery' or the paradox of 'poverty in the midst of plenty' Owenism was well calculated to speak to the condition of thoughtful working men.

There was, however, little evidence of any substantial immediate gain in all the protest and revolt of these turbulent years. The Chartists did not win their six points, and Owenite socialism was forgotten after 1848. Not until many years later were working people able to establish a tolerable position for themselves in capitalist society. Yet the reminiscences of old Chartists and Owenites do not convey a sense of failure. Looking back on their early struggles from the vantage point of the 1870s and 1880s they insisted that what they did and thought was right, and that subsequent developments had vindicated them. Like Ben Wilson they remained convinced that the Chartists were 'the true pioneers in all the great movements of their time'.[20]

9. Self-help and Respectability

The problems arising from the new industrial civilization were also tackled by the working class in ways other than protest and revolt. Especially after the mid-century, when some of the worst excesses of capitalist industrialism had been mitigated, numbers of working people turned to movements of reform and adaptation to improve their lot. No hard and fast line can be drawn between movements whose object was to change the nature of society itself, and those designed to change conditions within that society; though the distinction is useful as a means of assessing different types of action. Some Chartists and Owenites wanted fundamental changes in the structure of society; but most riots and protests of the traditional type were directed only against specific grievances, without any long-term objectives. Nor is the distinction primarily one between revolutionaries and reformists, for there were in fact very few of the former; but rather between different modes by which the working classes sought economic betterment and social emancipation. The mode most widely adopted to achieve peaceful social change was self-help, which appeared in a variety of forms.

Self-help is usually associated with the name of Samuel Smiles and his widely influential book, *Self-Help: with illustrations of Character and Conduct* (1859). Middle-class enthusiasm for the virtues of self-help later integrated it into the dominant Victorian philosophy of individualism, and it was preached to the working classes as an answer to their demands for better social conditions. But in its original expression, self-help was a spontaneous response to working-class needs, and frequently assumed a collective form. The mutual improvement society, the friendly benefit society and the cooperative store were organizations set up by working men to do together something which they could not do so well alone. This collective self-help developed its most powerful potential in trade unionism.

The early trade unions were not direct descendants of the gilds which, although designed to protect the interests of all members of a trade, were in practice dominated by the masters. From the second half of the seventeenth century the gilds began to crumble and the journeymen had therefore to look elsewhere for the protection of their interests. Apprenticeship, wage rates, price lists, tramping, and hours of work had all previously been regulated by gild rules and in some cases by municipal law and act of parliament. In the eighteenth century combinations of journeymen were formed to assume these functions. The early unions were often small and local, and were largely limited to skilled craftsmen: hatters, printers, bookbinders, weavers, woolcombers, shearmen, stockingers, cotton spinners, steam-engine makers, shipwrights, brushmakers, masons, ironfounders, miners, potters, shoemakers, tailors, cutlers, coopers, bricklayers, carpenters – in short, all those known in the nineteenth century and later as the 'trades'. Not until the end of the nineteenth century was it considered either practical or desirable to organize labourers. From 1799 to 1824, under the Combination Acts, such combinations of workmen (and also of employers) were illegal. One result of this was to put a premium on secrecy. Even after the repeal of the Combination Acts in 1824 secrecy was continued because of the hostility of employers, who in some cases sought to impose the 'document' requiring their men formally to renounce the union. When the pioneer labour historians, Sidney and Beatrice Webb, were collecting material for their great *History of Trade Unionism* ninety years ago they discovered that every union which dated from before the 1830s possessed legends of 'the midnight meeting of patriots in the corner of the field, the buried box of records, the secret oath, the long terms of imprisonment of the leading officials'.[1] The records of such happenings are extremely elusive; but in the case of the secret oath it is possible to recapture something of the atmosphere of this early unionism.

The oath was taken at the time of initiation into the union, usually in a private room at a tavern at eight or nine o'clock in the evening. On one side of the apartment was a skeleton, above which a drawn sword and a battle axe were suspended, and in front stood a table upon which lay a bible. The officers of the union wore surplices and addressed each other by their titles of president, vice president, warden, principal conductor, and inside and outside tiler. The new members were blindfolded for part of the ceremony, which included the singing of hymns and the recitation of prayers; and the ritual was generally reminiscent of the Freemasons and Oddfellows. After an address by the president, in which he reminded them of the awful solemnity of the occasion, the climax of the ceremony was reached. The 'strangers', as the new members were termed, placed their right hands on the bible and repeated the following oath:

I, A.B., woolcomber, being in the awful presence of Almighty God, do voluntarily declare that I will persevere in endeavouring to support a brotherhood, known by the name of the Friendly Society of Operative Stuff Manufacturers, and other Industrious Operatives, and I solemnly declare and promise that I will never act in opposition to the brotherhood in any of their attempts to support wages, but will, to the utmost of my power, assist them in all lawful and just occasions, to obtain a fair remuneration for our labour. And I call upon God to witness this my most solemn declaration, that neither hopes, fears, rewards, punishments, nor even death itself, shall ever induce me directly or indirectly, to give any information respecting any thing contained in this Lodge, or any similar Lodge connected with the Society; and I will neither write nor cause to be written, upon paper, wood, sand, stone, or any thing else, whereby it may be known, unless allowed to do so by the proper authorities of the Society. And I will never give my consent to have any money belonging to the Society divided or appropriated to any other purpose than the use of the Society and support of the trade, so help me God, and keep me steadfast in this my most solemn obligation; and if ever I reveal either part or parts of this my most solemn obligation, may all the Society I am about to belong to, and all that is just, disgrace me so long as I live; and may what is now before me plunge my soul into the everlasting pit of misery. Amen.[2]

It was for adminstering such an oath that the most famous episode of early trade union history came about. In March 1834 six agricultural labourers from the Dorsetshire village of Tolpuddle,

273

who formed a trade union lodge, were sentenced to seven years' transportation under an Act of 1797 forbidding 'unlawful oaths'. George Loveless, their leader, described how the farmers of Tolpuddle progressively reduced wages below the rate paid in the surrounding district:

> From this time we were reduced to seven shillings per week, and shortly after our employers told us they must lower us to six shillings per week. The labouring men consulted together what had better be done, as they knew it was impossible to live honestly on such scanty means. I had seen at different times accounts of Trade Societies; I told them of this and they willingly consented to form a friendly society among the labourers, having sufficiently learnt that it would be vain to seek redress either of employers, magistrates or parsons. I inquired of a brother to get information how to proceed, and shortly after, two delegates from a Trade Society paid us a visit, formed a Friendly Society among the labourers, and gave us directions how to proceed. This was about the latter end of October 1833.[3]

Loveless seems to have been in contact with Robert Owen's Grand National Consolidated Trades Union, and as soon as the significance of the sentence was realized the GNCTU organized a sustained campaign of petitions and mass demonstrations. Two years later the six victims were pardoned. After some delay they returned home; and later five of them emigrated to Canada. The Tolpuddle martyrs found themselves caught up in a great outburst of trade union militancy and attempts at forming national organizations. But the main and continuing union experience throughout the 1830s and 1840s was at the local level and among skilled men. After 1850, when the turmoil of the Chartist years gave place to a period of relative social harmony, some unions, notably the Amalgamated Society of Engineers and the Amalgamated Society of Carpenters and Joiners, developed a centralized organization and a comprehensive system of benefits for members on strike, unemployed or sick. They were headed by full-time officials – working men who formed an efficient labour bureaucracy. In the 1860s they threw their weight behind the agitation for the Second Reform Bill; and in the 1870s they were successful in securing a series of legal reforms which established the position of trade unions and provided protection for workmen. The hallmarks of this type of unionism were the creation of a stable organization, respectability and moderation: 'If you do not wish to stand as you are and suffer more oppression,' advised the Birmingham *Flint Glass Makers' Magazine* in 1850, 'we say to you get knowledge, and in getting knowledge you get power. . . . Let us earnestly advise you to educate; get intelligence instead of alcohol – it is sweeter and more lasting.'[4]

With hindsight the early unions appear very significant as the forerunners of what is today the largest and most powerful trade union movement in the world. But in the nineteenth century their proportions were very much smaller. At mid-century membership was probably less than 250,000; and in 1888, when numbers had increased to 750,000, this was only about 5 per cent of the labour force or 10 per cent of the adult male working population. Until the last quarter of the nineteenth century unionism was mainly among craftsmen, textile workers and miners; and was strongest in London, the northeast, and the engineering, iron-working and shipbuilding centres of the northern counties. Because of the uneven concentration of unions in certain towns and regions, the strength of organized labour was more obvious in some areas than others. Yet even where they came to be increasingly recognized as a permanent part of the working-class presence, they represented only a minority of the productive classes. Very few women were organized before 1874, and those mainly in textiles.

To try to measure the influence of trade unions (perhaps the most 'advanced' of the indigenous institutions of the working class) solely by membership statistics is, however, somewhat misleading. In the 1830s popular institutions had not attained the degree of differentiation that they did later. The idea of a trade union was not clearly demarcated from a friendly benefit society or a cooperative store. The terminology used by working men suggests a central concept of union – union societies, trade unions, union exchange societies, the National Union of the Working Classes. At this stage the processes of production, consumption and exchange were not necessarily to be isolated in separate institutions, but could be served by multi-purposive bodies. The idea of union suggested several roads for working-class self-help.

For example, many of the early trade unions functioned as friendly benefit societies as well: the woolcombers' oath referred to a 'Friendly Society', as also did George Loveless. It may have been that in some cases the title of friendly society was used as a front during the period of illegality to cover up activities of a trade union nature, and later as a means of protecting the funds. But the long continuance of friendly society type benefits in the old trade societies suggests that there was a genuine working-class need for this side of unionism.

Friendly societies can be traced back to the late seventeenth century, but their rapid growth began about 1760. In return for a small weekly or monthly contribution paid into a common fund, they provided sickness and funeral benefits. The members met monthly in a local public house to transact business and, more interestingly, to drink beer and have a convivial time. An annual feast was held, and the funerals of deceased members were usually followed by a supper. Ceremony and ritual were an essential part of the societies' life. They held open-air processions with bands, banners and uniforms on all possible public occasions. Indoors, they conducted secret initiation rites, using mystical symbols, grandiloquent titles and regalia, mostly in imitation of the Freemasons and similar to the trade union rites already described. Originally, friendly societies had been local institutions with seldom more than a hundred members. But in the 1830s and 1840s these were eclipsed by the growth of the affiliated orders, with their organization into a unity (headquarters), districts and lodges. The oldest and largest was the Manchester Unity, Independent Order of Oddfellows. There were also the Ancient Order of Foresters, the Loyal Order of Ancient Britons, and the Antediluvian Buffaloes.

In point of numbers, the friendly societies far exceeded any other social organization except the churches. From an estimated 925,000 members in 1815 they grew to about 4 million in 1872 (compared with nearly 400,000 in the cooperative movement and 500,000 trade unionists in the same year). By 1892 probably 80 per cent of the 7 million male industrial workers were members of friendly societies. The strongholds of the societies were the industrial heartlands of the North and Midlands, but smaller benefit clubs (often unregistered) were found in rural areas and small towns. With the rise of the affiliated orders there was some friction between the lodges and the central body; and in true sectarian fashion the discontented members split off and formed a new society. In general, friendly societies were not agents of social change but rather of social adjustment. The ruling classes (in contrast to their attitude towards trade unions) were prepared to welcome (and control) the friendly societies as institutions of working-class self-help, while regretting that they 'wasted' time and money on conviviality. Yet without the opportunities for social intercourse which they provided, the friendly societies would not have flourished as they did. They catered to a need for community and a craving for fellowship. For many thousands of working men they satisfied a longing for membership in some institution to which they could feel they belonged, a place where they would be welcomed as a 'brother', not treated as a 'hand'. Such opportunities were not very numerous in the new industrial society.

Critics of the friendly societies, however, pointed out that they benefited the rich more than the poor, by relieving the former of their obligation to provide relief. William Cobbett, advising labourers against 'the folly of putting their money into clubs', observed:

It is the general practice of those who invent something to delude and cheat the people, to give a good name to the thing . . . and accordingly those who have invented this scheme for inducing you to give up your earnings, to prevent them from paying poor-rates, have christened these clubs 'BENEFIT clubs', instead of calling them . . . clubs to wheedle money out of the hard-earned pence of working people, in order to spare the purses of the landowners, big farmers, and other rich men.[5]

A similar conclusion was reached by the advocates of cooperation:

Benefit Societies relieve the capitalist even more than they do the workman. They first give him additional capital to make more profit of the labour of the workman: they then save him the trouble and expense of supporting the workman in sickness and old age. All the capital which is saved by a Benefit Society is so much comfort sacrificed by the members for the benefit of the capitalist . . . a Benefit Society is an ingenious contrivance on the part of workmen to rob themselves and benefit the upper classes.[6]

The alternative was a superior type of self-help: cooperation.

In its simplest form self-help through cooperation meant collectively buying a bag of meal and dividing it out among the purchasers. A next step was to extend this to other commodities and establish a small trading store. This type of venture spread quite rapidly in the 1820s, and by the early 1830s there were perhaps as many as 500 local societies with 20,000 members. William Lovett, who was storekeeper of one such cooperative in London, recalled that:

> like many others I was sanguine that those associations formed the first step towards the social independence of the labouring classes, and . . . I was induced to believe that the gradual accumulation of capital by these means would enable the working classes to . . . ultimately have the trade, manufactures, and commerce of the country in their own hands.[7]

But few of these stores managed to survive long, and the Owenite visions of some of their founders were gradually replaced by more practical and immediate aims. The modern cooperative movement traces its direct ancestry to the store set up in Toad Lane, Rochdale, by a small band of Owenites in 1844. Their original hopes of a community faded, but their store prospered. The Rochdale principle of paying an annual dividend to each member according to the amount of purchases soon spread, and after a slow start in the 1850s the movement grew steadily. In 1863 it extended beyond consumers' stores to a national Cooperative Wholesale Society, which supplied the stores and had its own factories. As with trade unionism, cooperation chiefly benefited the better-off sections of the working class, those with a fairly steady income and some security of employment. For the poor, who needed weekly credit and who could afford only goods of inferior quality, the cooperatives had little to offer: for them it was the pawnshop or the little store on the corner. Although experiments in producers' cooperation, involving schemes of co-partnership and profit-sharing, were made periodically throughout the nineteenth century and later, the main impact of the movement was in retail trading. By the end of the century the 'co-op' and the 'divi' had become established institutions of working-class life in all the industrial towns of the North and Midlands. In the 1930s many a working-class household relied on their year's divi to finance a week's holiday at the seaside. The cooperative shops, concentrating heavily on groceries, milk, meat, clothing and footwear, were the mainstay of the movement: in 1938 there were 1085 societies with 8·4 million members. The Women's Cooperative Guild, the youth movement, libraries and educational classes were reminders of the wider social ideals which had inspired the founders.

In addition to these indigenous labour bodies there was one further major institution making for respectability and social adjustment: the nonconformist (and particularly the Methodist) chapel. The hundreds of Zoars, Zions, Ebenezers and Little Bethels which appeared in the nineteenth century were not working-class institutions in the same sense as a trade union branch, but they did attract (and in some cases were financed and built by) working people. Their total membership numbers were large, the degree of commitment demanded was total, and they involved the whole family, not just the male breadwinner. Chapel membership was not exclusive of other allegiances: indeed, the artisan at his trade union or friendly society lodge night was quite likely to meet some of the same brothers as he did in chapel on Sundays. Four of the Tolpuddle martyrs were Methodists, two being local preachers. Methodism was first feared and then looked down on by the ruling classes – a sure sign that it had found favour among the common people. It had begun as an attack on the worldliness and complacency of early eighteenth-century church and society, and had grown under John Wesley's fifty-year leadership to the *de facto* status of an alternative church. At his death in 1791 there were 72,000 members of Methodist societies and perhaps nearly half a million adherents. By 1850 membership had increased to about half a million and it was estimated that perhaps 2 million persons (a tenth of the total population) were under direct Methodist influence. In Yorkshire as many as one-sixth, and in Cornwall a third of the total population attended Methodist services in 1851. As long as Wesley was alive there was no open breach with the Church of England, but after his death the gap widened, and the schismatic tendencies already observable in early Methodism led to successive breakaways from the parent (Wesleyan) body and the founding of new connexions.

Methodism was in many respects a paradoxical movement. Most of its members in the eighteenth century were originally humble people without any advantages of education, wealth or social position. But their puritan virtues brought them worldly wealth, which Wesley feared would endanger their souls. Wesley himself was autocratic, and conservative in his social views, and official Methodism in the nineteenth century continued in this tradition. The growing wealth of many middle-class members of the societies, and the consequent desire to be considered respectable, naturally inclined them to shun anything that might carry the taint of radicalism or disloyalty, especially in the period after 1815; and by the 1830s and 1840s the big down-town Wesleyan chapels in the northern towns were dominated by prosperous mill-owners and businessmen.

Yet underlying the dominant conservatism of official Methodism was a more liberal and democratic spirit. From the time when John Wesley took to preaching salvation in the open air and humble men were converted, Methodism was a popular movement, and most of the schisms which rent the central Wesleyan body until 1849 were attempts, in one form or another, to reassert this basic characteristic. The breakaway churches (such as the Methodist New Connexion, Primitive Methodists, Bible Christians, Protestant Methodists, Barkerites, Wesleyan Reformers) were characterized by differences of organization and personalities, not of doctrine. Methodism, unlike the Church of England, was essentially a layman's religion. In addition to the full-time ministers (who had the superintendence of a number of chapels in a circuit), there was an army of active lay helpers, numbering in 1850 some 20,000 local preachers, over 50,000 class leaders, together with trustees, stewards, prayer leaders and Sunday school teachers. How many of these were working men is difficult to ascertain, and the class composition of Methodism differed between connexions and between individual chapels in the same connexion. While the Wesleyan Methodists in most places were predominantly a middle-class body, the Primitive

Methodists had a pronounced working-class flavour. In some of the industrial towns and villages of the Midlands, and in rural areas too, the Primitive Methodists successfully pioneered a type of religion adapted to the needs of labouring men and women. Thus in the East Riding of Yorkshire a Primitive Methodist circuit was established at Driffield in 1837, after which societies in the villages on the Wolds multiplied rapidly. Farm labourers attended the 'Ranters'' meetings, held in a crowded cottage or plain, humble village chapel, and listened to a local preacher who was himself a working man and spoke their idiom. They felt at home there in a way they seldom did in the parish church with its liturgy, ritual and sermon by a middle-class parson.

Incidents like that described by Joseph Arch in his autobiography go far to explain the success of Methodism in attracting independently minded working men. Arch was a Warwickshire agricultural labourer and Primitive Methodist local preacher, who organized the National Agricultural Labourers' Union in 1872–3, and later entered parliament. In 1833, when he was seven years old, he observed the class divisions in the parish church of Barford, where he lived:

One Sunday my father was going to stop to take the Communion, and I, being a boy, had of course to go out before it began. I may here mention that the church door opened then in a direct line with the chancel and the main aisle, so that anybody looking through the keyhole could easily see what was going on inside . . . I was a little bit of a fellow, and curious, I said to myself, 'What does father stop behind for? What is it they do? I'll see.' So I went out of church, closed the door, placed my eye at the keyhole and peeped through, and what I saw will be engraved on my mind until the last day of my life. The sight caused a wound which has never been healed. My proud little spirit smarted and burned when I saw what happened at that Communion service.

First, up walked the squire to the communion rails; the farmers went up next; then up went the tradesmen, the shopkeepers, the wheelwright, and the blacksmith; and then, the very last of all, went the poor agricultural labourers in their smock frocks. They walked up by themselves; nobody else knelt with them; it was as if they were unclean – and at that sight the iron entered straight into my poor little heart and remained fast embedded there. I said to myself, 'If that's what goes on – never for me!' I ran home and told my mother what I had seen, and I wanted to know why my father was not as good in the eyes of God as the squire, and why the poor should be forced to come up last of all to the table of the Lord. . . .

There was no chapel in our village, but when I was about fourteen years of age some dissenters began to come over from Wellesbourne. They used to hold meetings in a back lane. When the parson got wind of it, he and his supporters, the farmers, dared the labourers to go near these unorthodox Christians. If we did, then good-bye to all the charities; no more soup and coals should we have. And it was no idle threat. . . . I well remember going with my mother to listen to these dissenters. They used to preach under an old barn in the back lane. Rough and ready men were they, dressed in their fustian coats, earnest and devoted to the truth as they saw it.[8]

The popular roots of Methodism meant that it could contribute to working-class movements like trade unionism or Chartism. The Methodist class system provided a useful model for Chartist and radical organization, and a class or band meeting could as easily study the works of Thomas Paine as the Old Testament. Camp meetings and chapels were institutions which could serve secular as well as religious purposes, and the eloquence and self-discipline acquired through preaching from a chapel pulpit was a useful training for addressing mass meetings of Chartists or Short Timers. As schools of practical democracy and self-government the Methodist chapels rendered valuable service to popular movements. Not only did working men utilize directly Methodist forms and techniques for other causes, but they also assimilated Methodist thought and attitudes into movements for social and political reform. At the great Chartist meeting at Peep Green on Whit Monday 1839,

the proceedings opened with prayer by Mr William Thornton, at the close of which Feargus O'Connor put his hand on his shoulder and said, 'Well done, Thornton, when we get the

People's Charter I will see that you are made the Archbishop of York.'[9]

Thornton, a leading West Riding Chartist, was a Methodist local preacher; and the writer of this description, Ben Wilson, was also a Chartist and a member of the Wesleyan chapel at Salterhebble.

It is not an accident that almost every self-educated working man in early and mid-Victorian England who came to write his memoirs paid tribute to the beneficial influences of Methodism in his youth. The accounts of self-educated men show a pattern of Methodist domestic piety, help in a local Sunday school, conversion, membership of a Methodist class, preaching, and then (usually) a progression beyond the original Methodism to some new intellectual position. Methodism for them was almost a natural stage in their educational and moral development; and for thousands of less distinguished labouring men and women it remained an intellectual and philosophical resting place. Joseph Barker, the son of a Bramley (Leeds) handloom weaver, was brought up in his father's trade. At the age of six or seven he was already a 'believer in the great doctrines of religion', and his Methodist parents brought him up to look for salvation through conversion.[10] After attending Sunday school he became a member of a Methodist class, and was helped in his studies by a Methodist travelling preacher stationed at Bramley and also by a local schoolmaster who was a Methodist local preacher. Barker himself became a local preacher for the Wesleyan Methodists while still working as a handloom weaver, but after a time joined the Methodist New Connexion, becoming first a travelling preacher and later a chapel minister. In 1841 he was expelled from that Connexion, taking with him some twenty-nine chapels and over four thousand members, mostly in the West Riding. Thereafter he progressed through several different religious positions and became a radical journalist.

Around the chapel there developed an intense world of personal and social relationships, which lasted into modern times. Friendship, marriage partners, help and support in time of need, a sense of security and personal worth, were assured to Methodists, who were exhorted to 'watch over one another in love'. A typical programme of chapel activities in the first half of the twentieth century was: Sunday – spent almost entirely in the chapel, with services, Sunday school, and prayer meetings; Monday – preaching service; Tuesday – class meeting; Wednesday – Christian Endeavour; Thursday – choir practice; Friday – free; Saturday – special efforts. Other chapels might include Band of Hope and Independent Order of Good Templars (temperance).[11] The general direction of this Methodist culture was toward respectability, through living a temperate, thrifty, hard-working life. This had been so since the beginnings of Methodism, and the effects in disciplining 'unruly' elements among the working class were noted early. Among the Durham miners, for instance, a remarkable transformation took place in the nineteenth century: the Methodists

> fought the evils of drunkenness, gambling, and improvidence. They took away from the pitman his gun, his dog, and his fighting cock. They gave him a frock coat for his posy jacket, hymns for his public-house ditties, prayer-meetings for his pay-night frolics.[12]

The convenience of religion as a work discipline was well understood by Victorian employers; and the more enlightened members of government came to recognize that Methodism could be a force making for stability rather than conflict in a working-class community. Indeed, according to a famous theory of the French historian, Elie Halévy, it was Methodism that prevented revolution in England during the revolutionary decades, 1789–1848, when the rest of Europe was convulsed.

In one important respect Methodism was different from the other movements described in this chapter, in that its dynamic was primarily not social or economic, but religious. To thousands of ordinary men and women it offered a view of man's nature which harmonized with, and interpreted their own experiences.[13] In a world full of disease, early death, injustice and all kinds of insecurity, Methodism (unlike much official Anglicanism) did not play down the tragic elements in the life of the common people, but instead emphasized the doctrine of original sin and the ubiquity of evil. All were in need of salvation – and all could be saved, through divine grace. The search for salvation, as immortalized in *The*

Pilgrim's Progress, echoed again in the hearts of new generations of seekers. Much has been written recently about the pessimism, repression, guilt feelings and psychic inhibitions encouraged by Methodism; and certainly some of its popular manifestations – crude, emotional, narrow, and self-righteous – were unlovely enough. But the message that comes through innumerable accounts of the great central Methodist experience of conversion is one of joy and hope. When a miner or farm labourer or domestic servant 'found Jesus', their life was transformed. Their religion brought happiness, and a cheerful conviction that in God's providence there was a place for everyone, however humble. One's own little life history was part of God's ultimate plan for the universe, no matter how many tribulations and disappointments as well as successes and rewards came one's way. Methodism, it has been said, was born in song; and one of Charles Wesley's hymns captures the notion that daily life and work is service to God:

> Forth in Thy name, O Lord, I go,
> My daily labour to pursue,
> Thee, only Thee, resolved to know
> In all I think, or speak or do.
>
> For Thee delightfully employ
> Whate'er Thy bounteous grace hath given,
> And run my course with even joy,
> And closely walk with Thee to heaven.

Beyond the world of denominational religion lay a sub-culture of popular religion. No hard and fast line can be drawn between the various brands of orthodoxy and the adventist and millenarian sects which flourished in different parts of the country. From Anglicanism and Wesleyanism, through Primitive Methodism and revivalism, there was a gradual shading off into the more extreme forms of Protestant sectarianism. Some of these sects were native, like the Plymouth Brethren, the Southcottians (followers of the prophetess Joanna Southcott who died in 1814) and their offshoot the Wroeites or Christian Israelites. Others came from abroad, like the Swedenborgians, the Millerites and the Mormons (who were strong in Lancashire and the Potteries in the 1840s). A local prophet or messiah had little difficulty in gathering round him a coterie of devoted followers – witness the case of 'Sir William Courtenay', a millennialist who claimed to be the messiah and who died fighting against the military in Kent in 1838. How large this underworld of popular religion was we do not know; but it is clear that it constituted a religious element among people untouched by the orthodox churches, people who found in the special values of sectarianism something that they needed and which they could not find elsewhere in Victorian society. Beyond the sects was the even wider influence of general nonconformist Christianity which coloured the thinking of members of the lower middle and working classes – people like William Lovett who desired a religion free from credal beliefs, conceding the right of private judgement, and unconnected with any ecclesiastical hierarchy. For those who could not stomach the claims of the churches, George Jacob Holyoake in the 1840s provided the religion of secularism.

Religion strongly encouraged another aspect of self-help and respectability – the increase in literacy. From the 1640s there had been a continued, though fluctuating, growth in the number of people who were literate. Using the statistics of the marriage registers, where brides and grooms who could not write their names signed with an 'X', the figures for the 1840s show that about two-thirds of the males and half the females were literate, at any rate to the extent of signing their names. Joseph Brook, a weaver who gave evidence before the Assistant Handloom Weavers' Commissioners in 1839, estimated that two-thirds of the adult weavers in Bradford could read but that not above a quarter could write. There were considerable regional differences in literacy rates which are not very easy to explain. After 1840 the percentage of literate persons increased, although for some time there was also an absolute increase in the number of illiterates because of the growth in population. Literacy and illiteracy of course are not objective categories, and have only a limited usefulness when applied to working people in the nineteenth century. What for instance should we make of the following letter, sent by Elizabeth Kellett of Catforth, Lancashire, to Florence Nightingale, the soldiers' friend, during the Crimean War?

Dear Madam
it is with reagret that inow persume to adress these few lines to you Beging won kind favour from you will you pleas dear madam to wright and let me no if hever my son Robert kellet has Been in this hospital they last account I herd of in he had Been Brought to they ospital iashure you that I have rote several times But has recived no answer from im dear madam they acount that iherd was that he was Brought to scutarion ospital in they later end of genuary and idoo ashure you that ifeel verry unapy about im and if he Bee dead pleas to let mee know what was is complaint I will now give you they discriptions of im he his a streight nice clean looking light complexioned young youth near twenty so now imust conclude with hevery kind regards towards you and Belive mee to Be yours affectionetley frend John and ElisaBeth kellet . . .

> privat Robert kellet
> No 3510 34th Rigiment
> Light Division[14]

Middle-class educational reformers in the nineteenth century assumed that the root cause of illiteracy was inadequate elementary education. They pointed out that in 1851 there were nearly 5 million children of school age, that is, between the ages of three and fifteen. Of these, 600,000 were at work, over 2 million were in school, and the remainder were neither at work nor in school. For the children of the working classes four main types of educational institution were available: the private day school (including the dame school), which had existed for the previous two hundred years; the ancient endowed and the charity school, which benefited poor children in some places; the Sunday school, which had grown rapidly since the 1780s, but which was handicapped by the part-time basis of its operation; and the factory school, established under the educational clauses of the 1833 Factories Act, and which was confined to the factory districts. The great majority of working-class pupils in these different schools were under the age of ten, and many attended for only two or three years.

In response to what seemed to be the challenge of perhaps a quarter or a third of the labouring poor who were totally illiterate, and a further percentage whose literacy was only rudimentary, the middle class set about increasing the provision of elementary school facilities. Encouraged by a modest annual grant of £20,000 from the government in 1833 (increased to £30,000 in 1839) and by the setting up of a small central administration and inspectorate, the voluntary religious school societies built a network of elementary schools across the country. Thanks to the rivalry between the two main providing bodies – the British and Foreign School Society (nonconformist) and the National Society (Church of England) – a system of public elementary education was established. Throughout the 1850s and 1860s this system of competition between the Anglicans and the nonconformists (free trade in education) continued to spread; but by 1870 it was still failing to provide schooling for more than half the children in London and for only a third to a fifth of the children elsewhere. State intervention thus became inescapable if adequate provision of this kind was to be made, and in 1870 the Education Act began the process of supplementing and, ultimately, replacing the voluntary schools with state schools.

This is not, however, quite how the matter appeared to many of the common people. The working-class view of education was essentially instrumental: literacy was a skill, to be learned, used and valued much as job skills. Not everyone needed to be 'a far-learned man' (as a good reader of the newspaper was revered in Pudsey in the 1830s), and even those who were unable to read were not entirely cut off from the culture of literacy. From this angle the nineteenth-century statistics of illiteracy do not appear so shocking as they did to educational reformers of the time. For instance, at Ramsbottom, Lancashire, with a reported illiteracy rate of over 50 per cent in 1839, only 11 families out of a total of 309 had no single reader among their number.[15] Moreover, until the last quarter of the nineteenth century, schooling was regarded by the common people as but one of several means of acquiring literacy. Children learnt to read, and sometimes to write, from their parents, relatives, friends or neighbours, in various informal settings and at times convenient to other tasks. When they did go to school it was frequently to a dame school, which was the truly indigenous institution for educational self-help of the working class.

Nothing better illustrates the way in which the perceptions of the common people have been systematically ignored, overlaid and finally forgotten, than the treatment of the working-class private venture school in the nineteenth century.[16] Historians of education have followed the lead of Victorian educationalists who were anxious to professionalize teaching, and who took every opportunity to denigrate working-class private schools, and ultimately drove them into extinction. These schools (sometimes called dame schools because they were often run by women) had between ten and thirty pupils as a rule, and were frequently held in the home of the teacher, who was without any formal educational training. There was no segregation of pupils by sex, age or ability; and the teaching and learning was individual and informal. Fees of 3d. to 9d. a week were paid to the teacher by the parents. Charles Shaw, the working potter, describes 'old Betty W.'s school' which he attended for three or four years in the 1830s:

> The school was the only room on the ground floor of her little cottage. It was about four yards square, with a winding, narrow staircase leading to the one bedroom above. The furniture was very scant, consisting of a small table, two chairs, and two or three little forms about eight inches high for the children to sit upon. There were a few pictures on the walls of the usual garish sort, blazing with colour, and all the figures upon them in strikingly dramatic attitudes. . . .
>
> The course of education given by the old lady was very simple and graded with almost scientific precision. There was an alphabet, with rude pictures, for beginners. There must have been something intensely vivid about these letters in the alphabet, for to this day when I see the letters Q and S as single capitals I see them rather as when I first saw them in old Betty's alphabet. I have often wondered whether other people carry the same weird impression of the capitals of their first alphabet. I have an impression, too, that the distinctness of that old alphabet had something to do with the success of old Betty's teachings, for though she never taught writing, her scholars were generally noted for their ability to read while very young. I know I could read my Bible with remarkable ease when I left her school, when seven years old. . . .
>
> Betty's next grade, after the alphabet, was the reading-made-

easy book, with black letters, making words in two, three and four letters.

The next stage was spelling, and reading of the Bible. . . . She taught both boys and girls who were successful in reading how to knit stockings. She was a remarkable knitter herself, and could carry on this occupation with the regularity almost of a machine, while her eyes were everywhere in her school. I knew boys who knitted stockings for their families. They thus learnt reading and knitting, instead of reading and writing. . . .

On fine days the little forms were taken outside her cottage, and placed under the windows. The children had their books, or their knitting, and the old lady, knitting herself incessantly, marched backwards and forwards, hearing lessons and watching work. The joy of the children was that they could see the passers-by, and their mothers.[17]

As rewards for good reading and spelling the pupils were allowed to take the ashes from under the fire-grate to the ash-heap outside the house, or sit on the top stair of the bedroom staircase. Thomas Cooper, who attended a similar dame school kept by 'Old Gatty' (Gertrude Aram) in Gainsborough, which was held in her cottage, noted that the room was always full, for 'she was an expert and laborious teacher of the art of reading and spelling', as well as being a fine knitter.[18]

Government inspectors and middle-class reformers condemned such schools as mere baby-minding establishments. They noted with strong disapproval the absence of settled or regular attendance. The pupils came and went at all times during the day. School hours were nominal and adjusted to family needs – hence the number of two- and three-year-olds who were sent to be 'out of the way' or 'kept safe'. The accommodation was overcrowded and sometimes stuffy, dirty and insanitary. The pupils were not divided into separate classes, and the teacher was a working man or woman who continued to work while teaching: 'I hears 'em read, an say their lessons; and it's no hindrance to my trade. My works a-going on all the same. Sometimes I lays down my tools a bit; and looks over their sums, an their writing, an sets 'em fresh lessons, to be larning; an then I goes on mending my shoe again,' explained John Pounds, a crippled Portsmouth cobbler, who for

many years until his death in 1839 ran a school for poor children.[19]
Very few books were available, or indeed considered necessary,
though sometimes a bible or testament would be used as a reader.
Pounds replied to a visitor who remarked that he needed some new
books:

'Why so?'
'Because those under that birdcage seem to be coming to pieces.'
'So much the better.'
'How can that be, Mr Pounds?'
'Why, ye sees, Sir, when a book's new like, an all tight together,
it sarves for only one at a time; but when it comes to pieces, every
leaf sarves for one. Besides, I doesn't always larn 'em out o'
books.'

To the middle classes such efforts appeared woefully inadequate: the schools were simply not real schools at all. Yet throughout the first three quarters of the nineteenth century their numbers
remained large: they provided the education 'of thousands in my
day', testified Charles Shaw. Official nineteenth-century inquiries
gave a ratio of attendance at working-class private schools to
public elementary (working-class) schools of about one to three. In
Bristol in 1875 (five years after the famous 1870 Education Act),
4280 pupils still attended private venture schools, which was 24
per cent of the number attending public elementary schools. Only
after 1875, when the state made a determined effort to eliminate
them, did the working-class private schools disappear, and even
then a few lingered on into the twentieth century.

Why did working people cling so tenaciously to an institution for
which they had to pay fees and which was in many ways inferior to
the alternative state-sponsored elementary school? The answer
must be that the private school offered the kind of education which
many of the working class wanted, rather than the education
which the middle class thought they should have. The grounds on
which Her Majesty's Inspectors objected to working-class private
schools were the very ones that endeared them to many of the
common people. Because they paid fees to the teachers (not always
punctually) the working classes controlled the schools completely.
The teachers were working people like the parents, not socially

superior, 'educated' persons, and they were prepared to take the children at the times and on the conditions acceptable to a working-class family. The schools were efficient in teaching basic literacy, as even the HMIs had reluctantly to admit. To many labouring people the atmosphere of a small, warm, stuffy dame's cottage may have seemed preferable to the cold, draughty and impersonal nature of large school buildings. They felt at home there, in the same way that they did when they knelt by the side of their chairs to pray at a Primitive Methodist meeting in a cottage kitchen. The working-class private school was in this sense a part of the culture of the common people, and its role raised class issues of a fundamental kind. Like the trade union, it was an agency of working-class self-help which the middle classes did not welcome. Schools for the people were one thing: the people's own schools were quite another.

For a minority of working men, educational self-help was extended far beyond the dame school. A pattern of autodidacticism emerges from the autobiographies of working men in the eighteenth and nineteenth centuries. After the three Rs came a perusal of any books in the home, however unsuitable, to practise reading; and then a headlong plunge into theology, mathematics and languages. With almost no guidance in the selection of books, and with almost no idea of systematic progression from the simpler to the more complex, the self-taught artisan had by his own unaided efforts to find his own level. That in so many instances he should have successfully wrestled with heavy classical works of philosophy, theology, science and political economy – and often studied them simultaneously – is some indication of the intellectual quality of a certain section of the working class in the nineteenth century. Equally important with intellectual ability was the moral stamina necessary to sustain the burden of home study amidst conditions of working-class life and labour. Great ingenuity and discipline was exercised to overcome the difficulties of lack of time and a quiet place for study. Learning while working was one solution. Thus Joseph Barker kept a book propped open on his loom; Thomas Cooper got up at 4.00 a.m. to study, and read during his breakfast and dinner times; and reading aloud in workshops or during the dinner hour was sometimes practised.

The fruits of this tradition of self-culture among the working classes were observable in several forms. Engels had often heard working men, whose fustian jackets scarcely held together, speak upon geological, astronomical and other subjects with great knowledge. The workman-naturalist became a familiar figure in many parts of Lancashire and the West Riding in the nineteenth century. Halifax and Todmorden were particularly rich in this respect. Interest in botany, geology, entomology and conchology was widespread, and local working men formed collections of fossils, insects, plants and mosses. Even more widespread was the workman-poet. There is a very large quantity of local poetry of the nineteenth century to be found in little volumes published locally by subscription, and in local newspapers and periodicals. The thirst for knowledge for its own sake was strong among many intelligent workmen, and a reverence for learning and the tools of learning appears to have been especially strong among weaver-poets and cobbler-philosophers.

The pursuit of knowledge under difficulties (as the Victorians loved to call it) could be eased by two institutions for educational self-help: the mechanics' institute and the mutual improvement society. Following the foundation of the London Mechanics' Institute in 1823, similar institutes soon appeared in all the main northern and Midland towns, and in the 1840s in rural areas as well. The original aim of most institutes was to provide lectures and classes in science for artisans; but only a few of them were able to profit from this provision, and the majority of the students were clerks, shopkeepers and members of the lower middle class, who preferred lighter and more literary subjects. In most cases control of the institutes was firmly in the hands of middle-class patrons, with at most a token mechanic or two on the management committee. Until late in the nineteenth century the local mechanics' institute – solid, stone-faced, Gothic, and blessed with civic pride – was a familiar sight. But it represented adult education for the working class rather than by them.

Less impressive than the mechanics' institute, but much closer to the people it was designed to serve, was the mutual improvement society. This consisted of a small number of members who met together either in each other's houses or in a small room hired for the purpose. A few simple rules, a programme of classes, essay readings and discussions were drawn up, and a small stock of books was collected as the basis of a little library. Weekly payments of 1d. or 2d. were made. The instruction was given voluntarily by the members themselves, and was designed primarily to promote proficiency in the three Rs; but in some instances was extended to geography, history, French and chemistry. A discussion circle and opportunities for practising public speaking in debates were also frequently provided. The very simplicity of these societies was their chief virtue, providing a seed which could germinate rapidly in many different kinds of soil. They could be attached to chapels, adult Sunday schools, Oddfellows' lodges, or Chartist branches. Smiles called them 'the educational Methodism of our day', and claimed in 1847 that there was scarcely a town or village in the West Riding without at least one. The society he knew best was started in Leeds in 1844 by four young men, who were soon joined by other operatives. They met at first in a room of a cottage of one of the members; but when summer came they migrated to an old garden house, where, amidst rakes and hoes and broken flowerpots, they taught themselves reading, writing, grammar and arithmetic. When winter came round again they hired a room which had been used as a temporary cholera hospital, and which for that reason they obtained cheaply as no one else would risk using it. By March 1845 their numbers had grown to about a hundred, and 'growing ambitious, they desired to have lectures delivered to them', and Smiles agreed to help them. From these lectures came the nucleus of his book, *Self-Help*.

The spontaneous formation of mutual improvement societies even in places where other means of adult education, such as mechanics' institutes, already existed, was an indication of the dissatisfaction with the latter institutions. Sometimes this dissatisfaction was expressed as a desire to discuss political and religious subjects which were forbidden in the mechanics' institutes; but more frequently it was simply that the type of class and the method of instruction in the institutes were felt to be alien to the ordinary working man. So strongly was this felt that in many instances he was prepared to try to struggle along with the help of a few untutored friends rather than avail himself of the opportunities for 'proper' instruction provided in the institutes. As with the dame school, the mutual improvement society was preferred to superior middle-class provision because it was the working man's own solution to his educational needs. Such societies by their very nature tended to be ephemeral: they sprang up rapidly and died away just as quickly when they had either fulfilled their purpose or exhausted their intellectual resources. They do not belong to any specific period, but flourished throughout most of the nineteenth century; though the decade after 1844 was particularly rich in the formation of such societies. When the Workers' Educational Association was founded in 1903 and tutorial classes were begun in Yorkshire after 1907, many of the first students were drawn from the mutual improvement societies and cottage meetings attached to the chapels and Sunday schools in Bradford and the Calder Valley.

Many, perhaps a majority, of working-class autodidacts were also advocates of temperance. Drinking customs pervaded all aspects of working-class life – at meals, markets, festivities, rites of passage, and also at work. Every trade had its distinctive system of footings, or payments for drink. In the Yorkshire woollen mills, for example, the first entry into the factory, the changing from one loom to another, the first lighting of the factory in autumn, or the first time a young man was seen by his mates with a young woman (the 'bull shilling'), were all made the occasion for payments to be spent on drink. At weekends the grosser results of working-class intemperance were manifest. Saturday night, Sunday and Saint Monday were commonly given over to prolonged drinking by artisans and labourers, though it is difficult to define the extent of this indulgence statistically. There is no shortage of evidence that a father's drinking habits could be a serious drain on the limited resources of a working-class family, and, if he were a drunkard, that this could cause misery and wretchedness for his wife and children. The culture of drink, with its pressures and temptations, was anathema to artisans striving to promote moral and intellectual self-improvement, and could not be condemned too strongly. William Lovett was of the opinion that:

If we look abroad in society we shall find that to this debasing vice, the inordinate thirst for intoxicating drink, may be traced a larger amount of human misery, suffering, and crime, than to all the collected vices of humanity.[20]

Drunkenness, he argued, is 'a species of temporary insanity', which 'degrades and sinks the man below the brute'. Excessive drinking meant a loss of self-control, a submission to non-rational influences, and therewith the sacrifice of that freedom and independence which was the hallmark of the respectable working man. Robert Lowery, a journeyman tailor and Chartist, found that the handloom weavers of Carlisle were

> intelligent, fond of reading, and well acquainted with the debated topics of the day . . . to a greater extent than with any other class of workmen. [Yet their drinking customs were] the stumbling block in the way of all improvement. . . . Low as their wages were, the public-houses were supported by them. The men who rarely saw beef too often got beer.[21]

The temperance movement, which was concerned to curb drinking and drunkenness, began in 1829–30 among middle-class, evangelical-type reformers, and was at first limited to abstention from spirits only. But in the early 1830s dissatisfaction with this moderate policy (which permitted beer and wine drinking and which even supported the 1830 Beer Act, resulting in the licensing of many new beershops) led to the introduction of the teetotal pledge to abstain from all forms of intoxicants. Born in Preston, Lancashire, among working-class and Methodist reformers, teetotalism became the dominant form of the temperance movement. The parade of reformed drunkards at public meetings and the secularized conversion experience which accompanied taking the pledge were not to everyone's liking; and some official leaders of church and chapel were suspicious of a movement which seemed to be almost an alternative religion. But at the local level teetotalism soon became an integral part of the nonconformist world. The Band of Hope for young people, begun in 1847, was closely associated with Sunday school work; and by the 1870s few chapels were without some form of adult temperance activity. Teetotalism was not exclusively working-class, but rather a reform movement which bridged the gap between the working and middle class. It strengthened the tradition of self-help and self-respect among an elite of working men and women, and emphasized their distance from the non-respectable labouring poor. Estimates of the size of this temperance elite vary considerably. In the 1840s teetotal membership was claimed to be about 1,200,000. By the 1860s estimates of 2 to 3 million teetotallers, including children, were being made. A cautious assessment would be that in the last three decades of the nineteenth century there were perhaps 100,000 to 200,000 active members of temperance societies, and a million adults who practised teetotalism, plus several hundred thousand juveniles in the Band of Hope. Lancashire, Cornwall and North Wales were strongholds of the movement; and temperance flourished wherever religious nonconformity was firmly rooted.

The centre of happiness for the sober, knowledge-seeking working man was his home and family. Not for him the delights and temptations with his workmates in the public house; after his long day of toil he was welcomed home to his favourite fireside chair by his admiring (and obedient) children, while his loving (and dutiful) wife prepared the 'viands' for his 'humble board'. This of course is the theme immortalized in Robert Burns's poem 'The Cottar's Saturday Night', much admired and imitated by weaver-poets and others. How far the working-class family approximated to this familiar Victorian ideal is hard to say. Skilled artisans apparently enjoyed some modest comfort at home. Their cottages were larger and in more salubrious areas of the town than those of the labouring poor. There was usually a small yard at the back, the windows were often well proportioned, and the doorways showed traces of simple Regency elegance. Inside the furnishings were usually described as comfortable, meaning something beyond the basic necessities of bed, table and chairs. Such things as clocks, pictures, books, ornaments, floor coverings, oak or mahogany chests of drawers were taken as signs of decency and prosperity. And if a parlour, separate from the everyday living room, could be maintained, then respectability was assured. Standards of housewifery were high, with much emphasis on scrubbing, scouring, polishing and (in northern towns) the whitening of doorsteps and window sills. Nowhere did the great Victorian virtues of frugality, cleanliness and sobriety appear more attractively and to greater purpose than in 'the cottage homes of England'.

But not all artisans accepted this cosy syndrome. Henry Price, a London cabinet-maker, reacted indignantly:

The Merry Homes of England Around their fires by night. Some one has sung about them. But they could not have known much about them. The vast majority of them in the Towns and Cities Have no room to be merry in. The Bread Winner has to be up and off early, and home late and too tired to be merry. His little ones are fast asleep. He gets a peep at them. God Bless them is his silent prayer. A look at the wife a painful one. What is the matter dear oh nothing. Poor Dear she has been hard at work too. Trying to earn a bit to keep them decent. If this is the case in ordinary times when employ was regular and dad comes straight home and denies himself a glass of ale till he gets there, his shirt wet with sweat and tir'd with a long walk were does the Merriment come in.[22]

For the majority of working people the family functioned in a way that was more traditional than the bourgeois model. As the basic social institution to which virtually everyone belonged, it was an agency for working-class self-help and stability in a sense that was different from middle-class notions. It was the main support in all the great crises of life, the source of help when most needed in times of illness, unemployment and death. Within the family the difficulties, tensions, satisfactions and deep affections of daily life were experienced, from the joys of love to the sorrows of bereavement. 'I was as fond of my wife Has a Cat is of New Milk,' recorded James Bowd, a Cambridgeshire farm labourer, in a rare moment of candid reminiscence.[23] Samuel Bamford lost his brother, sister, grandfather, uncle and mother in a smallpox epidemic, and was himself desperately ill: 'What a change we felt! What a void was around us – and what a diminished and unsheltered group we seemed to be!'[24] James Dawson Burn, a pedlar and later felt-hat maker, summarized his family experiences:

During my wedded life I have had eighteen births, and thirteen deaths to provide for, . . . and they have all been surrounded with many feelings of much joy and no little sorrow. I have always been blessed with the enjoyment of domestic love and sincerity. . . . The soothing pleasures and quiet enjoyments of home have always exercised a pleasing influence over my mind, and when the toils, trials, and vexations of the world have pressed upon me . . . the approving smile of my hoping and confiding wife would chase the melancholy gloom from my heart.[25]

The family, with its intertwining of the economic and affective sides of marriage, was for a working man something of a contradiction. On the one hand, the continuous struggle to feed and clothe an increasing family, the cost of childbirths, illnesses and funerals, and the frequency with which the household was reduced to utter poverty when the tenuous balance of its economy was upset by unexpected misfortune, was a major obstacle to financial security. On the other hand, in times of hardship a working man could find help, both material and emotional, in his family.

During the nineteenth century the working-class family as an institution was subjected to many pressures and as a result began to change. But the exact nature of that change is hard to assess, and at present we cannot write with assurance about many aspects of the family life of working people. On the relations between spouses, between parents and children, the regulation of sexual mores, or the authoritarian role of the father, there is very little hard data (as distinct from outsiders' impressions). It used to be thought that the Industrial Revolution broke up the traditional working-class family based on domestic industry. This was certainly the view of middle-class reformers at the time. As textiles set the pace of economic change, the strains and tensions within the family structure were felt earliest and most acutely in the manufacturing areas, though they were not confined to that part of the population.

The factory system, it was charged, affected the working-class family adversely in four main ways. First, it physically separated the members of a family for twelve to fourteen hours a day when some or all of them went off to work in the mill early in the morning and returned at night. The family as a unit was together only for purposes of sleeping, eating and (on Sundays and holidays) recreation, whereas under the domestic system the members had been together at work and leisure all day and every day. Second, when a married woman went out to work her efficiency as a wife and mother was greatly reduced. She did not have time to do the housework, sewing and cooking except in the evenings, when she was tired, and on Sundays (when she should have been at church). The children were neglected because she was not at home to look after them. Third, unmarried girls who worked in the factories had no time to develop housewifely skills and were also encouraged in sexual immorality by the conditions of mill life. It was also stated that the factory system diminished respect for chastity in marriage and thereby undermined the family. Fourth, the strength of the married man's position in the family was weakened. When his wife and children were also breadwinners, and when he was separated from them all day, his patriarchal authority was reduced. He was not able, as in domestic industry, to exercise the necessary control over his children, to train them daily in good habits and to exert an unchallenged leadership. Indeed, at times he might even be unemployed and at home, while his wife and daughters had to get work to support him.

On closer examination, however, it becomes apparent that this is by no means the whole story. Only a minority of workers were employed in factories; and even in the heart of industrial Lancashire in 1851 half the labour force did not work in them, but in artisan, trading and labouring occupations. The virtues of the domestic system, where the whole family worked together, are easy to appreciate. But the removal of industry from the home to the factory was from the housewifely point of view a blessing. A home that was also a workshop could become very squalid. Not all handicraft industry was carried on in a specially built loomshop in a substantial stone house like the Yorkshire weaver's. The low-ceilinged living room of the Leicester stockinger was almost completely filled with his great clumsy wooden knitting frame, and the Black Country nailer's shed was a lean-to at the back of his cottage. Emancipation from the noise and dirt and smell of domestic industry must have been welcome to housewives.

With regard to the separation of the family during the day, every effort was made by the textile workers to resist this change. In the cotton industry they succeeded until the 1820s in maintaining something of the family relationship within the factory. It was the custom for a skilled cotton spinner to hire his own assistants, usually two or three, and so he employed his wife and children or near relations. The family was thus kept together and the link between the economic and other functions of the family was preserved. In the 1820s, however, large mules with more spindles were introduced which required anything from four to nine assistants. The spinner could not normally provide this number of helpers from among his own children so had to hire others, which diluted or undermined the family unit. At the same time changes in the weaving branch of the cotton industry also worked against the preservation of the family within the factory. Powerlooms were introduced widely in the late 1820s and early 1830s, and were operated by women and boys, not by fathers of families. The powerloom weavers' assistants were appointed by the masters, not the operatives. No room was left for the employment of a family all together. This breakdown of the traditional family relationship within the factory accounts in part for the operatives' support of the factory movement in the 1830s. They agitated for a ten-hour day for children, knowing that this would mean ultimately a ten-hour day for adults as well. But the Factory Act of 1833 which emerged from these struggles limited children's labour to eight hours a day and made possible a relay system whereby adults would continue to work long hours with the assistance of different shifts of child helpers. This did not suit the operatives' needs at all. It broke up the family unit in the mill and did not reduce adult hours. From 1833, therefore, the operatives demanded first an eight-hour day for all, then a twelve-hour day including the children, and finally settled for a universal ten hours, which meant actually extending the hours of children. Successive Factory Acts in 1844 and 1847 did not go back on the 1833 Act, but rather strengthened it by separating still further the hours and conditions of children from those of adults. In this way the earlier efforts to maintain family relationships in the factory were effectively ended.

Women's work raised various questions about the nature and quality of family life. In the cotton districts in 1851, about 30 per cent of all married women were employed, and of these almost two-thirds were textile operatives. The percentage of married women who at some time had gone out to work would be higher than this. In Staffordshire the proportion of married women working in the potteries was about the same. Arrangements had to be made for looking after the home and the children. The most convenient solution of the wife's problems was to have a grandmother or a young daughter not in the mill to look after the babies and to do a little cooking and cleaning. Alternatively it was possible to hire a girl aged seven to eleven to do these chores for not more than 2s. a week. There were also day nurses, usually old women, to whom babies could be taken during working hours. Children of working mothers had to be weaned early – in contrast to most working-class children whose mothers breastfed them as long as possible, hoping thereby to avoid another pregnancy. Infants in such homes did not, by modern standards, get very much or very careful attention, and Godfrey's cordial (a pacifier containing laudanum) was administered liberally.

This pattern of domestic life did not accord with the middle-class family ideal in which the woman's place was firmly in the home, under the authority and dominance of the husband. Respectability required that she should not be associated with the male world of work and public affairs. But the working-class home was dependent on family earnings, not just the income of the male breadwinner. In the case of home-based crafts the woman helped her artisan husband; or else worked in some other capacity, as laundress, needlewoman or shopkeeper. For low-paid workers their children's earnings were essential for the family to function effectively. Factory work and the employment of women, married and single, did not necessarily disrupt this type of family economy. Put another way, the working-class family as an institution was sufficiently resilient to absorb the changes brought by industrialism, and strong enough to preserve many of its traditional attitudes and values. In the second half of the nineteenth century the elite of the working class drew closer to the bourgeois sentimental ideal of home and family. But for the majority of ordinary working-class families, self-help was the collective help of neighbours and relatives; and respectability was maintaining a steady income, preserving the respect of the local community, and avoiding the workhouse and a pauper funeral.

The lifestyle and aspirations outlined in this chapter were most fully developed among that upper 10 to 20 per cent of the working class who formed an aristocracy of labour in the nineteenth century. They enjoyed a combination of good wages, steady employment and craft skill that secured their independence and respect from those above and below them. It has been suggested that in their pursuit of respectability this elite accepted middle-class standards and values, and mediated them to the working class as a whole. Engels complained that in this most bourgeois of all nations even the working class was becoming bourgeois. More recently (and following the theories of the Italian Marxist, Antonio Gramsci) the labour aristocracy has been presented as an instrument of bourgeois hegemony, a mechanism by which the ruling classes maintain their supremacy less through force than by diffusing their ideology throughout all sections of society, who are thus persuaded to accept the status quo. Support for this view comes from the observation that at various points working-class culture converged with that of the bourgeoisie, which it would seem was imposed on the former. But this is not how the issue was seen by class-conscious artisans, who thought of their culture as indigenous and separate, though not necessarily always in conflict with middle-class aims and intentions.

Let us take the case of William Lovett. Here we have a working man who embraced wholeheartedly the doctrine of improvement through education, and accepted the ethic of respectability and individual effort. But he never became a member of the middle classes, nor accepted bourgeois radicalism. Lovett was the representative of a working-class culture which had some values in common with the middle classes, but which was essentially quite separate. When Lovett and his fellow-radicals talked of respectability and improvement they used the same words as their middle-class contemporaries, but their meaning was different. When the Victorian middle classes urged working men to become respectable, the intention was to make them deferential and secure in their allegiance to bourgeois values. But this was the very opposite of the qualities which Lovett looked for in respectability; namely, independence, dignity and deferring to nobody. His respectability has to be interpreted within an egalitarian working-class context. His ideal of self-help was not that associated later with Smilesian notions of getting on in the world. Lovett, of course, was a skilled artisan, and it might be argued that the culture to which he belonged was not that of the working class as a whole. Yet despite the great gulf between the labour aristocracy and the mass of unskilled workers, Lovett and other artisan leaders in the Chartist movement identified themselves with 'the working classes' against the middle class. Even when he later became somewhat soured by his experiences in trying to organize working-class movements, Lovett never conceded that the middle classes were in any way superior.

Although there was some upward mobility, the opportunities for this were limited, and it seems unlikely that most self-educated artisans were seeking to become members of the middle class. From some of their writings there emerges an alternative artisan ideal. W.J. Linton, a radical reformer and wood-engraver, writing of his friend James Watson (bookseller and radical), has this to say:

> He seemed always, and in private as well as public, to have before him the ideal of what an English workman ought to be. I think of him always as a workman, because, though he had a shop, he was in no sense a tradesman – a buyer and seller for gain.[26]

This suggests that the artisan ideal of respectability should not be defined simply in terms of social mobility, implying movement into a higher social class. Men such as Watson sought to define themselves in terms of a working-class culture; almost as if their intellectualism was an attempt to learn a new trade within the working class. Linton's image of what a workman ought to be implied things about the kind of society he ought to live in. Some years later the same idea was echoed by the early Workers' Educational Association with its message that the aim of workers' education was not to enable working men to rise out of their class, but to raise the whole class.

Nevertheless, the attainment of respectability was beyond the reach of large numbers of the common people in the nineteenth century. For the labouring poor and unskilled workers the suggestion of self-help through thrift and mental and moral improvement was simply advice to lift themselves by their own bootstraps. They remained outside the great Victorian institutions for the 'progress of the working class': the trade unions, friendly societies, cooperative societies, and chapels. Their advance required an altogether different approach: no less than the intervention by the state to secure their welfare, and this was not acceptable until the twentieth century.

10. In the Workshop of the World

The Victorians proudly proclaimed that Britain was the workshop of the world. They liked to compare society to a beehive, in which the whole population (except for a few aristocratic drones) busily worked away, providing goods and services of all kinds for their own needs and for export. However idealized this analogy might become among middle-class apologists of the new industrial civilization, it did have the merit of emphasizing the centrality of work in the lives of a majority of the people. But if it suggested uniformity and regularity of behaviour it was seriously misleading; for nothing is clearer than the enormous variety of occupations and types of work in the nineteenth century. When the first full census of occupations was taken in 1841 officials were completely surprised by this variety and were unable to make a precise classification, and even later censuses fail to give an adequate idea of the complexity of jobs actually done. So great is this diversity that generalization about the work experience of common people is impossible. Our problem is also compounded by the amount of information we have, which is much greater than for earlier periods. For the first time in their history, direct evidence from the common people themselves is reasonably plentiful, and increases the nearer we get to the present. We can draw upon working-class autobiographies and reports of interviews with working people in the Victorian era; and for the 1890s onwards the carefully collected and recorded views of old people, known as oral history, are available on tape and in transcription. The chronology of work is not clearly defined: many occupations pre-dated the nineteenth century, and some jobs were still performed in the 1930s in virtually the same way as a hundred years previously. Our dates and categories are therefore no more than general guides. All we can be sure of is that the common people, from the labouring poor, through factory operatives and skilled craftsmen to clerks and

305

shopkeepers and small farmers, had to perform some sort of work for their livelihood, and that that experience dominated their lives.

The diversity of occupations in the workshop of the world becomes apparent as soon as we attempt some form of classification, with implied contrasts and similarities. The Industrial Revolution created new types of job in industries which had not previously existed, such as factory textiles, machine-making, engineering and the railways. But older industries, like mining, quarrying, building and agriculture expanded production without requiring new types of skill. Although the factory was the symbol of the new machine age, home industry and out-work continued in many trades, as in tailoring, hardware, woodworking, blacksmithing, handloom weaving and scores of country crafts. Often the home industry existed alongside the main factory production, working the marginal, less profitable lines, and available always in times of heavy demand to take up the slack. The backyard workshop and the sweater's garret were as much a part of industrial England as the great cotton factory or the iron and steel mills. So too the divisions between hand and machine work, between skilled, semi-skilled and unskilled jobs grew throughout the nineteenth century. Some trades, such as tailoring and cabinet-making in London, were divided into 'honourable' (unionized) and slop (non-unionized) branches. The traditional gulf between the craftsman and the labourer remained; and everywhere there was a vast expenditure of muscular effort and sweat – sheer toil which was unalleviated by steam power or machinery. Some jobs were wholly indoors, as in factories, bakeries and offices; others wholly outside, as in agriculture; while some, like brick-making or the building trades, partook of both. The urban and rural divide was as deep as ever, the uniqueness of London was undiminished, and regional and local differences in the economic structure determined the kind of work and skills required. A few manual jobs offered security and full-time employment; most suffered from periods of over- and underemployment. The weather and the seasons dictated what could be done on outdoor jobs, which were therefore always irregular and unpredictable. Levels of pay were not necessarily related directly to degrees of skill or hardness of toil: miners and iron and steel workers, for instance, earned more

than dockers, dustmen or farmworkers: the silk weavers of Spitalfields were skilled but their earnings were low. Not all jobs were
primary occupations: out-work and women's work were frequently of an ancillary nature, and odd jobs and harvest work were
welcome means of balancing the family budget.

We do not know to what extent working people had an overall
view of this world of work, as distinct from their particular
occupation. Their primary concern was to make a living for
themselves and their families, and their experiences of work were
shaped accordingly. This may have given them a view of the
Victorian economy which was somewhat different from the one
usually reflected in economic histories of the nineteenth century. It
was no doubt a partial and incomplete view; but it was their own
perception and as such has a special validity for us. The following
accounts have been selected to illustrate something of the diversity
of ways of getting a living. They are in no sense a complete picture
of labour in the workshop of the world; nor can any such selection
avoid being arbitrary. Nevertheless the extracts are typical
expressions by some working people of their views and
experiences.

Our first vignette is of Ben Turner and work in a Yorkshire
woollen mill.[1] Turner, who was later a prominent trade unionist,
was the son of a Batley weaver, and began work at the age of
nine and a half by helping his aunt and uncle at handloom
weaving. In 1873 he entered the mill where his father worked:

The day I was ten years of age, I went into the mill as a
half-timer. I had several jobs, one being to squeeze the wobbly
sizing into small bits – a nauseating job – another to put sticks
into a big balloon used for drying the warps upon, and a third to
reach ends in for the warper, ready for the warp to be taken into
the loom.

We had to go to school one half-day and the mill the other
half-day. One week we started work at 6 a.m. and went on until
12.30 p.m., with a half-hour for breakfast. We then had to go to
school from 2 to 4.30 p.m. The opposite week we went to school
at 9 a.m. until 12 noon, and to work from 1.30 until 6 p.m. It was
a bit cruel at times – when on the morning turn at the mill – for it
meant being up at 5 a.m. getting a drop of something warm, and

trudging off to the mill a mile away to begin work. In winter, it was fearful. Of course, it was customary, and we didn't think there was anything wrong about it. . . .

When he was thirteen Turner left school and became a full-timer at 5s. per week. Shortly afterwards he moved to Huddersfield, where he considered himself lucky to get a job as a 'piecener in a woollen mulegate', working under the direction of a head spinner for 9s. a week. The hardships of strikes and unemployment came to him early:

My first glimpse of a strike was in Holmfirth in 1872, when I was nine years of age. My father was one of the strikers, and a Union Committee man as well. The weavers wanted a uniform weavers' piece rate scale applying at each mill. The employers opposed it, and for eleven weeks a dispute raged. I went and watched the processions of strikers as they marched round the district or went the six miles' walk to the mills at Huddersfield. The dispute pay was four shillings per week, and my mother had to allocate so much bread per day for the seven of us, and often we were hungry. . . .

Turner himself was unemployed in the 1880s, and was forced to turn to peddling lengths of drapery and garments, and to collecting money and canvassing as an insurance agent. Even without such dislocations the family economy could only function with the aid of credit from local shopkeepers, operated by means of a 'shop book':

Nearly all working-class families are poor until they get one or more of the children working. Men's wages have seldom, if ever, been enough to keep the house equipped with food and raiment when there have been three to seven children.

Side by side with Turner's account of the ups and downs of life for a woollen textile worker in the 1870s and 1880s may be set the classic description of life in the railway workshops at Swindon by Alfred Williams.[2] Unlike Turner, Williams's interest in later life was not trade unionism but literature, and his account of the Great

Western Railway workshops, where he worked as a forgehand and hammerman from 1892 to 1914, has unusual poetic qualities:

> Arrived in the shed the workmen remove their coats and hang them up under the wall, or behind the forges. . . . A terrible din, that could be heard in the yard long before you came to the doors of the shed, is already awaiting. Here ten gigantic boilers, which for several hours have been steadily accumulating steam for the hammers and engines, packed with terrific high pressure, are roaring off their surplus energy with indescribable noise and fury, making the earth and roof tremble and quiver around you, as though they were in the grip of an iron-handed monster. The white steam fills the shed with a dense, humid cloud like a thick fog, and the heat is already overpowering. The blast roars loudly underground and in the boxes of the forges, and the wheels and shafting whirl round in the roof and under the wall. The huge engines, that supply the hydraulic machines with pressure, are chu-chu-ing above the roof outside; everything is in a state of the utmost animation. . . . The furious toil proceeds hour by hour. Bang, bang, bang. Pum-tchu, pum-tchu, ping-tchu, ping-tchu. Cling-clang, cling-clang. Boom, boom, boom. Flip-flap, flip-flap. Hoo-oo-oo-oo-oo. Rattle, rattle, rattle. Click, click, click. Bump, bump. Scrir-r-r-r-r-r. Hiss-s-s-s-s-s. Tchi-tchu, tchi-tchu, tchi-tchu. Clank, clank, clank, clank, clank. The noise of the steam and machinery drown everything else. You see the workmen standing or stooping, pulling, tugging, heaving, dragging to and fro, or staggering about us though they were intoxicated, but there is no other sound beyond the occasional shouting of the forger and the jerking or droning of the injectors. It is a weird living picture, stern and realistic, such as no painter could faithfully reproduce. . . .

Life for the 12,000 workers in the railway workshops had its own yearly, weekly and daily rhythms. The factory year was divided into three periods: Christmas to Easter, Easter to 'Trip' (held in July), and Trip to Christmas; and there were the additional one-day bank holidays of Whitsuntide and August. From Christmas to Easter was a period of hope and rising spirits, looking forward to brighter days, longer evenings, and time spent in the garden. After Easter all thoughts were directed towards the Trip, or annual holiday. Trip Day was the most important day in the calendar of the railway town. For several months preceding it 'fathers and mothers of families, young unmarried men, and juveniles' had been saving up for the outing. Whatever new clothes were bought for the summer were usually worn for the first time at Trip. The trade of the town was at its zenith during the week before the holiday. A general exodus from the town took place, and some 25,000 people were hurried off by early morning trains to London, Weymouth and other resort towns. About half of the trippers returned the same night; the others stayed for a week. Return to work after Trip was painful; and after the August bank holiday there was nothing to break the monotony of labour until Christmas.

The week too had its characteristic pattern for the workmen. Monday was always a 'flat, stale day', especially up to dinner time. 'Everyone seems surly and out of sorts.' Tuesday was the 'strong day', when the most and best work was done. 'The men come to work like lions.' Wednesday was similar to Tuesday, though the pace was not quite as brisk. Thursday was 'humdrum day', when the men began to look 'tired and haggard', and more effort was required to maintain production. By Friday morning 'the barometer will have risen considerably'. Despite tiredness, the men were more cheerful because it was pay-day and the last whole day to be worked before the weekend. Saturday was 'the day of final victory', when the week's battle was almost finished. Sunday was a day of complete inactivity with most workmen; and Williams hazarded the opinion that it was 'possibly the weakest and the least enjoyed of all'. If the weather was dull and wet a great number stayed in bed till dinner time, and sometimes till Monday morning – when they would be all the more refreshed for the 'toil and battle' of the coming week.

Every day also had its divisions according to the temper and feeling of the workmen:

In the morning, before breakfast, nearly everyone is sober and quiet, very often surly, and even spitefully disposed. During that time the men in the shed rarely speak to each other, but bend down to the labour in silence. After breakfast the tone improves a little, and continues to do so till dinner-time, when the tempers of the men will have become about normal; they are restored to their natural humour and disposition. When they return after dinner a still greater improvement is discernible, and by five o'clock in the afternoon they are not like the same beings. In the evening, after tea, greater good-fellowship than ever prevails. . . .

Williams was convinced that exploitation of the workers had increased during this period in the workshops. 'The speeding up of late years has been general and insistent.' The output in some instances was increased tenfold, and the exertions of the workman were doubled or trebled; yet he received scarcely any more in wages. Again, the balance between day wages and piece work was altered to the detriment of the worker. 'On the hammers under my charge during the last ten years the day wages of assistants – owing to their being retained on the job up to a greater age – had doubled, and the piecework prices had been cut by one half. As a result the gang lost about £80 in a year.' Fear of illness and old age was greater among workmen than previously because of the management's ruthless policy of getting rid of anyone who was not one hundred per cent fit. The views of workers, even respected and experienced men, were rarely sought: 'If offered, they are belittled and rejected.' If a workman had a grievance it was useless for him to complain to the overseer (who was usually the cause of it); 'and if he takes it upon himself to go and see the manager he gets no redress. The manager always supports the foreman whether he has acted rightly or wrongly, and the man is remembered and branded as a malcontent.'

Another occupation requiring heavy manual labour as well as skill was coal mining. Between 1851 and 1911 the number of coal miners increased from 216,000 to 877,000. Unlike the cotton or engineering industries, coal-mining techniques remained primitive and unmechanized until recent times. Boys began work as trappers (opening and closing the ventilator doors), progressed to driving a pit pony, then became putters (supplying the face workers with empty 'tubs' and pushing the full ones from the coal face to the wagons for hauling to the shaft), and finally hewers, the key men who hacked out the coal from the seams with their picks at

311

the coal face. The coal seams varied in thickness from as little as eighteen inches in Durham to seven feet in Yorkshire, so that the hewer had sometimes to work lying down, sometimes in a crouching or kneeling position. 'The thin seams of Durham are a nightmare,' testifies a modern miner,

> and many's the nightmare I've had about them since. Strange to say you don't really become aware of what they actually mean, how terrifying they are, until you've left them and look back ... [and] you know what filthy little cracks and warrens they are.... Crawling down the seam, only inches would separate the roof from your prostrate body, your head would be turned to the side, flat against the floor with maybe a two-inch space above before you made contact with the roof.[3]

Each region had its own system of working. In the Forest of Dean the pits were run by the colliers themselves, as free miners claiming ancient rights. In the Midlands varieties of a sub-contracting system were common, whereby the 'butty' agreed a price with the mine-owner and then paid the miners to get the coal. The Durham and Northumberland pits were worked on a system of 'cavilling', in which the miners balloted every quarter for their place at the coal face, which they then worked with their 'marras' ('marrows') or mates. Thomas Burt worked from the age of ten as trapper, donkey-driver, putter and hewer in a number of pits in Durham and Northumberland. At the end of a successful career as the Northumberland miners' leader and one of the first working men to enter parliament in 1874 as Liberal-Labour member for Morpeth, he looked back on his days as a young miner in the 1850s:[4]

> At Seghill I worked with my uncle, Thomas Weatherburn. He was a strong, skilful hewer. For many years he had been an engine-man, and had been tempted, or starved, into the coal-mines that he might get higher pay. He worked with the steady stroke, the composure, and the effectiveness of a perfect machine....
>
> The hewer is paid by the ton. His earnings, therefore, depend partly upon his industry, strength, and skill, and partly upon his

luck. In extreme cases, I have known two or three shillings a day difference between one working-place and another. To give an equal chance to everybody, the places were 'cavilled', or balloted for, once a quarter. A good 'cavil' was, of course, a desideratum. The hewers grouped themselves into parties of four, these 'marrows' working together, two in each shift, and dividing the total earnings among them on the pay Friday, which came once a fortnight. The satisfaction and smoothness of the hewer's life depend in no small degree upon his having suitable 'marrows.' In this respect I could not have been better placed. At Seaton Delaval I worked all the time with my uncles, Robert and Andrew Burt, the other partner in the quartette being William, or Willie, Armstrong. My closest relations were with my uncle Robert, since he and I were always in the same shift, and for the most part in the same working-place. . . .

The hours of hewers at Delaval then, 1855–60, were about eight from bank to bank. The wage would run about 5s. a day. That was then deemed a good wage, and I think it would be above the average of the country. Certainly the wage at Delaval was higher than at some neighbouring collieries. During the winter months work was irregular. Taking the year round, the pits would probably work about nine days a fortnight. The miner then nearly always had his house and coal free, a small sum of sixpence a fortnight being charged for the carting of the fuel. After making deductions for powder, candles, and working tools, and for irregularity of employment, the hewer's wage at this period would probably average, the year round, from 21s. to 23s. per week.

Despite the danger and brutal hardness of mining, there were some compensations. At the coal face the miner was very much his own boss. There was little in the way of supervision, and he could choose his workmates. Hours of work were more flexible than in a factory. When Burt went to work at Cramlington in the 1850s he found things were what he called rough and irregular. 'There was no recognised starting time or ending time for the day's work of the fore-shift men. The coal-hewers went into the pit and came out when they liked, and some of them apparently liked to go in at ten or eleven o'clock at night and to remain till about noon the next day.' 'Laking', or taking a day off work from time to time, was traditional in the coalfields. Earnings were also higher than for many other types of manual work, as we are reminded in the traditional Lancashire song:

> Collier lads get gold and silver,
> Factory lads get nothing but brass,
> I wouldn't marry a spindle cleaner,
> When there are plenty of collier lads.

What the workshop of the world meant to a different class of workers is brought home by a series of interviews carried out by the pioneer social investigator, Henry Mayhew, and published in the *Morning Chronicle* in 1849–50.[5] Mayhew collected a mass of detailed material on the London trades, and analysed the various ways of organizing the labour of tailors, shoemakers, carpenters, toy-makers and other handicraftsmen. He discovered that while small masters and well-paid artisans dominated the superior or 'honour-able' end of the trades, they were under the constant threat of competition from the slop, or 'dishonourable' branches of the business. Thus, out of 21,000 working tailors in London, only about 3000 belonged to the honourable branch; the remaining 18,000 were engaged in cheap, slop or sweated work. A sweater described the working arrangements:

I employ persons to work under me – that is, I get the work, and give it to them to do. I generally have two men working at home with me. I take a third of the coat, and I give them each a third to do. They board and lodge with me altogether – that is, they have their dinners, teas, breakfasts, and beds in my place. I give them at the rate of 15s. a coat – that is, I take 1s. off the price I receive, for the trimmings and my trouble. The trimmings come to 9d., and the extra 3d. is profit for my trouble. They pay me at the rate of 2s. 6d. per week for washing and lodging – the washing would be about 6d. out of the money. They both sleep in one bed. Their breakfasts I charge 4d. each for – if 'with a relish', they are 5d. Their teas are 4d., and their dinners are 6d. – altogether I charge them for their food about 8s. 2d. a week, and this with lodging and washing comes to from 10s. 6d. to 11s. per week. The three of us working together can make six coats in the week, if fully employed – on an average we make from four to five coats – and never less than four.

A tailor who had worked at the honourable trade, but who had been unable to get employment for more than a third of his time, gave his version of working for sweaters:

The pay that I received by working for the sweaters was so little that I was forced to part with my clothes. When I first went to work for the sweater, I used to get 4s. 6d. for making the third part of a coat. It could take from 11 to 13 hours to make a third. I could have done as many as six thirds, but could not get them to do. The sweater where I worked employed more hands than he had work for, so that he could get any job that was wanted in a hurry done as quickly as possible. . . .

But workmen in the honourable part of any trade did better. A journeyman carpenter, working for the best shops at the best prices, told Mayhew:

I have known the London trade between twenty and thirty years. I came up from Lancashire, where I served an apprenticeship. I have worked all that time entirely at carpentering. No doubt I am a pure carpenter, as you call it, never having worked at anything else. . . . I have always had 5s. a day, and in busy times and long days have made 33s. and 35s. a week, by working overtime. I have always been able to keep my family, my wife and two children, comfortably, and without my wife's having to do anything but the house-work and washing. One of my children is now a nurse-maid in a gentleman's family, and the other is about old enough to go and learn some trade. . . . But then, you'll understand, sir, I'm a sort of exception, because I've had regular work, twelve months in the year, for these ten or twelve years, and never less than nine months before that. I know several men who have been forced to scamp it – good hands, too – but driven to it to keep their families. What can a man do? 21s. a week is better than nothing. I am a society man, and always have been.

I consider mine skilled labour, no doubt of it. To put together, and fit, and adjust, and then fix, the roof of a mansion so that it cannot warp or shrink – for if it does the rain's sure to come in through the slates – must be skilled labour, or I don't know what is.

The craftsman's special skill and knowledge, hinted at in this extract, was not something which he normally found easy to express. Wages, apprenticeship, working conditions and types of job he could describe to an interviewer; but the heart of the 'mystery' often remained veiled. One of the few successful attempts to penetrate this veil is George Sturt's account of wheelwrighting. In 1884 he entered the family firm of wheelwrights in Farnham, Surrey, in which his father and grandfather had worked. Under the tutelage of 'the men' (for his father died shortly afterwards) he learned the meaning of craftsmanship:

What we had to do was to live up to the local wisdom of our kind; to follow the customs, and work to the measurements, which had been tested and corrected long before our time in every village shop all across the country. . . . A good wheelwright knew by art but not by reasoning the proportion to keep between spokes and felloes; and so too a good smith knew how tight a two-and-a-half-inch tyre should be made for a five-foot wheel and how tight for a four-foot, and so on. He felt it, in his bones. It was a perception with him. But there was no science in it; no reasoning. Every detail stood by itself, and had to be learnt either by trial and error or by tradition. This was the case with all dimensions. I knew how to 'line out' a pair of shafts on a plank, and had in fact lined and helped saw on the saw-pit hundreds of them, years before I understood, thinking it over, why this method came right. So too it was years before I understood why a cart wheel needed a certain convexity although I had seen wheels fall to pieces for want of it. It was a detail most carefully attended to by the men in my shop; but I think none of them, any more than myself, could have explained why it had to be so.[6]

The men in Sturt's wheelwright's shop enjoyed two advantages which were denied to many workers: security of employment and job satisfaction. Between the workmen and the master there was an almost paternal, family relationship. The men had all been at Sturt's for many years, and were allowed to work at their own pace and in their own way. But for other types of worker this was far from the case, as two examples will show.

First was the custom of tramping. Artisans, even highly skilled men, often had difficulty in getting permanent employment, and so they were in the habit of leaving town and looking for work elsewhere. In this they were assisted by their trade society (union), which handed them on from branch to branch. The difficulties and hardships in finding work are described by Henry Broadhurst, an Oxfordshire stonemason who was forced to go on tramp during the trade depression of the late 1850s. For many months he wandered across southern England, working intermittently before finding a permanent job in Norwich:

Before I started on this . . . journey I had been out of work for a week or two, so that my entire capital amounted to less than ten shillings, and I finished the tour with the sum of sixpence in my pocket. At no time during my progress did I possess more than ten shillings, and on many occasions I was without even a penny. My trades-union had relieving-stations in nearly every town, generally situated in one of the smaller public-houses. Two of the local masons are appointed to act as relieving-officer and bed-inspector. . . .

When a mason on tramp enters a town, he finds his way to the relieving-officer and presents his card. . . . He is entitled to receive a relief allowance of one shilling for twenty miles and threepence for every additional ten miles traversed since his last receipt of relief money. . . . In addition he is allowed sleeping accommodation for at least one night, and if the town where the station is situated is of considerable size, he is entitled to two or three nights' lodging. . . .

Unfortunately, the stations did not exist everywhere, and when they were separated by forty or fifty miles − not a rare occurrence in the southern counties − the traveller's life became a hard one. I have frequently had to provide supper, bed, and breakfast on less than a shilling, so it may be readily imagined that my resting-places were never luxurious hotels. . . . During the whole of that tramp, and over all those hundreds of miles, I do not remember more than one occasion upon which I got a lift on the road. Even an ordinary drayman little cares to pick up for ever so short a distance any person having the appearance which I presented at that period. . . . In the course of my wanderings I fell in with many men bent on the same search as myself, though belonging to different trades. Sometimes it would be a bricklayer, sometimes a tanner, and sometimes an engineer.[7]

These were the skilled men. How the conditions of labour could be degraded for less fortunate workers is shown in a minor classic of the early labour movement, *The Ragged Trousered Philanthropists*. Robert Tressell (a pen-name for Robert Noonan) was a house painter in Hastings, Sussex, about 1902 and drew upon his experiences for his novel about life in the building trades. In this passage Hunter the foreman, nicknamed Misery, puts pressure on the painters to scamp their work:

Linden was still working at the vestibule doors . . . Misery stood watching him for some minutes without speaking. At last he said loudly:

'How much longer are you going to be messing about those doors? Why don't you get them under colour? You were fooling about there when I was here this morning. Do you think it'll pay to have you playing about there hour after hour with a bit of pumicestone? Get the work done! Or if you don't want to, I'll very soon find someone else who does. . . . There's plenty of better men than you walking about. If you can't do more than you've been doing lately you can clear out; we can do without you even when we're busy.'

Old Jack trembled. He tried to answer, but was unable to speak. . . . At last, with a great effort, for the words seemed to stick in his throat, he said:

'I must clean the work down, sir, before I go on painting.'

'I'm not talking about what you're doing, but the time it takes you to do it!' shouted Hunter. 'And I don't want any back answers or argument about it. You must move yourself a bit quicker or leave it alone altogether. . . .'

Downstairs, Misery was still going to and fro in the house and walking up and down in it. Presently he stopped to look at Sawkins' work. This man was painting the woodwork of the back staircase. Although the old paintwork here was very dirty and greasy, Misery had given orders that it was not to be cleaned before being painted. Just dust it down and slobber the colour on, he had said. Consequently, when he made the paint, he had put into it an extra large quantity of dryers. To a certain extent this destroyed the 'body' of the colour: it did not cover well; it would require two coats. When Hunter perceived this he was furious. He was sure it could be made to do with one coat with a little care; he believed Sawkins was doing it like this on purpose. Really, these men seemed to have no conscience. Two coats! and he had estimated for only three.[8]

Sturt's wheelwright's shop seems far removed from the usual image of the workshop of the world. Yet the two important crafts of the wheelwright and the blacksmith continued to flourish as long as society was horse-based – which (despite the railways) was the case essentially until 1914. Sturt's customers were farmers, and the business was centred in a country town. Rural England declined relatively in size and importance in the nineteenth century. Nevertheless, agriculture and the whole rural economy which it sustained was a vital part of the working life of the nation. In 1851 agriculture was still the largest single occupational category, employing over 2 million men and women (or over 21 per cent of the labour force); in 1901 the corresponding figure was under $1\frac{1}{2}$ million, which was less than 9 per cent of the occupied population. The absolute number of workers employed in agriculture remained high until the end of the nineteenth century, in spite of the slow erosion of rural ways noted by Sturt and others. Labouring life in the countryside was bound by the same seasonal rhythms and basic demands of husbandry as it had been in previous centuries. There was the same need for a great variety of aptitudes and skills (all too often glossed over in outsiders' descriptions of Hodge) and the continuation of local and regional variations in the organization of work. It is impossible to generalize the experience of agricultural labour from, say, the work of a Wiltshire shepherd, a Norfolk horseman, a Yorkshire cowman, and a

Warwickshire hedger and ditcher. But to recapture something of the feel of work in the fields we can turn to haymaking and harvest, the great peak of the agricultural year which drew in all who worked on the land, no matter what their normal job might be. In all parts of the country, as the time of the harvest approached, plans were made for the hectic work of getting in the crops. This was the time when the labourer did not have to beg for work, but for once was able to bargain freely with the farmer. The harvest contract was negotiated from a position of relative strength:

> We were allus hired by the week . . . except at harvest. Then it was piece-wukk. I dessay your've heard of the 'lord', as we used to call 'im? Sometimes he was the horseman at the farm, but he might be anybody. His job was to act as a sort of foreman to the team of reapers – there was often as many as ten or a dozen of us – and he looked after the hours and wages and such-like. He set the pace, too. His first man was sometimes called the 'lady'. Well, when harvest was gettin' close, the 'lord' 'ld call his team together and goo an' argue it out with the farmer. They'd run over all the fields that had got to be harvested and wukk it out at so much the acre. If same as there was a field badly laid with the wather, of course the 'lord' would ask a higher price for that. 'Now there's Penny Fields', he'd say – or maybe Gilbert's Field – or whatever it was; 'that's laid somethin' terrible', he'd say. 'What about that, farmer?' And when the price was named he would talk it over with his team to see whether they'd agree. The argument was washed down with plenty of beer, like as not drunk out of little ol' bullocks' horns; and when it was all finished, and the price accepted all round, 'Now I'll bind you', the farmer 'ld say, and give each man a shilling.[9]

Work in the harvest fields was very hard, for the weather was hot and the pace relentless. Thomas Ratcliffe of Worksop described how it was in the 1870s:

> Every man, woman and child went forth into the fields to help . . . and win the extra wage for harvest. . . . When the first corn field was ready . . . the sicklemen or scythemen with the gatherers and binders were at the field. The gatherers of the sheaves and the

binders were generally the wives and children of the men, and the whole work of the harvest was of the nature of a family outing . . . though a hard working one . . . the reapers or mowers fall in one by one behind the leader, the women and children as gatherers and binders following in their wake. The first stop was when the leader wanted to sharpen. He said 'Now', and all stopped at the end of his sickle or scythe swing. Then came the music of half a dozen tools sharpening as the stone rasped the steel blades. . . . The sharpening was often as not the time of 'lowance' as well, when from the wooden kegs or stone bottles came . . . the home-brewed as it fell into the horn ale-tots. . . .[10]

Women were an essential part of the harvest team. But their work was not limited to the special effort required at that time of the year. Of the 2 million people employed full-time in agricultural occupations in 1851, 11·5 per cent were women, and in 1901 the percentage was 5·9. Women worked in the fields at gleaning, potato-gathering ('tatering'), turnip-pulling, hoeing, weeding, thinning, hop-binding, and in all kinds of fruit and vegetable picking. In some jobs the children worked alongside their mothers. Field work on the Lincolnshire Wolds and in the east Midlands and East Anglia was sometimes organized in a gang system, with the women and children hired by a gangmaster who contracted for the work and paid the labourers. Women's work was usually paid at about half the men's rate, though in gangs it might be less. The working unit in agriculture was commonly taken to be the family: 'Wanted, a farm labourer with a working family,' ran an advertisement in the *Dorchester County Chronicle* in the 1860s. There was also indoor work for women on the farm, usually under the direction of the farmer's wife, in cleaning the house, milking, and working in the dairy at butter and cheese making. Cottage industries provided another source of women's (and children's) work: pillow-lace making in the south Midlands; straw-plaiting (for the hat and bonnet trade) in Buckinghamshire, Bedfordshire, Hertfordshire and Essex; hosiery work in Nottinghamshire and Leicestershire; glove-making in Oxfordshire, Worcestershire and the West Country; button-making in east Dorset; net-making on the coasts of East Anglia and Cornwall; and always the lingering on of handloom weaving.

In industry, as in agriculture, there was always paid work for women to do – in addition to the great unpaid burden of managing the home, cleaning, cooking, mending, sewing, nursing and bringing up the children. It was the woman who had to strive to 'make ends meet' on what her husband chose to hand over to her each week, supplemented by what she and the older children might earn. About 30 per cent of the total labour force in 1851 were women, and the figure was almost the same in 1901. Some of the work undertaken by women was rough and dirty, as in brick-making or sorting coal at the pit head. But mostly it was indoor employment and accordingly considered more respectable. In factory districts there was work in the mills; in the artisan trades wives helped their husbands; and out-work of all kinds, from sewing garments to making matchboxes, was done by women in London. Taking in washing, selling milk, keeping a dame school or corner shop, going out cleaning or nursing were all occupations for women, enabling them to add that vital bit to the family earnings which made all the difference between poverty and respectability.

The largest category of women's work, however, was domestic service. In 1851 the number of female domestic servants was over one million – second only to agriculture; and in 1901 they had grown to two million, which was 12·5 per cent of the total labour force. A growing demand for personal service was one of the signs of middle-class prosperity in the second half of the nineteenth century; and a steady supply of fresh servants was required, for the turnover was high in an occupation staffed heavily with girls and young women who shortly left to get married. The recruits came from the surrounding country districts or were the daughters of labouring men in the towns. The number of women who at some time had been in service was thus even larger than the census figures. A period as a lady's maid, housemaid, parlourmaid, cook, scullery maid, nursery maid, wet nurse, maid-of-all-work, char-woman or washerwoman was an experience shared by millions of working-class women. Lilian Westall, the daughter of a London craftsman, was seventeen when she went to work in the home of a Chiswick dentist in 1909:

> I was the only servant. I had to be up at six in the morning, and there were so many jobs lined up for me that I worked till eleven

o'clock at night. The mistress explained that she was very particular; the house had to be spotless always. After all, they were professional people and used to very high standards. I had to clean all the house, starting at the top and working down, sweeping and scrubbing right through. Hearthstoning the steps from the front door to the pavement took me an hour alone. I was most conscientious.

The meals I remember well. For breakfast I had bread and dripping. There were often mice dirts on the dripping to be scraped off first. Dinner was herring, every day; tea was bread and marge. I didn't have a bath during the month I was there, I wasn't given the opportunity; in fact there was no time to comb my hair properly, which was long – down to my waist; it grew so matted my mother had to cut a lot of it off when I finally came home again.

My room was in the attic. There was a little iron bed in the corner, a wooden chair and a washstand. It was a cold, bare, utterly cheerless room. At night I used to climb the dark stairs to the gloomy top of the house, go over to my bed, put the candle on the chair, fall on my knees, say my prayers, and crawl into bed too tired to wash. . . .[11]

Such testimony could be repeated many times over. Domestic service was continual, tiring and often monotonous; and the financial rewards were low. What could be said in favour of all the ceaseless fetching and carrying and emptying, brushing, polishing, scrubbing, dusting, cooking, waiting, answering calls, feeding, nursing, washing-up – which had to be performed, day in day out, in thousands of middle-class homes? The very design of a Victorian villa, tall and narrow, with the family sandwiched in between the servants' work area in the basement and their sleeping quarters in the attic, is a visible reminder of the expendability of human muscle in the cause of comfort.

The keeping of servants was a hallmark of the middle class, and even the humblest householders in the lower middle classes expected to be able to have a servant of some kind, though she might be only a girl of twelve or thirteen who made the fires and helped with the washing and cleaning. Yet the lifestyle of elite artisans of the labour aristocracy was close to that of clerks and small shopkeepers, the line between the upper working and lower middle classes becomes blurred, and it is a moot point how many of the latter should be included among the common people. Certainly their earnings were often less than the wages of highly skilled artisans, and in their work many white-collar workers such as clerks and shopmen suffered from exploitation and employer's tyranny as much as manual workers. H.G. Wells, the novelist, began his adolescent life as a draper's shopman in Southsea in 1881:

We apprentices were roused from our beds at seven, peremptorily, by one of the assistants. . . . We flung on old suits, tucking our nightgowns into our trousers, and were down in the shop in a quarter of an hour, to clean windows, unwrapper goods and fixtures, dust generally, before eight. At eight we raced upstairs to get first go at the wash basins, dressed for the day and at half-past eight partook of a bread and butter breakfast before descending again. Then came window dressing and dressing out the shop. I had to fetch goods for the window dresser and arrange patterns or pieces of fabric on the brass line above the counter. Every day or so the costume window had to be rearranged and I had to go in the costume room and fetch those headless effigies on which costumes are displayed and carry them the length of the shop, to the window dresser, avoiding gas brackets, chairs and my fellow creatures en route. Then I had to see to the replenishing of the pin bowls and the smoothing out and stringing up of paper for small parcels. . . . There were a hundred small fussy things to do, straightening up, putting away, fetching and carrying. It was not excessively laborious but it was indescribably tedious. If there was nothing else to do I had to stand to attention at the counter, as though ready for a customer, though at first I was not competent to serve. . . .

Half an hour before closing time we began to put away for the last time and 'wrapper up,' provided no customer lingered in the department. And as soon as the doors were shut and the last customer gone, the assistants departed and we junior apprentices rushed from behind the counters, scattered wet sawdust out of pails over the floor and swept it up again with great zest and speed, the last rite of the day. By half-past eight we were upstairs and free, supping on bread and butter, cheese and small beer. That was the ritual for every day of the week, thirteen hours of it, except that on Wednesday, Early Closing Day, the shop closed at five.[12]

Nevertheless, the work of the shabby clerks who appear in Dickens's novels, or of Mr Pooter in George and Wheedon Grossmith's *Diary of a Nobody*, unstable as it was in some respects, provided more security than was the lot of most manual workers. It was usually better paid, offered some prospect of promotion, and was not dependent on the weather or the seasons. The unemployed clerk or the draper's assistant who lost his 'crib' could of course be plunged into destitution; but poverty was not endemic in lower-middle-class life as it was for the lower-paid sections of the working class. In his great survey of working-class poverty in York in 1899 Seebohm Rowntree found that over 40 per cent of the wage-earning population (or 28 per cent of the total population) were living in poverty, defined as 'the minimum for food, clothing, and shelter needful for the maintenance of merely physical health'. His poverty line was drawn very strictly, to include only the barest essentials, and allowed nothing for such things as bus fares, newspapers, drink, tobacco, or subscriptions to church, chapel, sick club or trade union. Working people could expect to experience a cycle of alternate periods of want and comparative plenty. During childhood, unless the father was a skilled worker, the family would be in poverty. Then, when the older children began to earn and still lived at home, a more comfortable period would follow. The children would in their turn marry, leave home, and enjoy relative prosperity, until the number of their children forced them back into poverty. Finally, in old age, when they could no longer work, the labourer and his wife would again be in want. The proportion of the working class who at one period or other of their lives suffered from poverty to the point of being physically deprived was thus greater than the numbers below the poverty line at any given moment. Rowntree's findings for York were similar to those of Charles Booth in London in 1887–92 and for similar investigations in Northampton and Reading. His startling and inescapable conclusion was that 'in this land of abounding wealth, during a time of perhaps unexampled prosperity, probably more than one-fourth of the population are living in poverty'.[13]

For most of the time there was little opportunity in the workshop of the world for a majority of the people to do much beyond the confines of their work. But there were precious periods of leisure when life could offer something more than toil. To use the word leisure in its modern sense much before the mid-nineteenth century is probably anachronistic. In traditional society periods of non-work were filled by certain types of activity, though the demarcation between work and free time was not clearly drawn. With the development of industrialism and the establishment of new and more regular patterns of work, the enjoyment of customary popular recreations was increasingly replaced by a broader demand for leisure, defined as the very antithesis to work. To meet this demand (and also create new demands) a leisure industry, or industries, developed. Hours of work in industry generally increased during the first stages of the Industrial Revolution, but thereafter declined. A seventy-two-hour week was normal in northern textile mills in the 1820s and 1830s; but following pressure to reduce the hours of women and children this figure had fallen to fifty-four hours a week in the 1880s. By 1914 a fifty-two-hour week was common for skilled men in unionized industries. The attainment of first a ten-hour, then a nine-hour, and finally an eight-hour day became a major objective of the main industrial unions. Actual hours of work were of course often reduced by unemployment and also by absenteeism. The Saturday half-day off was granted the textile operatives under the Factory Act of 1850, and spread to other workers in the second half of the nineteenth century. In those categories of work which were little affected by mechanization – backyard workers, out-workers, agricultural labourers, domestic servants, shop assistants (until the Shops Act of 1911) – the hours of labour were long and unregulated. The extension of leisure, like the spread of industrialism, was therefore uneven, and traditional recreations continued side by side with newer forms of entertainment.

Despite the best efforts of temperance workers and reformers anxious to promote respectability and 'rational' recreation, the most popular institution for leisure activity was the public house. Its appeal to working men was shrewdly assessed by a domestic servant, recalling the 1920s in Hove: 'When you got in the pub you were your own master. Yes, then a man had money in his pocket regardless of the fact that it was supposed to last him all the week. So he let go.'[14] In town and country alike the social centre after work was the pub:

> We made our own life [said a Hackney housewife who had worked as a presser in a laundry until her marriage in 1927]. A lot of it revolved round the pub. You'd go in 'The Ren' [Rendlesham Arms] and have a drink. Then you'd all get together and have a sing-song 'Who's Sorry Now', 'Jealous of You', 'Nellie Dean', 'Old County Down' and so on. Somebody would say, 'let's take a couple of bottles' and you'd all go home. It was a happy place all the time. I used to be the life and soul of the party, singing and all that. My brothers and I used to sing in the pub. We enjoyed life. . . . Even the police used to come and have a drink. They weren't allowed to come in the pub, because they were on duty, but men used to take them drinks round the back. It was open to all. Women could go there as well – husbands and wives used to go in. Every Sunday morning my husband would go down to another pub, The Manor, in Rectory Road, and play darts. Then he'd come back past the window and whistle at about a quarter to two. We used to go down 'The Ren' for the last couple of drinks. It was really nice.[15]

In towns and cities, especially London, an alternative form of recreation was the theatre and music hall, which in the later nineteenth century became a favourite form of working-class entertainment. At their peak, from the 1880s to 1930, the music hall audiences of Lambeth, Whitechapel and the Mile End Road revelled in the songs and 'turns' of Marie Lloyd, Gus Elen, Dan Leno, Little Tich, Vesta Tilley and other stars. An East Ender remembered how, as a boy in the early years of this century, his sister Jo would take him to the local theatre:

> Sometimes on a Monday night she would come home from work and if she had a few coppers left over from the week-end she would say to Mum, 'Get yourself and the kids ready, we're going up to the Brit.' This was the old Britannia Theatre in Hoxton. Jo

loved the dramas that were performed there. If Mum could afford it we had a bag of peanuts or a ha'penny bag of sweets. We went in the 'gallery' for twopence – half-price for us kids. Among the dramas I remember was *The Face at the Window* – real horrible. Others were *Sweeney Todd, Maria Marten, Why Girls Leave Home*. Many times I have lain awake after going to the Brit, terrified to open my eyes for fear of seeing the murdered lying next to me. Sometimes we went to Collins Music Hall or the Islington Empire. That was different. They always had variety shows. We saw Harry Champion, Vesta Tilley, The Two Bobs, Hetty King, comedians of all sorts and stars of the day.[16]

In the countryside leisure was spent in a basically similar though somewhat quieter environment, nevertheless often polarized between pub and chapel. The significance and flavour of a rural pub in northeast Oxfordshire in the 1880s and 1890s is beautifully conveyed by Flora Thompson, the daughter of a stonemason:

In the taproom of the Wagon and Horses . . . the adult male population gathered every evening, to sip its half-pints, drop by drop, to make them last, and to discuss local events, wrangle over politics or farming methods, or to sing a few songs 'to oblige'.

It was an innocent gathering. None of them got drunk; they had not money enough, even with beer, and good beer, at twopence a pint. Yet the parson preached from the pulpit against it, going so far on one occasion as to call it a den of iniquity. . . .

Only about half a dozen men held aloof from the circle and those were either known to 'have religion', or suspected of being 'close wi' their ha'pence'.

The others went as a matter of course, appropriating their own special seats on settle or bench. It was as much their home as their own cottages, and far more homelike than many of them, with its roaring fire, red window curtains, and well-scoured pewter.

To spend their evenings there was, indeed, as the men argued, a saving, for, with no man in the house, the fire at home could be let die down and the rest of the family could go to bed when the room got cold.

So the men's spending money was fixed at a shilling a week, sevenpence for the nightly half-pint and the balance for other expenses. An ounce of tobacco, Nigger Head brand, was bought for them by their wives with the groceries.

It was exclusively a men's gathering. Their wives never accompanied them; though sometimes a woman who had got her family off hand, and so had a few halfpence to spend on herself, would knock at the back door with a bottle or jug and perhaps linger a little, herself unseen, to listen to what was going on within.[17]

In addition to the daily and weekend enjoyment of leisure there were also longer periods of escape from work. The custom of an annual holiday, to be spent if possible away from home, spread rapidly among the middle classes from the 1840s, but was still not common among working people by 1900. Holidays with pay, which professional and white-collar workers had enjoyed from the 1870s, were not generally available for manual workers before the Holidays with Pay Act of 1938. In the nineteenth century even the three days of Christmas, Easter and Whitsuntide (officially sanctioned, together with a fourth day in August, by the Bank Holidays Act of 1871) were not always paid for. Most workers' holidays were centred, as they had been for centuries, round the traditional religious festivals and local fairs, fêtes and race meetings. In the North and Midlands the main popular holidays were the wakes, when all the factories and workshops in the locality were closed for a period of three or four days and sometimes for a whole week. Until the 1840s these holidays were celebrated with rush-bearing ceremonies and traditional amusements such as cock fighting, bull and badger baiting, wrestling, bare fist fighting, together with a good deal of hard drinking, gambling and blood sports. But in the second half of the century leisure patterns changed. In the drive for respectability and improvement the old forms of recreation were condemned as coarse, brutal, disorderly and immoral. The traditional holidays were still observed, but they were tamed by a combination of direct attack on the old sports, regularization of work habits, and the provision of attractive alternatives. Above all, the building of the railways, and the introduction of excursion fares, made possible a day (and, for those who could afford it, a week) at the seaside. In the 1870s a London artisan could take his family of four persons to Brighton and back for 9s. The day trip and the excursion fare did not kill the wakes and the old holidays, but they gradually transformed them, as Alfred Williams testified. The old holy days were turned into the modern holidays. In the workshop of the world free time, like work, had to be measured and disciplined. Leisure became something quite distinct from work – to be planned, organized, and looked forward to.

PART IV

The People (1880–1980)

11. The Labour Movement

There was a time, and not so very long ago, when a history of the common people during their last two hundred years could be written almost exclusively round the theme of the labour movement. Events before and after 1880–1914 were interpreted as either leading up to or developing from this pioneer period of modern trade unionism and socialism. That such Whiggish history is no longer acceptable is not to diminish the importance of the labour movement but rather to set it in the perspective of the people as a whole, instead of the labour activists and their institutions. Working-class history can emphasize either the radical, even revolutionary potential of the working class, or their passivity, long-suffering and inward-lookingness. The first sees them as agents of change, the second as forces of conservatism. To some extent the difference stems from where we look for evidence: from skilled artisans or the casual poor, from trade unions and socialist parties or families and neighbourhoods. The labour movement was, and probably still is, the most powerful expression of the common people organized for action. It was a truly popular movement in that its inspiration and control was in the hands of individuals and groups drawn from the common people rather than from other classes. But it did not include all the people, or even a majority of the working class.

For most of their history the common people were not part of the political nation. Very few of them had the vote, and the basic assumptions about political authority excluded them. Not until the Reform Act of 1884 extended the franchise to two-thirds of the adult male population was anything approaching popular democracy possible, and the female half of the population was excluded until 1918 and 1928. It is therefore hardly surprising that a sympathetic observer could claim in 1884 that

The mass of persons in England take a languid interest in political action, and a capricious line on social questions. They have had reason to believe that politics are the mere game of two hereditary and privileged parties, in which it signifies little which gets a temporary ascendancy. They are convinced of the hollowness of political cries, and are under the impression that the public service is a phrase by which politicians mean private advantage.[1]

Because of such disenchantment the typical attitude of large numbers of the common people was not political but populist. Their social philosophy was no more than a simple feeling that they were somehow the victims of the system and its ruling elites. A deep-seated conviction that the world was divided into 'them' and 'us', a kind of secular Manichaeism or dualism, provided a basis of support for causes (rather than movements) which seemed to demonstrate a clash between the people (right) and the Establishment (wrong). Throughout the nineteenth century there was no lack of opportunity for the display of such sentiment, much of it of the flag-wagging, jingoistic, xenophobic, no-popery kind. A typical rallying point of populist sentiment in the 1870s was the Tichborne cause, when the fraudulent claimant to a baronetcy and estates in Hampshire became the hero of thousands in his attempt to prove his case. The legal proceedings lasted from 1867 to 1874, a Magna Charter Association was founded, and its periodical, the *Englishman*, had a weekly circulation of 70,000. By support of the claimant the Tichbornites were expressing their opposition to the Establishment and their approval of a champion who appeared to challenge its codes and practices. Thoughtful working men and their middle-class sympathizers could regret this 'flood of human idiotism', as John Ruskin called it. But elements of populism have remained strongly entrenched down to our own day, as witness the delight of the popular press in reporting the discomfiture of 'them' who are supposed to be superior to ordinary people but who are evidently no better, or even worse.

Populism, however, is a form of social protest without much organization or ideology, dependent upon heroes and adventurers, and reactionary in its attitudes. It arises when people feel alienated from the centres of power, and are prone to believe in conspiracies and corruption in high places. But because it attacked symptoms rather than causes it offered little satisfaction to intelligent working men, who saw the need for more lasting organizations for effecting social change. The outcome of their efforts was the labour movement, designed to extend the area of industrial freedom, open up the possibilities of democratic politics, and achieve a wide measure of social emancipation. Its dynamic came from two sources: trade unionism and socialism.

By the early 1870s a small minority of workers – mainly skilled craftsmen, textile operatives, coal miners, shipbuilders, engineers and metal workers of various kinds – had succeeded in getting their trade unions accepted and recognized by employers and government. From this base expansion began immediately following an upswing in the trade cycle; but some of the gains, notably among agricultural workers, were not permanent, and with hindsight the growth in the 1870s appears as a false dawn. The truly massive advance began in 1889 and continued, with some fluctuations, as follows:

Trade Union Membership in UK (in thousands) at selected dates[2]

1888	750	1926	5,219
1892	1,576	1930	4,841
1900	2,022	1939	6,274
1910	2,565	1950	9,289
1914	4,145	1960	9,835
1918	6,533	1968	10,049
1920	8,347	1979	12,173

This growth took the membership from about 5 per cent of the labour force in 1888 to 23 per cent in 1913 and a record 45 per cent in 1920 (a figure not reached again until 1948). The increase was in the membership of existing trade unions and also (more significantly) among unskilled and semi-skilled workers who had hitherto been largely outside the trade union orbit. This 'new unionism' was symbolized by the great dock strike of 1889, which in August successfully closed the London docks and wrested from the employers 'the dockers' tanner' (a day wage of 6d. an hour) and abolition of the sub-contracting system. Daily, disciplined marches across London secured favourable publicity for the strike, and its colourful leaders – John Burns, Ben Tillett and Tom Mann – became nationally known figures. Earlier in the year the London gas workers formed a union and won a reduction in working hours; and in the summer of 1888 the matchgirls' strike at Bryant and May's factory had shown that it might be possible to organize even the poorest and most exploited groups of workers. Across the country a fever of unionism spread rapidly, and the number of trade unionists doubled between 1889 and 1891. The employers fought back, and further union gains were bitterly contested. Ben Turner, who was in the thick of the struggles in the West Riding, recalled that when he joined the Huddersfield Weavers' Union in 1882 it was so weak that it could not even collect regular contributions: 'It was really playing at Trade Unionism, but was as far advanced as the old Radical section felt able to go.'[3] Yet ten years later the whole industrial climate had changed: old unions were revivified and hundreds of unorganized workers – gas workers, tramway workers, blue dyers, plasterers' labourers, tailors and tailoresses – were recruited into new unions in Yorkshire. Nationally the membership of unions reached 2 million by 1900, and by the outbreak of war in 1914 had doubled to 4 million.

The great achievement of trade unionism was that by 1914 in most of the major industries a system of collective bargaining had been evolved: the workers, through their representatives, were able to secure improvements in wages and conditions of work. It was however only too apparent that there were limits to industrial negotiation. The workers wanted, above all, a steady wage and some degree of security against reductions and unemployment in times of recession. But these goals were not easily negotiable, and while the leaders were deeply committed to collective bargaining the rank and file were often less enthusiastic. The gap between trade union officials and their members which opened up, and which has plagued labour ever since, contained elements of the familiar syndrome of them and us.

The need to transcend the limits of what trade unions alone could do for their members was recognized from the 1870s, when legislation favourable to labour was secured by political action. After the extension of the suffrage in 1867 and 1884 the two main political parties were prepared to court the working-class vote, which provided organized labour with a certain amount of political power. On this basis was built a Liberal-Labour alliance, by which a few labour candidates were returned to parliament on the Liberal ticket. Thomas Burt was one of these in 1874, as also was his fellow-MP, Alexander Macdonald. The arrangement worked best in mining constituencies, where the area was socially homogeneous and the union strong. At the general election of 1885, following the Third Reform Act, the number of Lib-Lab MPs increased from two to eleven, and of these six were miners. Since the demise of Chartism such working men as were enfranchised usually voted Liberal, except in Lancashire and parts of London. Indeed, the Liberal Party remained the party of most working men up to 1914. But discontent with Lib-Lab'ism began to be voiced in the 1880s and gathered momentum in the 1890s. It sprang basically from the reluctance of the Liberal Party to appoint more working-class candidates and support the trade unions in their legal struggles with employers. To many working men in the North it became increasingly anomalous to be expected to support politically at the polls the very men they had been fighting industrially in the mills. There arose therefore a demand for independent labour representation, free from the constraints of alliance with either Liberals or Conservatives. This movement was reflected within the Trades Union Congress, set up in 1868 to act as a national parliament of labour. Every year from 1887 to 1899 the issue of independent labour representation was raised and hotly debated. On the one side were the new unionists, the socialists, and the advocates of direct sponsorship of working-class candidates, led by the Scottish miners' leader, Keir Hardie, who had himself been refused adoption as a candidate by the Liberals; on the other were the old unionists and the upholders of Lib-Lab'ism as exemplified by Henry Broadhurst, who had left his stonemason's bench, as he said, for the Treasury Bench of a Liberal government. The climax came in 1899–1900, when a carefully worded motion was passed to call a special conference of representatives from 'Co-operative, Socialist, Trade Union, and other working-class organizations' to 'devise ways and means for the securing of an increased number of Labour members in the next Parliament'. Out of this conference emerged the Labour Representation Committee (LRC), which in 1906 became the Labour Party.

The second element in the dynamic of the labour movement was socialism. What precisely the term meant to the many hundreds (later thousands) of earnest working men and women who so described their beliefs is not an entirely straightforward matter. Membership of most socialist organizations signified a commitment to certain principles (of which some version of 'the collective ownership of the means of production, distribution and exchange' was the most important) followed by a list of 'immediate' reforms, such as the eight-hour day, state pensions, and free, secular education to sixteen. But it is clear from the reminiscences of old socialists that while they subscribed to these objectives, they often had a variety of other expectations and motivations. For some, the revolt against Victorian society and all that it stood for was paramount; some were appalled by the waste and inefficiency of capitalism and wished to replace it by a more rational system; others found in socialism a new religion; and a few believed in class struggle and the hope of revolution. Socialism was not only an instrument for the realization of certain social and political goals. It also had an expressive function in the lives of many of its more active adherents; they needed socialism as much as the movement needed them. In the 1880s and 1890s they had a choice of organizations. The oldest was the Social Democratic Federation (SDF), founded in 1881 as the Democratic Federation from various radical clubs in London. It was basically Marxist, and most of the leading English socialists were for a short while in its ranks. The Socialist League, under the leadership of William Morris, split off from the SDF in 1884; and in the same year the Fabian Society was formed by a group of middle-class intellectuals, who derived their socialism not from Marx but from utilitarianism. In 1893 the Independent Labour Party was founded at a conference in Bradford, and despite its title was committed to socialism.

Numerically the socialists were only a small body – probably no more than two thousand in the 1880s and perhaps twenty or thirty thousand by 1900 – but their influence was widespread, especially in London and the industrial North. Their activities, and above all their propaganda, set up a ferment of social ideas which captivated a whole generation of young people in the 1890s and carried over into the first decade of the new century.

It is curious indeed [reflected the socialist guru Edward Carpenter in 1916] to see how, of all the innumerable little societies – of the S.D.F., the League, the Fabians, the Christian Socialists, the Anarchists, the Freedom groups, the I.L.P., the Clarion societies, and local groups of various names – all supporting one side or another of the general Socialist movement – not one of them has grown to any great volume, or to commanding and permanent influence; and how yet, and at the same time, the general teaching and ideals of the movement have permeated society in the most remarkable way, and have deeply infected the views of all classes, as well as general literature and even municipal and imperial politics.[4]

In Yorkshire, the home of the ILP, local socialist and labour societies flourished vigorously. Ramsay MacDonald gave a typical picture of such a group in 1894:

Nothing is too hard for the members in their virgin enthusiasm to do. They run their little prints, they sell their stock of pamphlets, they drop their pennies into the collecting box, they buy their I.L.P. tea and cocoa etc. as though they were members of an idealistic Communist society. Their poverty is nothing. I know of one Labour Association that conducted the registration of a town of 40,000 inhabitants for the sum 14s. 6d. The same work used to cost the Liberals £40 to £50 and it now costs the Conservatives three times that much.[5]

In the larger towns there was a whole variety of labour clubs, in addition to the trade union branches and the central political organizations. Around the *Clarion* newspaper was developed a series of social activities, especially attractive to youth – cycling clubs, glee clubs, field clubs and scouting. Parties of young socialist pioneers went out into the villages at the weekends distributing leaflets, holding meetings, consciously spreading the new gospel. In the towns of the West Riding the coffee-houses (the traditional debating grounds for Radicals and others) provided admirable opportunities for the dissemination of socialist ideas.

To many of the pioneers, socialism had the appeal of a religion; they spoke often of their faith in socialism. Margaret McMillan saw that the new party in Bradford sprang from an impulse that had nothing in common with the older political parties. 'It was called the Independent Labour Party. In reality it was a new religion – a heresy.'[6] Philip Snowden, after addressing his first socialist meeting at Keighley in 1894, experienced the same discovery: 'It was an inspiration. It was like a revival gathering. Socialism to those men and women was a new vision.'[7] There was a tremendous feeling of being part of a movement which would make a reality of this vision, a feeling of taking part in a great crusade. 'England, arise! The long, long night is over,' proclaimed Edward Carpenter in a hymn that was sung at labour gatherings for many years. 'Socialism', said Keir Hardie, 'is not a system of economics but life for the dying people.'

The new movement was educational, both in its methods and its broad effects. Socialist Sunday schools, adult schools and discussion classes were established by the labour clubs, and socialist lectures found their way into existing institutions such as the Secular Sunday Schools wherever possible. Lecturing was one of the ways in which a meagre livelihood could be secured for those who wished to devote themselves whole-time to the cause. Margaret McMillan and Philip Snowden were itinerant ILP lecturers of this order, travelling from place to place and spending the nights in the homes of local comrades. The new socialism was educational also in a broader sense; the flood of pamphlets and journals which it released stimulated intellectual activity and sustained prolonged debate on the fundamentals of democracy and politics which lasted until the First World War. A steady stream of Fabian tracts, Fabian book-boxes, and ILP, SDF and Secularist pamphlets provided food for endless discussion and debate. Local journals like the *Yorkshire Factory Times*, the *Bradford Labour Journal*, *Labour Champion* and the *Huddersfield and Colne Valley Labour News* were read along with the national papers such as *Justice*, *Commonweal*, the *Labour Leader* and *Clarion*. Robert Blatchford's *Clarion* (begun in 1891) was labour journalism of a new kind, reaching out to the masses, and presenting the socialist case to them in a simple, good-humoured way. Not since Cobbett had any popular political journalist been so effective. In 1894 Blatchford reprinted some of his articles on socialism, as *Merrie England*, and sold 75,000 copies at once, and over 2 million during the next fifteen years. The circulation of *Clarion* rose to 80,000. The intelligent young workman who read *Merrie England* was not encouraged to stop there; in the appendix at the end of the book was a reading list which extended far beyond socialist tracts to Emerson, Ruskin and Carlyle. Behind this stood the long tradition of working-class self-education and self-improvement.

There was nothing inevitable in the association of this enthusiasm for socialism with the bread-and-butter issues of trade unionism, although the most prominent leaders of the new unions were socialists. Theories of socialism, as Lenin pointed out, were not the product of the working class but of intellectuals from the educated classes. Neither revolutionary socialists nor Fabians were overoptimistic about the potentialities of trade unions for bringing about fundamental social change. From their side the old unionists were deeply distrustful of the socialists, whom they suspected of merely wanting to capture the union membership for ulterior ends. Nevertheless, the unique achievement of British labour was the building of a political alliance between these two movements, resulting in the Labour Party. In Europe and America, which also had trade union and socialist movements, no comparable structure developed, although the seeds were there.

The chief architect of what he called the Labour Alliance was Keir Hardie, and the crucial steps in its formation were taken in the generation before the First World War. It had been hoped that the ILP would become a mass socialist party, but its failure to do so in the 1890s was interpreted as showing the need to redouble the efforts to win trade union support. A counteroffensive by the employers, who hoped to emulate the success of their American rivals in union breaking, convinced some unionists that they might be unwise to rely on industrial action alone. And in this mood the LRC was established by delegates from the ILP, SDF, Fabian Society and the unions. The three largest unions – of the miners, cotton workers and engineers – at first held aloof, in contrast to the new unions and the railwaymen. But after the Taff Vale case in 1900–1, when the House of Lords ruled that a union could be liable for all the damages resulting from a strike (thereby undercutting the very roots of trade union power) the need to exert political pressure to change the law in labour's favour was clear, and there was a rallying of the unions behind the LRC. Success came in

341

1906, when twenty-nine LRC candidates were elected to parliament, where they assumed the name of Labour Party. The new party did not adopt a socialist programme until 1918, and Lib-Lab'ism, especially among the miners, took some time in dying. The socialism of the Labour Party when it finally emerged was of a peculiarly insular kind: empirical, reformist and welfare statist.

How these movements affected the life of an obscure but rather uncommon common man can be seen in the case of George Meek, the 'bath chair-man'. His autobiography is a vivid presentation of the life of a non-industrial working man in an area far removed from the traditional strongholds of labour and socialism.[8] He was born in Eastbourne in 1868 and brought up by his grandparents in villages in east Sussex. Although literate and fond of reading he had no trade or skill, and his eyesight was poor. He lacked the physical strength necessary for labouring work and after a succession of dead-end jobs became a bath chair-man in Eastbourne. Every day he stood at a street corner or on the front with his heavy wheeled chair, weighing about three hundredweights, waiting for customers. The work was seasonal, casual, and subject to petty exploitation by middlemen. A few chair-men owned their chairs, but most rented them from a chair-owner. Like the framework knitters of the 1840s, the chair-men could find themselves in debt if there was insufficient work to cover the rent. Meek had been told by a friendly village shoemaker ('a strong Radical and an atheist who lent me books') that the Liberals were the natural friends of poor working men, and so 'I became an ardent Liberal'. In 1888 he got work as Liberal registration agent and then as assistant steward at the Liberal Club and collector for the Working Men's Liberal Association. But in the early 1890s he began to read socialist papers – the *Clarion, Justice* and the *Workman's Times* – and also *Looking Backward*, a utopian socialist novel by the American, Edward Bellamy. At the same time, and accelerated by disappointment in love, he lost his religious (Baptist) faith: 'My Socialism made me more humanitarian, and I wanted to live a fuller life than the bondage of religious tenets would permit.' He was expelled from the Liberal Party in 1893 for advocating the formation of a branch of the ILP; and from then on was active in local groups of Fabians, Clarion Scouts and the SDF, as well as in organizing a chair-men's union. After the 1906 election he became secretary of a South Eastern Federation of socialist societies.

From the distance of 1910 he claimed that thirty years earlier, and before ever he had heard of socialism, 'I was imbued with a sense of class-consciousness, which has intensified since.' This latent class-consciousness was endemic and was strengthened by his subsequent experiences of the poverty, insecurity and frustrations of working-class life: 'I have always longed to be able to earn enough to be able to pay my way honestly. I hardly ever have.' He married in 1895 and his wife worked as an ironer in a laundry to try to make ends meet; yet they could never afford a home of their own – only furnished or unfurnished rooms, to be shared with a lodger. 'I have never been able to keep anything saleable or pawnable we could do without,' he concluded sadly. His socialist reading provided Meek with an explanation of this experience; and his work for the 'cause' gave him comradeship and a badly needed sense of worth. He also found a belief and a hope for the future:

> Some day the workers will tire of mere politicians of every shade and will organise themselves for the definitive struggle with Capitalism. Then, thoroughly grounded in the economics *and* ethics of Socialism, they will know what to do. It will be no great loss to the idle rich for them to have to live useful, healthy lives, nor to the business man to be relieved of the ever-increasing strain of competition. The worker will have no fear of unemployment or of want through sickness or old age. The reign of hatred engendered by the competition of individuals and the war of classes will give place to that of 'Peace on earth, goodwill to men'.

This was to be the familiar tone of the British labour movement for the next forty years, inspiring sufficient support for two minority Labour governments in 1924 and 1929, and reaching its apogee in the Labour victory of 1945 with its ensuing programme of nationalization and welfare legislation. For committed socialists the Labour Party was inadequate yet inescapable. The tie with the unions and their philosophy of labourism hampered the development of a full-blooded socialist programme; but to win sufficient support to elect a socialist government required the backing of the trade union movement. Some socialists sought to preserve a more militant stance by membership of the ILP, which until 1932 was affiliated to the Labour Party; and those who favoured revolutionary policies found a home in the SDF and after 1920 in the Communist Party. At times the labour movement functioned as an umbrella under which the socialists, like other radical and reform groups, could shelter. This was particularly noticeable at the local level, where trade unionists, socialists, cooperators, workers' educationalists and women's organizations flourished together.

The measure of the success of the Labour Party, however, lay ultimately not with the activists but with the electorate. Labour's task was to convince the general public that it was a truly national and not just a sectional party. The election statistics tell an important part of the story. In 1906 Labour polled 330,000, which was 5·9 per cent of the total vote; by 1918 this figure had increased to 2·4 million (22·2 per cent); in 1929 it was 8·4 million (37·1 per cent); and in 1945, 12 million (47·8 per cent). This does not mean that the common people had all become enthusiastic Labour Party supporters, and there is no reason to suppose that a majority of the population took more than an intermittent interest in politics. It does mean that during the first half of the twentieth century a sizeable part of the population turned away from the Conservative and Liberal parties and identified with Labour. The extension of democracy to the whole people could not be contained within the framework of the traditional parties, despite their efforts to retain the working-class vote by passing welfare legislation. There was need of a new image of what a popular political party might be if the electorate was to be anything more than voting fodder. Old attitudes died hard:

> Look at them there Labour members of Parliament – a lot of b—rs what's too bloody lazy to work for their livin'! What the bloody 'ell was they before they got there? Only workin' men, the same as you and me! But they've got the gift o' the gab,

declared one of Tressell's painters.[9] To overcome such cynicism, to break away from the them-and-us dualism, was one of the hardest tasks facing the labour movement. In the long run it could

344

be achieved only by demonstrating new political possibilities to the people and raising the whole horizon of their expectations.

In the advance to effective mass democracy no issue was more important than the popular attitude to the state. Throughout their long history the common people had good reason to distrust state power, which in their experience was almost always wielded in the interests of the ruling classes. The medieval peasant faced with demands for taxes, the seaman impressed or soldier conscripted, the trade unionist struggling against the law, saw the state as a natural enemy. Of all the state authorities likely to be encountered by working people the Poor Law was the commonest, and their experience of that was full of bitterness and fear. The idea that the state might be benevolent or a source of social security was almost too much to be believed. Flora Thompson recalled how the introduction of old age pensions by the Liberal government in 1908 transformed life for aged cottagers:

> They were relieved of anxiety. They were suddenly rich. Independent for life! At first when they went to the Post Office to draw it, tears of gratitude would run down the cheeks of some, and they would say as they picked up their money, 'God bless that Lord George! [for they could not believe one so powerful and munificent could be a plain 'Mr'] and God bless *you*, miss!' and there were flowers from their gardens and apples from their trees for the girl who merely handed them the money.[10]

The Liberals' remarkable programme of social welfare between 1906 and 1911 undermined the assumption that the working class had nothing to hope for from state action; and the parliamentary socialism of the Labour Party was a programme to use the power of the state for social reform. Once the possibility of a benign instead of a repressive state began to be recognized, the way was open (via Fabian socialism) to the goal of the welfare state. Along this increasingly attractive path numbers of the common people were prepared to follow the Labour Party.

The weakening, if not abandonment, of popular distrust of the state had the effect of incorporating the working class more fully into the political life of the nation. Yet paradoxically the popular attitude to politics probably changed very little. Modern democracy operates on the basis of a consensus. The difference between the various parties must not be too great to allow of agreement on fundamental constitutional and political principles; otherwise the system will be disrupted. The enfolding of the labour movement within this consensus, which was effected so successfully by the labour leadership between 1906 and 1945, was not without its price or its critics. It brought recognition, stability and power for labour; but in the process labour assimilated many of the attitudes, values and priorities of the traditional parties and bourgeois society in general. For their part the Conservatives overcame their bogy-fears of ruin and blood-red revolution occasioned by Keir Hardie's triumphal entry to parliament in 1892 dressed in a tweed jacket and cloth cap, and in due course had little difficulty in adopting the most popular planks in Labour's platform. The two main parties began to look like different versions of the same set of general liberal values. Some socialists reacted to this by demanding much bolder and more radical measures; but there was little evidence of support for complete rejection of the consensus and an 'extreme' or revolutionary alternative. The voters, faced with a choice, not about fundamentals, but about the means of attaining more or less agreed ends and the leaders who were to accomplish them, might be forgiven if they were sometimes less than enthusiastic about politics and politicians: 'there's nowt to choose between 'em'; 'they're all talk and no do'; or, 'politics never did anybody any good'.[11]

Historians have puzzled over the apparent problem of why more working people did not support Labour than was in fact the case, and have propounded complex and ingenious explanations. But the reality was perhaps simpler. Arthur Harding, an East Ender born in 1886 in one of the most notorious slums of late-Victorian London, explained:

> My father's family . . . were all true-blue Conservatives, quite simple. The Conservatives were rich and powerful and they distributed large gifts to their supporters. The Radicals and Liberals were too poor, they were out to get something for themselves so what was the good of voting for them? These political beliefs have remained with all the off-spring . . . all who hold our name vote Conservative.[12]

Even so, Harding bought a Liberal-Radical paper – because it was 'a racing man's paper'. He identified the Conservatives with the publicans: 'In every pub you would see a Conservative picture at election times. In the pubs you couldn't argue politics. The landlord would say, "Here, none of that 'ere".' Conversely, 'The Liberals were against the pubs. That's why so many of the working men's wives were for them.' His father, who was a carver and gilder, and his uncles who were cabinet-makers, were persuaded that they needed the protection of tariff reform: 'The cabinet-maker was told by his governor that he had to vote Conservative, because if they voted Liberal they would be out of work because of Free Trade. The market would be flooded with cheap furniture from abroad and the cabinet-makers would end up in the work-house.' Harding's own attitude to politics was frankly opportunistic. In 1922 he 'helped the Liberals in St George's in the East, protecting them against the Labour', and in the general strike of 1926 he 'made a lot of money' by organizing bodyguards to terrorize the dockers; in the 1930s he supported Mosley's Blackshirts; and in 1945 he voted Labour.

It is not easy to reconcile this perspective of politics from below with the idealism and loyalty of working people outlined earlier, for whom the labour movement was 'the cause'. Harding's underworld of organized crime and cheap-jack cabinet-making was far removed from the respectable working class who were the heirs of a long tradition of artisan radicalism reaching back to Chartism, the Corresponding Societies and the Levellers. Among the army of the unskilled, the casual poor and the petty criminals Labour awakened only a feeble echo. The driving force of the labour movement came from other elements in the heritage of the common people: religious nonconformity, a sense of social justice and equity, belief in self-help, a desire for the freedom of independence, and a longing for dignity and security.

12. War and the Dole

The life of everyone who lived through the years between 1914 and 1945 was likely to be scarred by two great memories: war and unemployment. These were not the only formative events in the first half of the twentieth century; but they affected the lives of more people, either directly or indirectly, than at any other time in English history. There had been wars before, and lack of work was one of the well-known hazards of working-class life; yet the general verdict was that this time things were somehow different. The two world wars were total wars in a way that no previous conflict had been. They mobilized very large numbers in the armed forces and also involved the whole civilian population. For ten years altogether the economy of the country was geared to all-out effort for war, drawing directly upon the labour of millions of ordinary people. Between the two world wars stretched twenty-one uneasy years, marked first by acute industrial strife and then by unemployment on a scale beyond anything in living memory. War, by its very nature, disrupts the historical pattern of stability and steady evolution; it provokes rapid social and technological change, and heightens social consciousness. We should therefore expect to see significant changes in the lives of the common people during this period; and in fact historians have had little difficulty in demonstrating that this was so. Before outlining some of these changes, however, it is well to remember that our primary concern is with the experience of the people themselves rather than with the historian's broad assessments of what happened, and that things sometimes look different from below. A recent writer gives a salutary warning from his description of the changes which the First World War brought to rural Oxfordshire:

When the war was over not only had the young men gone but things had changed completely. This is a platitude of history, but one which is repeated by practically every old man and woman that one talks to. An old man in Headington once said 'It was all different after', and when I asked why he said 'The donkeys and rabbits had gone'.[1]

The statistics of the First World War tell a relentless story. About 6 million men were recruited into the armed services and another 3 million men and women were in reserved occupations, mostly connected with munitions. Three-quarters of a million men were killed in the war and 1·6 million wounded. Battle casualties were at times horrifying: 420,000 on the Somme (60,000 casualties, including 21,000 killed, on the first day) in 1916; 142,000 at Arras early in 1917; 324,000 at Passchendaele (late 1917). On the western front 56 per cent of all soldiers became casualties and 12 per cent of those were killed. In Britain as a whole 9 per cent of men under forty-five were killed in the war. Only the cadre of this vast army were regular soldiers; the rest were civilians who, until conscription was introduced in 1916, volunteered. Such a flocking to the colours was the more extraordinary since the popular attitude to soldiering was traditionally hostile. To 'go for a soldier' was regarded as only a little less degrading than going to prison, and the only justification was poverty. Respectable working people shunned the army, associating it with low life and danger: 'I would rather bury you than see you in a red coat' were the sentiments of many a mother when her son suggested enlisting. Yet within six months of the autumn of 1914 the call for the 'first hundred thousand' had been answered by over a million volunteers. A small minority of socialists, Liberals and pacifists opposed the war from the beginning, but the Labour Party and the trade unions supported it. The common people swung behind the enthusiastic and patriotic lead given by the middle classes and the government, and responded to the appeal that 'Kitchener [War Secretary and hero of the Boer War] needs you'. There was a widespread belief that the war would be over by Christmas. Reasons for 'joining up' were usually personal and immediate, and if an explanation was called for later, working men often referred to a sense of duty or the need to go with their mates. Equally strong was the desire for adventure, for a break in the monotony of everyday life, and for the economic security of army pay.

I cannot remember that I ever thought of soldiering as anything but a better way of life than sitting at a desk [wrote Llewellyn Wyn Griffith]. None thought of it as a noble calling – it was what your friends were doing.[2]

Others were like a young Berkshire roadman who recalled joining Kitchener's army:

I worked for the County Council and, one morning, I left to go to work; we were repairing the roads in Windsor Park at the time, but on the way I met a friend who was going to enlist. Instead of going on to work, I went back home, changed into my best clothes and went with him to the Recruiting Office in Reading.[3]

Few of the first recruits had any idea of what war or the army would be like, and the experience when it came was traumatic.

Until fairly recently accounts of the fighting were mainly by officers and poets. The First World War was a very literary war, and a spate of memoirs and poems published in the interwar period helped to create a no-more-war mentality. In the last few years many diaries, letters and reminiscences by ordinary soldiers have come to light, and from these it is possible to see the war through the eyes of the 'Other Ranks'. Almost all of these confirm the view that 'war is hell'; but they also emphasize the resilience and ingenuity of the common people when faced with totally new, unwelcome and ultimately horrible experiences. As was noted in the case of the civil war, the private soldier's view of a war is very different from his commander's. The ordinary soldier is concerned not so much with winning a battle as surviving. A machine gunner commented:

In a sense it was an advantage being a private for nobody told you anything. You just waited in a day-to-day kind of existence until things happened. It didn't do you any good to know that you were going to be in a great battle next Wednesday.[4]

The private soldier thinks of himself in the first instance as a member of a small group – perhaps half a dozen 'pals' – with whom he recognizes his survival is bound up. This is the root of the comradeship which old soldiers remembered as the best part of their war service – enshrined for posterity in posed studio photographs of three or four young men in soft caps, puttees and polished boots. Like loyalty at the workplace or solidarity in the family, comradeship was not always on the surface.

The importance of this relationship was brought out most fully by experience in the trenches on the western front. After the first few months of free manoeuvring in Belgium and northern France, the war settled down into a stalemate, with each side dug into a system of parallel trenches stretching some 475 miles from the North Sea coast in Belgium to the Swiss border. The British held about ninety miles of this line, including the two important sectors of the Ypres salient in Flanders and the Somme area in Picardy, with about 800 battalions of 1000 men each. The trenches were normally three deep: the front line trench, the support line two hundred yards behind, and further back still the reserve trenches. Perpendicular to the line were communication trenches, and running out at right angles from the front line were 'saps' leading to the most forward positions of all, manned as observation or machine gun posts. Dugouts in the sides of trenches provided deeper shelter for command posts and officers' quarters. A front line trench was between six and ten feet deep, and four or five feet wide. On the enemy side was a two- or three-foot parapet of sandbags, and on the back wall of the trench a corresponding but lower parados. About two or three feet from the bottom of the trench was a ledge or fire step, on which the defenders stood when facing the enemy. The trench was not a straight line but a zig-zag, with frequent traverses, in order to minimize damage from shells and avoid enfilade fire by attackers. The floor was covered with wooden duckboards below which were sumps to collect water. Between the German and Allied lines was no man's land, varying in width from sector to sector but usually a few hundred yards across. Each side put up entanglements of barbed wire in front of their lines and sited machine guns to cover them. Flanders and Picardy have a high rainfall and in parts are low-lying, with the result that the British trenches were always ankle-deep in mud and often flooded several feet deep. Nor were they (unlike the German trenches) always very well constructed. For ninety miles of front (perhaps 6000 miles of trenches in all) an army of men lived for four years below ground level in holes and ditches.

Trench duty was normally rotated. After three days to a week in the front line trench, a unit would move back to the support trench for a similar period, then to the reserve, and finally spend a week of 'rest' (i.e. training) behind the lines, before returning to the line again. The changeover, and indeed the movement of all rations, ammunition and stores, took place at night. Once arrived in the line, the soldier's day settled into an intense twenty-four-hour cycle which revolved round the ritual of stand-to, just before dawn and again at dusk, when everyone mounted the fire step with his rifle ready to repel an attack. When the Germans did not attack at dawn the stand-down was given and everyone began preparing his breakfast from the rations of tea, bread and bacon (fried in mess tins over small fires). During the day there was an endless succession of sentry duties, inspections, repairs to the trenches, and fatigues of all kinds. At night patrols, raiding parties and wiring parties were out in no man's land. Sleep was snatched in short intervals; but throughout the twenty-four hours a majority of the men were awake and busy – and very tired. While all this was going on they were harassed by enemy shells which fell almost daily on the trenches, killing, wounding or burying a few unfortunates. Before an attack the bombardment would reach a crescendo, with shells bursting incessantly and the whole earth transformed into an inferno of noise and uproar: 'all hell was let loose', as every account by a survivor testifies. Learning how to live through shelling was the main business of an infantryman. Some did not manage to do so, and were reduced by 'shell shock' to a state of mental breakdown.

The second painful experience was 'going over the top'. This usually meant a night patrol into no man's land to gain information about the enemy. An officer and one or two men would crawl forward on their stomachs, listening for enemy activity. It was a nerve-racking business as they crouched in a shell hole or lay flat beneath a bursting flare, knowing that at any moment a sentry might be alerted or a machine gun open up. For those who got back to their own trench a sense of utter exhaustion followed. On other nights wiring parties would be out, repairing and reinforcing the protective entanglements. A bigger and more dangerous exploit was the raiding party, made up of about thirty men, whose object was to break into the enemy lines with bombs and bayonets and bring back a few prisoners. But the bloodiest enterprise was a general attack, when thousands of men simultaneously scrambled out of their trenches and attempted to advance across no man's land and capture the German positions. Before the attack, rumours and the inevitable massive preparations first alerted the men back in the rest positions that a 'big push' was in the offing. Next they would be officially told by their commanding officer that they would soon be in action. Then the order came to dress in battle order with extra ammunition and grenades; and finally they marched up to the front line, occupied the trenches at nightfall, and waited apprehensively for the dawn. There are many accounts in poems and memoirs of what this experience meant to the men involved, but none more powerful than Frederic Manning's fictional yet autobiographical voice from the ranks. The little group of friends are about to take part in an attack. Private Bourne (i.e. Manning) notes the heavy drumming of the guns in the distance:

'What do you make of it, sergeant?' he asked.

'I don' know what to make of it. What the bloody hell do you make of it, yourself? After all, that's what matters. I suppose we'll come through all right; we've done it before, so we can do it again. Anyway, it can't be more of a bloody balls-up than some o' the other shows 'ave been. . . .'

'You don't want to get the bloody wind up, you know,' he said kindly.

'Who's getting wind up?' replied Bourne, resentfully. 'Don't you worry about me, sergeant. I can stick it all right. If I do get it in the neck, I'll be out of this bloody misery, anyway.'

'That's all right, ol' son,' said the sergeant. 'You needn't take me up the wrong way, you know. I'm not worryin' about you. I'm a bit windy myself. It'll be all right when we get started. We'll pull it off somehow or other.'

The next night they entered the front line trenches.

There was a reek of mouldering rottenness in the air, and through it came the sour, stale odour from the foul clothes of the men. Shells streamed overhead, sighing, whining, and whimpering for blood; the upper air fluttered with them; but Fritz was not going to take it all quietly, and with its increasing roar another shell leaped toward them, and they cowered under the wrath. There was the enormous grunt of its eruption, the sweeping of harpstrings, and part of the trench wall collapsed inwards, burying some men in the landslide. It was difficult to get them out, in the crowded conditions of the trench. . . .

The noise of the shells increased to a hurricane fury. There was at last a sudden movement with some purpose behind it. The men began to fix bayonets. Someone thrust a mug into Shem's hands.

'Three men. Don't spill the bloody stuff, you won't get no more.'

Shem drank some of the rum and passed it to Bourne.

'Take all you want, kid,' said Bourne to Martlow; 'I don't care whether I have any or not.'

'Don't want much,' said Martlow, after drinking a good swig. 'It makes you thirsty, but it warms you up a bit.'

Bourne emptied the mug, and handed it back to Jakes to fill again and pass to another man. It had roused him a little. . . .

They shook hands, the three among themselves and then with others near them.

'Good luck, chum. Good luck. Good luck.'

He felt his heart thumping at first. And then, almost surprised at the lack of effort which it needed, he moved towards the ladder.

Martlow, because he was nearest, went first. Shem followed behind Bourne, who climbed out a little clumsily. Almost as soon as he was out he slipped sideways and nearly fell. The slope downward, where others, before he did, had slipped, might have been greased with vaseline; and immediately beyond it, one's boots sank up to the ankle in mud which sucked at one's feet as they were withdrawn from it, clogging them, as in a nightmare. It would be worse when they reached the lower levels of this ill-drained marsh. The fear in him now was hard and icy, and yet apart from that momentary fumbling on the ladder, and the involuntary slide, he felt himself moving more freely, as though he had full control of himself.

They were drawn up in two lines, in artillery formation: C and D Companies in front, and A and B Companies in the rear. Another shell hurtled shrieking over them, to explode behind Dunmow with a roar of triumphant fury. The last effects of its blast reached them, whirling the mist into eddying spirals swaying fantastically: then he heard a low cry for stretcher-bearers. Some lucky beggar was out of it, either for good and all, or for the time being. He felt a kind of envy. . . .

He knew, they all did, that the barrage had moved too quickly for them, but they knew nothing of what was happening about them. In any attack, even under favourable conditions, the attackers are soon blinded; but here they had lost touch almost from the start. They paused for a brief moment, and Bourne saw that Mr. Finch was with them, and Shem was not. Minton told him Shem had been hit in the foot. Bourne moved closer to Martlow. Their casualties, as far as he could judge, had not been heavy. They got going again, and, almost before they saw it, were on the wire. The stakes had been uprooted, and it was smashed and tangled, but had not been well cut. Jakes ran along it a little way, there was some firing, and bombs were hurled at them from the almost obliterated trench, and they answered by lobbing a few bombs over, and then plunging desperately among the steel briars, which tore at their puttees and trousers. . . .

After bombing up and down the German trenches the order was given to go back:

They moved back very slowly and painfully, suffering a few casualties on the way, and they were already encumbered with wounded. One of the Gordons was hit, and his thigh broken. They carried him tenderly, soothing him with the gentleness of women. All the fire died out of them as they dragged themselves laboriously through the clinging mud. Presently they came to where the dead lay more thickly; they found some helplessly wounded, and helped them. As they were approaching their own front line, a big shell, burying itself in the mud, exploded so close to Bourne that it blew him completely off his feet, and yet he was unhurt. He picked himself up, raving a little. The whole of their front and support trenches were being heavily shelled. Mr. Finch was hit again in his already wounded arm. They broke up a bit, and those who were free ran for it to the trench. Men carrying or helping the wounded continued steadily enough. Bourne walked by Corporal Jakes, who had taken his place in carrying the wounded Gordon: he could not have hurried anyway; and once, unconsciously, he turned and looked back over his shoulder. Then they all slid into the wrecked trench.[5]

For all who participate in a war first-hand its images remain in the memory with special sharpness. It is so unlike any other experience in the normal world that it sets apart those who have been in it from those who have not. Even at the time, soldiers on leave were constantly amazed by the ignorance and lack of understanding of the true horrors of the war betrayed by their civilian friends and relatives. The world of the trenches was so very near and yet so very far away. Before an attack the sound of the gunfire could be heard distinctly on the Kentish coast, and letters and parcels (often containing perishable food) were delivered to the front line within four days of posting from home. The sense of isolation from the normal world was reinforced by the military system, which deliberately aimed to turn the private soldier into a disciplined automaton who would instantly obey orders, no matter how fatuous. By constant harassment, petty humiliations and daily punishments the 'men' were made part of another world, bounded by regimental tradition and army ritual. They were not required to think for themselves, simply to do as they were told. In the expressive army nomenclature they were the Other Ranks.

This intense personal experience was borne by hundreds of thousands of common soldiers in a way that defies useful generalization. From some of their letters and reminiscences one can discern the same qualities which sustained them in civilian life. After all, it was no new experience for the working class to discover that they were always at the receiving end, and that they would be blamed by their superiors for anything that went wrong. There was therefore a natural scepticism about all official statements, coupled with a hatred of all 'brass hats' who directed operations from a safe distance behind the lines without any apparent regard for the lives of the thousands of troops involved. The men at the 'sharp end' had their own views of the war: for them the Somme offensive was known simply as the Great Fuck Up, and they were the 'bloody sacrifice'. In reaction to the knowledge of their impotence and the sense that their lives were at the disposal of some power which cared nothing for them as individuals, private soldiers tried to preserve fragments of their civilian life and working-class values. A fatalism and matter-of-factness helped them to keep going and to maintain some form of identity: 'cheer up, cockie, it's your turn next'; 'we're not dead yet'; 'we're 'ere because we're 'ere because we're 'ere'. Many soldiers used their old skills of foraging, scrounging, 'skyving' (and 'swinging the lead') to make themselves as comfortable as possible; and there was always the hope of a non-serious 'blighty' wound which would mean a period of home-leave. A peculiar vocabulary and army style of humour was current:

> Dear Mother, It's a bugger. I am sending you £5; but not this week.
> Dear Aunty, hoping this finds you as it leaves me. We are wading up to our necks in blood. Send fags and a life-belt. Some fell by the wayside, and the Sergeant-Majors sprang up and choked them.
> Are we downhearted?
> No!
> Then you bloody soon will be!

The western front was not the only theatre of war; but it absorbed more men than any other, and the memory of the Great War was derived overwhelmingly from images of the trenches.

For those who remained at home the experience of war was very different. Casualties were light: fewer than 1500 killed in air attacks during the whole of the war, though the Zeppelin raids were novel and frightening. The main impact on the lives of ordinary people came from the vast extension of state control into vital areas of the economy. First was the need for munitions, which led to a comprehensive control of all industries involved in war production. Second was the danger of food shortage. This required the reversal of the trend of the previous forty years from arable to pasture which had left the country dependent on imports for four-fifths of its wheat and 40 per cent of its meat. Direction of labour, price controls, rationing and queues were some of the outward signs of war collectivism. And there were also jobs for everyone. Arthur Harding, on his return home in 1916 after a five-year gaol sentence, discovered:

> The First World War had made a great change in Bethnal Green. Before then it was practically impossible to find work. But with the war every firm was getting busy and the people they said was 'unemployable' became the people to fill the jobs. Even the people round the corner in Gibraltar Buildings got jobs. People who'd been scroungers all their bloody lives. They got to Aldershot, building the army huts, and on Hounslow Heath. . . .
>
> At Lebuses, the great furniture place, instead of cabinets they were turning out ammunition boxes and cases to put the shells in. Many people went to work there. They got a good living. As long as you could use a saw and a hammer you were all right. Making packing cases. They got much more money out of ammunition boxes than out of furniture.[6]

The war brought definite gains to two sections of the community: organized labour and women. In the years immediately preceding the war growing labour unrest had been accompanied by violence and syndicalist ideas; but on the outbreak of war this was suddenly checked and the trade union leadership declared its support for the war effort. On its side the government was forced to recognize the crucial role of labour in an industrial economy at war and the consequent need to secure trade union cooperation. The unions were soon deeply involved in committees, arbitration and advisory roles on a scale which brought them new rights and status. So much was this so that some militant workers felt that agreements between government and the trade union leadership amounted to a betrayal of labour. In South Wales and Clydeside discontent led to strikes in 1915. A very significant development was the emergence of shop stewards in the engineering industry. They were elected from the shop floor and provided a militant rank-and-file leadership which was a thorn in the flesh of the

358

official trade unions. A key issue was 'dilution'. As there were not enough skilled workers to meet the demand for munitions, new machines which needed only semi- or unskilled labour were introduced into engineering works; and this was possible only with the agreement of the trade unions, who were concerned to protect the status and differentials of skilled men. In this process of dilution there was a heavy recruitment of women, who became in effect a new industrial proletariat.

By November 1918 there were 947,000 women working in the munition industries. The attraction of becoming a munitionette is not difficult to fathom:

> I was in domestic service and 'hated every minute of it' when war broke out, earning £2 a month working from 6.00 a.m. to 9.00 p.m. So when the need came for women 'war workers' my chance came to 'out'.
>
> I started on hand cutting shell fuses at the converted war works at the ACs Thames Ditton, Surrey. It entailed the finishing off by 'hand dies' the machine cut thread on the fuses that held the powder for the big shells, so had to be very accurate so that the cap fitted perfectly. We worked twelve hours a day apart from the journey morning and night at Kingston-upon-Thames. Believe me we were very ready for bed in those days, and as for wages I thought I was very well off earning £5 a week.[7]

Women were also employed as nurses, bus and tram conductresses, railway ticket collectors, ambulance drivers, land workers, dockers, clerical workers, as well as in the services (WAAC, WRNS and WRAF) and the police. In 1914 the number of women in paid employment in Great Britain was nearly 6 million; by the end of the war this had risen to between 7·2 and 7·5 million. The most visible area in which women replaced men was in public transport. But in the long term the more significant development was the entry of women into commerce, banking, business, national and local government, and education. Unlike the new opportunities in other fields of employment, which largely came to an end after the war, the creation of thousands of jobs as shorthand typists, secretaries and office clerks signalled the rise of a new category of women employees, recruited from a wide spectrum of the people. The war also provided a temporary relief from domestic service, whose numbers dropped from 1·6 million in 1914 to 1·2 million in 1918. The social effects of these changes have often been commented on, sometimes exaggeratedly. It has been claimed that the war introduced a looser attitude to sexual morality, that women and young people gained a greater degree of personal freedom, and (patronizingly) that as a reward for their efforts women over thirty were granted the vote in 1918. These changes, however, did not produce a sudden social revolution. Rather, the war accelerated trends towards women's emancipation which had already begun in the previous twenty years. The war served to raise female consciousness. As a shrewd observer concluded: 'Women grew in social stature and gained an authority they have never lost since.'[8]

In some respects the Second World War began where the first one left off. But history repeats itself only with a difference. Statistically there was the same massive dedication of the whole society to total war. By June 1944 5·2 million men and women were in the armed services and 7·8 million were engaged in civilian war production, out of a total working population of some 23 million. This was an intensity of war effort greater than in the First World War or than either the German or American mobilization. The cost in casualties however was much less for Britain in the Second than in the First World War: a total of 300,000 in the armed forces, 60,000 civilians and 30,000 in the merchant navy were killed. The total nature of the Second World War was brought home by the civilian experience of air raids. Talk of the home front became a reality, unlike in the First World War, when blighty was a world of comparative peace in contrast with the battle zone. The blitz replaced the trenches as the archetypal war experience.

In popular memory two experiences seem to predominate: evacuation and life in the shelters. The government had estimated that very heavy casualties from bombing (perhaps 600,000 people killed and twice that number injured) could be expected as soon as war broke out. To counter the enemy's objective of destroying or demoralizing the civilian population plans for the evacuation of women and children from large cities were drawn up. In the first days of September 1939 1·5 million persons voluntarily accepted evacuation under the official plans from London, Clydeside,

Tyneside, Merseyside, the industrial Midlands and the southern ports. An additional 2 million people evacuated themselves, mostly into the West Country, Wales and Scotland. The expected bombing, however, did not materialize, and after some weeks many evacuees returned home. A year later (after some months of 'phoney war', then the return of the defeated army from Dunkirk, and the RAF's Battle of Britain) the blitz began, and evacuation to the country was renewed, though not on such a large scale as the first time. Mass exodus produced a rich variety of experiences, not all of them happy. Stories of billeting difficulties, social mismatching, and dirty or vermin-ridden children from the slums were legion. For the children the separation from their homes and mothers could be traumatic. An East Ender remembered her departure from London and arrival in the 'reception area':

I was nine when I was evacuated during the war. We were evacuated from St Luke's School in Old Street and we were taken to Dunstable. We were all scared; we were all crying. You can't explain it. Your mums and dads weren't even allowed to the station. You were left in St Luke's Church until the coach came and got you, then you were packed straight into trains. I don't know about evacuees, you felt like refugees. You didn't know where you were going or who was going to have you. It was terrible. Before we were taken there we were given our gas masks and a big label on our collar to say our name, address, where we'd come from and where we were going to. When we got to Dunstable, we were put into a big school hall, and people came up and sorted you out. I was with two sisters and one brother. My dad told us we weren't to be parted – we should go with one another. A church lady came, and the WVS lady said, 'There you are, there's a nice little family.' The woman said, 'I don't want her – she's too ugly.' That was me. I cried. The voluntary worker said, 'Well look, let your brother and sisters go with this lady, and you go with this other one.'[9]

The first bombs of the blitz on London were dropped on 7 September 1940. Thereafter for seventy-six consecutive nights (except for 2 November when bad weather ruled out raiding), and sometimes by day as well, the bombing went on. From 14 November the raids were switched from London to other towns, but London continued to be raided intermittently until mid-1941. In the last phase of the war, from June 1944 to March 1945, there was a final blitz of V1s and V2s (pilotless planes and rockets). Total civilian casualties from air raids were 295,000, of whom 60,000 were killed. On the worst night of the London bombing, 10 May 1941, 1436 people were killed and 1752 injured. At Coventry on the night of 14 November 1940 the centre of the city was obliterated and 554 persons were killed and 865 seriously injured. Destruction of property was enormous: 4 million (out of a total 13 million) homes were damaged during the war and about 220,000 totally destroyed. The East End suffered particularly badly in the raids: in Stepney two-fifths of the houses were destroyed or damaged by 11 November 1940. In London as a whole 1·5 million homes suffered bomb damage. After the great raid on Coventry nearly a third of the houses in the city were uninhabitable. In Hull, which was vulnerable to air raids from across the North Sea, only 6000 of its 93,000 homes had not been damaged by the end of the war.

Living through the blitz was primarily a matter of finding adequate shelter, and most reminiscences have something to say about it. In the early months of the war the government distributed 2·25 million 'Anderson' shelters. These consisted of two curved pieces of corrugated steel which met in a ridge at the top. The Anderson was sunk about three feet into the ground, covered with eighteen inches of earth, and the entrance protected with a blast wall. It could be fitted out with bunks for up to six people. Its disadvantage was that it was damp, if not actually flooded, and it did not shut out the noise of the raid. Many working-class homes did not have gardens in which to put an Anderson, and the inhabitants therefore had to use public surface shelters, built of brick and concrete and intended for about fifty people. The basements of large buildings and cellars of all kinds were also utilized. But the most spectacular action was the occupation of the London tube stations, at first against the wishes of officialdom. On 27 September 1940 a peak of 177,000 people were sleeping in 79 underground stations. At first arrangements in the tube shelters were chaotic and insanitary; but soon the whole operation was regularized. People queued all day to be sure of their place at night. Once admitted, after the trains had stopped running, they settled down on the platforms with their blankets, pillows and thermos flasks. A new sub-culture of shelter life developed. Nevertheless, when a census of London shelters was taken in November 1940 only 4 per cent of the population were sleeping in the tube and other large shelters; 9 per cent were in public (street-type) shelters; and 27 per cent in domestic (mostly Anderson) shelters. This left about half the population still in their homes, either upstairs in bed or sheltering under the stairs or kitchen table. The problems of life in an Anderson are not difficult to imagine. A young housewife and laundry worker, whose husband had been called up, describes how she shared the next-door neighbour's shelter in a backyard in Hackney:

> We hadn't got a proper light in there – they wouldn't let us fix a light up, in case they could see it from the planes. So we'd stand a box on end and put a lantern in it.
>
> To go to the toilet, we had to wait till the planes had gone over a bit, then go out one after the other. Mrs. Harper used to say, 'Hurry up and come back!' We used to wear pyjamas with slacks and that over the top.
>
> The trouble with the shelter was that you had to go down there so early – about 6.00 at night. You got fed up with knitting and trying to read, because you hadn't got a proper light down there. You'd fall asleep, but then you woke up and thought it was time to get up, you'd find it was only 10.00 at night. So it would be back to knitting. We used to unpick jumpers and knit them up again. Mrs. Harper used to go out and bring jugs of cocoa and suet puddings. She was very good to us. We didn't get cold – there were too many of us down there. By the time you'd all packed in at night and you'd got your slacks and jumpers on over your pyjamas, you couldn't really feel cold. When the bombing first started we only had old wooden kitchen chairs in the shelter. We used to sit up all night, with a door on the floor to put our feet on. When we went to sleep, we used to lean on one another. But at 7.00 in the morning you'd got to come out, wash yourself and go to work, day after day. In the finish you would just lay on the dirt at night because you couldn't keep awake. We thought, 'This is no good', so we took mattresses down. . . .

But it was ridiculous down there. It was work and shelter, work and shelter – no life, really.[10]

A good deal of what is now 'remembered' about the blitz and the home front turns out upon close examination to be myth. The war was such an intense experience, and the pressures of the mass media and national propaganda were so powerful that certain images and slogans have become implanted in the popular mind as universally acknowledged truths. From Churchill's 'their finest hour' to 'London can take it' and 'keep smiling through' there is a whole mythology about national unity, heroism and humour in the blitz, and the unshakable morale of the people. 'Your courage, your cheerfulness, your resolution, will bring us victory,' declared the posters; and forty years later it is only too easy for those who were on the home front to believe that such was the case. In fact, at the time the government was very anxious about civilian morale; the first air raids demonstrated the inadequacy of the provisions made to deal with homelessness and bomb damage; at the local level there was dismay and rage at the ineptitude of officials, and widespread trekking into the surrounding countryside to avoid the bombing. For most of the war and for a majority of the people the home front meant not the blitz but something much less horrific and altogether unexciting. Boredom in time became a greater problem than bombs. The true experience of the war for many of the common people lay elsewhere.

First, it meant jobs for the 1·5 million who were unemployed in 1939, though their absorption in some cases took over a year. 'I experienced something I had not known since 1925, the year we were married,' wrote a Hackney shoemaker. 'A full week's work, every week.'[11] Second, it meant separation and disruption of normal family life: evacuation of children, the call-up of husbands and sons, removal to new and sometimes remote places to work in war factories. The war lasted a long time – six years, as opposed to the four years of the First World War – and weariness set in long before the final stages of the invasion of Europe. There was the poignancy of parting and the hopelessness of not knowing when or whether one would meet again. In the First World War it was possible to organize regular leave home for troops in France; but in the Second World War, when active service could be in almost any part of the world, there was little or no home-leave, and men could be abroad continuously for three years or more. 'We'll meet again, don't know where, don't know when,' sang Vera Lynn, 'the Forces' Sweetheart', and her most famous song echoed the sentiment and longings of millions. Paradoxically the enforced mobility for many people was accompanied by 'staying put' for others. This led to boredom, disinterest and just 'carrying on'. A 1943 survey of a war factory concluded that for most of the girl workers:

Life has become for them a formless vista of days and weeks, from which most physical discomforts have been smoothed out, most cares lifted, and most pleasures and interests gone . . . their interest in the war has been blacked out by this sort of life. . . . Instead of feeling 'in it' (as the newspapers would lead one to suppose working in a war factory makes one feel) they feel out of it, in every way. . . . [Nothing is] more insulated from the struggles of real life than is working twelve hours a day at an unexacting job in a humanely run war factory.[12]

Third, it was an era of shortages, rationing and queues. Food, clothes, fuel and furnishings were strictly limited in quantity; and great ingenuity was exercised in 'making do' or 'knowing a friend' who could obtain 'a little extra' on the black market or 'under the counter'. An index of grumbles compiled by observers in 1943 put food second only to blackout as the main grievance. Even beer was in short supply and diluted:

BARMAID (handing Yorkshireman his pint): It looks like rain.
YORKSHIREMAN: Aye, I thought it wasn't beer.[13]

Yet one is left with the impression that ultimately the people as a whole came to terms with the war. Faced with a situation in which literally the whole population was conscripted and directed and organized and inconvenienced, the most practical response was to 'carry on' and if possible turn things to one's own advantage. The war became just a stage in one's life.

For those in the armed forces the experience of the Second World War was different in many respects from 1914–18. The theatres of war were much more widespread, for the conflict was truly global. But, as the lower casualty figures reflected, actual battle experience was much rarer than in the First World War. The proportion of combat troops was lower, and for the British army there was nothing approaching the carnage of the trenches on the western front. For the minority directly engaged in the fighting, however, the experience was similar in both wars. Digging in on the Anzio beach-head in Italy in 1944 was reminiscent of the Somme or Ypres in 1916; an infantry attack in Normandy or North Africa or Burma provoked the same kind of feelings in the individual soldier as earlier; the effect of being shelled, the death of a comrade by one's side, the tiny limited world of the private soldier and his friends were not essentially different, despite the altered context. The boredom and pointlessness of military life was always apparent to civilian-soldiers; and the class distinction between officers and men (still called the Other Ranks) had not lessened to any significant degree. It did not escape notice that the men who had suffered unemployment in the 1930s were often those who were still at the sharp end.

Nevertheless for a majority of the 2·75 million men who served overseas in the British army the Second World War was not so dangerous or unpleasant as the First. Many did not have experience of actual fighting; but, as they admitted later, had a 'cushy' war. Their experience was basically a compound of foreign travel and army discipline: 'seeing the world at the king's expense'. What the long-term effect of this was on a whole generation of young Britons is hard to say. For some it probably only reinforced their parochialism ('What, no fish and chips?'); but for others it was an educative and broadening process. Ironically they were taken to all parts of the British Empire on the very eve of its dissolution. During the previous seventy years the main benefit from imperialism for the common people was that their standard of living was higher than it would otherwise have been. The exploitation of the colonies brought wealth to Britain and some of this passed to sections of the working class. But this was an indirect and concealed benefit. The popular idea of Empire was expressed in music hall songs and enthusiastic demonstrations over events such as the relief of Mafeking in May 1900 during the Boer War. Virtually the only direct experience which the common people had of Empire was through army service, especially in India. The other great contact with the wider world was through emigration. Between 1815 and 1914 nearly 17 million people left the United Kingdom to make new homes for themselves in the United States, Canada, Australia, New Zealand and South Africa. Some of these were never heard of again; but in other families the ties were maintained by the occasional letter. In the great invasion of Britain by allied American and Commonwealth troops in 1942–4 family connections were sometimes renewed.

The two world wars were separated – perhaps only interrupted – by what in retrospect seemed no more than a 'long weekend'. When the war ended in November 1918 there was a deep feeling of 'never again', a yearning for a return to 'normalcy', and hope that some of the politicians' promises of a better world would be realized. Within a few months disappointment and disillusion set in. George Coppard, badly wounded and with four and a half years' service as a machine gunner, voiced the experience of thousands of his generation:

> Lloyd George and company had been full of big talk about making the country fit for heroes to live in, but it was just so much hot air. No practical steps were taken to rehabilitate the broad mass of demobbed men, and I joined the queues for jobs as messengers, window cleaners and scullions. It was a complete let-down for thousands like me. . . .[14]

For the next six years the economy alternated between boom and slump, accompanied by inflation, high unemployment, strikes, and revolutionary talk on the left. The workshop of the world was in dire straits. Essentially Britain's nineteenth-century pre-eminence in the markets of the world had come to an end, and her staple industries – coal, iron and steel, shipbuilding and textiles – were in decline, and were not yet offset by the rise of new industries. Labour had emerged from the war greatly strengthened and determined to resist any attempt by employers or government to reduce wages or working conditions. The resulting industrial struggles culminated in a unique event, the general strike. Outwardly the 'national strike', as the TUC preferred to call it, was a miners' strike supported by the transport workers and others; but basically it was a violent readjustment of the relations between capital and labour in the postwar period.

For nine days in May 1926 the life of the nation came to a halt. The TUC, in support of the miners, called out the railwaymen, dockers, transport workers, printers, and workers in iron and steel, chemicals, building, gas and electricity. These were the 'first line', and (continuing the wartime imagery) the government countered by mobilizing troops and calling for volunteers to man essential services. Like the blitz, the general strike has become part of folklore. The stories of strikers and police good-humouredly playing football together, of Oxford undergraduates trying to drive trains, and local trade unionists running affairs through 'councils of action' are well known. For most of the 2·5 million workers called out it was a time of holiday, and the weather was conveniently good; for the trade union and political activists it meant a heady whirl of committees, meetings and demonstrations. The solidarity of the strike was much commented on; and when it was called off by the TUC the news was received incredulously by the rank-and-file, who felt that they had been betrayed. Jack Langley was a young carriage-painter in the Brighton railway workshops at the time. Later he reflected:

[The general strike] was a ruthless strike, absolutely ruthless. The strange part about it, what wasn't realised, was the strength of the trade union movement. It was so strong that it overwhelmed us. Everybody was coming out, our foreman, everybody in authority came out with us, so long as they were on a wage basis. We stopped everything, we were so powerful. And yet we weren't prepared to govern with it. We couldn't, because we didn't have the organisational ability to manoeuvre all that great power. There was terrific enthusiasm for it. It was remorseless. It was so remorseless that it got serious. There was civil strife everywhere. Even in Brighton . . . we were up in arms attacking blackleg transport, and the police. They came out on their horses with whacking long sticks, and they were smashing people down in the streets. I went to a meeting and the policeman walked all along the road at the side kicking my feet, trying to make me fall down, so that I should only just clutch hold of him. . . .

We had the power then, and we should have gone on, but it

was too much for us. The power was too big. We couldn't grasp it – it was like going to the moon.[15]

Langley's experience of clashes with the police was repeated in other towns. There was more violence and a great deal more bitterness than is sometimes recognized: about 4000 arrests were made during the strike, and another 3000 persons were charged afterwards. The general strike was not a rehearsal for the British Revolution but it did drive home the reality of class divisions in British society. The government, the army, the police, and virtually the whole of the middle and upper classes were openly ranged against the working class; and after the strike, despite official assurances to the contrary, there was victimization, particularly on the railways.

Most bitter of all were the miners. They refused to accept the ending of the strike and vainly fought on for another seven months, suffering great hardship. The miners were at the centre of the postwar labour struggles. In 1926 coal mining employed over a million workers (today there are 200,000), and it was an industry in which wages accounted for over 70 per cent of the cost of production. The coal-owners were an obstinate and unenlightened group of employers, and they were faced by one of the largest and most militant unions, the Miners' Federation of Great Britain. The defeat of the miners was a major set-back for the labour movement. In the coalfields it had disastrous results: wages were reduced, working hours lengthened and pits were closed. By 1929 a quarter of all coal miners were out of work. The memory of the general strike haunted the mining areas for the next two generations.

The mass unemployment which appeared in Britain in the early 1920s continued to grow. In 1922 the total number registered as unemployed was 1·5 million, and throughout the 1920s the figure never fell below 1 million. By 1931 2·6 million were out of work, and a peak of just under 3 million was reached in the winter of 1932–3. From 1935 the numbers declined from 2 million to 1·5 million on the outbreak of the Second World War. Behind these official figures (which almost certainly underestimate the total of unemployed) lies a wealth of painful experience, which has left a grim image of the 1930s. A working man from the Newcastle area recalled that in the depression 'when you met somebody . . . the greeting wasn't "Hello, how are you?" or "How's the family?" but "Hello, are you working?"' Many of the miseries of working-class life associated with poor housing, ill-health and poverty were not directly attributable to being without work. But unemployment highlighted and exacerbated these social problems, and is remembered as the biggest scourge of the time. The out-of-work fell into three categories. First were those temporarily out of work for a few weeks because of the seasonal or casual nature of their jobs; second were young people who had either never had a job or who had been employed only as long as they could not claim an adult's wage; and third were the long-term unemployed who had not worked for a year or more, and some of whom seemed unlikely to work again. The last were the most desperate. A forty-eight-year-old village carpenter and wheelwright from East Anglia said that he felt 'isolated and hopeless'. He had returned to his native village after serving abroad during the war and was now unemployed:

> We ordinary folk were rushed into that job [i.e. the First World War] before we knew what we were about. We were told then: Your king and country need you! It is no consolation now to be told: Your king and country *don't* need you! I have not been wanted now for nearly two years, and I sometimes think I shall never be wanted again.[16]

The insecurity that had always characterized their employment left working men completely vulnerable in times of depression like the 1930s. Men who had given years of service to a firm could be dismissed at a week's notice. A shoe-laster from Leicester, who had worked thirty-seven years with one firm, confessed:

> When I heard the new manager going through and saying: 'The whole of this side of this room, this room, and this room is to be stopped', I knew it would be uphill work to get something.[17]

The incidence of unemployment was very uneven. In general, the most distressed areas were the old heartlands of the Industrial Revolution – Lancashire, the northeast, industrial Scotland, west Cumberland, South Wales and Northern Ireland. By contrast

London, the southeast and the Midlands were much less afflicted. For instance, in 1934 Jarrow ('the town that was murdered') had 67·8 per cent of its workers unemployed and Merthyr Tydfil 61·9 per cent; whereas Greater London had 8·6 per cent, Coventry 5·1 per cent and St Albans 3·9 per cent. There were in fact several Englands, not one, in the 1930s; and the England of the unemployed was largely unknown to the comfortable classes in the suburbs of the south. The impact of unemployment was also different between one person and the next. Some people went completely to pieces, psychologically and physically; others were more resilient and became fatalistic or militant. Memoirs of the period generally recount familiar working-class problems and anxieties but greatly heightened by lack of work; the shortage and monotony of food; the strain on family life; the struggle to keep up appearances; feelings of shame, inadequacy and loss of self-respect.

To cope with the effects of heavy and continuous unemployment in the postwar years the government was forced to extend the provisions for relief. Through a series of piecemeal measures a system of unemployment benefit was elaborated, which was soon stigmatized as the 'dole'. Unemployment benefit could be drawn by insured workers for a period of twenty-six weeks; thereafter they had to apply for 'transitional payments', which were granted only after a household means test carried out by the local Public Assistance Committee (successors to the Poor Law guardians). All forms of income, including the earnings of sons and daughters, together with savings, pensions, and even household possessions, were taken into account. No aspect of the 1930s was more hated and remembered more bitterly than the means test. It often involved officials coming into the home; it penalized thrift and encouraged tale-telling and petty tyranny. An unemployed miner from the northeast recalled:

If you'd been on the dole for so long you had to go on what they called the Tribunal. A man would come down to the house to interview you. So, you went up before the Tribunal. And he would say 'Where have you been looking for work?' If you weren't 'looking for work' they'd suspend your Dole or stop it altogether because you weren't trying to get work. Well, looking for work then was absolutely farcical . . . everywhere you went there were hundreds of men sitting around. . . . Anyway, we had to go in front of this chap to explain. And he'd say 'Where were you on Monday?' and you had to have the name of the place where you'd been looking for work. 'Where were you on Tuesday?' right through the week. Then they'd try to trip you up, 'Where were you on Tuesday again?' And if he tripped you up and you couldn't remember or give the same name, he'd scratch your name off and stop your Dole.[18]

The effect of being struck off the dole is described in the most famous novel about the unemployed, *Love on the Dole*. Harry Hardcastle is informed that in the opinion of the Public Assistance Committee his father's dole and his sister's wages are sufficient for the household and therefore he is not entitled to any more benefit:

'Y' what . . .? What did y' say?' he asked, staring, incredulously, at the unemployment exchange clerk on the other side of the counter.

'A' y' deaf?' retorted the clerk, pettishly: he added, snappily: 'There nowt for y'. They've knocked y' off dole. Sign on of a Tuesday for future if y' want y' health insurance stamp. Who's next?'

The man behind Harry shouldered him away. Dreamlike, he turned and paused, holding the dog-eared, yellow unemployment card in his hand. This was catastrophic: the clerk was joking, surely; a mistake must have been made.[19]

The means test touched the common people on the raw, for it smelled strongly of the Board of Guardians and the workhouse. Too often the old sentiments of the Poor Law slipped out: saving the pockets of the taxpayers and making the poor support themselves; the insinuation that somehow the unemployed were to blame for their plight, and that they ought to be grateful for anything they received; the continuation of old attitudes based on charity, deterrence and the 'prevention of nuisance'.

The government's policy of maintaining the unemployed and their families out of public funds was successful in its main aim of preventing social revolution. But thinking men and women could not be prevented from asking fundamental questions about 'poverty in the midst of plenty' and 'capitalism in crisis', or reflecting that 79 per cent of the population owned only 12 per cent of the nation's money and goods. There was a general intellectual turning to the left, and increasing concern with the threat of fascism at home and abroad as the 1930s wore on. The biggest protests were the hunger marches and demonstrations organized by the National Unemployed Workers' Movement, largely under Communist Party leadership. The movement had begun in 1921; in the 1930s it mobilized thousands of unemployed workers to protest against the means test and cuts in benefit. Yet the best-known hunger march, the Jarrow Crusade, was organized by the Labour MP for the town, Ellen Wilkinson, and the mayor and council, and was carefully 'non-political'. In October 1936 two hundred marchers set off for London, and were given food and shelter by well-wishers in the towns they passed through:

A few high spots stand out . . . wealthy Harrogate where the Territorial officers looked after us . . . Leeds where the chief newspaper proprietor gave us a meal the men still talk of . . . and with free beer! Barnsley, where Joseph Jones the miner's leader and Mayor – how we blessed him! – had the municipal baths all heated ready for the men, and where I had the muscle-easing luxury of the women's municipal foam bath. Or the awful days like the twenty-mile stretch from Bedford to Luton when it rained solidly all day, and the wind drove the rain in our teeth. Except for the hospitality at the end of the day, one day's tramp was much like another. The one thing that mattered was the weather. The men were up at 6.30, the cooks having got up earlier to prepare breakfast. They had all slept together on the bare boards of a school or drill hall . . . if lucky on palliasses borrowed from somewhere.[20]

Little was done for Jarrow; the town became a symbol of what unemployment did to working people.

The England of the dole was not the whole picture of the interwar years. At the worst of the depression nearly 25 per cent of the labour force was unemployed; but over 75 per cent was still at work. The experience of many millions of the common people outside the depressed areas was not entirely gloomy. Real wages rose between 1924 and 1938, and there was some transfer of wealth from the rich to the poor by taxation and social services. Whereas in 1914 60 per cent of the income of the average working-class family went on food and 16 per cent on rent, by 1937 the figures were 35 per cent and 9 per cent. One of the greatest changes was in housing. The construction of houses and flats was a major form of capital investment and functioned like a programme of public works to bring recovery from the slump. Between 1919 and 1939 over 4 million houses were built in England and Wales, which means that about a third of all families moved into a new home. About 2·5 million of the new houses were built by private enterprise and were for sale; the remainder were for rent from local authorities. This massive building effort transformed housing conditions in the centres of big towns: nineteenth-century slums were pulled down and replaced by blocks of flats or estates of neat houses in the suburbs. The rehousing of families by local councils was matched by those who managed, with a £25 deposit and a twenty-five-year mortgage at 4½ per cent from the building society, to buy a £350–£450 house. A semi-detached England established itself in the 1930s, recruited from the lower middle and upper working classes, with its own lifestyle and aspirations. Lining the arterial roads out of every major city or laid out in uniform suburban estates, the little three-bedroomed houses with 'all mod.cons.' represented a new type of respectability and rectitude. Their pebble-dash and mock timbering, garden front and rear, bathroom and indoor toilet, were a far cry from the rows of terrace houses opening straight on to the street and with a privy in the backyard. The thrill of a move from West Ham to the new suburbia is described in this passage from a novel about life in the 1920s. Herbert Common, a clerk in a Covent Garden warehouse, and his wife Florrie inspect the new and uncompleted house:

> The house was meant for them. They knew this the moment they set eyes on it, as they balanced along the planks across the muddy unmade road, this fresh spring Saturday afternoon. Actually it was a bungalow, not a house. Mr. Roberts junior – son of the Mr. Roberts – sized them up at once: a desperate young couple with a small boy, clutching at a straw, too poor to

buy even the cheapest semi-detached house without half-starving themselves. . . .

They stared with disbelief: the newness, of the red brick, the green tiles of the gabled roof – tiles, not slates! The pebble-dash, glinting in the sunshine, the chimney against the vast sky, the warm country smells in the moist air! The woodwork was newly painted – green.

'Lattice windows!' Florrie breathed it – a prayer.

'Look at the porch!'

'A glass door!'. . . .

The bathroom – so small they had to shut the door to stand inside together – was completely finished, decorated, everything. The panelled bath glittered in the light from the frosted window. The chromium taps, the lavatory pan, the porcelain wash-basin, were still pasted with strips of brown paper. The lower half of the room – up to their shoulders – was tiled: white, with green medallions. The little cupboard, behind the door – for the meters, of all places – gas and electric – was painted white. They couldn't speak. They could make only silly noises, feel for each other's presence, gratefully. This was it, the authentic magic which had evaporated, too soon, from their marriage. It was more than the house of their dreams – it was a fresh start.[21]

More soberly the daughter of a skilled engineer noted the effects on her parents of a move from a terrace house in a working-class area of Nottingham:

By 1936 the financial situation seemed to improve. My brother was earning enough to keep himself and pay my Mother a few shillings, and when I got a job at fourteen, it was decided that we could afford a better house in a 'nicer' neighbourhood. We moved a couple of miles out of Nottingham to a detached modern house with a garden. We rented it for £1 per week. We were all thrilled with it and took on a new lease of life. The joy of a bathroom can only be appreciated when you've lived without one. The ritual of lighting the copper, dragging the zinc bath up the cellar steps, emptying the dirty water every time anyone had a bath, was at last over.

The new house was only a few minutes walk from the woods so very soon we acquired a dog, a Springer Spaniel which of course had to be exercised. My parents started to take him for walks together, and through him began to communicate with each other. A strange new relationship developed. Dad would say, 'Ask your mum if she wants to go for a walk' or 'Tell your mum we're going for a drink'. And when they were out, the dog was asked which way he wanted to go and whether he was ready to go home yet. . . .[22]

If bathrooms and indoor toilets were the most highly prized gains inside the home, the 'pictures' were a central preoccupation outside. The 1930s and the Second World War were the heyday of the cinema as a popular art. By 1939 20 million tickets were being sold each week. It was estimated that in Liverpool 40 per cent of the population went once a week, and 25 per cent twice or more. Total attendances reached a peak of 31 million in 1946. The picture palaces, built by Odeon, ABC and Gaumont-British, competed with each other in their modernistic exteriors and flashing lights. Inside, the Wurlitzer organs, the chromium-plated fittings and plush seating provided a relaxed setting for escape into the Hollywood dream. For a couple of hours everyday life could be forgotten in a world of adventure and romance.

13. Citizens and Wage Earners

The nearer the historian gets to the present, the more difficult is it for him to recognize phases and periods, and to distinguish fashions and incidental happenings from long-term trends and developments. The pattern of history is not yet in sharp focus. Everyone is agreed that the years since 1945 have been a period of rapid social change. But when we try to chart this change it proves to be paradoxical and elusive. On the one hand we are struck by the obvious effects of relative prosperity and consumerism; on the other we keep running into examples of unbroken continuity with the 1930s and earlier. There is already a received wisdom of what were the important changes in British history over the last thirty-five years, encapsulated in such phrases as the end of Empire, Britain in Europe, the age of affluence, and post-industrial society. Whether much of this history accords with the experience of the common people appears to be doubtful: the loss of Empire, for instance, had little discernible impact on ordinary manual workers; nor did the affluence of the 1960s add up to the social revolution proclaimed by some writers. In this chapter we shall pick up the basic themes introduced earlier and see how they developed in a new context.

The years immediately after the Second World War were very different from those after the First. In 1945 there was no enthusiasm for a return to the normalcy of the 1930s. On the contrary, the electorate repudiated Churchill and those whom it held responsible for prewar conditions, and returned the first majority Labour government. Wartime shortages continued for several years: food was rationed and raw materials controlled; consumer goods were channelled into export markets and so were in short supply at home; and conscription ('national service') lasted until 1960. From the later 1950s this austerity was relaxed, and the 'swinging sixties' were a time of expansion and much talk of affluence. This mood lasted until the early 1970s; but thereafter was replaced by economic uncertainty, cut-backs and increasing social tensions. Politically the period was shared by the two main parties. After the Labour government of 1945–51, the Conservatives were in power for the next thirteen years, to be followed by Labour again from 1964 to 1970. The 1970s saw the Conservatives in office from 1970 to 1974 and again in 1979, and Labour from 1974 to 1979. The proportions of the electorate voting Labour and Conservative remained fairly constant, with each party usually winning between 43 and 48 per cent of the total vote. However, the themes which most embodied popular experience, such as participation in the welfare state, cut across the political divide (though they did become party issues), and were not entirely limited to specific decades.

Underlying all working-class experience in the post-1945 period was the tremendous boon of a high level of employment. From 1942 the country enjoyed thirty years of virtually full employment. Only in the second half of the 1970s did unemployment begin to rise from 2·5 per cent or less to 5 per cent and upwards. Labour and Conservative governments alike were committed to policies for the avoidance of mass unemployment. It was the basis for a steady increase in the standard of living which, if measured in the conventional way by relating wages and earnings to prices, meant that the average earnings of a manual worker rose from the equivalent of £31 a week in 1951 (using 1975 prices) to £54 a week in 1975. Misleading as such average figures can be, there is no mistaking the evidence from many other sources that most British working people in the 1960s and early 1970s were better off than they had ever been. Already by 1959 the Conservative Party was able to campaign on the slogan 'You never had it so good'. Freedom from the fear of unemployment, and an income above the level necessary for basic necessities, were something new in the history of a majority of the common people.

At the centre of this new commitment by government was the welfare state. In 1942, partly as a morale-booster when the fortunes of war were at their nadir, the Beveridge Report was published. It was widely publicized in the press, discussed in the forces, and in a shortened form became a bestseller – which, to put it mildly, was unusual for a government report on such an unglamorous topic as 'social insurance and allied services'. The Report, in language almost reminiscent of Bunyan, called for an attack on the Five Giant Evils of Want, Disease, Ignorance, Idleness and Squalor. Social security, by means of a scheme of social insurance, with which the Report was concerned, was only an attack on want; but Beveridge made it clear that his proposals were part of a comprehensive social policy to remove the other four evils as well, by means of medical services, housing, education, and the maintenance of full employment. Whether this wartime ideal of social services 'from the cradle to the grave' penetrated the popular imagination as deeply as was later suggested may be doubted. The blueprint for a welfare state was a promise of social engineering from above, and the working class had long acquired a robust scepticism about politicians' promises. Arthur Newton, the Hackney shoemaker, commented:

> Later came some talk about forming some kind of welfare state after the war. A sort of Utopia where nobody would be in need, where the sick would be cared for, where a person unemployed would receive enough to see him through, where everybody, from the cradle to the grave, would be cared for.
>
> But looking back, I don't think many ordinary people took much notice. 'After all, wasn't we still fighting the war? One thing at a time, we've got enough on our plate at the moment. Besides, where was the money coming from? The war was leaving us poorer and poorer. We might have another three million unemployed like last time. Wait and see!'[1]

Nevertheless, in a hectic spate of legislation between 1945 and 1951 the Labour government created a welfare structure which soon brought very tangible benefits: a comprehensive, compulsory system of national insurance for unemployment and sickness benefits, retirement pension, and supplementary assistance; industrial injuries compensation; family allowances; maternity and death grants; a national health service; subsidies to local authorities for the building of council houses; new towns to take the overspill and rehousing requirements of London and other big towns. The measurement of the impact of such legislation is notoriously difficult; but a noble attempt was made by the pioneer sociologist, Seebohm Rowntree. In his third social survey of York he found that the proportion of the working-class population living in poverty had been reduced from 31·1 per cent in 1936 to 2·77 per cent in 1950. Without the welfare legislation the figure would have been 22·18 per cent. Within ten years a new pattern of social expectation had been created. Gone were the days of selecting a sixpenny pair of glasses from a heap on a counter in Woolworths. So strong was this expectation that no government dared to thwart it. The Conservatives, who had not originally been too enthusiastic about the Beveridge Report, declared their belief in the need for the welfare state. Yet there were important differences in the way the two parties regarded their commitment. For Conservatives the social services were essentially redistributive, in the sense of taking from those who have to give to those in need. The object was to help the weak and unfortunate to lead a full and decent life, to provide a safeguard against poverty and misfortune. The concept of the welfare state did not imply that the state was a machine constructed to produce welfare; but in a well-run state there would be a high degree of welfare for all. For socialists and others in the Labour Party the social services were not only redistributive, but also a means to a more equalitarian society, a step on the road towards the elimination of great inequalities in wealth and property. Participation in the benefits of the welfare state was not to be limited to the weak and unfortunate, but was itself a mark of full membership of the community, of citizenship. The emphasis was on benefit as a right, not as charity. The stigma of the Poor Law approach was to be finally eradicated.

Progress towards equality and redistribution of wealth in the thirty years after 1945 was fairly modest, despite widespread belief to the contrary. In 1977 the richest 1 per cent of the population still owned 24 per cent of all personal wealth: this was a decrease from 42 per cent in 1960 and 70 per cent before the First World War. Income distribution was somewhat less unequal: in 1974 the top 1 per cent received 6·2 per cent, and the top 10 per cent, 26 per cent of all personal income: these figures had been 8·4 per cent and 29·4 per cent in 1959. But the bottom 50 per cent of the population increased their share of total income only from 23·1 per cent to 24·3 per cent between 1959 and 1975. Nor did taxation effect any drastic redistribution of income. Differences in wealth and income between classes declined slowly; but the changes which affected the common people most directly were probably more the result of overall economic growth than redistribution.

Within the workforce the trends already apparent in the 1930s continued after 1945. Male manual workers, who in 1911 constituted 73·6 per cent of the occupied population, had declined to 68·4 per cent in 1951 and 58·8 per cent in 1971. The shift in the female labour force was even more marked: from 76·7 per cent in manual jobs in 1911 to 43 per cent in 1971. The corresponding growth in non-manual occupations was in the number of shop assistants, sales personnel, clerical and office workers, supervisors, technicians and lower professional and administrative staff. These changes in the occupational structure reflected the transformation of the economy: a shift away from manufacturing into the 'tertiary' (trade and services) sector; the introduction of new technology and larger-scale enterprises; the growth of public institutions in place of private provision. More and more of the common people were in white-collar jobs. Within industry the shift in emphasis was away from the traditional staples of mines and textiles and shipbuilding to automobiles, electronics, plastics, chemicals and light engineering. Certain industries (coal, iron and steel) and utilities (gas, electricity, railways) were nationalized. The old definitions of skill became less relevant, and the differentials between skilled and unskilled workers narrowed. Whereas in Victorian times the skilled man's wage rate was normally twice that of the labourer, by 1914 the difference was only 50 per cent, and in 1952 it was 16 per cent. The net result of changes in the economy was to increase the diversity of types of job and status, and to make generalization about work experience even more hazardous. Such evidence as we have suggests that many workers' perceptions of their job were still closer to the curse of Adam than the realization of personal identity through job satisfaction. The following account by a Coventry car worker in the 1970s is not far removed from Alfred Williams's experiences in the Swindon railway workshops seventy years earlier:

As soon as you get off the bus you can smell the factory. It's the foundry, a smoky sort of vapour. They process the smoke now, because so many of the residents of the area complained. They filter it now and scent it with a disinfectant. So now it discharges scented soot instead of filthy soot, and the people seem satisfied. . . .

Work starts at seven-thirty. You get into your overalls, boots, goggles, masks, gloves, hats, barrier creams, and you advance like a Dalek to your machine. The thing that keeps you human is the companionship, although even the possibility of that has been reduced in some jobs. The assembly and sub-assembly jobs engender more friendship than the machine shop, for instance, because in those there is still a sense of collective working. In the machine shop, you have an isolated function, with only a few thousand pounds' worth of equipment for companionship. If you're on the tracks, your work dovetails into that of other people. . . .

There's something irresistible about the tracks, always on the move; you see men bend over this piece of metal, bowing down, on their knees sometimes, contorting themselves round it. The metal governs their lives, they have to adapt themselves to it.

I'm on measured day work, and it's just a question of beating the clock. You have a quota, scientifically established and agreed, which you have to get through. My job is making manifolds for the cylinder head in the engine and I have to achieve four an hour. If you under-achieve, you have to account for yourself; but there's no medals for over-achievement. Everything is established by custom and practice; there's no rule book. The machine I work at, it's a radial driller, single spindle; and there's no one in the factory old enough to know where it came from. It had nothing to do with cars. It's probably over seventy years old. The concept of the machine dates from when they had old belt drives, overhead power shafts.

There's a tea-break at 9.50. The kiosks are open, and you see people start to take the shape of human beings again. The factory blots out the senses. There can't be much communication, hearing is about 90 per cent impaired. In the machine shop you can't talk because of the noise and the distance of people from each other. All sense of feeling is muffled, people are insulated from each other.

After that, the next landmark isn't till dinner time. Then human patterns of acquaintanceship and communication get re-established. . . . The afternoon is more relaxed. Most of the work is out of the way by the end of the morning. By then I should think about three-quarters of the day's work is finished. You start off with a relentless burst of energy, and that exhausts itself, and you can anticipate the rest of the day more comfortably. There's a ten-minute break at 2.50. . . .

Although the days follow an identical pattern, each day is subjectively different. There's a cycle in the week, just as there is within the day. Friday, for instance, is a strange day. The administrative staff and clerks are tidying up for the week, getting out quotas and statistics, the manual workers are preparing for the weekend. Friday night is a night out for a lot of the lads. Friday is a happy day: finish at three instead of four, it's a seven-hour day. Quite a few go for a jug at dinner time, there's a feeling of end-of-the-week elation. A weekend in prospect seems somehow longer than it really is. But because the time at the weekend is your own, it expands in anticipation. You get an illusion of freedom.

Monday is the reverse. I know it's a cliché about Monday, but if you experience it, you feel it afresh every week, the self-control needed, the constraint of having to get up for work. People are more grey, more subdued on Mondays. Thursday is pay day, so that has its own feel about it. Wednesday is a sort of half-way day, you're pleased to have reached the mid point of the week.[2]

The stress and strain of certain types of work are conveyed in an interview with a worker in a hosiery factory in the 1960s:

Watching the cones, checking the fabric, attending the machines which constantly break down, you're on the go all the time. If a machine stops, it must be started, and when it's going the cones are running out and have to be replaced. Hour after hour without break, from one machine to another and back, putting up ends, changing cones, starting the machines and trying to watch the fabric. The machines aren't designed for the operator. You bend low to see the fabric, and climb up on the machine to reach the arms holding the thread. To see all the cones you have to walk twenty-five feet round. Usually an operative has three machines with a total of 150 cones – many of which you can't see immediately because they're on the other side of the machines; you have to memorize which cones are going to run out. With bad yarn the machines snag constantly; it's gruelling keeping everything running. . . .

Hey, the machine's stopped. A top red light? Find a stick, disentangle the thread – break off the balled-up yarn, put the end up, check the thread is not caught, press the button, throw the handle. Peer at the fabric – needles? lines from tight yarn? Feel the yarn as it runs, alter the tension; we're not supposed to, it's the supervisor's job but he's too busy. Change a tight cone. A red light above droppers – cone run out? press-off? A yellow light – the stop motion has come up, maybe something is out of position on the needles, a build-up of thread or a broken needle. Clear the build-up, change the needle, start the machine again. And the other machines, are they all right? One of them stops every other minute on average. Can't spend more than thirty seconds looking at one, leave it for the two others, make sure they're all right, come back to the first. May take five or ten minutes to clear. By the time the trouble's clear, another one's stopped. Break off the bad yarn, disentangle the cone, restart the machine – a few seconds later do the same again.[3]

No subject has received greater attention from social commentators than the new affluence of working people in the 1960s and early 1970s, especially when compared with their lot in the 1930s. The situation was comparable in some ways with the years after Chartism when Victorian prosperity spread outwards and downwards in the 1860s. Consumerism (a new name for the standard of living) produced impressive statistics. By 1981 93 per cent of all families had a refrigerator (compared with 66 per cent in 1970, 33 per cent in 1962 and 8 per cent in 1956) and 49 per cent had a deep-freezer (4 per cent in 1970). Television sets were in 95 per cent of all households (74 per cent being colour sets) in 1981 – up from 75 per cent in 1961; 78 per cent had a washing machine, 59 per cent of homes had central heating (30 per cent in 1970), and 75 per cent had a telephone (double the proportion in 1970). Until the mid-1950s car-ownership was confined to a small minority, but by 1979 58 per cent of families had the use of at least one car (and 13 per cent two or more). Home-ownership grew from 27 per cent of households in 1947 to 55 per cent in 1979. Holidays abroad rose from 2 million in 1951 to 12 million in 1980. And so one could go on, adding figures for hi-fis and other consumer durables.

The difficult problem of course is how to interpret these statistics. It is easy to take a superior and rather hypocritical view about the spread of materialism and to lament the loss of those virtues of stoicism and self-denial which nourished the old labour movement. But we shall probably be on firmer ground if we emphasize the positive gains which affluence brought through an increase in both comfort and freedom. When older people looked back from the vantage point of the 1970s that was the verdict commonly recorded. They had no doubts at all about the great benefits brought by washing machines and hot-water systems. Monday, the universal washday, left an indelible impression on young minds. It was for ever afterwards associated with the labour of boiling the clothes in the copper, hauling them out on the end of a stick, mangling them, and finally disposing of oceans of suds. The house was filled with steam, the walls ran with condensation, and there was cold meat and 'bubble and squeak' for dinner. There were no regrets when all this was gone. Nor were any tears shed for the decline of that other memorable institution of working-class life, the pawnshop. Affluence removed the need for the Monday morning journey to 'uncle' and the 'Golden Balls' to pledge Sunday clothes and watches and chains. A 1938 survey of three hundred poor families in all parts of the country showed that a third of them had currently 'popped' goods with a pawnbroker.

> Up and down the City road,
> In and out the Eagle,
> That's the way the money goes,
> Pop goes the weasel.

But by the 1970s the meaning and origins of this children's song were as obscure as most nursery rhymes.

Buying things for the home and for leisure-time enjoyment increased domestic comfort. Spending was also a form of freedom for many people, especially the young. With steady employment and higher incomes, a smaller percentage of earnings was required for the basic requirements of food and shelter, and more was available for spending on what had hitherto been regarded as luxuries. Consumer-capitalism thus became acceptable as a means of increasing enjoyment. The popularity of 'sales' and spending sprees at Christmas and holiday times lay not simply in the acquirement of more and bigger things, but in the feeling of independence and power which money in the pocket or credit via the charge-card engendered. Consumerism provided one of the few areas in which a majority of ordinary people had the power to make real choices and decisions affecting their daily lives. To that extent it was valued as an enlargement of freedom.

At present it is too early to judge the lasting impact of consumerism or to separate the myths of affluence (fostered so assiduously by the media) from the reality of what was happening to ordinary people. Beneath the bright and glittering exterior there were changes in society of a more fundamental kind, affecting the family and the position of women. As we saw earlier, the most basic unit of the common people, the family, is also the most difficult to describe and analyse because of its taken-for-granted character: familiar means simply what everybody knows. The evidence from demography alone, however, would suggest the likelihood of changes in the structure of the family. From about 1880 the birth rate began to fall, and the death rate also continued its decline. The population continued to grow, but at a decreasing rate. Families became smaller, beginning with the middle classes and spreading to manual workers later. The decline in fertility had dramatic personal implications: for instance, in 1900 a quarter of all married women were in childbirth every year; by 1930 this proportion had fallen to one in eight. Although there was a sharp rise in the number of children born immediately after the Second World War, the demographic pattern soon settled into a new equilibrium of low fertility and low mortality rates.

A series of studies of working-class families in Bethnal Green in the 1950s and 1960s suggested movement away from the extended kinship network of the old working-class neighbourhood to a more home-centred, 'symmetrical' family on a new housing estate. The new type of family, consisting simply of a couple and their children, led a more private life: 'The neighbours round here are very quiet. They all keep themselves to themselves. They all come from the East End but they all seem to change when they come down here.'[4] There was less segregation into what was regarded as women's work and what was men's. It also appeared that the central figure of the old extended family, the working-class mum, was in process of being dethroned. The close mother-daughter relationship which continued after marriage was greatly weakened when the family no longer lived a few doors or streets away from mum and other relatives. Most inhabitants of the new housing schemes welcomed the improved physical conditions for living, but few were not without regrets for the friendliness and sense of community of the old East End, which they still talked of as 'up home'. For the children it was different. Bethnal Green was to them a strange, legendary place: 'When we go back to Bethnal Green – to see relations – the children hang about and say "Come on Mum, when are we going home?" '[5] The old urban landscape of tenements, back-to-backs, pubs, corner shops, factories and the friendly life of the street was being replaced by blocks of flats, housing estates and new towns. How resilient the closely knit, deeply textured culture of urban working-class life was in this new environment we do not yet know. But it seems safe to assume that the family was subjected to a process of change resulting from fewer children, the domestication of men, and an increase in women's freedom.

The emancipation of women was the most fundamental of these changes. Testimony to the burden of unwanted pregnancies in previous generations is plentiful:

I was my mother's seventh child, and seven more were born after me – fourteen in all – which made my mother a perfect slave. Generally speaking, she was either expecting a baby to be born or had one at the breast. At the time there were eight of us the oldest was not big enough to get ready to go to school without help.[6]

But by 1951 the effects of the decline in fertility were apparent.

It would seem that the typical working-class mother of the 1890s, married in her teens or early twenties and experiencing ten pregnancies, spent about fifteen years in a state of pregnancy and in nursing a child for the first year of its life. She was tied, for this period of time, to the wheel of childbearing. Today, for the typical mother, the time so spent would be about four years. A reduction of such magnitude in only two generations in the time devoted to childbearing represents nothing less than a revolutionary enlargement of freedom for women brought about by the power to control their own fertility. This private power, what Bernard Shaw once described as the ultimate freedom, can hardly have been exercised without the consent – if not the approval – of the husbands.[7]

A simple method of contraception for working people had been advocated by Francis Place in the 1820s, and there was renewed agitation by the Malthusian League in the 1860s and 1870s; but effective help for working women did not come until Dr Marie Stopes opened the first birth-control clinic in Holloway in 1921. The movement spread, though comparatively slowly, in the 1930s. From the 1950s new methods of contraception were developed, notably the 'pill', and were made cheap and easily available, though it was not until the later 1960s that the pill seems to have been at all widely used. Limitation of the size of the family, which had been practised by the middle classes and some of the working classes since the 1870s, was now available to all. The trend towards smaller families removed one of the traditional causes of working-class poverty and changed traditional attitudes to childbearing and the place of children in the home. The increase in women's freedom made for a more equal (or symmetrical) relationship between husband, wife and children. For women especially, effective contraception brought the freedom to control their own lives and bodies in a way they had not known before.

Another powerful reinforcement of emancipation was the increase in women's, including married women's, employment outside the home. In 1931 10 per cent of married women went out to work – virtually the same proportion as in 1911; by 1951 this figure had risen to 22 per cent and by 1976 was 49 per cent. Studies carried out in the 1960s concluded that women were motivated, first, by a desire to increase the family earnings and thereby the general standard of living (a more modern and attractive home, better food, holidays abroad, a car). Second, was the desire for social contacts and the wish to escape boredom. 'It's another interest. I enjoy meeting the other women at work,' said a young Dagenham housewife, working as a part-time secretary. 'You miss your children when they leave home. . . . You get lonely. You're glad of something to do outside the home,' testified a married part-time machinist from Watford.[8]

Freedom, however, was not without its problems. Easier divorce laws had long been on the agenda of the women's rights movement and bodies such as the Women's Cooperative Guild, but it was only from the 1950s that the law was progressively relaxed in favour of cheaper and less complicated procedures. The Divorce Act of 1969 accepted the principle of divorce by mutual consent; and divorce also became possible without consent if the parties had been separated for five years. In the early 1950s the average number of divorces per year was 33,000; in 1969 this had risen to over 50,000, and by 1980 to 160,000. The proportion of marriages where one or both partners had been divorced increased from one-fifth in 1971 to one-third in 1980; and there were nearly a million single-parent families with dependent children by the end of the decade. The stereotype of a married couple with one or two children was true for only a quarter of all British households in 1982.

How general the trend towards a new type of family life was by the end of the 1970s is uncertain. Even in traditionally male-dominated communities such as mining villages there were signs of change. But what exactly that change amounted to is confusing. We cannot assume that all, or even a majority, of husbands became enthusiastic do-it-yourselfers about the heavily mort-gaged house or were prepared to take their turn at baby-minding and washing up. The old male-segregated world of work, pubs, working men's clubs and football matches did not suddenly disappear: rather, it was infiltrated, modified, or perhaps overlaid by new social attitudes.

Affluence brought changes in leisure. It introduced new activities like TV watching and trips in the car, and modified existing habits such as going to the pub and the football match. The most popular leisure activity of both men and women was watching television. A government survey in 1969 showed that it occupied nearly a quarter of their leisure time – far ahead of the next most popular activities which were crafts and hobbies for women (17 per cent of leisure time) and gardening for men (12 per cent of leisure time). Another survey, this time by the BBC in 1961, found that at 8.30–9.00 p.m. on Sundays 48 per cent of the population were watching television, and 38 per cent on weekdays at the same time. The average hours of viewing per week during the period 1977–9 were sixteen in summer and twenty in winter. What the real effects of the massive impact of this new medium were it is too early to judge. It seems likely that it strengthened the trend towards consumerism and towards home-centred enjoyment. It is tempting to speculate that it also affected the popularity of the public house on the assumption that time spent in front of the telly at home was time absent from the pub. But we do not have any reliable figures for pub attendances. Between the two world wars the number of pubs declined. When Mass-Observation carried out an investigation of 'the pub and the people' in 1938–9 they could still begin their report: 'In Worktown [i.e. Bolton] more people spend more time in public houses than they do in any other buildings except private houses and work-places.'[9] Whether this is true today we do not know. The general decline in the number of pubs and their centrality in male working-class culture has continued during the last thirty years. Yet the appeal of the pub was still strong. For instance, darts, which an official household survey in 1977 identified as the most popular sport, involving 15 per cent of the men interviewed, was primarily a pub game. At the same time many pubs changed in accordance with the times, offering a higher standard of comfort, bar snacks, and a less proletarian atmosphere.

Similarly the great spectator sport of football remained highly popular, but had to change the conditions of its existence. From the 1880s and throughout the interwar period the football crowds grew ever larger, reaching a peak of over 41 million attendances in 1948–9. The Cup Final was a national event, watched by 95,000 people in the stadium at Wembley in 1949. From the early 1920s gambling on the football pools was an added enhancement: in 1946 there were perhaps 7 to 8 million people sending in their coupons each week. But from 1952 attendances began to fall, and by 1973 were reduced to 25 million. The televising of football transformed the nature of the sport. On the one hand the numbers watching it increased: the BBC's weekly coverage of league football on Saturday's 'Match of the Day' was watched regularly by 10 million people in the 1970s. On the other hand fewer and fewer people cared to spend their time on the cold, wet terraces to encourage their local teams. The players themselves, who until the 1960s were paid and treated as ordinary working men, discovered that they had economic power, and an elite group of highly paid stars emerged. In 1966 football received its first knighthoods, and top players became household names. Nevertheless, the clubs retained their strong working-class flavour. At the non-professional level football was played by thousands, perhaps millions, of men and boys every weekend. It was, both for those who played and those who watched, the people's game.

But the benefits of affluence were not enjoyed by all. Even in the prosperous and expanding 1960s certain groups either existed in, or were prone to fall into a state of poverty: old people, single-parent (usually fatherless) families, and some black immigrants. To these must be added the unemployed, whose numbers increased rapidly in the later 1970s and by the early 1980s had surpassed even the grim totals of the 1930s. A combination of demographic, social and economic changes had by the end of the 1970s removed a sizeable proportion of the common people from anything that might be called affluence. Although real disposable incomes more than doubled between 1951 and 1978, the poor made up 23 per cent of all families in the United Kingdom and a fifth of the total population. At the end of 1977 1,260,000 families were living on incomes below the subsistence level set by supplementary benefits. Another 2,650,000 families were receiving supplementary benefit, and 2,010,000 families had incomes above that level but within 20 per cent of it. Together these families consisted of 10,070,000 people, 4,600,000 of them over pension age. This was a sobering reflection on the extent to which the welfare state had failed to eradicate poverty. Deprivation and disadvantage appeared to be deeply rooted in the structures of a society which still maintained very unequal opportunities and life chances.

One new element in post Second World War Britain was the presence of a coloured population. A shortage of labour in the late 1940s and early 1950s attracted immigrants from the West Indies, India and Pakistan, and the number of newcomers reached a peak in 1961. By 1981 this ethnic minority was over 2 million people, of whom a million were Indian and Pakistani, and half a million West Indian or Guyanese. They were not distributed evenly over the country, but clustered in London and the large conurbations of the North and Midlands, finding jobs in low-paid occupations or in the heavy and less attractive industries such as steel and textiles. In the London boroughs of Brent, Hackney and Lambeth; in the Midland towns of Wolverhampton, Leamington Spa, Birmingham and Leicester; and in Bradford, Huddersfield and southeast Lancashire, coloured people became a familiar part of the population – whereas before the Second World War a coloured person on the street was a rare sight. The reception of large numbers of working-class immigrants was a new experience for British people. Previous groups, like the Irish, had been absorbed fairly painlessly, or concentrated in small ghettos like the Jews and Huguenot weavers in the East End. But the new immigrants were more visible by virtue of their skin colour and distinctive dress. They kept their own religion and social customs, and in most respects seemed to be foreigners. Their acceptance as full members of the community presented problems for a working class as ethnically homogeneous and insular as the English. Inevitably there was a certain amount of racial tension and also discrimination against coloured people. Studies showed that in earnings, job opportunities, housing and education the immigrants were seriously disadvantaged. In 1965 it became necessary for the first time to pass a Race Relations Act, setting up a Race Relations Board to deal with discrimination on grounds of race or colour. Probably a majority of people were confused in their attitudes towards the immigrants. Labour leaders and working-class activists were outraged by the idea of discrimination by race, creed or colour; but they came up against an ancient and deeply rooted xenophobia among some sections of the working class.

Attitudes and beliefs, as we discovered earlier, are much more difficult to chronicle than the outward changes in life. For most of their history the beliefs of ordinary people had been influenced, to a greater or lesser degree, by Christian teaching; but by the second half of the twentieth century there were signs that religion and its institutions were greatly weakened, that society was becoming increasingly secularized. This was not a sudden collapse. Ever since 1900 church attendances had been falling. For instance, in York 35·5 per cent of the adult population attended some place of worship on Sunday in 1901, 17·7 per cent in 1935, and 13 per cent in 1948.[10] Surveys in other places confirmed that not more than 10 per cent of the population went to church regularly. Contrary to the assumption of some religious leaders, there had never been a golden age when all, or nearly all, of the people attended church. Even the intensely religious Victorians had been shattered to learn from the religious census of 1851 that less than half the population attended public worship, and that in particular 'the masses of our working population' were absent. Nevertheless, a substantial number of the respectable working classes supported their chapels or attended church services until the Second World War. At the local level and in small communities the religious bodies maintained their customary role after 1945, but to diminishing numbers. A study of Methodism in one of its traditional strongholds, for example, found that in four Durham coal-mining villages in 1970 chapel life still centred on the Sunday services, the Sunday schools (the anniversary being the highlight of the chapel year) and funerals. But half the members were over the age of sixty-one and more than three-quarters were over fifty, and numbers had declined drastically. The culture of the chapel had lost its vigour and its relevance to the mining community which it had enjoyed fifty years earlier.[11] The same experience could be documented in other places and for other denominations.

The decline of institutional religion, however, does not necessarily imply an increasing secularization of belief. In fact, a survey carried out by Mass-Observation in a London borough in 1947 showed considerable confusion of thought and attitude on the subject of religion. Although no more than one person in ten was associated regularly with any of the churches, and about two-thirds never went to church, two-thirds of the men and four-fifths of the women interviewed said they believed in God. 'Yes, there's a God all right, but I don't bother with these things,' said a thirty-year-old man, who was representative of many others.[12] Belief in life after death was expressed by 32 per cent of those who did not go to church and by 54 per cent of Church of England attenders. Popular views about religion deviated widely, even among churchgoers, from the orthodox teachings of the churches.

The Mass-Observers found an attitude of goodwill towards the idea of religion and religious faith, but hostility or indifference towards the church and parsons. Opinion polls in the 1960s and 1970s showed that 60 per cent of the population described themselves as Church of England, but that most of them never entered a church except for a christening, marriage or funeral. In other words, a substantial number of people thought of themselves as religious, but did not go often, or at all, to church. As a young woman told an interviewer in the Mass-Observation survey,

> Of course, I think you should do right as much as you can, I don't mean people should live, anyhow. But I don't see that going to church and doing a lot of praying in public and putting your money in the collection plate is going to do much good. I think people don't believe in that sort of thing any more. It was the fashion once. It isn't nowadays.[13]

For a minority who desired a more intense commitment a number of evangelical, biblical-fundamentalist and charismatic churches came to life in the 1960s and 1970s. But the majority of the common people were content with that primary religion described by Richard Hoggart:

> They believe, first, in the purposiveness of life. Life has a meaning, must have a meaning. One does not bother much about defining it, or pursue abstract questions as to its nature or the implications which follow from such a conclusion; but clearly it is so. 'We're 'ere for a purpose,' they say, or 'There must be some purpose or we wouldn't be 'ere.' And that there is a purpose presupposes that there must be a God. . . .
>
> In so far as they think of Christianity, they think of it as a system of ethics; their concern is with morals, not metaphysics. . . . The emphasis is always on what it is right for them to do, as far as they can, as people. . . .
>
> Here, round the sense of religion as a guide to our duty towards others, as the repository of good rules for communal life, the old phrases cluster. Ask any half-dozen working-class people what they understand by religion, and very easily, but

not meaninglessly, they will be likely to answer with one of these phrases:

'doing good',
'common decency',
'helping lame dogs',
'being kind',
'doing unto others as y' would be done unto',
'we're 'ere to 'elp one another',
''elping y' neighbour',
'learning to know right from wrong',
'decent living'.[14]

There was a general approval of the ethical principles of Christianity insofar as they implied being kind, neighbourly and observing the Golden Rule: hence the approval of teaching religion in schools, or, in some cases, sending the children to Sunday school, 'to give them an idea of what's right and wrong'. The majority belief was in a vestigial Christianity and a rejection of religious institutions. A minority still believed in the traditional teachings of the churches, though with varying degrees of orthodoxy. If this seems a poor legacy for the heirs of the Lollards, Bunyan and Wesley we should remember that in their day they too represented a minority. Like has to be compared with like; and the crowd whose commitment to religion goes little further than singing 'Abide with me' at the Cup Final or 'Jerusalem' on the last night of the Proms is not the equivalent of the village Methodists or persecuted Saints of the past. We have no way of knowing the beliefs of the majority of people before the present century. Such clues as we have suggest that their beliefs were not the same as their leaders', but were vague, inconsistent and sceptical of orthodoxy. The old syndrome of them and us dies hard.

Coda

In 1884 the Fabian Society published its first tract, with the arresting title, *Why are the Many Poor?* A hundred years later we may or may not accept their answer, namely, that it was because of competition and capitalism. It is not the fashion to speak of the poor today, though if we translate this into some such term as underprivileged we may recognize a continuity with the past. Certainly when we look back over the history of the common people it is clear that until very recently the majority were, by modern standards, poor. Poverty of course is relative. Compared to a medieval peasant or a labourer in 1830 a person on supplementary benefit today is well off. But for most of their history the common people had little material wealth and many of them were in want. The basic reason for this was that society as a whole was poor. With a low ceiling on the output of total wealth even a more equal distribution of that wealth could have improved conditions only to a limited degree. The Industrial Revolution changed this. For the first time material abundance became a realistic possibility, though the common people had to struggle hard to win a small share of the new wealth.

The second theme which runs through their history is that the common people did not exercise power. They did not, for the most part, make the decisions which affected their lives, but were in effect controlled by others. Inevitably therefore they found themselves underprivileged, and remained so even in times of prosperity. Affluence, for example, did not extinguish the inequality of conditions of work in the 1960s, as the accompanying table makes clear. Similarly, despite the extension of secondary and higher education to many more people since 1945, inequalities of educational opportunity between the working and middle classes have remained. Explanations of why the majority should for so long have been subordinated to the will of a minority range from the Marxist theory of hegemony, whereby the ruling class persuades or brainwashes the majority into accepting the status quo, to the

Conditions of Employment, 1968

Terms and conditions of employment (percentage of establishments where the condition applies)

Selected conditions of employment	Operatives	Foremen	Clerical workers	Technicians	Management Middle	Senior
Formal sick pay scheme available	46	65	63	65	63	63
Sick pay provided for more than 3 months	49	58	55	57	65	67
Coverage by formal pension scheme	67	94	90	94	96	95
Pension calculated as fixed amount per year of service	48	18	16	14	13	12
Holidays, excluding public holidays, of 15 days or more a year	38	71	74	77	84	88
Choice of time at which holidays taken	35	54	76	76	84	88
Time off with pay for domestic reasons	29	84	84	86	92	93
Period of notice of dismissal in excess of statutory requirements	13	29	26	29	53	61
Clocking on to record attendance	92	33	24	29	2	4
Pay deduction as penalty for lateness	90	20	8	11	1	–
Warning followed by dismissal for frequent absence without leave	94	86	94	92	74	67

From Dorothy Wedderburn (ed.), *Poverty, Inequality and Class Structure* (Cambridge University Press, 1974), p. 144. Reprinted by permission.

concept of stratified diffusion (derived from de Tocqueville's view that what the few have today the many will demand tomorrow) which defuses the danger of revolution.[1]

Despite, or perhaps because of, their poverty and exclusion from power the common people developed their own consciousness and aspirations, which were different from their rulers'. For instance, the longing for freedom asserted itself continuously throughout the years. It was not restricted to the liberal demand for rights under the law, but embraced the artisan's notion of independence (as opposed to the slavery of wages) and the labourer's expectation of material sufficiency for himself and his family. Above all, there emerges from these pages the elemental desire in all human beings to feel that they are wanted, that their efforts are recognized and rewarded. When this is denied there is a loss in human dignity and sense of worth. Hence the affront of unemployment, which bit so deeply into the common consciousness. The denial of some of the basic needs of ordinary people, and the constant belittling of their opinions by the educated classes, perpetuated the gulf between them and us. There was a natural retreat into a working-class or popular religious world, where there were other values which recognized men and women for what they were worth, despite the contrary view of the dominant society. The 'sons of want' knew that they had only themselves to turn to for help. Experience taught self-help through reliance on the family, the village community, the chapel, the friendly society or the trade union.

As writers like Thomas Hardy have noted, there is a certain timelessness about the common people, which means that in the last resort their experience can be expressed by myth as well as by history. Their true allegory is the story of the Garden of Eden. The curse of Adam was that man had henceforth to work ceaselessly for his daily bread. Paradise was lost; but the future was not without hope as the first man and woman set out on their journey through life:

> Some natural tears they dropped, but wiped them soon;
> The world was all before them, where to choose
> Their place of rest, and Providence their guide:
> They, hand in hand, with wandering steps and slow,
> Through Eden took their solitary way.[2]

Notes and References

Introduction: the Contours of Popular History

1. William Wordsworth, *The Prelude*, Book IX, lines 123–4.
2. Ecclesiasticus, chapter 44, verse 9.
3. Hugh Trevor-Roper, 'History and Imagination', in *Times Literary Supplement*, 25 July 1980.
4. Philip Dunne (ed.), *Mr Dooley Remembers* (Boston, 1963), p. 305.
5. Thomas Hardy, *In Time of 'The Breaking of Nations'* (1915).
6. Thomas Hardy, *A Pair of Blue Eyes* (London, 1911), p. 316.
7. Dunne, *op. cit.*, p. 307.

1. Villeins and Serfs

1. W.G. Hoskins, *The Making of the English Landscape* (London, 1967), p. 80.
2. *Domesday Book*, I, 176, quoted in A.E. Bland, P.A. Brown and R.H. Tawney (eds.), *English Economic History: Select Documents* (London, 1933), pp. 16–17.
3. N.E.S.A. Hamilton, *Inquisitio Comitatus Cantabrigiensis . . . Subjicitur Inquisitio Eliensis* (London, 1876), p. 97.
4. G.G. Coulton, *The Medieval Village* (Cambridge, 1931), p. 37.
5. Sussex Record Society, *Publications*, vol. XXXI, p. 48, quoted in H.S. Bennett, *Life on the English Manor* (Cambridge, 1971), p. 66.
6. W.G. Hoskins, *The Midland Peasant* (London, 1957), p. 17.
7. Camden Society, *Chronicon Petroburgense*, ed. T. Stapleton (1849), quoted in Doris Mary Stenton, *English Society in the Early Middle Ages* (Harmondsworth, 1977), p. 140.
8. Aelfric's *Colloquy*, written in 1005 by a Canterbury monk as a textbook of conversational Latin, in which men of different occupations describe their daily lives. Quoted in Coulton, *op. cit.*, p. 307.
9. Hampshire Record Office, MS. Eccl. Comm. 2/159286 [1291/2], quoted in J.Z. Titow, *English Rural Society* (London, 1969), p. 183.
10. Coulton, *op. cit.*, p. 136, quoting from Froissart, *Chroniques*.
11. See Titow, *op. cit.*, pp. 78–93.

12. M.M. Postan, in *The Cambridge Economic History of Europe* (Cambridge, 1966), vol. I, pp. 619–20.
13. Quoted in Bennett, *op. cit.*, pp. 185–6.
14. Emmanuel Le Roy Ladurie, *Montaillou* (Harmondsworth, 1980), is a detailed study of the peasantry in a French Pyrenean village, 1294–1324, based on depositions made to the Inquisition.
15. William Langland, *Piers the Ploughman*, trans. J.F. Goodridge (Penguin edn, Harmondsworth, 1978), p. 108.

2. Craftsmen and Journeymen

1. James E. Thorold Rogers, *Six Centuries of Work and Wages*, 2 vols. (London, 1884), vol. 1, p. 121.
2. Guildhall Letter-Book F, f. 126, reprinted in Bland, Brown and Tawney, *Select Documents*, pp. 136–8.
3. Guildhall Letter-Book H, f. 309, in *ibid*, pp. 138–41.
4. *Ibid*, p. 147.
5. This account is based on Douglas Knoop and G.P. Jones, *The Medieval Mason* (Manchester, 1967).

3. The Growth of Freedom

1. R.H. Hilton, *The Decline of Serfdom in Medieval England* (London, 1970), p. 31. As will be clear, this chapter owes much to the work of Professor Rodney Hilton.
2. Robert of Avesbury, *Historia de Mirabilibus Gestis Regis Edwardi III*, ed. E.M. Thompson (Rolls Series, London, 1889), p. 177. See also Charles Creighton, *A History of Epidemics in Britain*, 2 vols. (Cambridge, 1891–4; repr., London, 1965), vol. I, pp. 122–3.
3. Giovanni Boccaccio, *The Decameron*, trans. J.M. Rigg (Everyman edn, 2 vols., London, 1955), pp. 5–6.
4. John Hatcher, *Plague, Population and the English Economy, 1348–1530* (London, 1977), pp. 21–3.
5. Augustus Jessopp, *The Coming of the Friars* (London, 1899), pp. 200–4.
6. Zvi Razi, *Life, Marriage and Death in a Medieval Parish: Economy, Society and Demography in Halesowen, 1270–1400* (Cambridge, 1980), p. 103.
7. Henry Knighton, *Chronicon*, ed. J.R. Lumby, 2 vols. (Rolls Series, London, 1889–95), vol. II, pp. 58–65; quoted in R.B. Dobson (ed.), *The Peasants' Revolt of 1381* (London, 1970), pp. 60–1, on which I have relied heavily in this chapter.
8. Hatcher, *op. cit.*, pp. 68–71.

9. Reprinted in Dobson, *op. cit.*, pp. 63–8.

10. Ancient Indictments, PRO, quoted in G.M. Trevelyan, *England in the Age of Wycliffe* (London, 1929), p. 188.

11. Razi, *op. cit.*, p. 110.

12. Dobson, *op. cit.*, p. 73.

13. Langland, *Piers the Ploughman*, pp. 89–90.

14. J. Gower, *Mirour de l'Omme*, in G.G. Coulton (ed.), *Social Life in Britain from the Conquest to the Reformation* (Cambridge, 1938), p. 353.

15. Dobson, *op. cit.*, p. 371.

16. Quoted in Charles Oman, *The Great Revolt of 1381* (Oxford, 1906; new edn, 1969), pp. 51–2.

17. Dobson, *op. cit.*, pp. 164–5.

18. *Ibid*, p. 277.

19. Quoted in Rosamund Faith, 'The Class Struggle in Fourteenth Century England', in Raphael Samuel (ed.), *People's History and Socialist Theory* (London, 1981), p. 59. See also R.J. Faith, 'The "Great Rumour" of 1377 and Peasant Ideology', in Past and Present Society Conference, *The English Rising of 1381* (London, 1981). This paragraph is based on Dr Faith's articles.

20. Dobson, *op. cit.*, p. 381.

21. Langland, *op. cit.*, p. 260.

22. G.R. Owst, *Preaching in Medieval England* (Cambridge, 1926), pp. 295–6.

23. Langland, *op. cit.*, p. 28.

24. R.H. Hilton, *Bond Men Made Free* (London, 1977), p. 229.

25. Caroline Barron, *Revolt in London: 11th to 15th June 1381*, Museum of London (London, 1981), p. 8.

26. The classic work on this theme is Norman Cohn, *The Pursuit of the Millennium* (London, 1957). See in particular pp. 209–17, 'Marginalia to the English Peasants' Revolt'.

27. For which see E.P. Thompson, *The Making of the English Working Class* (London, 1963), pp. 484–97.

28. See the contributions in the Past and Present Society Conference proceedings, note 19 above.

29. See Faith, *op. cit.*

30. M.T. Clanchy, *From Memory to Written Record: England 1066–1307* (London, 1979), pp. 203–8.

31. Coulton, *Medieval Village*, pp. 126–7.

32. Coulton, *Social Life in Britain*, p. 353.

33. 'A song of freedom', c. 1434. Dobson, *op. cit.*, p. 385.

34. Quoted in Coulton, *Medieval Village*, p. 332.

4. Living and Working

1. S.T. Bindoff, *Tudor England* (Harmondsworth, 1981), p. 8.
2. William Harrison, 'Description of England' (1577), repr. in *Elizabethan England*, ed. F.J. Furnivall (London, n.d.), pp. 12, 13–14.
3. Peter Laslett, *The World We Have Lost* (London, 1965), p. 22. These paragraphs owe much to Dr Laslett's stimulating book. For a contrary view see Christopher Hill, *Change and Continuity in Seventeenth-Century England* (London, 1974), chapter 9.
4. *Ibid*, pp. 1–2.
5. See S.T. Bindoff, *Ket's Rebellion, 1549* (London, 1968).
6. Keith Thomas, *Religion and the Decline of Magic* (London, 1971), p. 403.
7. R.H. Tawney, *The Agrarian Problem in the Sixteenth Century* (London, 1912), p. 331.
8. Bland, Brown and Tawney, *Select Documents*, pp. 247–50.
9. Sir Thomas More, *Utopia*, ed. Maurice Adams (London, n.d.), pp. 89–90.
10. Following Tawney's great work, *The Agrarian Problem*.
11. Notably in Eric Kerridge, *Agrarian Problems in the Sixteenth Century and After* (London, 1969).
12. Tawney, *op. cit.*, pp. 303–4.
13. Thomas Hardy, *The Woodlanders* (1887; London, 1906), p. 123.
14. Harrison, *op. cit.*, pp. 128–9.
15. Hoskins, *Midland Peasant*, p. 296.
16. Richard Carew, *The Survey of Cornwall* (London, 1602), quoted in Joan Thirsk (ed.), *The Agrarian History of England and Wales, vol. IV, 1500–1640* (Cambridge, 1967), pp. 443–5.
17. G.E. Fussell, *The English Rural Labourer* (London, 1949), p. 8.
18. Harrison, *op. cit.*, p. 119.
19. Richard Baxter, *The Poor Husbandman's Advocate* (1691), ed. Frederick J. Powicke, as *The Reverend Richard Baxter's Last Treatise* (Manchester, 1926), p. 25. The quotation in the next paragraph is from p. 22.
20. Tawney, *op. cit.*, p. 332.
21. Bland, Brown and Tawney, *op. cit.*, p. 327.
22. Daniel Defoe, *A Tour through the whole Island of Great Britain* (London, 1724–6), vol. III, letter VIII.
23. E.P. Thompson, 'Time, Work-Discipline, and Industrial Capitalism', *Past and Present*, no. 38 (December 1967), pp. 72–3.
24. William Hutton, *A History of Birmingham* (Birmingham, 1781), p. 69.
25. Paul Mantoux, *The Industrial Revolution in the Eighteenth Century* (1928; New York, 1962 edn), p. 76.
26. Benjamin Franklin, *Autobiography* (Everyman edn, London, 1960), p. 42.

27. William Hutton, *Life of William Hutton* (2nd edn, London, 1817). The quotations in this and the following paragraphs are from pp. 8–163.
28. Lawrence Stone, *The Family, Sex and Marriage in England, 1500–1800* (London, 1977), p. 56.

5. Attitudes and Beliefs

1. Milton Rokeach, *Beliefs, Attitudes and Values: a Theory of Organization and Change* (San Francisco, 1970), p. 2.
2. Laslett, *The World We Have Lost*, pp. 71–3.
3. Thomas, *Religion and the Decline of Magic*, p. 163.
4. Norman P. Tanner, *Heresy Trials in the Diocese of Norwich, 1428–31* (London, 1977), pp. 56–9.
5. John Foxe, *The Acts and Monuments* (1563), ed. Rev. George Townsend, 8 vols. (New York, 1965 facsimile edn), vol. III, pp. 594–6.
6. Tanner, *op. cit.*, p. 86.
7. Carlo Ginzburg, *The Cheese and the Worms: the Cosmos of a Sixteenth-Century Miller* (London, 1980).
8. John A.F. Thomson, *The Later Lollards, 1414–1520* (Oxford, 1965), pp. 67, 71, 83, 241.
9. Foxe, *op. cit.*, vol. V, p. 147.
10. *Ibid*, vol. VIII, pp. 323–4.
11. For literacy figures see David Cressy, *Literacy and the Social Order: Reading and Writing in Tudor and Stuart England* (Cambridge, 1980); Margaret Spufford, 'First steps in literacy: the reading and writing experiences of the humblest seventeenth-century spiritual autobiographers', *Social History*, vol. 4, no. 3 (1979); Lawrence Stone, 'Literacy and Education in England, 1640–1900', *Past and Present*, no. 42 (1969).
12. Keith Wrightson and David Levine, *Poverty and Piety in an English Village: Terling, 1525–1700* (New York, 1979), p. 150.
13. John Bunyan, *Grace Abounding* (1666; London, 1966 edn), p. 7.
14. Hutton, *Life*, pp. 29–51.
15. Dixon Ryan Fox, *Ideas in Motion* (New York, 1935), p. 102.
16. John Bunyan, *A Few Sighs from Hell* (1658), quoted in Roger Sharrock, *John Bunyan* (London, 1968), p. 98.
17. John Bunyan, *The Pilgrim's Progress* (1678; London, 1966 edn), p. 185.
18. *The Stranger in Reading* (Reading, 1810), p. 117, quoted in Stephen Yeo, *Religion and Voluntary Organisations in Crisis* (London, 1976), p. 299.
19. Thomas, *op. cit.*, p. 294. My debt to this great work will be obvious in the following pages on folklore, magic and witchcraft.
20. The *Athenaeum*, 2 January 1828.
21. Thomas, *op. cit.*, p. 223.

22. John Heydon, a seventeenth-century astrologer and writer on Rosi-crucian mysticism, quoted in Richard Alford Davenport, *Sketches of Imposture, Deception and Credulity* (London, 1837), p. 300.

23. William Blake, *Poetry and Prose*, ed. Geoffrey Keynes (London, 1967), p. 862 (letter to Butts, 22 November 1802).

24. E. Peacock in *Notes and Queries*, 2nd series, i (1856), p. 145, quoted in Thomas, *op. cit.*, p. 666.

25. The following quotations are from Thomas Cooper, *Life, Written by Himself* (London, 1872), pp. 18–19, 34–5; William Lovett, *Life and Struggles* (London, 1876), p. 18; Joseph Barker, *Life, Written by Himself*, ed. John Thomas Barker (London, 1880), pp. 19–22; Samuel Bamford, *Passages in the Life of a Radical*, 2 vols. (London and Man-chester, 1841–3), pp. 130–1 and chapters 20, 21, 22.

26. John Harland and T.T. Wilkinson, *Lancashire Folk-Lore* (London, 1867), p. 145.

27. Robert Southey, *Letters from England*, 3 vols. (London, 1807), vol. II, pp. 283–4.

28. Robert Burton, *The Anatomy of Melancholy* (London, 1924 edn), p. 294.

29. John Wesley, *The Journal of John Wesley*, ed. Nehemiah Curnock, 8 vols. (London, 1909–16), vol. VI, p. 109.

30. p. 1. The following quotations are from pp. 42, 43, 54, 71, 192.

31. Harland and Wilkinson, *op. cit.*, p. 10.

32. C.L'Estrange Ewen (ed.), *Witch Hunting and Witch Trials* (London, 1929), pp. 171, 239. The other quotations in this paragraph are from pp. 231, 68.

33. Thomas, *op. cit.*, p. 557.

6. The World Upset

1. Bunyan, *Pilgrim's Progress* (1966 edn), p. 146. The quotations in the following paragraphs are from pp. 147, 216, 219.

2. *A Relation of the Imprisonment of Mr John Bunyan*, in *ibid*, pp. 130–2.

3. Richard Baxter, *Autobiography* (London, 1931 edn), pp. 34–5. The quotations in the next paragraph are from pp. 38, 80, 82.

4. See Brian Manning, *The English People and the English Revolution* (Harmondsworth, 1978), to which I am indebted for this and the following paragraph.

5. A.S.P. Woodhouse (ed.), *Puritanism and Liberty: Being the Army Debates (1647–9) from the Clarke Manuscripts* (London, 1974), pp. 53–69, 82.

6. Richard Overton, *A Remonstrance of Many Thousand Citizens* (1646), in Don M. Wolfe, *Leveller Manifestoes of the Puritan Revolution* (London, 1944; repr. 1967), pp. 113–14. The following quotations in this

paragraph are from Leveller pamphlets, quoted in Manning, *op. cit.*, pp. 286, 320.

7. John Lilburne, *The Upright Man's Vindication* (1653), in H.N. Brailsford, *The Levellers and the English Revolution* (London, 1961), p. 239.

8. John Lilburne, *A Whip for the Present House of Lords or the Levellers levelled* (1648), in David W. Petegorsky, *Left-Wing Democracy in the English Civil War* (London, 1940), p. 110.

9. Woodhouse, *op. cit.*, p. 381.

10. George Fox, *Journal*, ed. John L. Nickalls (Cambridge, 1952), pp. 71–2.

11. John Reeve and Lodowick Muggleton, *A Volume of Spiritual Epistles* (1755; London, 1820), p. 5.

12. *Archaeologia*, vol. xxxv (1855), repr. in T.H. McGuffie (ed.), *Rank and File* (London, 1964), pp. 162–5, 179–80, 247–8.

13. Henry Foster, *A True and Exact Relation of the Marchings of the Two Regiments of the Trained Bands of the City of London* (London, 1643), in *ibid*, pp. 256–7, 297.

14. Quoted in D.R. Guttery, *The Great Civil War in Midland Parishes* (Birmingham, 1951), p. 60.

7. The Emergence of the Working Class

1. Samuel Bamford, *Early Days* (London, 1849), pp. 98–118.

2. *Stephens' Monthly Magazine* (March 1840), pp. 52–3.

3. William Cooke Taylor, *Notes of a Tour in the Manufacturing Districts* (London, 1842; repr. 1968), pp. 30–6.

4. William Dodd, *The Factory System Illustrated* (London, 1842; repr. 1968), pp. 108–10.

5. *Report . . . by a Statistical Committee of the Leeds Town Council*, in *Journal of the Statistical Society of London*, vol. II (1839–40).

6. Thomas Cooper, *Life, Written by Himself* (London, 1872), pp. 140–2.

7. 'Enclosure', in John Clare, *Selected Poems*, ed. James Reeves (London, 1964), p. 23.

8. *Annals of Agriculture*, vol. 36, p. 508, quoted in J.L. and Barbara Hammond, *The Village Labourer* (London, 1911; repr. 1978), pp. 63–4.

9. Hammonds, *op. cit.*, p. 59.

10. Thompson, *Making of the English Working Class*, p. 11.

11. Charles Shaw, *When I Was a Child* (London, 1903; repr. Firle, Sussex, 1980), pp. 96–108.

8. Protest and Revolt

1. E.P. Thompson, 'The Moral Economy of the English Crowd in the Eighteenth Century', *Past and Present*, no. 50 (1971), p. 79, on which this paragraph is based.
2. W.B. Crump (ed.), *The Leeds Woollen Industry, 1780–1820* (Leeds, 1931), pp. 229–30.
3. Frank Peel, *The Risings of the Luddites, Chartists and Plug-Drawers* (Brighouse, 1895), pp. 47–8.
4. *Ibid*, p. 263.
5. *Proceedings at York Special Commission, January 1813* (London, 1813), pp. 209–10.
6. Hammonds, *Village Labourer*, p. 184.
7. E.J. Hobsbawm and George Rudé, *Captain Swing* (London, 1969), p. 204.
8. *Ibid*, p. 210.
9. Hammonds, *op. cit.*, pp. 218–19.
10. *Ibid*, p. 214.
11. Hobsbawm and Rudé, *op. cit.*, pp. 274–5.
12. London Corresponding Society, *To the Nation at Large* (24 May 1792), quoted in Albert Goodwin, *The Friends of Liberty* (London, 1979), p. 197.
13. Francis Place, *Autobiography*, ed. Mary Thale (Cambridge, 1972), p. 131.
14. Samuel Bamford, *Passages in the Life of a Radical*, 2 vols. (Manchester, 1839–41), vol. 1, pp. 206–8.
15. William Lovett, *Life and Struggles* (London, 1876), p. 68.
16. *Political Register*, 2 April 1831.
17. *The Poor Man's Guardian*, 12 November 1831.
18. W.E. Adams, *Memoirs of a Social Atom*, 2 vols. (London, 1903), vol. 1, p. 237.
19. R.G. Gammage, *History of the Chartist Movement* (Newcastle, 1894), p. 94.
20. Benjamin Wilson, *The Struggles of an Old Chartist* (Halifax, 1887), p. 14.

9. Self-help and Respectability

1. Sidney and Beatrice Webb, *The History of Trade Unionism* (1894; London, 1911 edn), p. 57.
2. E.C. Tufnell, *The Character, Objects and Effects of Trade Unions* (London, 1834), repr. in G.D.H. Cole and A.W. Filson (eds.), *British Working*

Class Movements: Select Documents, 1789–1875 (London, 1965), pp. 280–1.

3. George Loveless, *The Victims of Whiggery* (London, 1837), repr. in *ibid*, p. 287.

4. Webbs, *op. cit.*, pp. 179–80.

5. *Cobbett's Two-Penny Trash*, vol. II, no. 7 (1 January 1832), pp. 154–5.

6. *The Co-operator*, no. 12 (1 April 1829), repr. in T.W. Mercer, *Co-operation's Prophet* (Manchester, 1947), pp. 97–8.

7. William Lovett, *Life and Struggles* (London, 1876), p. 41.

8. Joseph Arch, *Joseph Arch: the Story of his Life*, ed. Countess of Warwick (London, 1898), pp. 19–22.

9. Wilson, *The Struggles*, p. 3.

10. J.T. Barker (ed.), *Life of Joseph Barker, Written by Himself* (London, 1880), p. 25.

11. Robert Moore, *Pit-men, Preachers and Politics* (Cambridge, 1974), pp. 129–30.

12. E. Welbourne, *The Miners' Unions of Northumberland and Durham* (Cambridge, 1923), p. 57.

13. See John Walsh, 'Methodism at the End of the Eighteenth Century', in Rupert Davies and Gordon Rupp (eds.), *A History of the Methodist Church in Great Britain*, vol. 1 (London, 1965), pp. 311–15.

14. F.B. Smith, *Florence Nightingale* (London, 1982), p. 41.

15. *Journal of the Statistical Society*, vol. 1 (1839), p. 539.

16. The most recent research on working-class private schools in the nineteenth century is by Dr Philip Gardner, to whom I am greatly indebted for material and ideas in the following paragraphs.

17. Shaw, *When I Was a Child*, pp. 1–4.

18. Cooper, *Life*, p. 7.

19. Henry Hawkes, *Recollections of John Pounds* (London, 1884), pp. 63–4, 135.

20. Lovett, *op. cit.*, p. 44.

21. Brian Harrison and Patricia Hollis (eds.), *Robert Lowery: Radical and Chartist* (London, 1979), p. 114.

22. Henry Edward Price, 'Diary' [MS autobiography], quoted in David Vincent, *Bread, Knowledge and Freedom* (London, 1981), to which I am indebted.

23. James Bowd, 'The Life of a Farm Worker', *The Countryman*, vol. L1, no. 2 (1955), quoted in *ibid*, p. 42.

24. Bamford, *Early Days*, p. 64.

25. James Dawson Burn, *The Autobiography of a Beggar Boy*, ed. David Vincent (London, 1978), p. 200.

26. W.J. Linton, *James Watson* (Manchester, 1880), p. 87.

10. In the Workshop of the World

1. Ben Turner, *About Myself, 1863–1930* (London, 1930), pp. 36–42, 53.
2. Alfred Williams, *Life in a Railway Factory* (2nd edn, London, 1920), pp. 136, 217, 254–5.
3. Dave Douglass, in Raphael Samuel (ed.), *Miners, Quarrymen and Saltworkers* (London, 1977), p. 211.
4. Thomas Burt, *An Autobiography* (London, 1924), pp. 110–12.
5. E.P. Thompson and Eileen Yeo (eds.), *The Unknown Mayhew* (London, 1971), pp. 218–20, 342–3.
6. George Sturt, *The Wheelwright's Shop* (Cambridge, 1923), pp. 19–20.
7. Henry Broadhurst, *The Story of his Life . . . Told by Himself* (London, 1901), pp. 21–4.
8. Robert Tressell, *The Ragged Trousered Philanthropists* (London, 1965 edn), pp. 40–3.
9. C. Henry Warren, *Happy Countryman* (London, 1939), p. 119, quoted in Raphael Samuel, *Village Life and Labour* (London, 1975), pp. 45–6.
10. *Notes and Queries* (26 August 1905), pp. 164–5, quoted in *ibid*, p. 32.
11. Lilian Westall, 'The Good Old Days', in John Burnett (ed.), *Useful Toil* (London, 1976), pp. 216–17.
12. H.G. Wells, *Experiment in Autobiography*, 2 vols. (London, 1934), vol. 1, pp. 150–1.
13. B. Seebohm Rowntree, *Poverty: a Study of Town Life* (London, 1903 edn), p. 304.
14. Margaret Powell, *Below Stairs* (London, 1976), p. 19.
15. Minnie Ferris, in *The Island* (London, 1979), p. 32.
16. A.S. Jasper, *A Hoxton Childhood* (London, 1974), pp. 46–7.
17. Flora Thompson, *Lark Rise to Candleford* (London, 1945), pp. 53–4.

11. The Labour Movement

1. Thorold Rogers, *op. cit.*, p. 14.
2. Sources: B.R. Mitchell and Phyllis Deane, *Abstracts of British Historical Statistics* (Cambridge, 1962), p. 68; and A.H. Halsey (ed.), *Trends in British Society Since 1900* (London, 1972), pp. 123–4.
3. Turner, *About Myself*, p. 90.
4. Edward Carpenter, *My Days and Dreams* (London, 1916), p. 126.
5. *Seedtime*, July 1894, quoted in Henry Pelling, *The Origins of the Labour Party, 1880–1900* (London, 1954), pp. 164–5.
6. Margaret McMillan, *Life of Rachel McMillan* (London, 1927), p. 89.
7. Philip Snowden, *An Autobiography*, 2 vols. (London, 1934), vol. I, p. 67.
8. George Meek, *George Meek: Bath Chair-Man* (London, 1910). Quot-

ations in this and the following paragraph are from pp. 34, 84, 171, 208, 243, 281.

9. Tressell, *op. cit.*, p. 261.
10. Thompson, *op. cit.*, p. 86.
11. Richard Hoggart, *The Uses of Literacy* (London, 1957), pp. 86–7, 229.
12. Raphael Samuel (ed.), *East End Underworld: Chapters in the Life of Arthur Harding* (London, 1981), pp. 30, 262–7.

12. War and the Dole

1. Alun Howkins, *Whitsun in 19th Century Oxfordshire* (Oxford, 1972), p. 64.
2. W. Griffith, *Up to Mametz* (London, 1931), quoted in Denis Winter, *Death's Men* (London, 1978), p. 34.
3. Pte J.H. Harwood, 6th Royal Berkshire Regiment, in Martin Middlebrook, *The First Day on the Somme* (London, 1971), p. 7.
4. George Coppard, *With a Machine Gun to Cambrai* (London, 1976), p. 30.
5. Private 19022 [Frederic Manning], *Her Privates We* (London, 1930), pp. 378–404.
6. Samuel, *op. cit.*, p. 236.
7. Mrs H.A. Felstead, quoted in Arthur Marwick, *Women at War, 1914–1918* (London, 1977), pp. 67–8.
8. Robert Roberts, *The Classic Slum* (Harmondsworth, 1977), p. 200.
9. *'Where's Your Horns?': People of Spitalfields talk about the evacuation* (London, 1979), p. 29.
10. Nellie Priest, in *The Island* (London, 1979), p. 43.
11. Arthur Newton, *Years of Change* (London, 1975), p. 62.
12. Tom Harrisson (ed.), *War Factory: a Report by Mass-Observation* (London, 1943), p. 113.
13. Susan Briggs, *Keep Smiling Through* (London, 1976), p. 160.
14. Coppard, *op. cit.*, p. 133.
15. John Langley, *Always a Layman* (Brighton, 1975), pp. 43–4.
16. H.L. Beales and R.S. Lambert (eds.), *Memoirs of the Unemployed* (London, 1934), p. 182.
17. Pilgrim Trust, *Men without Work* (Cambridge, 1938), p. 145.
18. Henry Ashby, in *Hello, Are You Working?* (Whitley Bay, 1977), pp. 35–6.
19. Walter Greenwood, *Love on the Dole* (London, 1933), p. 259.
20. Ellen Wilkinson, *The Town that was Murdered* (London, 1939), p. 207.
21. Frank Tilsley, *Heaven and Herbert Common* (London, 1953), pp. 177–9.

22. Margaret Perry, unpublished autobiography, in John Burnett (ed.), *Destiny Obscure* (London, 1982), pp. 323–4.

13. Citizens and Wage Earners

1. Newton, *Years of Change*, p. 64.
2. Jeremy Seabrook, *What Went Wrong?* (London, 1978), pp. 194–6.
3. R. Fraser, *Work 2: Twenty Personal Accounts* (Harmondsworth, 1969), pp. 88–9.
4. Michael Young and Peter Willmott, *Family and Kinship in East London* (London, 1957), p. 121.
5. *Ibid*, p. 137.
6. Mrs Layton, 'Memories of Seventy Years', in Margaret Llewelyn Davies (ed.), *Life as We Have Known It* (London, 1931; repr. 1977), p. 1.
7. R.M. Titmuss, 'The position of women', *Essays on 'The Welfare State'* (London, 1958), p. 91.
8. Michael Young and Peter Willmott, *The Symmetrical Family* (London, 1973), pp. 102–3.
9. Mass-Observation, *The Pub and the People* (London, 1943), p. 17.
10. B. Seebohm Rowntree and G.R. Lavers, *English Life and Leisure* (London, 1951), p. 343.
11. Moore, *Pit-men*, pp. 214–21.
12. Mass-Observation, *Puzzled People* (London, 1947), p. 25.
13. *Ibid*, p. 11.
14. Hoggart, *The Uses of Literacy*, pp. 95–8.

Coda

1. See Young and Willmott, *Symmetrical Family*, pp. 19–22.
2. John Milton, *Paradise Lost*, Book XII, lines 645–9.

Further Reading

(The place of publication is London unless shown otherwise)

The following suggestions are limited to such standard works of political and economic history as have some relevance to the condition of the common people, together with certain monographic studies which I have found stimulating and useful. Most of these works have good bibliographies which list the substantial specialist literature on all the main episodes and themes in this book. For general history, the series of volumes in the *Oxford History of England*, the *Pelican History of England* and the *Pelican Social History of Britain* should be consulted. Much of the best and most up-to-date writing appears as articles in periodicals, and the reader is well advised to look at recent numbers of *Past and Present*, *History Workshop Journal*, *Oral History*, *Social History* and the *Journal of Social History*. As an alternative to the 'macro' approach to history, the 'micro' study (or what used to be called local history) has much to recommend it. Excellent examples are: Rowland Parker, *The Common Stream* (1976); J.R. Ravensdale, *Liable to Floods* (Cambridge, 1974); M.K. Ashby, *The Changing English Village* (Warwick, 1974); M.F. Davies, *Life in an English Village* (1909).

1. Villeins and Serfs

As an introduction one should start with Doris Mary Stenton, *English Society in the Early Middle Ages* (Harmondsworth, 1977), and A.R. Myers, *England in the Late Middle Ages* (Harmondsworth, 1978); but older works such as P. Vinogradoff, *Villainage in England* (Oxford, 1892), and F.W. Maitland's magnificent *Domesday Book and Beyond* (Cambridge, 1897; repr. London, 1960) are well worth reading. Two classic works in the field are H.S. Bennett, *Life on the English Manor* (Cambridge, 1937; repr. 1971), and George Caspar Homans, *English Villagers of the Thirteenth Century* (Cambridge, Mass., 1951; repr. New York, 1975). Also useful are Frank Barlow, *The Feudal Kingdom of England, 1042–1216* (1955); Reginald Lennard, *Rural England, 1086–1135* (Oxford, 1959); and H.E. Hallam,

Rural England, 1066–1348 (1981). Two works by W.G. Hoskins, *The Making of the English Landscape* (1967) and *The Midland Peasant* (1957), may be introduced at this point. On Domesday see H.C. Darby, *Domesday England* (Cambridge, 1977); R. Welldon Finn, *The Domesday Inquest* (1961); and Public Record Office, *Domesday Re-Bound* (1960). Of G.G. Coulton's many books, perhaps the most useful at this stage is *The Medieval Village* (Cambridge, 1931). For documents and essays on current issues in medieval history, see J.Z. Titow, *English Rural Society, 1200–1350* (1969); and also J.A. Raftis, *Tenure and Mobility: Studies in the Social History of the Medieval English Village* (Toronto, Canada, 1964). A comparative note can be introduced by reference to Teodor Shanin, *Peasants and Peasant Societies* (Harmondsworth, 1979); A.V. Chayanov, *The Theory of Peasant Economy* (Illinois, 1966); and Emmanuel Le Roy Ladurie, *Montaillou* (Harmondsworth, 1980).

2. Craftsmen and Journeymen

Many of the works recommended for Chapter 1 are also relevant here. Two economic histories provide useful material: J.H. Clapham, *A Concise Economic History of Britain* (Cambridge, 1949); and M.M. Postan, *The Medieval Economy and Society* (Harmondsworth, 1978). The works of Professor Rodney Hilton are essential reading throughout Part I. In particular see R.H. Hilton, *The English Peasantry in the Later Middle Ages* (Oxford, 1979); *A Medieval Society: the West Midlands at the End of the Thirteenth Century* (1966); *Bond Men Made Free* (1977); and *The Decline of Serfdom in Medieval England* (1970). Medieval building workers are dealt with in Douglas Knoop and G.P. Jones, *The Medieval Mason* (Manchester, 1933; repr. 1967). An older, and perhaps unjustly neglected work, is James E. Thorold Rogers, *Six Centuries of Work and Wages* (1884). There is no satisfactory study of medieval religion from the perceptions of the common people. Bennett, *op. cit.*, has a chapter on the church, and there are a few suggestive asides in G.R. Owst, *Preaching in Medieval England* (Cambridge, 1926; repr. New York, 1965). B.L. Manning, *The People's Faith in the Time of Wyclif* (Cambridge, 1919; repr. Hassocks, Sussex, 1975), despite its promising title, does not really present religion from below.

3. The Growth of Freedom

For general reading on the period, G.M. Trevelyan, *England in the Age of Wycliffe* (1899; repr. 1929), can still be recommended. On population changes a valuable summary, with bibliographical references to all the latest work in the field, is John Hatcher, *Plague, Population and the English Economy, 1348–1530* (1977). Also useful for long-term trends and problems in population, 1066–1800, is J.D. Chambers, *Population, Economy, and Society in Pre-Industrial England* (1972). A fascinating case study is Zvi Razi, *Life, Marriage and Death in a Medieval Parish: Economy, Society and Demography in Halesowen, 1270–1400* (Cambridge, 1980). On the Black Death, Charles Creighton, *A History of Epidemics in Britain*, 2 vols. (Cambridge, 1891 and 1894; repr. London, 1965), is the most useful work; but see also J.F.D. Shrewsbury, *The History of Bubonic Plague in the British Isles* (Cambridge, 1970); and Philip Ziegler, *The Black Death* (1969). The best introduction to the Peasants' Revolt is R.B. Dobson, *The Peasants' Revolt of 1381* (1970), which has an excellent essay and plentiful extracts from the main chroniclers. Charles Oman, *The Great Revolt of 1381* (Oxford, 1906; repr. 1969), is a good narrative account, and the 1969 edition has a new introduction and bibliography by E.B. Fryde. See also the Historical Association pamphlet by E.B. Fryde, *The Great Revolt of 1381* (1981). André Réville, *Le Soulèvement des Travailleurs d'Angleterre en 1381* (Paris, 1898), is still essential, though the text is in French and mainly limited to Hertfordshire, Suffolk and Norfolk; but it reprints a large number of documents and also has an index of names of persons involved. Analysis of the rising is best followed in Hilton, *Bond Men Made Free*. Edgar Powell, *The Rising in East Anglia in 1381* (Cambridge, 1896), does not add much to the above works; but is useful for the documents reproduced. James Anthony Froude, 'Annals of an English Abbey', *Short Studies on Great Subjects*, vol. III (1898), is an older essay on the troubles at St Albans, based on the chroniclers. For recent research, see the reference in note 19 of this chapter; also Caroline Barron, *Revolt in London: 11th to 15th June 1381* (1981); and W.H. Liddell and R.G.E. Wood, *Essex and the Peasants' Revolt* (Chelmsford, 1981). The European dimension is brought out in Michel Mollat and Philippe Wolff, *The Popular Revolutions of the Late Middle Ages* (1973). The best introduction to the controversies surrounding the Robin Hood legend is R.B. Dobson and J. Taylor, *Rymes of Robyn Hood: an Introduction to the English Outlaw* (1976). The exchange of views in *Past and Present* is reprinted in R.H. Hilton (ed.), *Peasants, Knights and Heretics: Studies in Medieval English Social History* (Cambridge, 1976). See also M. Keen, *The Outlaws of Medieval Legend* (1961); J.C. Holt, *Robin Hood* (1982); and E.J. Hobsbawm, *Bandits* (1969).

4. Living and Working

General reading for the period 1500–1800 will be found in S.T. Bindoff, *Tudor England* (Harmondsworth, 1981); Christopher Hill, *Reformation to Industrial Revolution* (Harmondsworth, 1980); Keith Wrightson, *English*

Society, 1580–1680 (1982); and Roy Porter, *English Society in the Eighteenth Century* (Harmondsworth, 1982). A stimulating but controversial interpretation is presented in Peter Laslett, *The World We Have Lost* (1965). For economic and social changes the essential reading is R.H. Tawney, *The Agrarian Problem in the Sixteenth Century* (1912), and Eric Kerridge, *Agrarian Problems in the Sixteenth Century and After* (1969). On enclosures see Joan Thirsk (ed.), *The Agrarian History of England and Wales, vol. IV, 1500–1640* (Cambridge, 1967); and the Historical Association pamphlet by Joan Thirsk, *Tudor Enclosures* (1981). Also, W.E. Tate, *The English Village Community and the Enclosure Movements* (1967); and J.A. Yelling, *Common Field and Enclosure in England, 1450–1850* (1977). For industrial life the following are useful: George Unwin, *Industrial Organization in the Sixteenth and Seventeenth Centuries* (Oxford, 1904); W.E. Minchinton (ed.), *Wage Regulation in Pre-Industrial England* (Newton Abbot, 1972); John Rule, *The Experience of Labour in Eighteenth-Century Industry* (1981); C.R. Dobson, *Masters and Journeymen: a Prehistory of Industrial Relations, 1717–1800* (1980). There is a useful essay by L.A. Clarkson on the extent of wage labour, 1500–1800, in Kenneth D. Brown (ed.), *The English Labour Movement, 1700–1951* (1982). Two older works which can be recommended because of their very full documentation are M. Dorothy George, *London Life in the Eighteenth Century* (1925; repr. New York, 1965); and Paul Mantoux, *The Industrial Revolution in the Eighteenth Century* (1928; repr. 1961). Maurice Dobb, *Studies in the Development of Capitalism* (1946), is a thoughtful book which many scholars have found helpful. For Ket's rebellion one can begin with S.T. Bindoff's Historical Association pamphlet, *Ket's Rebellion, 1549* (1968), and Anthony Fletcher, *Tudor Rebellions* (1973), both of which have bibliographies; but the fullest account is in the now rare book by Frederic William Russell, *Kett's Rebellion in Norfolk* (1859). A recent article and debate about Ket's rebellion appeared in *Past and Present*, number 84 (August 1979) and number 93 (November 1981). An important study of sixteenth- and seventeenth-century risings is Buchanan Sharp, *In Contempt of All Authority: Artisans and Riot in the West of England, 1586–1660* (Berkeley, Cal., 1980). Information about marriage and the family has to be gleaned from various sources, none of which is very adequate: but see Laslett, *op. cit.*, and also his later study, *Family Life and Illicit Love in Earlier Generations* (Cambridge, 1978); Lawrence Stone, *The Family, Sex and Marriage in England, 1500–1800* (1977); Edward Shorter, *The Making of the Modern Family* (1977); Alan Macfarlane, *The Family Life of Ralph Josselin* (Cambridge, 1970) and his *The Origins of English Individualism* (Oxford, 1979); Jack Goody, Joan Thirsk and E.P. Thompson (eds.), *Family and Inheritance: Rural Society in Western Europe, 1200–1800* (Cambridge, 1979). There is a need for local studies along the lines of Keith Wrightson and David Levine, *Poverty and Piety in an English Village: Terling, 1525–1700* (New

York, 1979), using the techniques of family reconstitution. See also Margaret Spufforth, *Contrasting Communities: English Villagers in the Sixteenth and Seventeenth Centuries* (1974), for three Cambridgeshire villages; and Hoskins's study of Wigston, Leicestershire, in *The Midland Peasant*. The definitive work on population figures is now E.A. Wrigley and R.S. Schofield, *The Population History of England, 1541–1871* (1981).

5. Attitudes and Beliefs

Religion in the late Middle Ages and sixteenth century is well presented in two important books: Claire Cross, *Church and People, 1450–1660* (1979); and A.G. Dickens, *The English Reformation* (1964). On Lollardy the following will be found useful: J.A.F. Thomson, *The Later Lollards, 1414–1520* (Oxford, 1965); A.G. Dickens, *Lollards and Protestants in the Diocese of York, 1509–1558* (1959); Margaret Aston, *Lollards and Reformers* (1983); Norman P. Tanner (ed.), *Heresy Trials in the Diocese of Norwich, 1428–31* (1977); Gordon Leff, *Heresy in the Later Middle Ages*, 2 vols. (Manchester, 1967). Foxe's *Book of Martyrs* was for long a popular favourite and was available in many abbreviated forms. The full edition is *The Acts and Monuments of John Foxe*, ed. Reverend George Townsend, 8 vols. (New York, 1965). For literacy the basic work is David Cressy, *Literacy and the Social Order: Reading and Writing in Tudor and Stuart England* (Cambridge, 1980); but see also the reference in note 11 of this chapter. Also important are Jack Goody (ed.), *Literacy in Traditional Societies* (Cambridge, 1968), and Thomas Laqueur, 'The Cultural Origins of Popular Literacy in England, 1500–1850', *Oxford Review of Education*, vol. 2, number 3 (1976). For chapbooks and popular literature Victor E. Neuburg, *Popular Literature: a History and Guide* (Harmondsworth, 1977), provides an excellent introduction and bibliography. On magic, astrology, folklore and popular beliefs of all kinds Keith Thomas's great book, *Religion and the Decline of Magic* (1971), is essential. Not only does it make fascinating reading, but it has very full notes and bibliographical references. See also Bernard Capp, *Astrology and the Popular Press* (1979). There is similar material for the eighteenth and nineteenth centuries in the early chapters of J.F.C. Harrison, *The Second Coming: Popular Millenarianism, 1780–1850* (1979). A recent study of custom is Bob Bushaway, *By Rite: Custom, Ceremony and Community in England, 1700–1880* (1982). For witchcraft, see Thomas, *op. cit.*; A. Macfarlane, *Witchcraft in Tudor and Stuart England* (1970); C. L'Estrange Ewen (ed.), *Witch Hunting and Witch Trials* (1929; repr. 1971); Peter Haining (ed.), *The Witchcraft Papers* (1974); Christina Hole, *A Mirror of Witchcraft* (1957).

6. The World Upset

There are many editions of Bunyan's *The Pilgrim's Progress*. The Oxford University Press edition (1966) also includes Bunyan's spiritual auto-biography, *Grace Abounding*, and his trial and imprisonment. The best short biography is Roger Sharrock, *John Bunyan* (1968). For puritanism see Christopher Hill, *Society and Puritanism in Pre-Revolutionary England* (1964), and his *Puritanism and Revolution* (1958). Most of the books on the English Revolution and civil war have little to say about the common people, but among the more informative and sympathetic are the following: E.W. Ives (ed.), *The English Revolution, 1600–1660* (1975); Brian Manning, *The English People and the English Revolution* (Harmondsworth, 1978); J.S. Morrill, *The Revolt of the Provinces* (1976); Ian Roy, 'The English Civil War and English Society', in Brian Bond and Ian Roy (eds.), *War and Society* (1975); C.H. Firth, *Cromwell's Army* (1902; repr. 1962); Austin Woolrych, *Battles of the English Civil War* (1961). Radicalism in the seventeenth century has attracted many eminent scholars. One cannot do better than begin with Christopher Hill, *The World Turned Upside Down* (1972); and then go on to A.L. Morton, *The World of the Ranters* (1970), and Perez Zagorin, *A History of Political Thought in the English Revolution* (1954). The story of the Levellers and Diggers is told in Chapters 9 and 10 of Manning, *op. cit.*, and in H.N. Brailsford, *The Levellers and the English Revolution*, ed. Christopher Hill (1961); and David W. Petegorsky, *Left-Wing Democracy in the English Civil War* (1940). Collections of documents are: William Haller and Godfrey Davis (eds.), *The Leveller Tracts, 1647–1653* (Gloucester, Mass., 1964); Don M. Wolfe (ed.), *Leveller Manifestoes of the Puritan Revolution* (1944; repr. 1967); A.S.P. Woodhouse (ed.), *Puritanism and Liberty: Being the Army Debates (1647–9) from the Clarke Manuscripts* (1938; repr. 1974); Gerrard Winstanley, *Selections from his Works*, ed. Leonard Hamilton (1944). A rare account of village life in the later seventeenth century by a contemporary is Richard Gough, *The History of Myddle*, ed. David Hey (Harmondsworth, 1981).

7. The Emergence of the Working Class

Of the great number of books on the Industrial Revolution the most suitable for introductory reading are T.S. Ashton, *The Industrial Revolution, 1760–1830* (1948), and Phyllis Deane, *The First Industrial Revolution* (1965). David S. Landes, *The Unbound Prometheus* (1969), sets British development in a European context. Two excellent economic histories are E.J. Hobsbawm, *Industry and Empire* (1969), and Peter Mathias, *The First Industrial Nation* (1969). The important matter of population growth is dealt with in D.V. Glass and D.E.C. Eversley (eds.), *Population in History* (1969); H.J. Habakkuk, *Population Growth and Economic Development Since 1750* (1972); and Wrigley and Schofield, *op. cit.* On agricultural changes, the most useful work is J.D. Chambers and G.E. Mingay, *The Agricultural Revolution, 1750–1880* (1966). See also G.E. Mingay, *Enclosure and the Small Farmer in the Age of the Industrial Revolution* (1968). The most important study of the development of the working class in the late eighteenth and early nineteenth century is of course E.P. Thompson, *The Making of the English Working Class* (1963), which is essential reading for all students of the period. Thompson's work is in the tradition of the pioneer social historians, J.L. and Barbara Hammond, whose three books *The Village Labourer* (1911), *The Town Labourer* (1917) and *The Skilled Labourer* (1919) are still immensely readable and rewarding. A stimulating and original interpretation is Harold Perkin, *The Origins of Modern English Society, 1780–1880* (1969). R.J. Morris, *Class and Class Consciousness in the Industrial Revolution, 1780–1850* (1979), is an excellent introduction to the issues and literature in this important area. For the debate about the standard of living of the people see Arthur J. Taylor (ed.), *The Standard of Living in Britain in the Industrial Revolution* (1975). The autobiographies of working people become increasingly numerous from the late eighteenth century, and some of these are referred to in the notes to this chapter.

8. Protest and Revolt

There is a large literature on the movements mentioned in this chapter, and only a tiny selection of it can be given here. A useful introduction is John Stevenson, *Popular Disturbances in England, 1700–1870* (1979). For crowd history it is convenient to begin with George Rudé, *The Crowd in History* (1981), and E.P. Thompson's article cited in note 1 of this chapter. The Corresponding Societies are dealt with in Albert Goodwin, *The Friends of Liberty* (1979). For Cobbett see George Spater's definitive biography, *William Cobbett: the Poor Man's Friend*, 2 vols. (Cambridge, 1982). Artisan radicalism in the first half of the nineteenth century is analysed in a most perceptive and scholarly fashion in I.J. Prothero, *Artisans and Politics in Early Nineteenth-Century London: John Gast and his Times* (1979). Varying and conflicting interpretations of Luddism are given in Thompson, *Making of the English Working Class*; Hammonds, *Skilled Labourer*; Malcolm I. Thomis, *The Luddites* (Newton Abbot, 1970); Duncan Bythell, *The Handloom Weavers* (Cambridge, 1969); and E.J. Hobsbawm, 'The Machine Breakers', *Labouring Men* (1964). An important source for the oral tradition of Luddism in Yorkshire is Frank Peel, *The Risings of the Luddites, Chartists and Plug-Drawers* (Brighouse, 1895; repr. London, 1968).

Accounts of Peterloo will be found in Donald Read, *Peterloo: the 'Massacre' and its Background* (Manchester, 1958); Joyce Marlow, *The Peterloo Massacre* (1969); and (most exhaustively) in Robert Walmsley, *Peterloo: the Case Reopened* (Manchester, 1969). For the Swing riots see E.J. Hobsbawm and George Rudé, *Captain Swing* (1969), and the Hammonds, *Village Labourer*. The unstamped press agitation is well covered in Patricia Hollis, *The Pauper Press* (1970); and Joel H. Wiener, *The War of the Unstamped* (Ithaca, NY, 1969). For the factory reform movement see Cecil Driver, *Tory Radical: the Life of Richard Oastler* (New York, 1946); J.T. Ward, *The Factory Movement, 1830–1885* (1962); and R.G. Kirby and A.E. Musson, *The Voice of the People: John Doherty, 1798–1854* (Manchester, 1975). Owen and Owenism can be studied in J.F.C. Harrison, *Robert Owen and the Owenites in Britain and America* (1969), and in the two biographies: Frank Podmore, *Robert Owen: a Biography* (1906; repr. 1923), and G.D.H. Cole, *Life of Robert Owen* (1925; 3rd edn, 1965). Some idea of the large amount of material on Chartism may be gathered from J.F.C. Harrison and Dorothy Thompson, *Bibliography of the Chartist Movement, 1837–1976* (Hassocks, Sussex, 1978). Recommended introductory reading is: David Jones, *Chartism and the Chartists* (1975); J.T. Ward, *Chartism* (1973); Dorothy Thompson (ed.), *The Early Chartists* (1971); F.C. Mather (ed.), *Chartism and Society: an Anthology of Documents* (1980); Asa Briggs (ed.), *Chartist Studies* (1959); James Epstein and Dorothy Thompson (eds.), *The Chartist Experience* (1982). Some voices from below (in this case, of common seamen, 1780–1840) can be heard in Henry Baynham, *From the Lower Deck* (1969).

9. Self-help and Respectability

Asa Briggs, *Victorian People* (1954), is an excellent introduction to Victorian self-help, and an important later study is Trygve R. Tholfsen, *Working Class Radicalism in Mid-Victorian England* (1976). The classic study of early trade unionism is Sidney and Beatrice Webb, *The History of Trade Unionism* (1894; and later edns). This should now be supplemented with Henry Pelling, *A History of British Trade Unionism* (1963); E.H. Hunt, *British Labour History, 1815–1914* (1981); and Kenneth D. Brown, *The English Labour Movement, 1700–1951* (1982). Important documents are reprinted in G.D.H. Cole and A.F. Filson (eds.), *British Working Class Movements: Select Documents, 1789–1875* (1965), and in A. Aspinall (ed.), *The Early English Trade Unions* (1949). For the friendly societies see P.H.J.H. Gosden, *Self-Help: Voluntary Associations in the 19th Century* (1973); and for cooperative societies G.D.H. Cole, *A Century of Co-operation* (Manchester, 1944). For popular Methodism the official connexional and chapel histories are not of much help. Instead one has to turn to reminiscences such as

Henry Woodcock, *Piety among the Peasantry: being Sketches of Primitive Methodism on the Yorkshire Wolds* (1889). H.B. Kendall, *The Origin and History of the Primitive Methodist Church*, 2 vols. (1903), conveys something of the tone of chapel life. For general reading the following are recommended: Maldwyn Edwards, *After Wesley* (1948) and *Methodism and England* (1944); and Robert F. Wearmouth, *Methodism and the Working-Class Movements of England, 1800–1850* (1947) and *Methodism and the Struggle of the Working Classes, 1850–1900* (Leicester, 1954). Some excellent local studies are now available, such as James Obelkevich, *Religion and Rural Society: South Lindsey, 1825–1875* (Oxford, 1976), and Robert Moore, *Pit-men, Preachers and Politics: the Effects of Methodism in a Durham Mining Community* (Cambridge, 1974). See also Stephen Yeo, *Religion and Voluntary Organisations in Crisis* (1976); Hugh McLeod, *Class and Religion in the Late Victorian City* (1974); and Alan D. Gilbert, *Religion and Society in Industrial England* (1976). Statistics of church membership are provided in Robert Currie, Alan Gilbert and Lee Horsley, *Churches and Churchgoers: Patterns of Church Growth in the British Isles since 1700* (Oxford, 1977). Literacy and popular literature are dealt with in R.K. Webb, *The British Working Class Reader, 1790–1848* (1955), and Richard D. Altick, *The English Common Reader* (Chicago, Ill., 1957). For education and self-help see Brian Simon, *Studies in the History of Education, 1780–1870* (1960); and J.F.C. Harrison, *Learning and Living, 1790–1960* (1961). David Vincent, *Bread, Knowledge and Freedom: a Study of Nineteenth-Century Working Class Autobiography* (1981), is very useful for autobiographical material on self-education, the family, and much else. On Sunday schools the best study is Thomas Laqueur, *Religion and Respectability: Sunday Schools and Working Class Culture, 1780–1850* (New Haven, Conn., 1976). The authoritative work on temperance is Brian Harrison, *Drink and the Victorians* (1971), which is also extremely perceptive on nineteenth-century reform movements in general. For the full flavour of the temperance movement one should sample P.T. Winskill, *The Temperance Movement and its Workers*, 4 vols. (1891–2). There is no satisfactory history of the working-class family in the nineteenth century; but Michael Anderson, *Family Structure in Nineteenth Century Lancashire* (Cambridge, 1971), is a sociological case study of Preston using historical material. A useful collection of family budgets is Frances Collier, *The Family Economy of the Working Classes in the Cotton Industry, 1784–1833* (Manchester, 1968). On the labour aristocracy E.J. Hobsbawm's essay in his *Labouring Men* is still the best general account; but more detailed studies are Geoffrey Crossick, *An Artisan Elite in Victorian Society: Kentish London, 1840–1880* (1978), and Robert Q. Gray, *The Labour Aristocracy in Victorian Edinburgh* (Oxford, 1976).

10. In the Workshop of the World

The economic histories listed for Chapter 7 are relevant here, together with J.H. Clapham's magisterial (and eminently readable) work, *An Economic History of Modern Britain*, 3 vols. (Cambridge, 1926–38). Two collections of essays contain a variety of topics touching on Victorian working people: H.J. Dyos and Michael Wolff (eds.), *The Victorian City*, 2 vols. (1973), and G.E. Mingay (ed.), *The Victorian Countryside*, 2 vols. (1981). For the mid-century Henry Mayhew's great *London Labour and the London Poor*, 3 vols. and extra vol. (1861–2, 1864; repr. 1969), provides many fascinating case histories. Mayhew is best approached via the introductory study, E.P. Thompson and Eileen Yeo (eds.), *The Unknown Mayhew* (1971). Comparable material for the later nineteenth century is contained in Charles Booth, *Life and Labour of the People in London*, 17 vols. (1892–1903). Two important studies of the 'workplace situation' are Richard Price, *Masters, Unions and Men: Work Control in Building and the Rise of Labour, 1830–1914* (Cambridge, 1980); and Patrick Joyce, *Work, Society and Politics* (1982), which deals with the northern textile workers in the later Victorian period. Standish Meacham, *A Life Apart: the English Working Class, 1890–1914* (Cambridge, Mass., 1977), draws upon a wide selection of primary sources relevant to many aspects of working-class life. From the 1860s two books by 'A Journeyman Engineer' (Thomas Wright) are available: *Some Habits and Customs of the Working Classes* (1867; repr. 1967) and *The Great Unwashed* (1868; repr. 1970). See also James Hopkinson, *Memoirs of a Victorian Cabinet Maker*, ed. Jocelyne Baty Goodman (1968); the autobiography of Joseph Gutteridge, reprinted in Valerie E. Chancellor (ed.), *Master and Artisan in Victorian England* (1969); and Guida Swan (ed.), *The Journals of Two Poor Dissenters, 1786–1880* (1970). The nearer we get to the present, the more plentiful become the autobiographies of working people. In addition to the few cited in this chapter, reference should be made to the following collections: John Burnett (ed.), *Useful Toil* (1976) and *Destiny Obscure* (1982); and David Vincent (ed.), *Testaments of Radicalism* (1977). See also Paul Thompson, *The Edwardians* (1975), which draws heavily on oral sources; Robert Roberts, *The Classic Slum* (1977) and *A Ragged Schooling* (1976); Charles Shaw, *When I Was a Child* (1903; repr. Firle, Sussex, 1980); James Hawker, *A Victorian Poacher*, ed. Garth Christian (1961); George Hewins, *The Dillen* (1982); C. Stella Davies, *North Country Bred: a Working-Class Family Chronicle* (1963). There are several good accounts of domestic service, mostly referring to the early twentieth century: Margaret Powell, *Below Stairs* (1976); Daisy Noakes, *The Town Beehive* (Brighton, 1975); and references in Janet Hitchman, *The King of the Barbareens* (Harmondsworth, 1976), and Winifred Foley, *A Child in the Forest* (1978). In the 1970s community publishing ventures have produced autobiographies and reminiscences by working people reaching back to the early 1900s: among these are Centreprise (Hackney); QueenSpark (Brighton); Bristol Broadsides; and Strong Words (Tyne and Wear). Ruskin College, Oxford, has also produced a series of *History Workshop Pamphlets*, ed. Raphael Samuel (1970–3), drawing upon the researches and experiences of working-class students. For labouring life in the countryside in the nineteenth and early twentieth centuries see, first, two old classics: W.H. Hudson, *A Shepherd's Life* (1910; and later edns), and Richard Jefferies, *Hodge and His Masters* (1880; repr. 1946). Then turn to Fred Kitchen, *Brother to the Ox* (1940); George Bourne [Sturt], *The Bettesworth Book* (1901; repr. Firle, Sussex, 1978) and *Memoirs of a Surrey Labourer* (1907; repr. 1930); Sybil Marshall (ed.), *Fenland Chronicle* (Cambridge, 1980). The books of George Ewart Evans are a mine of information, stretching back to the 1890s: *Ask the Fellows who Cut the Hay* (1965), *The Pattern under the Plough* (1966), *The Farm and the Village* (1969), *Where Beards Wag All* (1970), *The Days that We Have Seen* (1975), *The Horse in the Furrow* (1967) and *Horse Power and Magic* (1979). Also based on oral tradition is Ronald Blythe, *Akenfield: Portrait of an English Village* (1969). There is much original material from labouring people in Raphael Samuel, *Village Life and Labour* (1975); and Pamela Horn, *Labouring Life in the Victorian Countryside* (1976). The lower middle classes are not adequately represented in most of the literature: at present the most vivid accounts of their lives are probably in the novels of Charles Dickens, Arnold Bennett and H.G. Wells. Leisure is a subject much studied recently. The following can be recommended: James Walvin, *Leisure and Society, 1830–1950* (1978); Robert W. Malcolmson, *Popular Recreations in English Society, 1700–1850* (Cambridge, 1973); Hugh Cunningham, *Leisure in the Industrial Revolution, 1780–1880* (1980); John Lowerson and John Myerscough, *Time to Spare in Victorian England* (Hassocks, Sussex, 1977); Eileen Yeo and Stephen Yeo (eds.), *Popular Culture and Class Conflict, 1590–1914* (Brighton, 1981); Bernard Waites, Tony Bennett and Graham Martin (eds.), *Popular Culture: Past and Present* (1982); and Robert D. Storch (ed.), *Popular Culture and Custom in Nineteenth-Century England* (1982).

11. The Labour Movement

Much the most useful work for the study of English populism is Michael Roe, *Kenealy and the Tichborne Cause* (Melbourne, Australia, 1974). There is a large bibliography of the history of industrial relations and trade unionism. The standard account, which up-dates the Webbs, is H.A. Clegg, Alan Fox and A.F. Thompson, *A History of British Trade Unions since 1889, vol. 1, 1889–1910* (Oxford, 1964), but the works by Pelling, Hunt and

Brown, listed for Chapter 9, provide a shorter account. For the Labour Party it is best to begin with Henry Pelling, *The Origins of the Labour Party, 1880–1900* (1954; repr. Oxford, 1966), and the successor volume, Frank Bealey and Henry Pelling, *Labour and Politics, 1900–1906* (1958). A general history is provided in Henry Pelling, *A Short History of the Labour Party* (1962). Some of the older work by G.D.H. Cole is also still useful, for example his *A Short History of the British Working-Class Movement, 1789–1947* (1948). An important critical account is Ralph Miliband, *Parliamentary Socialism: a Study of the Politics of Labour* (1961). See also R. McKibbin, *The Evolution of the Labour Party, 1910–1924* (1975). Biographies and autobiographies of Labour leaders are plentiful, and the main titles are referred to in the above histories. Likewise the early socialists were extremely articulate and have left plenty about themselves and their views. A good introduction to the various groups and theories are the two books by Stanley Pierson, *Marxism and the Origins of British Socialism* (Ithaca, NY, 1973) and *British Socialists: the Journey from Fantasy to Politics* (Cambridge, Mass., 1979). Useful collections of documents are: E.J. Hobsbawm (ed.), *Labour's Turning Point 1880–1900* (1948); and Henry Pelling (ed.), *The Challenge of Socialism* (1954). An indispensable work of reference is Joyce M. Bellamy and John Saville (eds.), *Dictionary of Labour Biography*, 6 vols. (1972–82).

12. War and the Dole

The general impact of the First World War is portrayed in Arthur Marwick, *The Deluge* (1965), and in C.S. Peel, *How We Lived Then, 1914–1918* (1929). There are now a number of accounts of the fighting from the perspective of the private soldier, for example George Coppard, *With a Machine Gun to Cambrai* (1976). This and many others are quoted in such works as Denis Winter, *Death's Men: Soldiers of the Great War* (1978); Michael Moynihan (ed.), *People at War, 1914–1918* (Newton Abbot, 1973); Martin Middlebrook, *The First Day on the Somme* (1971) and *The Kaiser's Battle* (1978); and John Ellis, *Eye-Deep in Hell* (1976). Two fascinating studies, essential for perspective, are Paul Fussell, *The Great War and Modern Memory* (1975); and John Keegan, *The Face of Battle* (Harmondsworth, 1978). The part played by women is described in Arthur Marwick, *Women at War, 1914–1918* (1977), and Gail Braybon, *Women Workers in the First World War* (1981). The lot of working-class women generally in this period is brought out in several recent reprints: Maud Pember Reeves, *Round About a Pound a Week* (1913; repr. 1979); Margaret Llewelyn Davies (ed.), *Life as We Have Known It* (1931; repr. 1977); Margaret Llewelyn Davies (ed.), *Maternity: Letters from Working-Women* (1915; repr. 1978); Margery Spring Rice, *Working-Class Wives* (1939; repr. 1981). At this point it is appropriate to mention a feminist interpretation of events: Sheila Rowbotham, *Hidden from History* (1977). For the Second World War there is no shortage of memoirs, popular films, TV series and paperback accounts of prison escapes – all of which constitute a hazard rather than a help when searching for what ordinary people felt at the time. Michael Moynihan (ed.), *People at War, 1939–1945* (Newton Abbot, 1974), and John Ellis, *The Sharp End of War* (1982), deal with battle experience. The economic background is covered in W.K. Hancock and M.M. Gowing, *British War Economy* (1949), and Alan S. Milward, *The Economic Effects of the Two World Wars on Britain* (1977). The best general account of the home front is Angus Calder, *The People's War: Britain, 1939–1945* (1969); and see also the Mass-Observation reports in Tom Harrisson, *Living Through the Blitz* (1967). A popular and very readable account is Leonard Mosley, *London Under Fire, 1939–45* (1972). Susan Briggs, *Keep Smiling Through* (1976), and Arthur Marwick, *The Home Front: the British and the Second World War* (1976), have rich collections of illustrations which are marvellously (perhaps nostalgically) evocative of the time. Norman Longmate, *How We Lived Then* (1971), contains plenty of detail about everyday life during the Second World War. Much the best history of the interwar years is Charles Loch Mowat, *Britain between the Wars, 1918–1940* (1955; and later edns), which has very full bibliographical references in the footnotes. This can be usefully supplemented with: John Stevenson and Chris Cook, *The Slump* (1979); Noreen Branson and Margot Heinemann, *Britain in the Nineteen Thirties* (1971); and Robert Graves and Alan Hodge, *The Long Week-End: a Social History of Great Britain, 1918–1939* (1941). The fiftieth anniversary of the general strike prompted several histories, of which Margaret Morris, *The General Strike* (Harmondsworth, 1976), and Jeffrey Skelley (ed.), *The General Strike, 1926* (1976), are representative. For unemployment see the works cited in the notes for this chapter, and also Wal Hannington, *Unemployed Struggles, 1919–1936* (1936); George Orwell, *The Road to Wigan Pier* (1932); and J.B. Priestley, *English Journey* (1934). John Hilton, *Rich Man, Poor Man* (1944), is a short but perceptive comment on the economic condition of ordinary people. Several of the surveys by Mass-Observation are mentioned in the notes: see also Humphrey Jennings and Charles Madge (eds.), *May the Twelfth* (1937), the date of the coronation; Charles Madge and Tom Harrisson, *Britain by Mass-Observation* (Harmondsworth, 1939); and Mass-Observation, *The Pub and the People* (1943).

13. Citizens and Wage Earners

The most useful history of the period after 1945 is Arthur Marwick, *British Society Since 1945* (Harmondsworth, 1982). A valuable compilation of statistics is A.H. Halsey (ed.), *Trends in British Society Since 1900* (1972). For social change see A.H. Halsey, *Change in British Society* (1982), which has an up-to-date bibliography of recent work in the field. One important study, however, should be mentioned specially: J.H. Goldthorpe *et al.*, *The Affluent Worker*, 3 vols. (1968–9). Thanks to the efforts of sociologists and anthropologists there is now a considerable documentation of various working-class communities and neighbourhoods: Norman Dennis, Fernando Henriques and Clifford Slaughter, *Coal is Our Life* (1956); J.M. Mogey, *Family and Neighbourhood: Two Studies in Oxford* (Oxford, 1956); Michael Young and Peter Willmott, *Family and Kinship in East London* (1957) and *The Symmetrical Family: a Study of Work and Leisure in the London Region* (1973); Peter Townsend, *The Family Life of Old People* (Harmondsworth, 1963); Brian Jackson, *Working Class Community* (1968). A wonderfully convenient and revealing digest of government statistics on everything from the percentage of homes with TVs and washing machines to population trends and divorce rates is the series *Social Trends*, published annually since 1970 by HMSO. For leisure, see A. Howkins and J. Lowerson, *Trends in Leisure, 1919–1939* (1979); and James Walvin, *The People's Game: a Social History of British Football* (1975). There is much of general social interest in Geoffrey Gorer, *Exploring English Character* (1960) and *Sex and Marriage in England Today* (1971). Two classics of the period are: Richard Hoggart, *The Uses of Literacy* (1957); and Michael Young, *The Rise of the Meritocracy, 1870–1933* (1958).

Index

Index

429

Index